REAL ESTATE
MARKET ANALYSIS
Trends, Methods, and Information Sources

THIRD EDITION

Deborah L. Brett

Urban Land Institute

ABOUT THE URBAN LAND INSTITUTE

The Urban Land Institute is a global, member-driven organization comprising more than 44,000 real estate and urban development professionals dedicated to advancing the Institute's mission of providing leadership in the responsible use of land and in creating and sustaining thriving communities worldwide.

ULI's interdisciplinary membership represents all aspects of the industry, including developers, property owners, investors, architects, urban planners, public officials, real estate brokers, appraisers, attorneys, engineers, financiers, and academics. Established in 1936, the Institute has a presence in the Americas, Europe, and Asia Pacific regions, with members in 81 countries.

The extraordinary impact that ULI makes on land use decision-making is based on its members sharing expertise on a variety of factors affecting the built environment, including urbanization, demographic and population changes, new economic drivers, technology advancements, and environmental concerns.

Peer-to-peer learning is achieved through the knowledge shared by members at thousands of convenings each year that reinforce ULI's position as a global authority on land use and real estate. In 2018 alone, more than 2,200 events were held in about 330 cities around the world.

Drawing on the work of its members, the Institute recognizes and shares best practices in urban design and development for the benefit of communities around the globe.

More information is available at uli.org. Follow ULI on Twitter, Facebook, LinkedIn, and Instagram.

Urban Land Institute
2001 L Street, NW, Suite 200
Washington, DC 20036-4948

Recommended bibliographic listing:
Brett, Deborah L. *Real Estate Market Analysis: Trends, Methods, and Information Sources*, 3rd ed. Washington, DC: Urban Land Institute, 2019.

ISBN: 978-0-87420-428-5

Primary Author

Deborah L. Brett
President
Deborah L. Brett & Associates
Plainsboro, New Jersey

Reviewers and Contributors

Elizabeth M. Beckett
President
Real Estate Strategies Inc./RES Advisors
Paoli, Pennsylvania

Tony Biddle
Principal
Biddle Hotel Consulting
Philadelphia, Pennsylvania

Jon B. DeVries
Founding Director
Marshall Bennett Institute of Real Estate
Roosevelt University
Vice President, Research
Lambda Alpha Foundation
Chicago, Illinois

Valerie S. Kretchmer
President
Valerie S. Kretchmer Associates
Evanston, Illinois

M. Leanne Lachman
ULI Foundation Governor
Executive in Residence
Columbia Business School
New York, New York

Stephen H. O'Connor
Associate Professor of Practice in Real Estate
Freeman College of Management
Bucknell University
Lewisburg, Pennsylvania

Project Staff

James Mulligan
Managing Editor

Publications Professionals LLC Editorial Team
Manuscript Editors

Brandon Weil
Art Director

Amy Elfenbaum, Arc Group Ltd
Book Design and Layout

Craig Chapman
Senior Director, Publishing Operations

ABOUT THE AUTHOR

Deborah L. Brett, AICP

Deborah L. Brett is a real estate and planning consultant to a wide range of private and public organizations for which she provides project-related market studies, consumer surveys, and trend analysis. Areas of specialization include demographic and economic analysis, survey research, and project planning for commercial and residential developments, including mixed-use plans, commercial revitalization, market-rate and affordable housing, and transit-oriented development.

In 1993, Brett formed Deborah L. Brett & Associates, an independent consulting practice. She previously was senior vice president and director of consulting services at Real Estate Research Corporation in Chicago. In her 18-year career there, she directed major land use policy analyses for many government agencies. She also prepared development strategies, housing analyses, and retail and office market studies for private clients, including developers, lenders, investors, and nonprofit organizations.

Brett holds a master's degree in urban and regional planning from the University of Illinois at Urbana-Champaign.

She is a longtime member of ULI and a frequent contributor to its publications. With Adrienne Schmitz, she wrote the first and second editions of *Real Estate Market Analysis* and was a contributor to three editions of ULI's *Real Estate Development: Principles and Practices*. Both books are used by real estate and planning programs at many universities.

With M. Leanne Lachman, she cowrote two editions of *Global Demographics: Shaping Real Estate's Future* in 2008 and 2009. Also with Lachman, Brett conducted two national surveys of millennials' shopping habits and housing preferences that were published by ULI as monographs in 2013 and 2015, respectively. For ULI Washington, they cowrote two surveys of millennials' housing circumstances and satisfaction with living in the District of Columbia and its close-in suburbs; the surveys were published in 2015 and 2018.

Brett is a member of the American Institute of Certified Planners (AICP) and Lambda Alpha, the real estate and land economics honorary society. She taught online classes in residential and retail market analysis for Rutgers University's Bloustein School of Planning and Public Policy.

ACKNOWLEDGMENTS

Completing this textbook would not have been possible without the help of colleagues, clients, and friends who shared their skills and experience as contributors and reviewers. They highlighted trends that were important to identify and provided examples of tables and maps. In addition, they sent links to reports and timely articles from government sources and the real estate press. Special thanks to Beth Beckett, Jon DeVries, Valerie Kretchmer, and Leanne Lachman, all of whom I have had the pleasure to work with for many years. The contributions of Adrienne Schmitz, coauthor of the first and second editions of this book, shaped the structure and content of this updated edition. Numerous professional organizations, real estate brokerages, and consulting firms shared current information about market conditions, property performance, and analytical methods. They are cited in the webliography, figures, sidebars, and quotations throughout the book.

This effort would not have been successful without the efforts of ULI senior editor Jim Mulligan, Barbara Hart and the editorial team at Publications Professionals LLC, ULI art director Brandon Weil, and designer Amy Elfenbaum. They substantially improved both the text and the visual appeal of the book.

PREFACE

Like the first two editions, this third edition of *Real Estate Market Analysis* was conceived as a practical guide for analyzing the market potential of real estate development and property acquisitions. Other textbooks on this topic have emphasized economic theory and mathematical formulas, but most practitioners combine data analysis with their understanding of the subjective aspects of real estate. This book emphasizes the importance of fieldwork and hands-on experience: seeing the subject property and its competition, talking to brokers and property managers, and understanding the needs and preferences of tenants and buyers in today's economy. It also provides guidance about data sources and their limitations, as well as ways to present data to support market conclusions.

This book does not focus on aspects of development finance—sources of equity and debt capital, loan terms, and expected rates of return—that are critical to project feasibility. Nor does it closely examine the various financial or tax incentives available from government agencies to encourage commercial and industrial development or affordable housing construction. For all but the smallest deals, multilayered financing has become the norm. The availability of equity capital and the terms that can be obtained for construction loans or permanent mortgages are influenced by results of market studies, which is why market research is so important.

This book is organized around real estate product types: the first three chapters introduce that topic, discuss the basic approaches, and instruct readers on where to find and how to present or interpret data (with an emphasis on employment information). Chapter 4 highlights demographic information needed to understand demand; discusses residential product types (both for sale and rental); and introduces niche developments that target students, seniors, and low-income households. Chapter 5 covers retail development, where market changes have been most dramatic since the second edition was published.

Chapter 6 covers office markets, including growth in shared office spaces (typically referred to as "coworking") as a growing source of tenancy, especially in urban centers. Chapter 7 presents an expanded discussion of industrial real estate as it reflects on how the growing importance of e-commerce and omni-channel retailing affects the market for warehouse or distribution space. It also notes the concentration of industrial development in major port and railroad intermodal centers. Chapter 8 provides information about hotels and other short-term lodging options. Chapter 9 explains mixed-use projects and what is needed for them to succeed. An appendix includes a glossary and a webliography.

Throughout the book, considerable attention is given to providing information about data that are available from both public and private-sector sources. Note, however, that new information sources (and providers) are always emerging, while established ones may merge or change, with their products evolving over time. With greater use of "big data" to guide real estate investment decisions, competition among information providers is heating up, and fewer supply-side sources are available to market analysts without paid subscriptions or one-time fees.

Where possible, we have provided examples of information that can be obtained free. Those examples come from publicly available reports that are commissioned by government agencies or provided on commercial brokerage websites (where quality data and analytic reports can help persuade property owners or tenants to use the brokerage firms' sales, leasing, financing, or property management services). The examples are not intended to suggest the full range of market information that can be obtained from private providers whose primary business is selling research services. Also, this book does not indicate prices for statistics obtained from private vendors because availability, geographic coverage, and costs change over time.

This book is intended for real estate, planning, architecture, and business students. It is also a useful reference for individuals who are starting a career with real estate investment, development, or property management companies, as well as related public sector agencies. It will also be helpful for experienced professionals who are shifting to different disciplines within the real estate development field and the public sector or for those who just want to gain an understanding of real estate market analysis methods and information sources.

CONTENTS

Abbreviations and Acronyms viii

CHAPTER 1
Understanding Real Estate Market Analysis 2

What Is Real Estate Market Analysis? 5

Why Do a Market Analysis? 5

How Does Market Analysis Fit into the
Development Process? 7

Who Uses Market Analysis? 7

Who Does Market Analyses? 9

Factors Affecting the Cost of a Market Study 11

Summary 12

Book Outline 12

CHAPTER 2
Basic Approach to Real Estate
Market Studies 14

Describing the Regional or Metropolitan Setting 15

Defining the Market Area 16

Inspecting the Site 18

Demand Analysis 19

Supply Analysis 20

Reconciling Demand and Supply 21

Recommendations 23

Importance of Illustrations 24

Providing an Executive Summary 25

CHAPTER 3
Market Conditions: Employment,
Demographics, Demand, and Supply 26

Economic Indicators 28

Visitor Profiles and Tourism Trends 36

Consumer Demographics 36

Demographic Data Sources 42

Consumer Surveys and Focus Groups 45

Documentation of Historical Supply Trends
and Current Conditions 49

Importance of Fieldwork 54

Documentation of Historical and Future
Construction Activity 55

Presentation of Findings 55

CHAPTER 4
Housing 58

Housing Stock Overview: Products and
Community Types 59

Single-Family and Multifamily Stock:
Size and Age 67

Cyclical Nature of New Housing Construction 68

Characteristics of New Single-Family Homes 69

New Multifamily Buildings: Styles, Sizes,
and Features 71

Housing Tenure 73

Demographic Trends Affecting
U.S. Housing Markets 77

Preparing a Housing Market Study 83

Recommendations and Monitoring 97

Data Sources 98

CHAPTER 5
Retail Space 104

Why Do a Retail Market Study? 105

Trends in Shopping and Spending 106

Types of Shopping Centers 112

Staying Competitive 119

Prospects for New Construction 121

Preparing a Retail Market Study.............................. 122

Defining the Trade Area 123

Trade Area Demand Demographics and
Purchasing Power... 125

Using Shopper Data Analytics................................. 129

Understanding the Supply Side 130

Construction Activity and Future Competition 131

Putting It All Together... 131

Data Sources 131

CHAPTER 6
Office Space **136**

Characteristics of Office Buildings 137

Using Office Market Studies.................................... 142

Preparing an Office Market Study 143

Defining the Market Area.. 143

Site Evaluation 144

Demand for Office Space... 144

Tracking Supply.. 149

Evaluating Competitive Buildings 151

Putting It All Together.. 152

Data Sources 153

CHAPTER 7
Industrial and Warehouse Space **156**

Characteristics of Industrial and
Warehouse Buildings 157

Specialized Markets 162

Demand for Industrial Space................................... 163

Defining the Market Area.. 164

Supply Analysis.. 165

Putting It All Together.. 169

Data Sources 169

CHAPTER 8
Hotels and Lodging **172**

Hotels as Real Estate 174

Product Types 175

Preparing the Market Study..................................... 183

Evaluating a Site.. 184

Determining the Competitive Market Area............... 184

Analyzing Demand Segments................................... 185

Fluctuations in Demand... 189

Competitive Inventory.. 190

Future Supply... 192

Projecting Performance 193

Data Sources 194

CHAPTER 9
Mixed-Use Development...................................... **196**

Background... 197

Analyzing the Market Potential of
Mixed-Use Projects 200

Understanding Synergy 202

Using Consumer Research and Social Media 206

Putting It All Together.. 207

Appendixes **210**

A. Glossary... 211

B. Webliography... 217

Index **224**

ABBREVIATIONS AND ACRONYMS

3PL	third-party logistics company
AAA	American Automobile Association
AARP	formerly known as American Association of Retired Persons
ACS	American Community Survey
ADR	average daily room rate
AGI	adjusted gross income
AHS	American Housing Survey
AMI	area's median income
APA	American Planning Association
ARDA	American Resort Development Association
ASHA	American Seniors Housing Association
B&B	bed-and-breakfast
BEA	Bureau of Economic Analysis
BEBR	Bureau of Economic and Business Research
BLS	Bureau of Labor Statistics
BOPUS	buy online, pick up in store
CAM	common area maintenance
CBD	central business district
CBP	County Business Patterns
CBSA	core-based statistical area
CCRC	continuing care retirement community
CES	Current Employment Statistics
CEX	Consumer Expenditure Survey
CMD	Construction Market Data (firm)
CPS	Current Population Survey
CRE	Counselors of Real Estate
FAR	floor/area ratio
FHA	Federal Housing Administration
FHFA	Federal Housing Finance Agency
FMR	Fair-Market Rents (HUD)
GAFO	general merchandise, apparel and accessories, furniture and home furnishings, and other goods
GIS	geographic information system
GLA	gross leasable area
HUD	U.S. Department of Housing and Urban Development
HVAC	heating, ventilation, and air conditioning
ICSC	International Council of Shopping Centers
IRS	Internal Revenue Service
JLL	Jones Lang LaSalle
LAUS	Local Area Unemployment Statistics

LED	Local Employment Dynamics
LEED	Leadership in Energy and Environmental Design
LEHD	Longitudinal Employer-Household Dynamics
LIHTC	low-income housing tax credits
LMA	labor market area
LODES	LEHD Origin Destination Employment Statistics
LQ	location quotient
MHI	Manufactured Housing Institute
MPC	master-planned community
MSA	metropolitan statistical area
NAA	National Apartment Association
NAHB	National Association of Home Builders
NAICS	North American Industrial Classification System
NAIOP	NAIOP, the Commercial Real Estate Development Association (formerly National Association of Industrial and Office Parks)
NAR	National Association of Realtors
NCHMA	National Council of Housing Market Analysts
NIC	National Investment Center for Seniors Housing & Care
NIMBY	not in my backyard
NLIHC	National Low Income Housing Coalition
NMHC	National Multifamily Housing Council
OM	offering memorandum
PPS	Project for Public Spaces
PUMS	Public Use Microdata Sample
QCEW	Quarterly Census of Employment and Wages
R&D	research and development
REIT	real estate investment trust
RevPAR	revenue per available room
RevPOR	revenue per occupied room
SMERF	social, military, educational, religious, and fraternal
SNAP	Supplemental Nutrition Assistance Program
STEM	science, technology, engineering, and math
TIF	tax increment financing
TOD	transit-oriented development
ULI	Urban Land Institute
USDA	U.S. Department of Agriculture
VA	U.S. Department of Veterans Affairs
Vrbo	vacation rental by owner
ZBP	Zip Codes Business Patterns

REAL ESTATE
MARKET ANALYSIS
Trends, Methods, and Information Sources

CHAPTER 1

UNDERSTANDING REAL ESTATE MARKET ANALYSIS

Real estate market analysis provides guidance for the many decision-makers—in both the private and public sectors—who are involved in real estate development. It is an ongoing process that conveys vital information during predevelopment, acquisition, development, marketing, and disposition of a property. The goal of market analysis is to minimize the risks to and maximize the opportunities for developers, investors, lenders, and public-sector participants. Good market analysis combines timely and accurate information from a variety of sources with nuanced interpretation of the data based on real-world experience and on-the-ground observations. Although market studies are filled with data, interpreting the data takes experience, conversations with knowledgeable local professionals, and fieldwork. Drawing conclusions from the data is more of an art than a science.

The word *market* can be used in a variety of ways. Businesspeople usually use the word to mean the various ways of grouping customers, including geographic location (the Pacific Northwest, a county, a group of zip codes, suburbs, or city neighborhoods); demographic profiles (millennials, empty nesters, seniors); and product types (off-price stores, big-box warehouses, upscale hotels, class A office space). Economists refer to both buyers and sellers when describing markets in terms of supply and demand, while marketing professionals consider sellers to be the client and buyers to be the market.

In real estate, *product* refers to property type (for example, apartment buildings, offices, warehouses), which is further classified by locational attributes, size or layout, quality, design features, project amenities, services, and prices or rents. Hotels are subdivided into convention and conference properties, full-service or limited-service establishments, and resort facilities oriented to tourists. Retail projects can include regional malls, neighborhood strip centers, "power" or "lifestyle" centers, outlet malls, and urban street retail. The housing sector can be segmented by physical characteristics into single-family detached or attached models or low-rise, mid-rise, and high-rise apartments, and by tenure (for sale or rental).

Industrial properties include warehouses with 36-foot-high ceilings; "last mile" distribution facilities serving e-commerce; research laboratories; and modest low-rise "flex" space used for offices, light assembly, and storage. Narrowly defining the market segment helps fine-tune the analysis.

A project's architecture, construction materials, layout, and finishes all influence perceived quality. Most types of real estate can be customized to some extent to meet the needs and wants of the buyer or tenant. For-sale housing offers numerous options, including upgraded appliance packages, a choice of exterior facades, bonus rooms for additional space, and decor (flooring, cabinetry, countertops).

Hotels offer rooms with different bed configurations and spacious suites. Office buildings typically offer a tenant improvement allowance to a company that is leasing new space or renovating its existing space as an incentive to remain in place; tenants may opt to spend more. Companies providing shared workspaces offer desks, private offices, or group project space with flexible arrangements by the day, week, or month.

A mid-rise apartment building with ground-floor shops at the Domain II in Austin, Texas. *(CBRE Austin office)*

Neotraditional homes on small lots in a suburban town center. *(Deborah L. Brett & Associates)*

Most rental property types offer standard tenant services (building management, maintenance of common areas, security, janitorial service). In today's marketplace—where up-to-date digital connections and high-tech capabilities are vital—high-speed internet, wi-fi, cable television, streaming video connections, and sophisticated security systems are required, not optional. Such features are not just for luxury properties. Enclosed shopping malls, town centers, and outlet malls typically provide joint marketing and promotional services for all the tenants, with the cost typically passed through on a pro rata basis. Office buildings, apartment complexes, and hotels offer an array of concierge services, exercise facilities, meeting and event space, and social activities. Housing for seniors might offer optional meals, maid service, and personal care on an as-needed basis, along with a variety of group activities. Hotels catering to business travelers often include shops, restaurants, and bars. Their fitness centers are more spacious and provide more equipment than offered 10 years ago, or a hotel may provide complimentary passes for its guests at a nearby gym. Depending on distance, hotels often provide airport shuttle service. Guests can enjoy free breakfast buffets—a time saver for business travelers and a stress saver for families with children. Some of those services provide additional income to management; others are covered by room revenue but are needed to be competitive. Developers must consider all of those "extras" when they evaluate the strengths of competitive properties.

Market analysis forms the basis for decisions regarding location and site, project size, design and quality, features and amenities, target audience, pricing, and phasing. Although market analysis examines demographic trends and forecasts sales, rents, vacancies, and absorption, further qualitative insights are increasingly important. For example, a housing market analyst looking at a proposed condominium building needs to know what design features appeal to homebuyers in certain communities. Surveys, psychographic research, and focus groups are useful tools in doing customer research.

A strong overall market does not necessarily equate to a good opportunity for development. Neither does a weak market mean that a good idea is not feasible. In other words, a good market from the perspective of demand may be oversupplied; at the same time, a good concept may overcome the challenges of a slow-growth market. Moreover, not all demand is driven by growth; many opportunities exist to replace obsolete properties—those buildings that are deteriorated, are poorly located, or are no longer meeting the needs of consumers. In-depth market analysis can reveal opportunities that may not be readily apparent. Poor implementation can undermine the most promising opportunities in any market, while even flawless execution cannot redeem a bad idea. Understanding the market is a prerequisite to generating good development ideas.

What Is Real Estate Market Analysis?

Real estate market analysis is the identification and study of demand and supply. On the demand side are the end users—the buyers or renters of real estate (homebuyers, apartment tenants, retail stores, businesses seeking office or warehouse space, visitors needing hotel accommodations). On the supply side are competitors—both existing properties and those at various stages in the development pipeline.

Market analysis identifies prospective users of real estate—both buyers and renters—and their characteristics. Some product types appeal to a relatively narrow market niche (for example, a for-sale residential development that is targeted to active seniors who like to play golf). Others reach broad segments of the potential market (for example, a supermarket-anchored retail center that a large percentage of residents in adjacent neighborhoods will patronize). Location influences the target market. A very desirable school district will draw families with young children. For childless households and empty nesters, the quality of schools will have little influence on the decision to rent or buy a home (although a home located in a good school district will have better resale prospects, all other things being equal).

Analyzing competition helps a developer determine how to set prices or rents. Homebuyers will pay more for a home if it offers more attractive or up-to-date features or styling than is found in another home. Tenants will be willing to pay the higher rents typical of a new building only if it has features, amenities, and locational attributes that are at least equivalent to those of established properties. It should be noted, however, that consumer preferences are always changing. Trendy features in today's market may quickly seem dated or unnecessary. Supply conditions also affect rents. If existing properties are experiencing high vacancy rates, prospective tenants may see opportunities to negotiate lower rents in older properties, thereby limiting the occupancy and income potential of a new building.

A market study can cover either a single land use or multiple property types. With the growing popularity of mixed-use development, a single report can cover more than one use, each with a distinct geographic area from which prospective buyers or tenants will be drawn (as discussed in chapter 9). A good example is a downtown, high-rise apartment building with retail space on the ground floor. The target market for the apartments could include young adults from throughout the city or county who want to live in a vibrant neighborhood or closer to their jobs. However, the main source of patronage for the retail space could be nearby workers, with residents of the building providing secondary market support.

Depending on the type of project proposed, the geographic scope of a market study can be national or regional, but more often it covers a relatively small geographic area. The market area (or *trade area* for retail properties) is the geographic region from which the majority of demand comes and where the majority of competitors are located. Market reports that cover an entire metropolitan area or report on countywide conditions will help set the context for project-level decision-making. For hotels and other lodging, competitive supply will consist of nearby properties with comparable services, amenities, and price points, but demand is not estimated on the basis of local population demographics.

A narrowly focused market study will yield the most useful results. For example, providing background information on performance for all hotels in a region is a good starting point, but more useful data come from focusing on directly competitive properties in the same price and amenity categories in nearby locations.

Most real estate market analyses examine both the market potential and the marketability, or competitiveness, of the proposed project. The analysis of market potential examines aggregate data about demand and supply. Demand is, by far, the more difficult half of the equation. Projecting the strength of demand requires a mix of research, experience, and intuition.

Why Do a Market Analysis?

Just as there are many types of market studies, there are many reasons for doing them, from researching the potential of a site to refocusing a marketing effort that has not been successful. Such studies accomplish the following:

- *Provide input for preliminary project planning.* Developers will often commission a market overview when they are deciding whether to exercise an option on a parcel or to proceed with the initial stages of land planning and engineering for a project. This type of market study is often a memo or brief report with supporting data. It analyzes the location's advantages and drawbacks, suggests the types of uses that would be appropriate, and provides general guidelines on the range of rents or prices that are possible given current market conditions. The developer can then decide whether it makes sense to hire a site planner to examine zoning requirements, how many units or buildings the site could accommodate, what traffic issues to consider, and whether detailed environmental studies will be necessary.

- *Generate inputs for financial feasibility analysis.* The results of the market analysis lead to assumptions that developers use to analyze the financial feasibility of a project. The market study's conclusions regarding achievable rents and prices, the potential for additional income from project amenities or upgrades, and the absorption and vacancy rate forecasts are important in determining projected cash flows and returns on investment. Developers can also run alternative scenarios to predict the effect on the bottom line if market conditions change.

- *Demonstrate the potential for a new product or an unproven location.* As demographics of an area change, existing property types may not meet current need. For example, a more upscale retail center may be appropriate for an evolving neighborhood even though it is untested in that marketplace. Sometimes a developer can create a market for a new product type. A new rental apartment community can quickly render existing apartments obsolete in the minds of renters, thus creating a market for more "on-trend" units. Using environmentally friendly design, materials, and equipment can enhance marketability, although not all tenants or buyers are willing to pay the additional short-term costs associated with ecofriendly features. The notion of what constitutes the most desirable hotel accommodations, office floor plans, retail locations, or apartment features can change seemingly overnight, thus forcing owners and managers to upgrade older buildings or lower their price points.

Locations once considered remote, unsafe, or inaccessible can become desirable. Expanding transit service, creating usable open space, providing a new highway interchange, or improving the perceived quality of public schools can change the attractiveness of available parcels, thereby offering opportunities to savvy, pioneering developers.

■ *Attract equity investors, debt financing, or government financial assistance.* Partners, lenders, and other parties that are providing capital for a project need evidence that the developer's expectations are well founded and that the proposed project can generate an attractive return, carry its debt load, or justify participation by government agencies. Investors and lenders will often commission their own market studies (separate from those submitted by the developer) as part of their due diligence requirements. Staff members or consultants may conduct those studies.

■ *Create a better, more marketable product.* Market studies can help fine-tune the product by revealing the characteristics and demands of consumers or commercial space users. For large projects, the market analyst should be an active member of the developer's pre-construction team, which will also include land planners, civil and environmental engineers, architects, traffic consultants, financial analysts, public relations specialists, and attorneys. Give-and-take among the development professionals is likely to result in a more successful project.

■ *Build community support for private development.* Few projects can proceed without some type of approval or assistance from a government agency, be it a zoning variance, a modification of site planning standards or permitted uses, or help in assembling land for a redevelopment project. When evaluating development proposals, local staff members, elected officials, and consultants usually focus on density, utility capacity, parking, and traffic. However, developers who are requesting public subsidy or tax increment financing (TIF) for a project may be required to submit a market study and financial projections that demonstrate the need for government funding and to conclude that the development has the potential to succeed.

A rooftop bar in New York City. *(Gregorio Koji/Shutterstock.com)*

- *Provide input for public-sector housing or economic development strategies.* Government agencies need to monitor real estate markets. At a minimum, local governments have a vested interest in keeping abreast of trends that affect property tax collections. And they may aggressively seek to attract development while hoping to diversify their tax base, revitalize a sagging business district, or provide needed workforce housing. State housing finance and economic development agencies often require that market studies be done before those agencies will issue revenue bonds or allocate tax credits for affordable housing or commercial projects.

How Does Market Analysis Fit into the Development Process?

Market studies are important at many stages of development. At the earliest point, an analyst might be asked to look at one or several metropolitan areas for development potential (sometimes called *market screening*). The analyst will then focus on a submarket and finally seek out a site that is most appropriate for the proposed development concept. But given the limited availability of developable land today, it is more common for a developer to have an eye on a specific site and ask that the site be studied.

If the site proves viable, the market analyst might provide a basis for determining its value so that a purchase price can be negotiated. In most cases, an appraiser will create a formal estimate of value. Either the market analyst or the land planner will investigate the development climate of the jurisdiction while looking for answers to the following questions:

- Is the proposed project likely to meet with public acceptance?
- Is the proposed development compatible with existing zoning for the site?
- If not, how likely is it that variances or rezoning will be approved in a timely manner?
- Are utilities readily available? For a residential project, which schools would additional children attend, and do the schools have the capacity to serve them?
- What public improvements are scheduled or planned for the area that would enhance the project's appeal?
- Are there difficulties that might slow or hinder development? Although the market analyst will not be qualified to deal with environmental and engineering issues, an analyst may identify potential problems that need further exploration.

Recognizing that entitlement authorities represent the citizens who must be sold on a project, experienced developers have learned that it is useful to address local concerns from the onset. A series of negotiations transpire as developers adjust their projects to respond to local issues. It is far better to identify and address community concerns early in the project approval process than to face a concerned (or hostile) audience at a public hearing. Elected officials are much more comfortable issuing approvals when the electorate is at ease with a project.

Although market analysis is a crucial part of the initial feasibility study for a real estate project, developers and owners must continue to monitor market conditions throughout the project design, approval, construction, sales or leasing, and management stages. Once the project has been completed for a few years, market analysts might be asked to evaluate the project's performance, comparing its occupancy, rent levels, and other metrics with predevelopment forecasts. It is very common for market analysts to be consulted for repositioning strategies after a project is up and running if the developer sees that absorption is not meeting projections. Property managers continually monitor their competitors, either through direct contact or by using data from third-party providers, checking to see how occupancy has changed, determining whether rents have moved up or down, and using new information to reposition the project as conditions change.

Who Uses Market Analysis?

Developers cannot rely solely on instinct or even experience to decide what to build or to assure prospective investors or lenders that a project will succeed. A rigorous market study early in the process stimulates development ideas, improves initial concepts, and helps control risk. However, developers are not the only players who benefit from market analysis. Research benefits not only the parties with a financial stake in the project but also the community whose well-being the proposed project will affect.

Developers

Real estate developers are probably the most frequent users of market studies, especially if they will continue to own or manage their buildings after construction is completed. Although the need for market analysis is most obvious during the predevelopment process, reports are often updated when a developer applies for construction financing and again when sales or leasing efforts are underway. A good market study helps a developer

- Determine whether a location is suitable for development, or consider alternative locations.
- Identify a product or mix of products that best meets the demands of the market.
- Understand existing and potential competition, and then evaluate their advantages and disadvantages when compared with the proposed project.
- Identify the nature and depth of demand.
- Provide guidance for land planners and architects and offer input for initial design concepts and later refinements.
- Suggest project pricing, sizing, and phasing.

The Wynwood Walls art installation in Miami has stimulated neighborhood reinvestment. *(Jenner Furst)*

- Generate key inputs for cash flow analysis in support of loan applications or equity syndication.
- Persuade elected officials and government agency staff members to provide entitlements, financial incentives, or utility services for a proposed development.
- Devise a marketing plan by identifying market niches or prospective buyers or renters and then suggest how to reach them.
- Learn why a completed product is not selling or leasing as expected.

Government Officials

As suggested earlier, government officials may ask developers to provide a market study as part of the approval process, or they may commission their own studies from either staff members or consultants. The scope of a public-sector real estate market study can cover conditions in an entire metropolitan area or county, or it can focus on a specific neighborhood, industrial area, local business district, or proposed development site. Examples of areawide studies are the "Comprehensive Housing Market Analysis" reports issued by the U.S. Department of Housing and Urban Development (HUD). In some cases, a municipality or authority will commission a market study for a specific development proposal; the government may hire the consultant, with the developer paying the fee. Or the

developer will hire a consultant who provides a scope of services that the government agency or department has approved.

Public officials use market studies to help with the following:

- Better understand community- or region-wide housing demand or the reasonableness of a proposed economic development strategy.
- Identify affordable housing needs and possible locations where new housing construction should be encouraged.
- Comply with state and federal grant requirements.
- Provide support for redevelopment plans.
- Review requests for zoning changes or expansion of utility service areas.
- Calculate the effect of new housing on schools.
- Determine the effects of new commercial development on parking or traffic conditions in an established business district.
- Justify creation of special improvement districts or TIF districts.
- Identify likely demand for transit-oriented development when new rail lines or multimodal facilities are being planned.
- Determine the fiscal impact of a proposed project to use when negotiating impact fees.

- Justify using incentives to stimulate a neglected market niche, such as artists' housing.

- Provide employers with information about housing stock, prices, rents, and vacancies for use when recruiting personnel.

- Support infrastructure investment in facilities that will draw tourists and other visitors.

Investors and Lenders

Market studies provide input for cash flow analysis, which demonstrates to lenders if a project's income is likely to cover its debt service and tells investors what returns they could expect on their investments. A lender will look at the developer's market study to decide whether to consider a loan application, but the lender may ultimately commission its own study. Lending institutions and government agencies that provide bond financing have their own standards for market-study content and may or may not deem a developer's study to be sufficiently detailed. Or the lender may be concerned about changes in market conditions that might have emerged over time. Equity syndicators, corporate investors, and limited partners may have similar concerns.

Lenders and investors need to feel comfortable that a proposed development, costly renovation, or adaptive use is appropriate for the site or building, as well as for the presumed market. More specifically, they will ask the market analyst to offer an opinion on whether

- Prospective buyers or tenants exist in sufficient numbers and can be attracted to the location.

- The project will lease-up or sell at the pace estimated by the developer's consultant or staff members.

- Proposed prices and rents make sense in light of what the competition is offering.

- The amenities to be offered are necessary or appropriate for the marketplace.

- The project will generate sufficient income to cover operating expenses and debt service, and still generate profits that will provide an attractive return on investment.

Market studies are also needed when developers buy or sell a piece of vacant land or when they acquire or dispose of an investment property. Generally, transactions are backed by an appraisal, but sometimes a market analysis report is completed either as part of the appraisal or instead of one. Researching recent transactions and competitive rents helps owners identify an appropriate selling price for a completed project. For a vacant tract, land value can be determined by having the purchaser use market study results to model total project value upon completion and then by assigning a share of the value to the land itself.

If a property's performance is not meeting expectations, a market study can suggest how upgrading or repositioning could improve occupancy or rent levels. Such a market study might be initiated by the owner's property or asset manager or by investors.

Tenants or Buyers

Commercial tenants, such as office-based businesses, retail stores, or warehouse users, may conduct their own market research when they consider signing or extending a lease. Large space users may look to the services of a broker or an independent market analyst to help them decide on the best locations for their operations. Corporate real estate managers will analyze the advantages of locating in different metropolitan areas or will examine the suitability of buildings that they are considering for purchase or lease. Apartment tenants and small businesses are not likely to commission market studies, but they will often rely on published market data from local real estate brokers or will consult online sources to determine the asking rents at nearby competitive projects.

Figure 1-1 depicts the many participants in the real estate industry who use market analyses and the reasons they do.

Who Does Market Analyses?

Many types of real estate professionals specialize in providing market analysis services. They may be employed by consulting firms that specialize in real estate research or services, by research departments of brokerage firms, or by commercial real estate appraisal firms. Large developers often have a team of in-house analysts. Contact information for market analysts can be found in the membership rosters of organizations such as the Urban Land Institute (ULI), Lambda Alpha International (the land economics honorary society), Counselors of Real Estate (CRE), and American Planning Association (APA). Other professional organizations represent analysts who cover niche markets. For example, the National Council of Housing Market Analysts (NCHMA) publishes a directory of market study providers, which is available on its website. Retail market specialists are likely to be members of the International Council of Shopping Centers (ICSC). Public accounting firms also have active real estate practices; their staff members include market analysts who specialize in hotels, resort and timeshare communities, affordable housing, and other real estate investments.

Larger market research firms often have multiple offices, and their analysts work in metropolitan areas throughout the United States and worldwide. Many firms concentrate their efforts in specific cities or regions. Specializing in only one or two land uses—housing or retail, office and industrial space, or hotels—is common because it allows staff members to develop in-depth knowledge and data sources that reflect their specialties.

Real estate brokerages also prepare summary market analyses covering national, regional, and local conditions. National firms use their networks of local offices to provide insight into local conditions, as well as statistics about market performance and future construction announcements. Brokerage reports tend to focus more on supply than on demand, but good reports will include an economic overview that covers trends in key indicators like employment or household growth. Major firms such as CBRE Group (formerly CB Richard Ellis), Colliers International, Cushman & Wakefield, JLL (formerly Jones Lang LaSalle), Marcus & Millichap, NAI Global, and Newmark Knight Frank publish data on their websites. Some data are available only to clients, but all such firms regularly release information and insights about market conditions for public use. Those data either are on their global websites or are available through local affiliates. When a brokerage represents a property that is being offered for sale, it often will prepare a market overview in addition to providing information and photographs for the specific property; thus, an offering memorandum (OM) for a sizable project or portfolio will be quite detailed.

The past two decades have seen dramatic growth in private subscription data services that provide overviews of market conditions for one or more land uses. Their reports cover broad trends and, like broker reports, emphasize the supply side. They provide information about the size and quality of the inventory, often classifying space as class A, B, or C (typically for apartment complexes, office buildings, and industrial space) or—in the case of hotels—by market niche (convention-oriented, luxury, budget, etc.). Some private data vendors focus on single-family housing or senior housing only. Vendors then further segment the inventory into geographic submarkets, with information about rent or price trends, occupancy, absorption, and construction activity. Unlike brokerage reports, some private data services permit customized geographies, which will allow the analyst to narrow in on the most competitive properties. In addition, private data vendors offer a wealth of historical information that may not be included in a publicly available brokerage report. This book's later chapters and annotated webliography in the appendix contain more information about data sources.

Trade associations also compile data that provide important insights into market conditions for the nation and larger metropolitan areas. For example, the website of the National Association of Realtors (NAR) provides regular updates on the median sales prices of homes in metropolitan areas. The National Association of Home Builders (NAHB) has resources on its website that focus on new home construction and affordability; some data are available free of charge, while other information requires a fee. Local

Figure 1-1

Market Studies: Clients and Their Objectives

Purpose or objective	Developer	Equity investor/ partner	Buyer	Seller	Lender	Redevelopment agency	Housing finance or economic development authority	Tenant/ owner	Realtor/ broker
Market overview for use in brochure and publications	X			X		X	X		X
Input for corporate location/ relocation/expansion decisions								X	
Devising/revising real estate investment strategies	X	X							
Product planning, design, pricing, phasing	X								
Obtaining zoning or other government approvals	X					X			
Input/assumptions for cash flow analysis	X	X	X		X				
Loan application support	X				X				
As part of a sales offering package				X		X			X
Acquisition due diligence			X					X	
Lender due diligence					X	X	X		
In ongoing asset management		X						X	

Source: Deborah L. Brett & Associates.

NAHB affiliates may provide more detailed data for smaller geographic areas, which allows the market analyst to compare price levels and sales activity in different parts of a state or in specific counties.[1] Local appraisers who specialize in residential development or resales may also have this information (available for a fee) in the counties where they work.

Factors Affecting the Cost of a Market Study

Developers often underestimate the value of an impartial assessment of the market. They understand that they will have to pay for the services of other professionals—an architect, land planner, and engineer, at a minimum—to get plans approved, but they see no need to pay for an outside market study unless a lender or a government agency asks them to do so. Even when they recognize the need for an objective analysis, they may not have a realistic sense of what a market study will cost.

The study objectives, the expertise needed, and the complexity of the research will all influence the cost of market research. A developer, lender, investor, or government agency that is considering hiring a consultant to conduct a market study must take into account a number of factors when budgeting for the work:

- *Number of land uses to be studied.* The volume of data that a consultant must collect and analyze is much greater for a multiuse project than for a single-use property. If a residential development will have both rental and for-sale components, data about the characteristics of household demand may be the same for both housing types, but the market analyst will have to visit many more potentially competitive properties. A mixed-use project comprising office space, a hotel, and condominiums will require more detailed analysis of employment data and sources of demand for hotel rooms than will a condominium study alone. There may be some economies of scale with multiple uses, but mixed-use projects are inherently more complex and thus riskier (as discussed in chapter 9) than are single-use projects. In some cases, more than one consultant will be necessary, and the scope of services for each expert analyst must be crafted carefully to avoid duplication of effort.

Adaptive use of the former Hahne & Company department store in Newark, New Jersey. The building provides apartments, retail space, a chef-branded casual restaurant, and arts collaboration space. *(Deborah L. Brett & Associates)*

- *Level of detail required.* At the early stages of the development process, an overview of local area demographics and key characteristics of the competition may suffice to provide ideas for project planning. In contrast, a report that will go to investors or lenders must include a careful exposition of methodology as well as detailed information about competitors and demand segments.

- *Using a market analyst with experience and credentials.* The level of experience that staff members need for a particular study will affect its cost. If senior consultants are needed, the study will obviously be more expensive than if it had been prepared by junior staff members. If relatively inexperienced personnel are doing field research or report writing in order to minimize fees, senior personnel who are familiar with all aspects of the work program should supervise them and review their reports and recommendations.

- *Fieldwork expenses.* Hiring a market analyst who is based in or near the location being studied can save on travel-related expenses. However, some developers or lenders and investors may prefer engaging a nationally known consultant or a person whose judgment they trust, even if doing so increases the fee.

- *Buying data.* Purchasing demographic data or supply inventories from private vendors can save time, but it can cost hundreds or even thousands of dollars, depending on the scope of the market study. Reports requiring high-quality photography, graphs, or mapping may also require outside assistance.

- *Hiring subcontractors.* If a consumer survey or focus groups are necessary for the market study, the consultant will probably need to find a specialist. Increasingly, consumer surveys are conducted online, but they must be structured by an experienced firm that can design a workable questionnaire, find the target audience, and tabulate responses. (See chapter 3 on the different types of consumer surveys.) Focus groups are still widely used, especially to get consumer reactions to proposed plans and designs. Such groups require experienced moderators who work with the client to structure the conversations, gauge reactions, and record comments.

- *Scheduling.* A developer or lender who asks a consultant to prepare a market study in a short time will often have to pay a premium; the consultant may need to bring in outside assistance to get the job done on time.

Summary

Market research is an investigation into needs and wants (*demand*) and into products (*supply*) that compete to satisfy those needs and wants. The availability of data has greatly improved over the years, but an experienced market analyst can and should ask questions about geographic coverage and breadth of building information. For example, industrial and office space statistics vary widely in what minimum building size they cover or whether the data include both single-tenant and multitenant occupancy. Reams of information must be synthesized using instinct born of experience, lest the analyst drown in the data and be unable to formulate conclusions. And nothing takes the place of old-fashioned shoe-leather fieldwork and driving the neighborhood for understanding the competition.

The importance of market research in real estate development, particularly in unfamiliar or highly competitive markets, cannot be overemphasized. Market research begins at the project's inception, when the idea to acquire a property or to develop a site first emerges, and it continues through the construction, marketing, and eventual disposition of the project.

Book Outline

This chapter has defined market analysis and discussed its uses and users. It has shown how market analysis fits into the development process as a way to improve decision-making at each stage. Useful research can be both broad (including national and regional economic overviews and development product trends) and highly focused (for example, fine-tuning features for kitchens at an apartment complex or the truck docking and loading facilities in a warehouse).

Subsequent chapters explain how to perform market analysis. Chapter 2 outlines the content of a market study, from researching the background of a region or metropolitan area to delineating a local market area, analyzing demand and supply, evaluating a site and its location, and documenting and illustrating the report. Chapter 3 provides general guidance about explaining economic trends and analyzing demand and supply, with a focus on labor force and employment information as a starting point for evaluating the need for all types of properties. Chapters 4 through 9 describe how to tailor the process to each product type by explaining how market areas differ for each land use, what product-specific methods are used for analyzing supply and demand, what types of data are needed, and where to find information. Each chapter includes commentary about national trends and how-to advice about interpreting available data. The appendix provides a glossary of terms used in real estate market analysis and an annotated webliography of public and private information sources.

This book focuses on conducting market studies in the United States. However, the basic approach to market analysis—methods and content—applies to real estate anywhere in the world. Product characteristics, consumer preferences, location considerations, and data sources are unique to each country; in many places, information about current conditions is relatively limited. The techniques for analyzing supply and demand, however, are the same no matter where they are used.

Note

1. Professional associations and trade groups—such as the National Apartment Association; National Association of Homebuilders; National Association of Realtors; NAIOP, the Commercial Real Estate Development Association; and National Multifamily Housing Council—can be useful sources of data and perspective about development trends and market conditions. Other organizations cover specialized properties, such as manufactured housing/mobile homes, senior housing, affordable housing, office parks, and tourism. Information on these organizations can be found in chapters 4 through 8 and in the webliography.

CHAPTER 2

CHAPTER 2

BASIC APPROACH TO REAL ESTATE MARKET STUDIES

This chapter outlines in general terms how to approach a real estate market analysis and what to include in a thorough report. It describes the basic tasks to be done, discusses the importance of field observations, and identifies the types of information needed to reach supportable conclusions. It also discusses how to use maps, tables, and illustrations to create persuasive reports.

Although the content and detail suggested in this chapter are most appropriate for a formal report on a proposed development plan, parts are relevant for shorter reports (for example, an overview of supply conditions, an update of performance indicators at competitive properties, or an examination of changes in demand demographics). Detailed how-to guidance for specific property types is presented in chapters 4 through 8; specific data sources are cited in the figures and sidebars throughout the book, as well as in the appendix.

Describing the Regional or Metropolitan Setting

The market analyst needs to set forth the regional economic context for a proposed development project. This introduction demonstrates to the reader that the report's conclusions and recommendations make sense in light of overall regional economic conditions. The analyst should provide background on the location of the site within the metropolitan area (for example, the distance to downtown, the airport, and other regional draws).[1] Some market analysts begin with an overview of key demographic indicators for the metropolitan area, such as population and household growth, and median household income. Others incorporate these indicators in sections of the report that discuss conditions in the local market area, thus providing an opportunity to easily compare and contrast regional or metropolitan areawide trends with conditions in the submarket or trade area where the project is proposed.

At a minimum, demographic and economic data should go back as far as the preceding decennial census. However, once the most recent census is more than a few years old,

the analyst will need to provide more current estimates and projections. For a fee, private data vendors such as Claritas and Esri issue current-year estimates and five-year projections for a variety of demographic indicators. Their data are available by subscription (which is usually more economical for analysts who use information for many places in a given year) or as a one-time-only custom order.

It is useful to compare current estimates from private vendors with those prepared by the U.S. Census Bureau (which issues metropolitan, county, and municipal population estimates every two years). For metropolitan areas and larger places, the Census Bureau's American Community Survey (ACS) provides selected demographic and housing statistics annually. The scope of the ACS has expanded over the past decade.[2] However, the ACS does not cover small suburbs and rural counties annually, nor does the Census Bureau issue population projections at the metropolitan and local levels.[3] State and regional planning agencies or universities often prepare projections, which can be compared with private estimates.

The overview of the region or metropolitan area should also include a discussion of employment trends, because job growth creates demand for real estate products. The data on employment should indicate how the number of jobs has grown over the preceding five to 10 years, with a discussion of industries that expanded or declined. A market study often includes a look at the characteristics of the area's largest employers. For hotel studies, the overview should discuss areawide trends in tourism, convention attendance, and business meeting bookings—data that are usually available from the convention and visitor bureaus in large cities or from state tourism agencies. Chapter 8 adds information about finding visitor data.

In addition to the federal government's Bureau of Labor Statistics (BLS), state labor departments are useful sources of information on employment by industry as well as trends in unemployment rates for metropolitan areas and counties. Analysts must look carefully at the data series when they create tables with historical information, because the BLS frequently benchmarks or revises the numbers. Also, some data series do not include self-employed workers, farm workers, military personnel, or workers who do not pay into state unemployment compensation systems. Most federal and state labor information sources do not provide data for small areas (individual suburbs, zip codes, or census tracts). Usually, states have information for individual counties or multicounty labor market areas (LMAs). Some local statistics are available through the Census Bureau's interactive OnTheMap program.[4] It is important for market analysts to use a consistent data series when they track trends and to note exclusions or omissions. Chapter 3 provides more information on employment data, where to find them, and how to present them.

The regional or metropolitan overview should also include information on construction activity. For housing studies, the analyst should track building permit information for at least five years, preferably with separate tabulations for single-family and multifamily activity. Because the Census Bureau collects residential permit data from individual permit-issuing jurisdictions, it is possible to calculate the percentage of permits in a metropolitan area that are captured in a local market with multiple jurisdictions. Some state websites tabulate the number of units for which permits were issued.

Free information on nonresidential construction activity is more difficult to find. Some state and regional agencies collect this information from local jurisdictions, but most do not. Local affiliates of large national commercial real estate brokerages will have this information; it may be available on the company's national website. Local brokers who track commercial and industrial construction activity can also be helpful. However, metro area data that are available on brokerage websites do not always provide the needed level of detail. Better information may be available from regional/local real estate professionals, government economic development staff members, and local business and real estate publications (online and in print).

Defining the Market Area

One of the initial challenges facing the market analyst is how best to define the boundaries of the property's market area (or the trade area in a retail market study). In reality, properties often have two market areas—one from which most potential tenants or buyers will be drawn and another in which key competitors are located.

Preliminary studies may define a market or trade area using three-, five-, or 10-mile radius rings to determine whether the population meets a minimum threshold size. Each ring includes the area within the stated number of miles from the subject site—without taking access, barriers, or density into consideration. Ring data are relatively inexpensive to obtain from private vendors.

For a retail market study, simple trade area rings are useful for an initial review of a market's population size or expenditure potential, but they will not accurately portray a site's actual "draw." A precise trade area definition will not extend equally in all directions because it needs to take into account transportation patterns, natural and built boundaries, and cultural or political factors. Devising an accurate market area definition will usually require first visiting the site of a proposed development or acquisition; analysts must also consider data availability and the cost of information collection when they draw a market area.

More precise trade areas for residential and retail properties are usually defined as a combination of census tracts, zip codes, municipalities, or counties from which the vast majority of customers (homebuyers, apartment renters, shoppers) will be drawn. In large cities, planning departments typically assemble census information for city-defined neighborhoods. (As noted earlier, decennial census counts become dated over time, especially in neighborhoods experiencing rapid change.)

The analyst should recognize that zip codes often do not conform to municipal boundaries, nor do they necessarily reflect neighborhood residents' sense of "turf" or local traffic patterns. However, private data vendors have sophisticated geocoded software that permits creation of customized market or trade areas that the analyst can specify—perhaps a polygon, an area between arterial streets, or a corridor with multiple highway interchanges—that realistically reflect where local residents will shop or where office tenants will look for space. Once the market area is mapped, the analyst can request demographic data for that geographic area.

For commercial properties, competitive market areas are likely to cluster in downtowns, in master-planned office parks, or at suburban retail nodes along highways or major arterials. Industrial/warehouse competition may be found near ports, airports, or at interchanges where two or more interstate highways connect. Distance (miles and travel time) to customers or local distribution centers are the key factor for highway-oriented warehouse properties. For manufacturing, key factors could be availability of natural resources, skilled labor, or utility services. Rail connections may be a consideration, depending on the types of goods being produced. For all types of industrial properties, the availability of labor and accessibility for workers (including public transportation) are increasingly important.

Factors to Consider

Seven key factors affect the size and shape of a market area:

- *Natural features.* In some cases, lakes, rivers, or mountains cannot be traversed easily. Roads might be narrow or winding, or bridges might be few and far between. In other cases, natural features act as psychological or social barriers. ("Nobody from around here would drive halfway around the lake just to go to the supermarket.")

- *Built barriers.* Highways, railroad tracks, large industrial areas, and airports can restrict access to a site from nearby neighborhoods, thereby limiting the size of the trade area. The impact of these barriers varies by the type

An office/warehouse building in a business park. *(Deborah L. Brett & Associates)*

and scale of the proposed development. As a general rule, households will not want to cross a major barrier for everyday needs but will accept some inconvenience to reach a large shopping center. The absence of bridges across bodies of water can have a similar effect.

▪ *Traffic congestion.* Chronic traffic congestion can limit the size of trade areas and discourage potential homebuyers, apartment renters, or office tenants from looking at an otherwise attractive location. Traffic can also diminish the market for a retail facility by reducing the distance people are willing to drive in order to shop.

▪ *Population density.* A shopping center proposed for a densely developed city neighborhood will have a much smaller market area than will one proposed for a small town in a rural county. In urban neighborhoods and in areas around train stations, the primary trade area might be defined on the basis of walking distance—usually no more than a half mile. In rural areas where shopping choices are limited, customers will travel farther to shop for everyday necessities.

▪ *Political boundaries between cities and suburbs or between school districts.* Residential properties in communities with low crime rates and good schools will draw from a large trade area, all other things being equal. Political boundaries also determine real estate tax rates for all types of development. Tax rates can vary dramatically among municipalities in the same general area.

▪ *Neighborhood boundaries and identity.* Household income, family composition, education levels, and the age of the population all play a role in defining market areas, for both residential and commercial properties. Community identity, insularity, and image influence where people are willing to live or shop.

▪ *Development size and mix of uses.* Sizable projects will draw from large areas; smaller projects from small ones. A mixed-use development can cover multiple trade areas (for example, housing, offices, entertainment, and retail space) and thus draw potential buyers or tenants from different parts of the metropolitan region.

Primary and Secondary Markets or Trade Areas

More sophisticated residential or retail market studies will define both a primary market area, from which 60 to 80 percent of residential or retail patronage will be captured, and a secondary market area, which will generate the balance of demand. For retail studies, a portion of demand will also be allocated to *inflow*—retail purchases made by tourists and other visitors who do not reside in either the primary or the secondary trade area. Inflow can account for a significant share of sales at upscale super-regional shopping centers or outlet malls. (See chapter 5 for definitions of different types of retail centers and an in-depth discussion of how retail trade areas are defined.) Demand from outside the local area can also be significant for retirement housing. In metropolitan suburbs, developers of retirement communities will certainly draw homebuyers from nearby municipalities, but there are examples of developments where a majority of residents moved from quite a distance to be closer to family members or friends.

Hotel, resort, and second-home properties will target consumers who live well beyond a metropolitan area.

Demand is less dependent on local demographics than on transportation access (easy interstate highway or air connections), conditions in the general economy (growth in tourism, increasing affluence), interest in natural and built features (ski slopes, beaches, golf courses, hiking trails), and price points of the proposed development. The nearest competition may be located outside the immediate area or even out of state.

Competitive Clusters

As discussed earlier, office and industrial land uses tend to cluster along transportation routes; at highway interchanges; or around activity centers such as airports, seaports, universities, hospitals, or regional malls. When developers evaluate a prospective location for such commercial buildings, ease of access—to a labor force, clients, customers, and suppliers—is critical. The availability and cost of land and utilities, along with appropriate zoning and supportive local government policies, are also important factors in attracting new commercial and industrial development. The number of nearby residents and the characteristics of their households are less important for hotel, office, and industrial projects than whether the community is stable or growing and has a good reputation in the real estate community. In fact, for industrial uses, having fewer residential neighbors is preferable, thereby avoiding conflicts over truck traffic, noise, odors, or other factors that could delay project approvals.

As already discussed, a metropolitan area will typically encompass several major office clusters located downtown, in suburban business districts, and along key highway corridors. Industrial and warehouse buildings can also congregate in multiple locations—near a port or airport, along freight rail lines, or at the junction of interstate highways. The analyst examines the marketability of a proposed new office or industrial development (or the economic potential of an existing property that is being considered for acquisition) in light of both regional economic conditions and the performance of similar properties within the cluster or submarket.

Inspecting the Site

Field observations are critical to a high-quality market study. Analysts can rarely get an accurate understanding of a site and its environs without visiting the property. Maps can show the property's size and shape, and Google Earth can show aerial views of its surroundings, but visiting the site itself gives an analyst a sense of its topography, natural features, and views. The presence of mature trees on the site can be an asset for selling single-family homes but may be a cost concern for projects that require clearing land. Attractive views (mountains, lakes, rivers, skylines, historic features) can bring premium prices, but building on a parcel with steep slopes will increase the cost of site improvements and, for commercial uses, may limit visibility.

Visiting the site also provides an opportunity to assess the compatibility of the proposed development with surrounding uses. Unattractive or deteriorating buildings adjacent to or across the street from a site could deter potential tenants. An inspection will also reveal potential visibility issues or problems with access from nearby roads. The field visit offers the opportunity to meet with local planners to learn about the existing zoning, whether any

Food hall vendors and customers in downtown Chicago. *(Valerie S. Kretchmer Associates Inc.)*

variances might be needed for the envisioned uses, and if future infrastructure improvements might affect the marketability of the site. Field interviews with government agencies can also yield important information about potentially competitive development projects in the area that are in the planning pipeline. The site analysis should conclude with an assessment of the advantages and drawbacks of the site and its surroundings.

Assessing the Site's Advantages and Disadvantages

If the site is unimproved, the report should discuss its size, shape, and dimensions. It should briefly note the site's topography and vegetation, along with the presence of streams, ponds, or wetlands. The analyst should mention both positive and negative characteristics of the property or its location.

Site advantages might include location in a historic district (although architectural restrictions could impose development constraints), attractive views of the downtown skyline, or presence of mature trees that will remain after construction. Incompatible neighboring uses such as deteriorating nearby buildings; proximity to environmental hazards or landfills; and noise from highways, rail lines, or airports are negative characteristics—especially for residential development. The analyst should note access or visibility problems that could hamper marketability and therefore require corrective action. (The developer may have to pay for certain off-site infrastructure improvements.) If any changes are planned (such as a new commuter-rail station, highway construction, road widening, intersection improvements, or new traffic signals), the report should note when these improvements might be completed.

The analyst can assess certain site attributes as either positive or negative, depending on the proposed land use. Proximity to a major airport would benefit absorption of hotel rooms or warehouse space but would be less than ideal for an upscale residential subdivision. High traffic counts would not draw seniors to a retirement community but would attract shopping center developers and their tenants.

In addition to studying the site and its immediate environs, the analyst must consider factors such as community character and reputation. Low crime rates and the proximity to services that are necessary for daily living are also important for assessing a location's suitability for residential use. If new housing is targeted to young families, information about the reputation of the local school district, the availability of nearby daycare, and the location of community park and recreation programs should be part of the report. For office space, proximity to transit may be important for attracting tenants in a tight labor market. The presence of shops, restaurants, and entertainment in the area creates an identity that can lend prestige to an office location.

The analysis should discuss the property's zoning and permitted uses and should note whether any zoning changes or variances will be necessary before development begins. Knowing the allowable density—calculated as a function of floor/area ratio (FAR) for a commercial or industrial property and as units per acre for housing—is critical for determining project feasibility.

Proximity to Amenities

Nearby amenities can be key when a developer is selling a location to prospective tenants and buyers. Proximity is obviously important for a resort or second-home property that is intended to attract skiers, golfers, or boaters, but it is also important for conventional residential development. Homebuyers and renters want to walk, bike, or take only a short drive to shopping, recreation, schools, and entertainment facilities. Access to public transportation can make all the difference to potential residents in urban neighborhoods or mature suburbs. However, certain homebuyers still prefer remote, semirural locations where lots are larger or purchase prices are lower. Homebuilders assume that buyers in these areas will be comfortable with driving long distances to shop and with sending their children to school on buses. The market analyst must also determine whether bus pickup for students is even available. Some districts do not pick up students who live within a mile or two from school.

It is important for the analyst to drive around the area near the subject property while noting the location of amenities that buyers or tenants will consider essential. For example, for a residential development, the analyst should note the location of neighborhood stores, parks, schools, houses of worship, libraries, and health care services, as well as other basics in daily life. For an office building, convenient access to highway interchanges, rail stations, or express bus service is key. In downtown locations, nearby parking garages and lots should be identified. Prospective tenants will be drawn to areas with food and retail services because these locations will be attractive to their employees. Office tenants may want to be close to hotels for visiting vendors, clients, or employees from other locations. Businesses whose staff must frequently travel out of town will require proximity to the airport. In contrast, a retail chain's regional warehouse/distribution facility must be within an overnight drive of dozens of stores, so a location at the intersection of north–south and east–west interstate highways could be advantageous. For other types of industrial properties, rail service and proximity to ports and cargo airports may be essential.

Demand Analysis

As indicated earlier, it is useful to compare demographic trends in the trade area with those in the larger region, metropolitan area, or county. However, local characteristics beyond total population and household estimates and projections should receive greater emphasis. Age characteristics are especially important when analyzing the market for senior housing or for apartments that cater to young adults. Household composition (families with children, empty nesters, and singles) should also be noted.

Class A apartments in southern New Jersey. All units have two bedrooms and two baths; some have a den and a one-car garage. *(Deborah L. Brett & Associates)*

Detailed income data, when cross-tabulated with household age or other demographic indicators, can enable the analyst to identify the depth of targeted consumers—those whose housing or shopping preferences are likely to match the planned residential or retail space and those who have incomes sufficient to afford the rents or prices. Chapters 4 and 5 provide more insights into presenting this information.

For retail market studies, information should be added on how local incomes translate into purchasing power for different store types. The analyst can prepare estimates of purchasing power using information from the BLS's Consumer Expenditure Survey, but this is a time-consuming task; it may be more efficient to purchase data from private vendors, as chapter 5 explains. Analysts should recognize, however, that the way Americans shop and where they make purchases have changed dramatically in the past decade. Omnichannel retailers generate both in-store and online sales, but government retail trade surveys do not always reflect this change in sufficient detail.

Demand calculations for retail centers located in downtowns or other business nodes, or in tourist destinations, must also identify the spending potential of office workers and the inflow from purchases by visitors to the market area. These calculations are difficult to complete, because purely local data sources are limited. Trade organizations can provide insight into the shopping habits of special consumer groups, such as college students. These estimates tend to be national or regional in geographic scope; data for individual metropolitan areas are nonexistent. In contrast, local convention and visitor bureaus may have estimates of spending by tourists and business visitors in individual markets.[5]

For office and industrial properties, demand analysis may be limited to an examination of employment trends, a review of recent job growth in the competitive submarket,

and a look at changes in space absorption over time. It is important for the analyst to discuss how growth in employment translates into need for office space. Chapters 6 and 7 discuss approaches to office and industrial market demand analysis in greater detail.

Hotel demand is a function of projected growth in convention attendance, local business activity, and leisure visitor generators such as historic sites, outdoor recreation areas, beaches, amusement or theme parks, indoor water parks, and similar draws. The market analyst must determine which of these factors will generate room demand for the proposed product and how that demand will be supplemented by other sources of hotel revenue, such as restaurants, meeting-space rentals, and banquets. In addition to examining housing and other commercial uses, national data vendors track the number of occupied hotel rooms in local markets—a good indicator of changing demand parameters. Chapter 8 provides more detail on the unique features of hotel market analysis.

Supply Analysis

To understand the supply side of the equation, the analyst must look at existing and planned competition. Competitors can be identified through readily available (free or inexpensive) secondary sources—a directory of office properties or apartment listings in print or online—but these sources may not be comprehensive, current, or accurate. Using information from data vendors to provide up-to-date supply information has grown in popularity (and can save time), but the analyst must still field-check data about competitors by driving around the area and by talking to building managers. Most market analysts will tell property managers or leasing agents that they are conducting research in the area, but others will "shop" competitive buildings while posing as a prospective buyer or tenant to see a model unit or to get information on vacancies. It is important to recognize that not all competitors will be cooperative about sharing such information.

Analysts use summary tables or individual project data sheets to show details about competitive properties in their reports, and they may also provide a brief narrative for each property. Either way, the supply analysis should also draw comparisons between conditions in the local market area and those in the metropolitan area as a whole. It should end with a discussion of how the proposed property (or a completed building being sold or acquired) compares with the competition.

The greatest detail in the report should be provided for those projects in the local market area that are most comparable to the planned development. Data sheets and summary tables typically include the following items:

- Property size—number of units for a residential project, square feet of space for a commercial building, number of hotel rooms.

- Year the property was built and when it was last renovated, if known.

- For residential properties, the number of models offered (by number of bedrooms and baths) and the size of each unit type; for business parks, the range of building sizes; for office space, the floor plate sizes.

- Project or building amenities (for example, green building features, concierge services, and ground-floor coffee shops in an office building; pool, jogging trail, and dog run in an apartment complex).

- In-unit amenities (tech features, balconies, fireplaces, and any above-standard appliances, flooring, cabinetry, countertops, or trim).

- Monthly rent (total and per square foot) for each unit size in an apartment property; annual rent per square foot for commercial and industrial space.

- Lease concessions offered (for example, months of free rent, above-standard tenant improvement allowances in office buildings).

- Utilities and services included in the rent; extra charges (for example, parking or exercise facility fees, common area maintenance in an enclosed mall).

- Anchor tenants, for a retail or office property.

- Occupancy rates, sublet space available, and comments on the size and location of vacant spaces in retail properties.

- Absorption rates for recently built projects (see discussion of absorption later in this chapter).

The analyst must also investigate projects that are still in the pipeline and that may ultimately become the direct competitors for the proposed project. Of course, many details about these projects will not be available, but it is useful to provide as much information as possible—the size of the project, the market niche it is targeting, if it has received the necessary government approvals, if any anchor tenants have been signed, and when it is expected to open. Much of this information can be collected by calling or visiting the local jurisdiction's planning office. In a trade area with multiple jurisdictions, however, finding information about future competition can be one of the analyst's most time-consuming tasks. In some localities, published lists might be available, but they provide little insight other than the number of residential units or the approved square footage for commercial projects. It is possible that the most competitive developments (the ones most similar to proposed projects or existing buildings being studied for an investor or lender) are located outside the local market area.

Reconciling Demand and Supply

Market studies should conclude with an unbiased assessment of how well a proposed project will be able to compete; they should provide estimates of achievable rents or prices, suggest how quickly the project will be absorbed (leased or sold), and indicate what the stabilized vacancy rate is likely to be. For the acquisition or refinancing of an existing building or complex, the report should spell out the key risk factors: Does the project face an overbuilt market? Is tenant turnover high? Does it require renovations or upgrades? If the market is currently oversupplied, the analyst should estimate how soon supply and demand will become more balanced and should use historical metropolitan area or submarket vacancy rates as a guide. The likely duration of rent concessions should also be discussed.

Comparing the Subject with Its Competition

The analyst should highlight how a subject property's main features compare with those of its competition. These features will vary by product type; not all of the ones listed here will be essential in every analysis:

- Location (access, convenience, visibility, prestige);

- Unit sizes and mix by number of bedrooms and baths, plus lot sizes for single-family homes;

- Observed condition of buildings and grounds;

- Occupancy costs (estimated monthly cost of utilities, property taxes, common area charges for shopping centers);

- Parking ratios and availability of garage spaces versus open lot spaces;

- Building or project amenities;

- Ability to support current and future technologies; and

- Security.

Of course, competitive rents or prices are critical to all land uses. When an analyst looks at new construction, it is important to compare asking rents in current dollars, even though a new building could take two or more years to complete.

Capture Rates and Penetration Rates

Growth in target market groups must be sufficiently strong that a new project will not swamp the market. As a result, market analysts look at *capture rates*—the share of projected demand growth that a project must attract to fill its rentable space (allowing for reasonable vacancy) or to sell its lots or homes. *Penetration rates*—the share of total demand that is captured by current competitors and how this share will change with construction of additional product—are also important, especially for specialized market niches (for example, affordable housing for seniors, who must meet strict income- and age-eligibility guidelines set by the federal government).

Determining whether a projected capture rate is reasonable or excessive requires judgment based on experience. There are no hard and fast rules. A well-conceived new project in a dynamic market (with a growing number of income-qualified households, a surge in high-paying jobs, or evidence that existing buildings are being renovated/upgraded) might succeed even if it has to capture a relatively high share of future demand. How high is too high depends on the amount of competitive space that will be coming on line at the same time. In contrast, a niche product serving a select group of

potential customers will, under the best of circumstances, attract only a small share of demand and should not expect a high capture rate.

Consider the following examples:

- A developer is considering construction of an 800,000-square-foot downtown office building that will take three years to complete. Employment in office-prone industries rose strongly over the past five years, vacancy rates dropped, rents escalated, and two other new multitenant structures have been started in response to positive market conditions. But with the economy slowing, much of the space already under construction has yet to be pre-leased. Whether this market can support a third new office building will depend on projected growth in office-type businesses and the number of jobs they provide. Because the other new competitors will not be completed for 18 months, the proposed building cannot be expected to capture all of the projected demand growth three years hence. Vacant space may remain available long after these three office buildings are completed.

- If a proposed housing development for seniors has to capture a third of all the age- and income-eligible households in the trade area in order to fill its units, the project will be risky and absorption will be slow. Relatively few seniors move in any given year, some will move outside the area, and many are simply not attracted to age-restricted living. Owners would have to spend

A historic building in Woodbury, New Jersey, converted to affordable housing for seniors. Ground-floor space was slow to lease. *(Deborah L. Brett & Associates)*

A clubhouse in a new single-family-housing development.
(Deborah L. Brett & Associates)

heavily on advertising outside the trade area to attract tenants. Thus, this project is probably too big for the local market area.

As a practical matter, capture-rate calculations assume that a portion of space (usually 5 to 10 percent depending on property type and local market conditions) will remain vacant and that some share of demand will come from outside the trade area (new firms relocating from other regions, corporate transferees buying or renting housing, retail sales to tourists, and so on).

Determining the Supply/Demand Balance

Analysts should be on the lookout for the following warning signs of an imbalanced or overbuilt market:

- Construction activity levels that will dramatically exceed new demand, as indicated by household or employment projections. Note, however, that some excess is tolerable (and even desirable). If supply and demand were perfectly balanced, vacancy rates would be very low, and rents would escalate, eventually forcing out price-sensitive tenants.

- Escalating vacancy rates that cannot be readily explained by the movement of a single large tenant.

- Negative net absorption, with more space being vacated than new leases being signed.

- Declining real (inflation-adjusted) rents.

- Chronically vacant space and abandoned buildings, which indicate obsolescence, lack of demand, or both.

Absorption Rates

Developers and investors will look for the analyst's estimated absorption rate—the pace at which the proposed project will be able to lease or sell space. Depending on the property type, the absorption rate could be expressed as

- The number of apartments that will be leased or homes that will be sold each month,

- The length of time it will take to sell building sites in an industrial park, or

- The number of months until an office building or neighborhood shopping center is fully (or nearly fully) leased.

Quarterly net absorption information for new apartments or for commercial and industrial properties in a given submarket can often be obtained from brokers or purchased from data providers,[6] but the average monthly or quarterly absorption experience of individual buildings is more difficult to find. It is important not to equate gross leasing activity with net absorption, which takes into account move-outs as well as new leases.

Absorption rates are important inputs in financial feasibility models; they determine how long investors will have to carry the property before it starts generating positive cash flow. Most analysts express absorption rates as a range—say 12 to 16 apartment units leased per month, or 20,000 to 30,000 square feet of retail space leased per quarter. Analysts must also factor pre-leasing (renting space before construction is completed) into the absorption rate.

To a large extent, the analyst will rely on the absorption experience of recently completed competitive projects, especially those that are still being actively marketed. He or she will consider the competitive strengths and weaknesses of the project relative to the competitors, as well as changes in economic conditions.

Calculating how fast a project will lease up or sell out is much more difficult in a location where no similar new construction has occurred in years. If demand trends are positive and the project is appropriately priced and well located, a large new apartment complex (say 200 or more units) should absorb at least 20 units per month initially, but the pace will slow as the most desirable unit types or floors are fully leased. The same is true of shopping center space. A community center in a growing trade area might have 60 percent of its gross leasable area (GLA) committed to two or three anchor tenants before construction starts, plus another 20 percent of the total GLA leased by the time it opens. Less desirable storefronts (with odd configurations or reduced visibility) will take much longer to lease; the center might not be 95 percent committed until a year after opening.

Recommendations

Some clients will ask the market analyst to recommend changes to the building or site development plans that would improve its competitive position. This function is one of the most valuable that an analyst can perform. Such recommendations might include the following:

- Shifting the mix of units in a proposed apartment building project to include more (or fewer) two-bedroom units.

- Offering tenants an amenity or service that was not originally envisioned (such as a concierge or rooftop lounge).

- Reducing rents to be more in line with what the competition is offering.

- Modifying the mix of large and small shop space in a proposed shopping center.

- Changing construction phasing in a multibuilding complex if a slowdown in absorption is anticipated.

Importance of Illustrations

When preparing a market study, the analyst must recognize that the report has many audiences. The client and its staff may be familiar with the subject property and its surroundings. However, others who read the report (for example, a limited partner investor or a lender) might be located elsewhere and unfamiliar with it. Using maps and photography helps orient the reader who does not know the local market area, the location of the site, or the competition.

A complete market study report should include a map that shows where the property sits within the metropolitan area or a major city. At a smaller scale, a map should show the boundaries of the primary and secondary market areas, location of the site, nearby interstate highways, and key

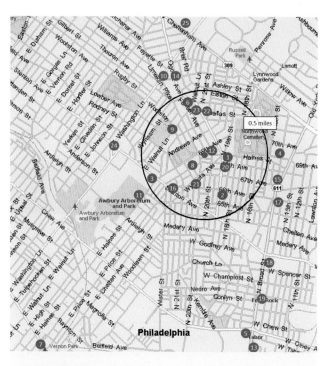

Transportation
1 SEPTA Bus Stop — Route 6
2 SEPTA Bus Stop —Routes 6 & K
3 SEPTA Bus Stop — Route L
4 SEPTA Bus Stop — Routes 16 and 22
5 SEPTA Olney Transportation Center

Recreation and Places of Worship
6 West Oak Lane Senior Center
7 Center in the Park — Senior Center
8 H&H Community Development Center
9 Simons Community Recreation Center
10 West Oak Lane Public Library
11 Awbury Arboretum
12 Mt. Airy Baptist Church

Social Services and Health Care
13 Albert Einstein Medical Center
14 Rite Aid — RediClinic
15 Wedge Recovery Center
16 Fresenius Medical Care-Olney

Shopping
17 CVS Pharmacy — North Broad Street
18 Aldi Grocery Store
19 PNC Bank
20 Mini-Market
21 8 Brothers Meat Market and Deli
22 Ogontz Avenue Retail Strip Center
23 Relish (Full-service Restaurant)
24 Citizen's Bank
25 Cheltenham Square

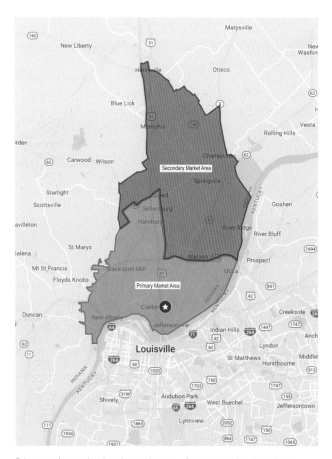

Primary and secondary housing market areas for a proposed assisted-living facility in Jeffersonville, Indiana, a suburb of Louisville, Kentucky.
(*Valerie S. Kretchmer Associates Inc.*)

A map of amenities and services near a proposed housing development in Philadelphia. The map key identifies shopping, bus routes, parks, and health services. The circle indicates a half-mile distance from the subject location.
(*Real Estate Strategies Inc./RES Advisors*)

arterial roads. For an industrial study, the map should show the location of (and distance to) airports, harbors, main highways, and freight rail service. If the market area includes many neighborhoods or political jurisdictions, they should be identified. Mapping software programs can enable the user to specify boundaries, place names, roads, and natural features.

Another map should point out the locations of key amenities to show their proximity. For example, a map accompanying a report on a proposed single-family subdivision should note the location of nearby convenience shopping, local schools, parks, recreation centers, and libraries. Reports about housing for seniors should include the locations of the nearest senior centers, hospitals, and medical offices. (If such facilities cannot be easily shown on the map, they should be noted in the text along with their distances from the subject site.)

For an office building, it will be important to show proximity to restaurants, hotels, and health clubs. The attractiveness of a downtown retail location is demonstrated by showing its proximity to cultural attractions and pedestrian traffic generators such as universities, courthouses, and hospitals. In all cases, the area map should show nearby highways and arterial roads, as well as transit stations.

Competitors should also be mapped to show how close they are to the proposed development site or the subject building being analyzed. If the map is not large enough to include property names and addresses, the analyst should substitute a number or letter key with the names and locations of the competitors.

Aerial photographs are useful to illustrate road access and nearby land uses. Photographs of the most comparable properties help the reader to visualize design, density, building heights, construction materials, and other features that are characteristic of the local market area. Reports should also contain pictures of the subject site (even if it is a tract of vacant land) and its immediate neighbors. Investors and lenders will want to feel confident that the surroundings are appropriate for the proposed development.

Providing an Executive Summary

Busy readers will greatly appreciate an executive summary. A thorough summary should cover key observations regarding the site and its surroundings, advantages and disadvantages of the location, demand indicators, and characteristics of the competition. It should conclude with the analyst's recommendations—that is, whether the development project should proceed as planned or, if not, how it could be modified to make it successful.

Notes

1. For a warehouse market study, it is also important to show other metropolitan areas within a day's driving distance.

2. The ACS replaced what used to be called the decennial census "long form," which provided detailed socioeconomic and demographic information derived from a sample of the population, rather than a full count.

3. ACS and other census data can be accessed through a new website that will be available after June 2019 at www.data.census.gov.

4. Provided through the Local Employment Dynamics (LED) partnership, which combines data collected by states with federal censuses and administrative records.

5. Estimation methods and information sources will not be consistent among metropolitan areas.

6. The Census Bureau conducts a quarterly sample survey of apartment absorption (rental and condominium) in buildings with five or more units, and it provides reports on absorption as of six, nine, and 12 months postcompletion. Data are provided at the national level and for the 45 largest metropolitan areas. https://www.census.gov/history/www/programs/housing/survey_of_market_absorption.html.

CHAPTER 3

CHAPTER 3

MARKET CONDITIONS: EMPLOYMENT, DEMOGRAPHICS, DEMAND, AND SUPPLY

National, regional, and local economic conditions all affect property demand. Macroeconomic variables (interest rates, inflation, unemployment rates, international trade imbalances, industrial productivity, and stability in the stock market) shape consumer confidence and business investment activity. The strength of the national economy influences whether businesses expand their space, what new online and bricks-and-mortar store concepts are introduced, when families move up to pricier homes, and whether travelers book more hotel room nights.

Thorough market analysis requires some consideration of the national economic climate. Even if the report does not include detailed data on national trends, the analyst should be aware of current and future macroeconomic factors when drawing conclusions about the advisability of starting a new project or investing in an existing building. At the same time, experienced researchers understand that the national economy is cyclical. Conditions observed today may change dramatically by the time a new building breaks ground, let alone by the time it is ready for occupancy.

Local conditions may not precisely mirror national trends. Not every metropolitan area benefits from a national economic boom, and some communities will survive a national recession relatively unscathed. As a result, real estate market studies usually give greater weight to metropolitan area economic indicators than to nationwide statistics. For example, employment growth at local businesses that use office space (banking, insurance, legal services, consulting, information providers, tech services) will be the key demand determinant for new class A office space. The need for additional hotel rooms depends on continued growth in local tourist, convention, and business visitation.

Metropolitan market dynamics are the most important factors considered in projecting housing demand. The only exceptions are for second-home or senior-housing projects that draw from a wide area or for projects that serve special-needs populations, such as persons with disabilities. Consumer demographics (population growth, household formation, mobility and immigration, age and family characteristics, income, and lifestyle choices) are critical in determining how much to build, which product types will sell or rent quickly, and how to set appropriate asking prices or rents. In turn, demand for convenience retail space is highly dependent on the location of new residential construction. Although online food shopping and expanded delivery services are growing in popularity, it is still true that most households prefer to buy groceries and other daily needs without traveling far from home. As population growth and the availability of relatively inexpensive land at the urban fringe turns farmland into subdivisions, demand for new convenience retail stores is generated. At the same time, the relatively recent growth of online shopping and off-price, discount, and outlet stores has negatively affected performance of all but the best enclosed super-regional shopping centers.

Developers and investors in residential and retail space look for population growth or new household formation. Housing developers may also want to see growth in particular types of households (families with children, empty nesters, seniors, young singles, or childless couples), depending on the product they plan to build or lease. Discount department store chains will want to locate in areas with middle incomes, while high-end retailers will gravitate to areas with affluent residents.

If demand analysis is based on employment growth, estimates of space per worker will be used to translate jobs into supportable space. These ratios vary dramatically by industry. Law firms use more space per worker than data processing firms do. Private-sector offices are generally more spacious than are those in government buildings. Flexible, shared offices (referred to as coworking spaces) are increasingly popular, especially in urban downtowns and mature suburbs. They provide little in the way of private space per worker. Standards for average space per worker have changed over time, as warehouses became more automated, executive offices were downsized, shared office operators offered flexible lease commitments, and so on. More information on this topic can be found in chapter 6.

Figure 3-1
Change in the Composition of U.S. Nonfarm Employment, 1980–2017

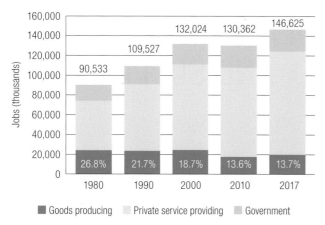

Source: U.S. Department of Labor, Bureau of Labor Statistics, Historical Data, Establishment Employment. www.bls.gov/data.

Note: Percentage figures are goods-producing jobs as share of total employment.

In some cases, real demand cannot be demonstrated on the basis of household growth or income gains. Housing market analysts must consider demand for replacement of deteriorated, abandoned, or uncompetitive units. An underserved city neighborhood—long neglected by retailers, entertainment venues, or restaurants—may already have sufficient purchasing power to support a proposed development, even if its household count is static. Analysts should include replacement demand for a small percentage of older or deteriorated housing units and class C commercial/industrial space.

The market analyst must also devote considerable attention to supply factors that affect development feasibility. Typically, supply-side analysis considers (a) macroeconomic trends affecting the market and current conditions (metropolitan area or countywide absorption, vacancy rates, and rents and prices); (b) local area market performance indicators and construction activity; and (c) characteristics of competitive buildings, both existing and proposed. As discussed in chapter 2, brokers and private data vendors are the usual sources of raw information on conditions in the metropolitan area and the submarket, both current and historical. However, market analysts, appraisers, and economic development professionals must verify, analyze, and interpret the statistics. To go beyond the numbers, they need to understand the physical character, tenancy, and performance of key competitors; learning about the competition requires field visits and personal or telephone interviews with building owners or managers.

Economic Indicators

A thorough market analysis begins with a review of the local economy and includes highlighting indicators that are most relevant to the particular land use or property type being studied. Real estate developers and their financial partners will want to understand the drivers of economic growth—the mix of industries, the area's largest employers, and the nature of new and expanding businesses. Investors must have confidence in the market's continued economic vibrancy, and so they look for evidence of a growing labor force and new job creation. Conversely, when labor markets are tight (unemployment rates are below 5 percent) or when the education and skills to support a specific type of business are lacking in the local area, businesses may be reluctant to expand or seek new locations.

Over the past 50 years, many metropolitan areas underwent a near-total economic transformation. Heavy industry departed, and even light assembly operations shifted overseas. Although there is some evidence that these trends have slowed as wages paid to overseas workers increased and shipping costs rose, U.S. domestic employment in manufacturing and other goods-producing industries is still below levels seen in 1980 and continues to be a declining share of total jobs, as shown in figure 3-1. Manufacturing, construction, and utilities workers totaled more than 24 million in 1980 and accounted for 26.8 percent of all nonfarm jobs. In 2017, only 20.1 million persons worked in these industries, and their jobs accounted for just 13.7 percent of nonfarm employment. Telecommunications, computer services, and data processing firms that did not exist in 1980 were formed, grew, and generated millions of jobs, despite outsourcing of customer service operations to overseas locations.

Although the share of jobs in manufacturing has declined, growth in technology-related industries has created new opportunities for well-paid work. In most metropolitan areas, health care employment has expanded (and will continue to do so as the population ages and as new approaches to medical care are introduced). Educational institutions, both private and public, became more important job generators

Bottling process at the Woodford Distillery in Versailles, Kentucky. (karenfoleyphotography/Shutterstock.com)

Figure 3-2

Comparing Sources of Employment Data from the U.S. Bureau of Labor Statistics

Topics	Current Employment Statistics (CES)	Local Area Unemployment Statistics (LAUS)	Quarterly Census of Employment and Wages (QCEW)
Description	Employment, average production worker wages, and average weekly hours by industry and geographic area (place of employment)	Employed and unemployed persons by geographic area (place of residence)	Employment, number of employers, average weekly wage, and total wages, quarterly and annual average, by industry and geographic area (place of employment)
Methodology	"Payroll survey" uses a sample of employers	"Household survey" estimates of employed and unemployed persons during a specified week each month	Census of all employers liable for unemployment insurance (97%–99% of total nonagricultural employment)
Populations excluded	Self-employed, agriculture, domestic workers, military	Individuals not in the labor force; persons in the military and in institutions	Self-employed, unpaid family workers, railroad workers, student workers, some agricultural workers
Currency	Monthly data available by the third week of the following month	Monthly data available by the third week of the following month	Quarterly data available six months after the close of the quarter
Geographic detail	United States, states, metropolitan statistical areas (MSAs), counties outside MSAs	United States, states, regions, MSAs, counties, cities larger than 25,000	United States, states, MSAs, counties
Advantages	Current employment data	Current household data	Complete universe of employers, and fine level of geographic and industry detail
Limitations	Uses statistical sample, not universe of employers; not an estimate of employed persons; person holding two jobs is counted twice	"Employed" can be working only a few hours per week; frequent revisions	Six-month time lag and some data confidentiality
Other products	Monthly press release	Monthly press release	

Sources: U.S. Bureau of Labor Statistics; New York State Department of Labor.

as college enrollments expanded and older adults sought "lifelong learning" opportunities both to meet the needs of a changing economy and for personal enrichment.

In today's economy, the largest employers in many markets are hospitals, universities, school districts, supermarket chains, and discount department stores. The mix of industries found in a metropolitan area will determine the strength of demand for different types of properties. For example,

- A community dominated by large, corporate-owned manufacturing facilities will need fewer multitenant office buildings than will one dominated by small high-tech businesses or financial services firms.

- Tourist destinations and convention cities (such as Honolulu, Las Vegas, New Orleans, and Orlando) will need far more hotel rooms than their resident populations would support.

- A city located at the confluence of three interstate highways is often a center for warehousing and distribution uses. Deepwater ports, intermodal rail centers, and international air cargo terminals also create above-average demand for warehouse space.

The market analyst must go beyond analyzing the existing economic base. It is important to learn about announced expansions, new business formations, and companies that may be moving into—or out of—the area.

Employment Statistics

Government agencies publish two types of employment data. *At-place* statistics count jobs according to their location; the data are calculated from sample surveys and reports filed by employers. Monthly and annual reports on employment by industry (published by the U.S. BLS and state labor departments) are workplace-based. In contrast, *worker-based* statistics (including unemployment rates[1] and much of the information about the occupation and education of the labor force) from the BLS are tabulated by the respondent's place of residence. In addition to the BLS's extensive online databases, state labor, employment, or economic development departments are good sources of information at the state, metropolitan, and county levels, as well as for larger cities.

Figure 3-2 shows the differences among three employment data series from the BLS. CES and QCEW data are based on place of employment; LAUS provides information on worker characteristics.

Real estate investors are interested in both the composition of the job base and how it has changed over time. Market studies should include current statistics on a metropolitan area's total employment by industry, using (at a minimum) two-digit North American Industrial Classification (NAICS) codes, as shown in figure 3-3. For office market studies, jobs in three-digit (and even four-digit) employment sectors may have to be tallied. Comparisons with state and national norms will be helpful in highlighting those industries that are underrepresented or overrepresented in the metropolitan job mix.

For most market studies, the economic overview should include data about total growth in nonfarm jobs over the preceding five to 10 years and about how those jobs are distributed by major industry group. In large metropolitan areas, at-place employment data may be presented for both the metropolitan area and submarkets (such as individual counties and large municipalities) to the extent they are available. Employment growth rates for the local market area can be compared with state and national statistics. Annual averages should be used when they are available. If monthly data series are used, the analyst should use the same month for every year shown to avoid inconsistencies resulting from seasonal variations.

State labor department websites are often the best sources of monthly and annual employment data for metropolitan areas, counties, and larger cities. Annual averages for selected metropolitan areas can also be found online on the BLS website.[2] BLS data are revised frequently, so it is important to use information from a single data series.

Because real estate developments take years to complete, the market analyst will want to obtain employment projections if they are available. The BLS's 10-year employment projections by industry and occupation are revised every two years. However, they are national in scope; therefore, market analysts should use them cautiously when looking at future employment prospects in a specific metropolitan area or county. Many states, large counties, and regional planning agencies issue their own employment projections but do not update the projections frequently. Private econometric firms such as Moody's Analytics and Woods & Poole Economics provide short- and long-term projections for a fee.[3]

Figure 3-3
Two-Digit Industrial Classifications Used in Employment Statistics

Code	Industry
11	Agriculture, forestry, fishing, and hunting
21	Mining, quarrying, and oil/gas extraction
22	Utilities
23	Construction
31–33	Manufacturing
42	Wholesale trade
44–45	Retail trade
48–49	Transportation and warehousing
51	Information
52	Finance and insurance
53	Real estate and rental and leasing
54	Professional, scientific, and technical services
55	Management of companies and enterprises
56	Admin, support, waste management, and remediation services
61	Educational services
62	Health care and social assistance
71	Arts, entertainment, and recreation
72	Accommodation and food services
81	Other services (except public administration)
92	Public administration

Source: U.S. Census Bureau, 2017, www.census.gov/eos/www/naics.

Seasonally Adjusted Data

Monthly employment statistics for the United States, individual states, and metropolitan areas are presented in two ways: seasonally adjusted and not seasonally adjusted. Seasonal adjustment is a statistical technique used by the BLS and state labor departments to measure and remove the influences of predictable seasonal patterns to more accurately reveal how employment and unemployment change from month to month.

Over the course of a year, the size of the labor force, levels of employment and unemployment, and other measures of labor market activity fluctuate because of seasonal events, including changes in weather, harvests, major holidays, and school schedules. Because these seasonal events follow a more or less regular pattern each year, their influence on statistical trends can be eliminated by adjusting the statistics from month to month. These seasonal adjustments make it easier to observe cyclical trends and other nonseasonal movements in the series.

As a general rule, the monthly employment and unemployment numbers reported in the news media are seasonally adjusted data, which are useful for comparing several months of data. Annual average estimates are calculated from the data series that is not seasonally adjusted.

Finding current employment data—let alone projections—for smaller areas can be challenging. But such information is important when an analyst is looking at the nature of employment in downtowns, city neighborhoods, or suburbs and is extremely useful in preparing market studies for office buildings and retail space. Local employment data can also suggest the size of the worker population that can be targeted for a new downtown residential development, as well as for shops and restaurants that depend on daytime population for revenue.

Sources of information on employment for municipalities or by zip code include the following:

- The U.S. Census Bureau's County Business Patterns (CBP) and Zip Codes Business Patterns (ZBP). This annual series has data for individual counties and zip codes covering private-sector businesses at the two-digit NAICS level, including the number of establishments, total employment, and establishments by number of workers. CBP information goes back to 1993, while ZBP data was first issued in 2004. This source does not cover self-employed workers or most government agencies.[4] Researchers should also understand that, in a small area, much of the data may be missing because the Census Bureau protects the confidentiality of information for individual businesses. Thus, if one employer is the only source of jobs in a particular NAICS industry in a given zip code, these data may be suppressed. Figure 3-4 shows how CBP data can be presented in a report.

- Employment data for small areas can be gathered from the U.S. Census Bureau's OnTheMap, a mapping and reporting application based on the 2002–2017 Longitudinal Employer-Household Dynamics (LEHD) Origin Destination Employment Statistics (LODES).

Figure 3-4
Example: Data from 2016 County Business Patterns
Douglas County, Colorado

Industry code	Industry code description	Number of employees	Number of establishments
	Total	110,124	8,997
11	Agriculture, forestry, fishing, and hunting	56	28
21	Mining, quarrying, and oil/gas extraction	292	46
22	Utilities	235	6
23	Construction	8,209	894
31–33	Manufacturing	7,701	150
42	Wholesale trade	2,612	363
44–45	Retail trade	8,413	913
48–49	Transportation and warehousing	861	102
51	Information	8,122	230
52	Finance and insurance	8,186	700
53	Real estate and rental and leasing	1,887	698
54	Professional, scientific, and technical services	8,243	1,802
55	Management of companies and enterprises	1,079	58
56	Admin, support, waste management, and remediation services	8,273	497
61	Educational services	3,442	200
62	Health care and social assistance	12,496	891
71	Arts, entertainment, and recreation	2,241	135
72	Accommodation and food services	12,453	546
81	Other services (except public administration)	5,273	724
99	Unclassified establishments	50	14

Source: U.S. Census Bureau, 2016 County Business Patterns, https://www.census.gov/data/datasets/2016/econ/cbp/2016-cbp.html.

Using Information from OnTheMap

The OnTheMap tool can be used to show the relationship between the location where workers are employed and the place where workers live. In the example shown in the figure below, a developer was considering constructing market-rate rental housing in a Chicago suburb and was hoping to attract employees of a nearby medical campus. OnTheMap allowed the market analysts to easily identify where medical center workers earning $40,000 or more per year currently live, as well as their zip code or distance/direction from their place of employment. This information helped the analyst determine if it might be possible to attract employees of the medical campus to the proposed development.

Example: Where Workers Live
Suburban Chicago Market Area, 2015

By municipality of residence	Count	Share (%)
All workers earning over $40,000 per year	17,924	100
City of Chicago	5,647	31.5
Specified West Cook County suburbs	2,481	13.8
Oak Park	573	3.2
Maywood	305	1.7
Berwyn	284	1.6
Forest Park	232	1.3
Bellwood	227	1.3
Westchester	223	1.2
Brookfield	202	1.1
Broadview	162	0.9
La Grange Park	143	0.8
Cicero	130	0.7
Other specified Cook County suburbs		
Orland Park	177	1.0
Oak Lawn	156	0.9
Skokie	138	0.8
Des Plaines	117	0.7
Specified DuPage County suburbs		
Naperville	330	1.8
Downers Grove	241	1.3
Elmhurst	241	1.3
Lombard	218	1.2
Bolingbrook	162	0.9
Westmont	126	0.7
Wheaton	120	0.7
Woodridge	114	0.6
Other specified suburbs		
Joliet city, IL	190	1.1
Aurora city, IL	174	1.0
All other locations	7,292	40.7

Sources: U.S. Census Bureau, OnTheMap (https://onthemap.ces.census.gov/); Valerie S. Kretchmer Associates Inc.

A major benefit of using the LODES database is the ability to download data not just for predefined geographies but also for market areas defined by the analyst. Data include jobs by worker age, earnings, NAICS industry sector, race, ethnicity, educational attainment, and sex. It is possible to download statistics from 2002 to 2017 for private- and public-sector jobs. The analyst can select only the primary jobs or all jobs held by area workers.

As of this writing, the most recent LODES data are from 2015. Data for 2017 will be available in 2019. Statistics on worker earnings may not be very helpful, because the highest annual income group shown is $40,000 or more.

- InfoUSA is a private, fee-based source of business establishment and employment data. Geographies include counties, municipalities, zip codes, and custom geographies (for example, blocks in a suburban Main Street area). Information is compiled using directories, U.S. Postal Service records, and government sources, and then verified. Lists purchased can then be

Interpreting the Data: Two Examples

As figure 3-5 shows, it is useful to compare local or metro area employment data with state averages. The figure shows the importance of the educational and health services sector in the economy of the Rochester, Minnesota, metro area—a sector that accounts for more than four in 10 jobs, which is an unusually high share. Rochester is home to the Mayo Clinic, a well-respected destination medical center that draws visitors from throughout the United States and around the world, and attracts medical-related ancillary service providers. Although Rochester also has an IBM research facility, medical instrument and optical design companies, and food/dairy-processing businesses, such employment is dwarfed by the number of jobs directly or indirectly related to the Mayo Clinic.

Figure 3-6 shows year-to-year growth in total at-place employment and percentage gains in the Newark Metropolitan Division as the business environment recovered from the economic downturn that began in 2008.

- Note that the area includes one county in Pennsylvania, along with five in New Jersey.

- The numbers illustrate a very slow economic recovery. Nonfarm employment peaked at more than 1.2 million jobs in 2007. Ten years later, total jobs had not yet returned to 2007 levels.

- However, the Newark Metropolitan Division is a very large area with a sizable and diverse job base. While the percentage gains look small, the number of jobs stabilized in 2011 and has increased each year after that.

downloaded using spreadsheet or database software. Businesses can be sorted by NAICS code, number of employees, or other indicators. The lists can be field-checked to generate names of stores or a list of office tenants in a given area.

■ Private data vendors provide current information on total numbers of employees for custom-created geographies. These reports include government employment.

The market analyst should also track trends in total employment in the local county, the metropolitan area, or both over time, going back at least five years. If the market area includes large cities or suburbs, the job data (if it is available) should also be used in examining employment growth or decline. Comparisons with statewide and national trends are helpful. (See figure 3-5.) Trends over time show whether a county or metro area has recovered from recession-related cyclical job losses, as shown in figure 3-6, or if it is experiencing booming job opportunities during a time of economic expansion.

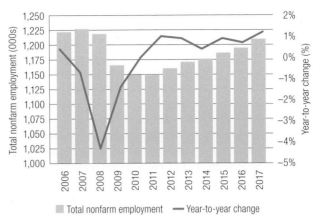

Figure 3-6
Example: Trends in Total Nonfarm Employment
Newark, New Jersey, Metropolitan Division, 2006–2017

Source: New Jersey Department of Labor and Workforce Development, https://www.nj.gov/labor/lpa/LMI_index.html.

Note: Newark Metropolitan Division includes Essex, Hunterdon, Morris, Somerset, and Sussex counties in New Jersey and Pike County in Pennsylvania.

Figure 3-5
Example: Nonagricultural Employment by Type of Business
Rochester, Minnesota, Metropolitan Area and Statewide, 2017

Type of business	Number of employees	Percentage of all employees	
		Rochester metro area	Minnesota
Mining, logging, and construction	4,580	3.8	4.3
Manufacturing	10,442	8.7	10.9
Wholesale trade	2,670	2.2	4.5
Retail trade	12,407	10.3	10.2
Transportation, warehousing, and utilities	2,799	2.3	3.6
Information	1,872	1.6	1.7
Financial activities	2,788	2.3	6.1
Professional and business services	5,415	4.5	12.8
Education and health services	49,275	41.0	18.2
Leisure and hospitality	10,807	9.0	9.2
Other private services	3,992	3.3	4.0
Government			
Federal	957	0.8	1.1
State	1,571	1.3	3.4
Local	10,529	8.8	10.0
Total	**120,104**		

Source: Minnesota Department of Employment and Economic Development, https://mn.gov/deed/data/data-tools/current-employment-statistics/.

Economic Diversity and Location Quotients

Most elected officials seek new industry that will shake up the mix of jobs and breathe new life into the economy. In general, greater diversity in a local economy makes it less vulnerable to economic downturns and less risky as a location for investment. An area that depends on a few large employers or a single industry will be more vulnerable to recession. This dependence will affect both absorption of new space and continued strong occupancy in existing buildings.

A thorough market study will go beyond employment numbers to discuss the key drivers of the local economy. One way to present these data is to use location quotients (LQs), which are ratios that compare the concentration of employment by industry in a defined area with that of the United States or of a state as a whole. A county where a particular industry's LQ is 1.00 has the same share of private-sector employment in that industry as can be seen nationwide. An LQ higher than 1.00 indicates a greater local concentration in a particular industry. LQs by industry are available online from the BLS's QCEW.[5]

■ For example, in Washoe County, Nevada (where Reno is the county seat), the LQ for Accommodation and Food Services (NAICS code 72) was 156 during the first quarter of 2018, which would be expected in an area with a high concentration of hotels, casinos, and restaurants that serve tourists. In contrast, the LQ for Educational Services (NAICS 61) was only 0.51, with 0.65 for Finance and Insurance (NAICS 52). Although casino businesses can continue to do well during economic downturns, convention and tourist demand will suffer. An area with many tourist-oriented businesses that thrive when consumers are prospering would be vulnerable during a broad-based recession.

Where STEM Occupations Are Concentrated

"Approximately half of all STEM jobs (science, technology, engineering and mathematics) are in the computer or mathematics fields, including information systems management, software development, programming and other IT support roles. The other half is focused on engineering and life, physical, and social sciences." According to location quotient data by occupation, the 10 metropolitan areas with the highest concentrations of STEM jobs in 2017 were (in descending order) San Jose and San Francisco, California; Seattle, Washington; Washington, D.C.; Boston, Massachusetts; Raleigh, North Carolina; Austin, Texas; Denver, Colorado; San Diego, California; and Baltimore, Maryland.

Source: Taylor Mammen and Ryan Guerdan, 2019 STEM Job Growth Index. The Advisory, RCLCO Real Estate Advisors, January 31, 2019. www.RCLCO.com.

■ Private universities have not located in Washoe County, nor is it a center for banking and the insurance industry.

■ The area may have potential for additional second-home development if it maximizes the appeal of its natural environment, offers frequent airline connections to gateway cities, and maintains good road access.

BLS location quotient data also enable market analysts to identify areas with above-average concentrations of well-paid occupations that require high-tech skills. This information is important for STEM (science, technology, engineering, and math) businesses looking for new locations where they will find a workforce with the skills they require.

Key Employers and New Industries

Noting the top 10 or 20 largest employers is also helpful for portraying the area's economic base. As previously cited, supermarket chains, discount department stores, universities, community colleges, countywide school districts, and hospitals are typically found in the top 20 list. Federal, state, and county governments may also be important to the economic base, especially in state capitals, communities with large public universities, or counties with military installations.

It is useful to focus extra attention on the area's largest private-sector businesses while noting whether their job counts or payrolls have grown over the preceding five years—if such information is available. Conversations with local economic development officials or utility companies can help clarify which segments of the economy are generating demand for space, bringing in new workers, and so on. If well-known Fortune 500 companies are expanding or relocating into the area, their plans should be noted. Similarly, if a key employer is contracting operations and layoffs have been announced or are anticipated, this change should also be cited. Companies are now required to notify state labor departments of major layoffs or facility closings. This information is often made available on the labor department websites.

Local chambers of commerce, economic development agencies, and business magazines or newspapers are the best sources of information on major employers and their future plans. Telephone or in-person interviews and agency websites can also provide announcements and statistics.

Labor Force Profile

Labor force availability and skills are important to employers and are carefully considered when businesses make location decisions. At a minimum, market studies should provide information on growth in the resident labor force and the local unemployment rate during each of the preceding five years.[6] The market analyst should then provide a brief interpretation of the data and their implications, if any, for the property. Comparisons with state and national unemployment rates and trends for the same time period are useful. If potential tenants will need specially trained or

Figure 3-7
Example: Resident Labor Force and Unemployment Trends
Akron, Ohio, Metropolitan Statistical Area, 2000–2017

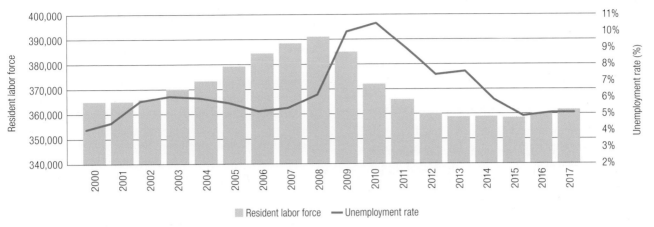

Source: Bureau of Labor Statistics, www.bls.gov/data.

Note: Numbers are annual averages.

well-educated workers, the report should provide background information about the educational attainment of the resident population, as well as brief descriptions of relevant community college training programs, nearby universities, and specialized trade schools. For properties that will target a small number of specific industries, information on wage rates and how they compare with state and national averages will be needed.

An economically healthy metropolitan area or county will be able to maintain or reduce its unemployment rate even as the number of potential workers grows. In most situations, low unemployment is a positive indicator for real estate: it boosts demand for homes and household services and sustains retail sales. However, if the supply of available workers is too limited—or if the necessary skills cannot be found in the area—labor costs will rise and businesses may look to other locations for expansion.

State labor departments compile monthly and annual average labor force estimates and unemployment rate statistics for metropolitan areas, counties, and larger cities. Data are also aggregated by the BLS and published on its website.[7] Market analysts should be aware that an economic slowdown may not be immediately visible in unemployment statistics; some employers will reduce hours or shift workers from full-time to part-time status before offering early retirement incentives or announcing layoffs.

The size and composition of the labor force reflects demographic trends and educational attainment, as well as economic opportunity. The labor force is fluid (workers enter, leave, or retire) and mobile (workers move in pursuit of more job choices, better pay, or a more attractive environment).

As with establishment-based employment estimates, an analysis of historical trends in labor force or unemployment rates must use similar data series. As discussed earlier, labor data series are either seasonally adjusted or not. Monthly estimates for counties or metropolitan areas are not seasonally adjusted. They do not take into account the variation that occurs during the holiday shopping season as retailers increase their hiring; neither would unadjusted data clearly indicate the unemployment situation in a beachfront resort area. To discuss trends using unadjusted monthly data, the analyst should compare the current unemployment rate to those of the same month during previous years. (See figure 3-7.)

Interpreting Labor Force and Unemployment Data

As shown in figure 3-7, annual average labor force counts and unemployment rates, which reflect seasonal differences, can be cited in market studies in lieu of monthly data. The figure shows that the size of the labor force in the Akron, Ohio, metropolitan area peaked in 2008. For the previous four years, Akron's unemployment rate was 6 percent, which undoubtedly encouraged residents to actively seek work. The onset of the recession caused a jump in the unemployment rate to more than 10 percent by 2010. It did not drop below 6 percent again until 2014. Despite economic improvement in recent years, the area's total labor force in 2017 was still below its peak 2008 level.

The market analyst should explore local reasons for labor force trends. The population of the Akron MSA is not growing, and the working-age population could be shrinking. Discouraged workers who were unemployed for years may have dropped out of the labor force.

Visitor Profiles and Tourism Trends

Visitor statistics are important in determining potential demand not only for hotels and resorts but also for entertainment, amusement, and cultural facilities that derive significant patronage from out-of-towners. A certain amount of retail business is supported by travelers as well. Visitor counts are obtained through a variety of methods and are not necessarily consistent from city to city.

As discussed in chapter 8 regarding demand for hotel rooms, tourist information can include a variety of statistics:

- Trends in occupied hotel room nights and average daily room rates—important indicators for analyzing both supply and demand;

- Estimates of out-of-town visitation—based on data collected from airlines, bus companies, Amtrak, and tour operators;

- Patronage at museums, theme parks, concerts, and sporting events—reflected in ticket sales and visitor surveys; and

- Breakdowns of visitors by type (convention attendees, business travelers, and pleasure visitors)—obtained from hotel bookings and visitor surveys.

In certain cases, some of this information can be obtained free from local tourism promotion agencies; those agencies may also estimate local spending by tourists at restaurants, stores, and entertainment venues using visitor surveys. In other locations, data must be purchased from private providers. Visitor spending estimates used in retail market studies should cover not only hotel guests but also "day-trippers" who do not stay in a hotel or other lodging, as well as persons who stay with friends or relatives. The U.S. Department of Commerce issues periodic reports on visitors to the United States from outside the country and the locations that attract them. Additional information on tourism data sources is provided in chapter 8 and in the webliography in the appendix.

Consumer Demographics

Housing and retail market studies require considerable detail on local population and household demographics. Along with population counts and trends (growth or decline over time), other data that are useful for understanding consumer characteristics include age distribution, median age, housing tenure (owners and renters), household size, household composition (for example, singles versus families, households with and without children), and median and average household incomes. Chapter 4 indicates how population and household characteristics have changed over time nationwide.

In housing market studies, data on the distribution of households by income are often cross-tabulated with data on the age of the householder. This tabulation allows the market analyst to zero in on the number of households that would be age- and income-qualified or targeted for a proposed development. For retirement housing, data on assets as well as current income help determine affordability.

As niche marketing grows in importance, sophisticated clients may also demand detailed market area segmenting that will provide insights into lifestyle choices, ethnic characteristics, educational attainment, and occupations. If the market analyst is working for a residential developer or owner with similar properties in its portfolio, obtaining information about existing tenants or buyers can be invaluable for identifying likely future customers. Shopping center management companies and store chains collect similar data indirectly from credit card holders or by using online shopper satisfaction surveys. (See chapter 5 for more information on consumer research for retail properties.)

Future projections are important, especially for larger developments that will be built and occupied over a period of years. Depending on the amount of time and money available for market research, the analyst can prepare his or her own demographic estimates, obtain forecasts from local or state planning agencies, or purchase projections prepared by economists or real estate consulting firms. Private demographic data vendors tend to look only five years into the future, which may be problematic for projects with long time horizons. Demographic models from private vendors use many factors to project population, households, and income but may not be sufficiently sophisticated with respect to household characteristics. It is important to remember that basing judgment on local knowledge and experience can be as important as sophisticated modeling for accurately determining future demand.

Office, industrial, and hotel market area studies require less demographic detail. Greater emphasis is placed on overall economic trends, labor force and employment growth, and occupation and wage data. However, even for a commercial or industrial property, the market study should feature an overview of the most recent census counts and current estimates of the population for the market area and the jurisdiction where the property is located, including trends in the number of persons and households, as well as the median and average household income. These statistics give the reader a sense of the community's overall economic health and status.

It is important to note that some office space users—such as medical professionals and allied health care workers, insurance agents, residential real estate brokers, accountants, financial planners, and other personal service providers—will want to learn about the potential customer base in the property's immediate area. Office leasing personnel must have this information on hand. Agents who lease space in shopping centers often include demographic data as part of their online descriptions of available space.

Clearly formatted tables help the reader understand what the characteristics of the population are and how they have changed over time. Comparisons with growth rates and population profiles statewide, in the metropolitan area,

Abandoned rowhouses in Baltimore.

Homes in Queens, New York, damaged by Superstorm Sandy in 2012.

or in the county where the property is located will demonstrate how the local housing market or trade area differs from the larger community. Key indicators should be highlighted in the text, and any unusual patterns or trends should be explained. Depending on the type of project being studied and the characteristics of the trade area, the analyst will emphasize some demographic indicators more than others in the report.

Population and Households

Population and household growth are the most obvious indicators of potential demand for housing or retail space. More often than not, an increase in population indicates that the local market or trade area is attracting new residents and shoppers, which will generate demand for additional housing and shopping facilities. However, it is possible for a trade area to show population growth without having much demand for additional housing units. Older households with only one or two people may be moving out and being replaced by larger, younger households with children. Or the neighborhood could be attracting recent immigrants or new ethnic groups living in multigenerational households with larger than average family sizes but no more spending power than smaller households. Conversations with knowledgeable local sources (such as real estate agents or community planners) can provide insights that help explain unusual population growth patterns.

Conversely, the absence of population growth does not necessarily signify a lack of demand for new space. A market area with little or no population growth may nevertheless need additional housing units or more stores. Neighborhoods that once served larger families with children could register a decline in population as those children grow up and move away, but these communities could still be attracting young singles and couples and retaining empty nesters and seniors.

Also, replacement demand can be significant in areas that do not show population and household growth. Replacement demand occurs when

■ Existing housing is lost as a result of fire or natural disaster;

■ Rental apartments are converted to condominiums;

■ Undesirable or deteriorated older housing units cannot be renovated or upgraded at a reasonable cost, and the location is valuable enough to merit redevelopment; and

■ Existing units are too big or too small for the types of households that want to live in the neighborhood.

For example, market studies for affordable housing often suggest demand for new units in areas that do not show growth in population or households. The new units will provide better quality, safer, or more spacious accommodations for low-income families. Demand for modern, physically sound units can be satisfied through new residential construction, renovation of existing housing, or conversion of obsolete commercial or industrial buildings to rental apartments or condominiums.[8] The key is to maintain the supply/demand balance through the selective demolition of deteriorated buildings.

Population loss is a greater concern for developers and owners of retail space. In general, households with a single wage earner—be it a young adult or a senior living alone— have fewer financial resources than two-wage households have. If the population of an area is declining because of housing unit conversion, demolition, or abandonment, total purchasing power is probably also declining.

Even so, supportable demand for retail space can exist even in trade areas with problematic demographics. For example, a trade area may have several grocery stores with enough total space to serve the market, but the stores could be undersized, poorly capitalized, or competitively

Figure 3-8
Example: Population and Household Characteristics
Downtown Chicago site

	1 mile	3 miles	5 miles
Total population			
2000	26,374	300,641	811,131
2010	49,610	330,257	793,494
2018 estimate	66,358	373,093	853,482
2023 projection	76,082	398,556	886,698
2018–2023 annual growth rate (%)	2.8	1.3	0.8
2018 estimated group quarters population	**5,508**	**12,466**	**32,630**
2018 population by age (% of total population)			
0–4	3.1	4.5	5.7
5–14	2.7	6.5	9.1
15–24	15.9	12.9	14.1
25–34	35.6	27.8	25.5
35–44	17.2	16.4	15.5
45–54	9.4	10.5	10.5
55–64	8.5	9.7	9.1
65–74	5.2	7.2	6.3
75–84	1.8	3.2	2.9
85+	0.7	1.3	1.2
Median age, 2018	**32.9**	**34.3**	**33.2**
2018 population by race/ethnicity (% of total population)			
White alone	67.6	59.3	53.1
African American alone	8.0	13.3	21.3
Asian or Pacific Islander alone	18.9	16.2	9.9
Some other race alone	2.4	8.3	12.5
Two or more races	3.2	3.0	3.4
Hispanic origin (% of total population)	7.4	17.6	26.4
Total households			
2010	27,906	169,592	355,173
2018 estimate	38,440	194,612	387,951
2023 projection	44,505	209,219	405,830
2018–2023 annual growth rate (%)	3.0	1.5	0.9
2018 average household size	1.58	1.85	2.12
2023 average household size	1.59	1.85	2.10
Family households			
2010	7,747	61,935	150,761
2018 estimate	10,370	68,909	160,458
Families as a % of total households, 2018	27.0	35.4	41.4
2023 projection	11,933	73,210	166,010
Families as a % of total households, 2023	26.8	35.0	40.9

Source: Data from Esri online sample report, June 2018, https://www.esri.com/en-us/home.

weak. A new chain could successfully enter the market and challenge the existing competitors. A new store with a stronger assortment of groceries could also attract additional smaller tenants that would benefit from proximity. Other factors that could enhance the desirability of a potential store location in an area with declining population include nearby employment sources that bring daytime population, strong traffic counts (bringing drive-by traffic), and tourist/seasonal visitation.

Demographic Characteristics

As discussed earlier, the age composition of the population and the characteristics of area households can strongly influence the demand for housing and retail space, the type of housing that will be marketable, and the types of stores that will be drawn to a business district or shopping center. For example,

- Younger households are more likely than others to occupy smaller units and to rent rather than own. Their retail expenditures are much different from those of families with children and those of seniors. Young people spend an above-average percentage of their incomes on restaurant meals and entertainment. Households with children spend more on food consumed at home and clothing.

- Segments of the older population will be drawn to different types of age-restricted housing. People between 60 and 70 could consider active adult developments (for sale or for rent), and persons age 80 and older may seek assisted-living buildings with supportive services.

- Recent immigrants are likely to rent, whereas homeownership rates for foreign-born persons who have been in the United States for more than 20 years will closely approximate those of native-born Americans.

- Seniors spend an above-average percentage of their income on health care and prescriptions but a lower share on clothing.

Although demand for housing and retail space depends more on household income than on ethnicity, developers and investors may nevertheless want to know about the ethnic composition of a trade area. If data from the decennial census or other sources suggest dramatic shifts, the market analyst should consult local sources to learn the reasons for such change. Ethnicity is important because it helps shape housing preferences and shopping habits. For example,

- In the past, housing for seniors held little appeal for certain Asian American cultures because elderly widows or widowers rarely lived alone; they continued to live with younger family members. However, Asian families have become more dispersed, following educational and employment opportunities across the country and internationally. As a result, demand for retirement housing and services is growing in neighborhoods with ethnic

Asian residents. Senior living communities that cater to Chinese, Japanese, or South Asian residents are appealing because of shared languages and food preferences. They can draw residents from a wide area in large metropolitan areas, as well as from nonresidents whose family members live locally.

- Research indicates that African American households will spend above-average amounts on name-brand apparel.

- Hispanic families allocate disproportionately high shares of their income to goods and services for their children. They spend an above-average proportion of their earnings on groceries for meals prepared at home, rather than dining at restaurants.

Figure 3-8 provides an example of demographic data from a private vendor for a one-, three-, and five-mile radius from a proposed development site. The figure shows that relatively few people live within a mile of the site, but density increases dramatically within three miles. The market analyst may think that there is considerable demand for retail space. However, before acting on population numbers alone, the analyst must critically examine existing or proposed competition. Note also that household size increases with distance from the subject site, as does the proportion of family households (as opposed to single or roommate households). The share of racial and ethnic minorities in the population also increases with distance. For a housing study, demographic data for a defined market area should be compared with data for the city as a whole or the MSA.

Household Income

Knowing that trade area residents have sufficient incomes to buy or rent in a proposed new housing development is very important to developers in deciding whether to build and what type of product to offer. Retail market studies use aggregate household income estimates for a trade area to calculate the expenditure potential for a proposed shopping center or a particular store type. Store chains look at a trade area's income profile to determine whether household characteristics are a good match with the merchandise lines, brand names, and price points those stores offer. They will compare the incomes for a proposed new location with those seen in the trade areas served by their successful existing stores.

A market report should provide a breakdown of the estimated number of households in the area by income bracket. It will also indicate the median and average household income in the area.[9] In some reports, the analyst will provide similar estimates and projections of *family* income.[10] Measuring family income is especially useful for residential subdivisions, because families, not singles, tend to make most home purchases.

Income breakdowns used in a market study will vary according to property type. For example, a market study for an affordable rental apartment development should show households by income in $5,000 or $10,000 increments for those earning less than the median income for the area. Higher income brackets can be shown in $25,000 increments because these households would not qualify for income-restricted units.

In contrast, a market study for a luxury single-family home or condominium development should focus its detailed income statistics on households or families that are most likely to be able to afford the proposed project. Figure 3-9 provides a sample breakdown of the number of households by age of householder and income using estimates and projections from a private data vendor.

In combination with household characteristics (such as race and ethnicity, age, income, presence of children, and tenure), income data can be used to estimate household retail expenditure potential. Private vendors use complex models to provide such estimates for trade areas defined by market analysts, relying on consumer expenditure surveys

Figure 3-9
Example: Households by Age and Household Income
Suburban Housing Market Area, 2017 Estimate and 2022 Projection

Income	Age cohort							Total households
	< 25	25–34	35–44	45–54	55–64	65–74	75+	
2017 households								
< $15,000	69	150	205	239	422	373	639	2,097
$15,000–$24,999	62	208	255	270	431	518	865	2,609
$25,000–$34,999	57	294	313	304	490	482	846	2,786
$35,000–$49,999	99	560	608	638	804	875	1,143	4,727
$50,000–$74,999	190	1,172	1,230	1,455	1,509	1,517	1,258	8,331
$75,000–$99,999	104	972	1,330	1,383	1,456	1,125	395	6,765
$100,000–$149,999	68	940	1,803	2,257	2,042	1,147	458	8,715
$150,000–$199,999	27	347	880	1,382	1,042	480	113	4,271
$200,000+	16	254	811	1,225	1,221	535	158	4,220
Total	**692**	**4,897**	**7,435**	**9,153**	**9,417**	**7,052**	**5,875**	**44,521**
2022 households								
< $15,000	63	148	206	191	349	385	708	2,050
$15,000–$24,999	55	190	196	188	342	493	925	2,389
$25,000–$34,999	39	240	247	203	375	457	856	2,417
$35,000–$49,999	84	459	457	449	617	807	1,219	4,092
$50,000–$74,999	171	1,058	1,067	1,125	1,289	1,565	1,423	7,698
$75,000–$99,999	122	1,065	1,403	1,311	1,513	1,419	539	7,372
$100,000–$149,999	71	1,131	1,988	2,265	2,266	1,494	698	9,913
$150,000–$199,999	32	449	1,025	1,436	1,219	659	182	5,002
$200,000+	17	336	967	1,293	1,374	762	263	5,012
Total	**654**	**5,076**	**7,556**	**8,461**	**9,344**	**8,041**	**6,813**	**45,945**
Absolute change in the number of households, 2017–2022								
< $15,000	–6	–2	1	–48	–73	12	69	–47
$15,000–$24,999	–7	–18	–59	–82	–89	–25	60	–220
$25,000–$34,999	–18	–54	–66	–101	–115	–25	10	–369
$35,000–$49,999	–15	–101	–151	–189	–187	–68	76	–635
$50,000–$74,999	–19	–114	–163	–330	–220	48	165	–633
$75,000–$99,999	18	93	73	–72	57	294	144	607
$100,000–$149,999	3	191	185	8	224	347	240	1,198
$150,000–$199,999	5	102	145	54	177	179	69	731
$200,000+	1	82	156	68	153	227	105	792
Total households	**–38**	**179**	**121**	**–692**	**–73**	**989**	**938**	**1,424**

Sources: Esri, RES Advisors.

conducted by the Bureau of Labor Statistics as inputs for their models.[11] Chapter 5 provides more information on how to use these estimates.

It is important to remember that Census Bureau income statistics are based on sample surveys of money income.[12] The Census Bureau relies on the willingness of respondents to fully and accurately report what they earn. Not all households are entirely forthcoming. In many communities, there is a thriving underground economy consisting of people who work "off the books," either legally or illegally in full- or part-time jobs. Income from babysitting, tutoring, domestic services, driving, moonlighting, and other occupations can add significantly to an area's purchasing power by allowing households to afford both necessities and extras. Also, while income data collected in Census Bureau surveys do include Social Security, pension, alimony and child support, and other cash payments, they do not include noncash payments such as housing subsidies or SNAP (Supplemental Nutrition Assistance Program, often referred to as food stamps although funds are now provided electronically). Nor do they consider the value of assets such as savings accounts or stock market holdings, which are significant in areas with above-average concentrations of retired persons.

Figure 3-10
Example: Household Net Worth, 2018
Households Age 65+, Vigo County, Indiana (Terre Haute)

	Number	Share of households
Age 65–74		
<$15,000	916	14.9%
$15,000–$34,999	170	2.8%
$35,000–$49,999	221	3.6%
$50,000–$99,999	564	9.1%
$100,000–$149,999	609	9.9%
$150,000–$249,999	959	15.6%
$250,000+	2,725	44.2%
Total	**6,164**	**100.0%**
Age 75+		
<$15,000	911	17.9%
$15,000–$34,999	221	4.3%
$35,000–$49,999	85	1.7%
$50,000–$99,999	516	10.1%
$100,000–$149,999	456	8.9%
$150,000–$249,999	971	19.0%
$250,000+	1,942	38.1%
Total	**5,102**	**100.0%**

Source: Valerie S. Kretchmer Associates Inc., from Esri data.

Note: Net worth is total household wealth minus debt. Assets include home equity; equity in pension plans, retirement accounts, and vehicles; and business equity and the value of stocks and other investments. Debt includes mortgage and vehicle loan balances, credit card debt, bank loans, and other outstanding bills.

In some neighborhoods, bartering is another source of noncash income. Consequently, census numbers provide a somewhat incomplete (and understated) estimate of households' ability to pay for housing or their retail spending potential. This limitation is especially problematic in low-income neighborhoods, where unreported income and noncash subsidies are key sources of purchasing power.

As discussed earlier, understanding household assets is also important, especially when analyzing the marketability of housing for seniors. The money income of senior citizens will usually fall well below the overall average, but many retirees have substantial savings and investment assets, as well as little debt. The Census Bureau does not publish information on household assets for counties or small areas (for example, a city neighborhood or groups of suburbs, census tracts, or zip codes). However, estimates are available from private vendors. Income statistics are also available in Internal Revenue Service databases, but there is a considerable time lag between reported income for a given tax year and when the data are published.

An example of asset estimates is shown in figure 3-10. The data suggest that more than one in five senior households lack the assets to pay for a year in market-rate senior housing or for private-pay nursing home care. However, well over half have assets exceeding $150,000.

Psychographics: Portraying Household Lifestyles

Information on age, income, ethnicity, and housing tenure may not fully portray important differences in trade area populations. Household composition (singles or couples; presence or absence of young children), education, occupation, reading and music preferences, hobbies, recreational pursuits, and community involvement can vary widely among residents in a given age or income bracket, and the differences influence shopping habits and housing preferences. As a result, today's market studies often include information on trade area psychographics. Market analysts can purchase lifestyle profiles of a trade area from private data vendors. For example, Claritas's PRIZM system and Esri's Tapestry are proprietary household lifestyle classification systems. Market analysts can find details on the characteristics of households in each segment and purchase counts of the number of households by segment in a specified geographic area—in much the same way they obtain current population and household counts or income estimates and projections.

Psychographic systems assign addresses, blocks, and census-defined block groups to a lifestyle "cluster" according to their location (urban, suburban, rural, small town), employment (white or blue collar, retired), education (high school versus college degree), affluence and wealth, social status, and age. For 2018, Esri had 14 LifeMode groups—with a total of 67 segments—in its Tapestry system. Claritas's PRIZM system defined 68 clusters. Claritas also offers Workplace PRIZM, which provides demographics for people who work in a defined geography, using tract-to-tract commuting data from the Census Bureau. This product is useful for conducting retail market analyses for downtown or suburban areas with large numbers of workers.

Information sources that are used to construct psychographic profiles include television and radio ratings services, newspaper and magazine circulation bureaus, stores' "frequent buyer" or "loyalty" programs, product warranty registrations, and the like. Local trade areas will typically contain at least two clusters; the larger the trade area, the more numerous the lifestyles within its boundaries. Data vendors assign colorful names to each socioeconomic cluster.[13]

Analysis of lifestyle clusters helps developers determine the types of stores, restaurants, and entertainment venues that would be best suited for a new shopping center. Retail chains use clusters extensively to see if the trade area surrounding a proposed location fits the profile of their existing customer base. Consumer preferences for home types, sizes, features, and amenities become more obvious when residential developers use lifestyle data.

Housing Tenure

The extent to which trade area households own or rent their homes, while not a population indicator per se, is important not only for housing market studies but also for retailers. Home improvement centers, lawn and garden shops, and home decor, flooring, and furniture stores prefer to locate in areas with a high degree of homeownership. In contrast, operators of self-storage properties (also known as mini-warehouses) look for sites in areas with a high percentage of apartment dwellers because tenants often need additional storage space.

For small areas, precise tenure estimates are difficult to obtain in census off-years. The Census Bureau provides annual estimates of homeownership rates only for the 75 largest metropolitan areas individually and for all metropolitan areas, principal cities, suburbs, and nonmetropolitan locations in the aggregate.[14] However, the Census Bureau's ACS can provide five-year tenure estimates for small areas—municipalities, zip codes, and groups of census tracts.

Building permits can be helpful indicators of the types of units constructed since the preceding decennial census. However, the analyst must recognize that multifamily permits cover condominium and cooperative units as well as rental apartments; they do not specify whether a multifamily unit is intended for ownership or rental. Chapter 4 offers more detail on using permit information in conducting housing market studies.

Demographic Data Sources

Demographic data can be obtained from the Census Bureau, private data providers, civic organizations, universities, or state and local public agencies. It is often necessary to rely on a combination of sources to assemble a complete picture.

Census Bureau Products

As indicated earlier, the U.S. Census Bureau's decennial counts form the basis for most demographic estimates and projections. Because conditions can change dramatically between census years, market analysts must use current demographic estimates.

To provide more current information in greater detail, the Census Bureau began to focus its resources on the annual ACS sample in 2005. The ACS has replaced the decennial census's "long form," which before 2010 generated detailed data from a sample of households regarding household income, occupation of employed persons, educational attainment, and other social and economic characteristics. The ACS now provides these data indicators each year for metropolitan areas, counties, and places with populations of 65,000 or more, along with five-year average estimates for all geographies (including rural places, small suburbs, census tracts, and zip codes). These estimates are based on sample surveys and are revised annually.

The ACS provides a wealth of information that can be accessed from preformatted data tables using the Census Bureau's data portal (www.data.census.gov). These tables include cross-tabs that provide additional insights. Indicators that are of greatest interest to real estate market analysts include these:

- Population and household estimates.
- Population characteristics (age distribution, median age, gender, educational attainment, race, Hispanic ethnicity).
- Geographic mobility in the past year, with limited information on destination of persons who moved.
- Marital status and marital history.
- Employment status; employed persons by industry and occupation.
- Commuting data (journey to work, place of work, transportation to work, travel time).
- Household size (persons per household).
- Household types: families (married couples, single-parent families, other related persons living together) and nonfamilies (unrelated persons living together, single-person households).
- Total housing units and occupancy/vacancy status.
- Owner/renter tenure.
- Age of housing units (year built).
- Housing unit types (single-family detached and attached, multifamily buildings by units per structure).
- Housing unit sizes (number of rooms, but not square footage).
- Rents (distribution of rents paid, median and average rent).
- Estimated home values (distribution, median and average).

- Household income and family income distributions (mean [average] and median incomes).

- Vehicles available to household members.

- Poverty status.

For market studies that require an understanding of population subgroups, the ACS also includes data about the following:

- Veteran status by period of military service.

- Persons with disabilities.

- School enrollment.

- Ancestry.

- Persons living in group quarters (college dormitories, nursing homes, correctional facilities, military housing).

The Census Bureau also prepares population estimates for states, counties, incorporated places, and minor civil divisions every year, separate from the ACS. Annual age, sex, race and Hispanic ethnicity breakdowns for states and counties can also be obtained from the Census Bureau website. However, the Bureau prepares population projections only for the nation as a whole and for states. The projections are updated infrequently and are of little help (except in comparisons) when studying a local housing market or forecasting growth in consumer spending.

Additional information on household characteristics and income is collected in March of each year in the Current Population Survey (CPS), a joint product of the Census Bureau and the Bureau of Labor Statistics. Its annual Social and Economic Supplement provides information on per capita, family, and household incomes by age, race, and Hispanic origin. It is also the source of oft-cited information

When to Use One-Year or Five-Year ACS Estimates

In choosing which dataset is most appropriate, the market analyst must think about the balance between currency and sample size/reliability/precision. For details, research implications, and examples, see "Understanding and Using ACS Single-Year and Multiyear Estimates" in section 3 of the Census Bureau's *General Data Users Handbook*.[15]

Further guidance on comparing annual information from the ACS with results from previous years and with the most recent decennial census is also provided on the website.

Distinguishing Features of ACS One-Year, One-Year Supplemental, and Five-Year Estimates

One-year estimates	One-year supplemental estimates	Five-year estimates
12 months of collected data	12 months of collected data	60 months of collected data
Data for areas with populations of 65,000+	Data for areas with populations of 20,000+	Data for all areas
Smaller sample size; higher margin of error	Smaller sample size; higher margin of error	Larger sample size
Less reliable than five-year	Less reliable than five-year	Most reliable
Most current data	Most current data	Least current
Released annually, 2005 to present	Released annually, 2014 to present	Released annually, 2009 to present

Best used when	Best used when	Best used when
Currency is more important than precision.	Currency is more important than precision.	Precision is more important than currency.
Analyzing large populations	Analyzing smaller populations	Analyzing very small populations
	Examining smaller geographies because the standard one-year estimates are not available	Examining census tracts and other smaller geographies because one-year estimates are not available

about living arrangements for young adults, a factor affecting housing demand (especially rental housing), and about marriage, which also influences housing needs. Although some CPS data on household characteristics are published online for states, analysts will have to download and manipulate large data files using the Census Bureau's Public Use Microdata Sample (PUMS) files. It may be more convenient and less time-consuming to purchase data.

State and Metropolitan Agency Sources

Many states and regional planning agencies prepare their own population estimates or projections. The data are used primarily for transportation planning or in areas with strong growth management programs. Where available, such data are usually presented for counties and municipalities; zip code or census tract projections are rare. The market analyst should examine projections to evaluate their reasonableness; state and regional planning agencies are loath to issue projections that show declines in population or households.

As discussed earlier, state labor departments or economic development agencies provide data on size of the labor force and unemployment statewide, by county, and—in some cases—for state-designated labor market areas. Statistics on employment by industry and by occupations are also provided. This information is helpful to employers trying to understand labor availability, as well as for job seekers who want to know more about where they might find opportunities. Occupation forecasts help community colleges identify the need for new curricula that improve skills that will be needed in the future.

Figure 3-11

Example: County Population Projections[a] from a State University
Miami–Fort Lauderdale–West Palm Beach MSA, 2017–2045

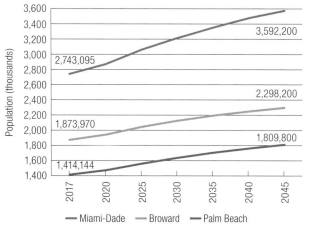

Source: University of Florida, College of Liberal Arts and Sciences, Bureau of Economic and Business Research. "Projections of Florida Population by County, 2020–2045, with Estimates for 2017." Florida Population Studies, Volume 51, Bulletin 180, January 2018. https://www.bebr.ufl.edu/population.

Note: All estimates and projections are for April 1 of the stated year.

a. Medium series. The bureau also prepares low and high projection series.

University Sources

Many universities, both private and public, have demographic and economic research institutes that provide instruction in analytic techniques and offer practical experience for current and future practitioners. Figure 3-11 shows county population projections to 2045 that were issued in early 2018 by the Bureau of Economic and Business Research (BEBR) at the University of Florida. The report includes three series (low, medium, and high) of long-range forecasts for each county in the state; the medium series is shown in figure 3-11. Because Florida counties vary significantly in size and their growth patterns are so different, BEBR researchers used four different methods to prepare their projections, evaluated the results, and reached conclusions about the best approach to use. Other states use a variety of techniques when examining future growth prospects for individual counties.

As the figure shows, all three counties in the Miami–Fort Lauderdale–West Palm Beach MSA are projected to grow significantly, with medium-series increases ranging from 18.2 percent in Broward County to 25.0 percent in Miami-Dade.

Private Sources

Not surprisingly, private data vendors have stepped in to provide estimates and projections not issued by the Census Bureau or state/local agencies. Firms that sell demographic estimates and projections include economic consultants and demographic data vendors.

Economic consultants use proprietary models to describe national, regional, and local economic conditions and then estimate and project population, households, income, and (in some cases) housing demand. Some of these firms provide customized research and consulting services in addition to selling standardized economic analyses and projections. Clients can subscribe to reports for the nation as a whole, for regions, or for one or more counties or metropolitan areas. Regular updates are available in a variety of media and can be purchased online, either by subscription or on a one-time basis. Two of the firms are Moody's Analytics and Rosen Consulting Group. These sources are best suited to market analyses for commercial and industrial properties because they can also provide detailed employment projections by industry.

Demographic data vendors focus on consumer demographics rather than econometric modeling. These firms provide additional detail on population and household characteristics. As a result, they are widely used in housing and retail market studies. The sources also supply estimates and projections of retail expenditure potential by type of store or by type of merchandise. Claritas and Esri are among the companies that provide clients with local area estimates that are based on distance from a particular site or for a combination of municipalities, zip codes, or census tracts or that are for custom-tailored geographies. They also offer five-year forecasts of population, households, age

characteristics, and income, as well as current estimates for other key demographic indicators. Their data are available by subscription or license or on a per report basis. Most vendors also offer detailed reports on employment by industry, daytime workforces, or estimates of retail purchasing power and sales by type of store. They have mapping capabilities (market area maps based on user-specified geography) and traffic counts, both of which can save time for the real estate market analyst.

Woods & Poole provides population, household, labor force, employment, and retail sales data (historical and current estimates, 25-year projections) for individual states, counties, and metropolitan areas. Data for a single county or metropolitan area are reasonably priced and popular with regional and county planning agencies.

Additional information on demographic data vendors and links to their websites are provided in the webliography appendix.

Consumer Surveys and Focus Groups

Surveys and focus groups can be very useful in real estate market analysis because they directly provide information on consumer opinions and preferences. In the real estate industry, consumers can refer to prospective homebuyers or renters, shoppers, or business-to-business targets, depending on the type of property being studied.

Using surveys and focus groups improves the accuracy of real estate market studies. The market analyst and the client can learn about what the characteristics of potential customers are and what aspects of a proposed real estate development are most important to them. Surveys are most commonly used in connection with retail market studies, especially when a community is trying to revitalize a sagging business district or a developer wants to re-tenant a declining shopping center. Surveys can tell a developer of housing for seniors about the choices being considered by persons 55 or older who live near a site. They also can provide feedback

to a homebuilder about model home features that were most appealing to visitors. More generally, survey research can accomplish the following:

- Tell owners of existing retail properties (or developers considering new construction or major renovations) where trade area residents are shopping and the extent to which they are buying merchandise online versus in stores.

- Indicate how frequently consumers are patronizing restaurants at various price points.

- Identify what previous customers (buyers or tenants) liked and disliked about a building or an entire development project.

- Gauge customer interest in new concepts or features not previously seen in the market.

- Reveal which factors (location, price or rent, and amenities) are most important in customers' decision-making.

- Suggest how much tenants or buyers would be willing to pay for space in a proposed project.

- Tell owners how current tenants feel about property management and maintenance.

- Provide information on prospects' demographic characteristics that can be cross-tabulated with their responses to substantive questions.

Surveys are most typically commissioned by a developer or a government agency; it is rare for a lender or investor to conduct a survey as part of its due diligence. Even for developers, direct consumer research is more the exception than the rule because of concerns about cost or timing. Real estate developers generally know their products well. They should be familiar with their competition, their market, and their industry and should know the characteristics of projects that have been successful in the past. Thus, they are tempted to assume that they know their future customers' needs and preferences. This assumption is a common, but potentially serious, misconception.

Owners of existing shopping centers, office buildings, or hotels can benefit from surveying their tenants or patrons when new competition enters the market. Anchor stores will track and reach out to shoppers periodically to stay informed regarding customer satisfaction. Customer satisfaction emails are now commonplace for online purchases. Apartment buildings have online portals allowing them to contact tenants and, in turn, tenants can send feedback to management. Hotel operators contact recent visitors after they check out. And in an era when store and hotel loyalty programs are commonplace, it is relatively easy for management to contact patrons to ask about their satisfaction with purchases or visits.

The two primary types of customer research are quantitative and qualitative. Quantitative research provides statistics on customer characteristics and the proportion

of respondents who react favorably to various aspects of a proposed project or an existing building. Respondents can be asked to comment on planned changes or to suggest ways a building or apartment complex could be improved. Qualitative research does not produce statistics; rather, it allows for more detailed exploration into customer perceptions of the product, competition, shopping habits, housing preferences, and so on.

Traditional methods of contacting existing or potential customers or tenants have changed in the past 10 to 15 years:

- Online surveys, which are relatively inexpensive to administer and tabulate, are replacing techniques such as on-the-street or in-the-mall shopper surveys (described later in this section).

- It is more difficult to reach a truly random sample of residents or businesses using telephone interviews when so many potential respondents use caller ID; they don't have to answer calls from unfamiliar numbers.

- Agents who staff residential leasing or sales offices can obtain email addresses from visitors and follow up with an online questionnaire link, but they do not reach potential customers who have not stopped in the office or responded to advertising.

- Survey research companies maintain respondent panels—households who agree to participate in surveys. The companies know the location and demographic characteristics of their panelists (age, race/ethnicity, gender, owner/renter tenure). If the panels are sufficiently large, the survey firm can send email links to panelists who live in the target market area. When responses are returned, the firm can check to be sure the respondents are representative of market area households as a whole, using Census sources such as the ACS.

Consumer surveying can apply scientific methods, but it is not an exact science and has limitations. Changing market conditions (a downturn in the economy or new competition) make research results time-sensitive and require that studies be updated periodically. Surveys provide an educated guide for developing a property, marketing the product, and keeping it competitive, but adhering to survey results cannot guarantee success. Using such data can, however, reduce the risk of making wrong decisions and maximize the likelihood of building a marketable product.

Identifying Targets and Respondents

Regardless of which type of research will be conducted, the first thing that must be done is to identify the characteristics of the people who should participate in the study. These characteristics can be either demographic or psychographic. They are used to select the area from which survey respondents will be drawn and to screen survey participants. For example,

- An office developer would want to learn more about the plans of existing tenants who are in the developer's market area and whose leases will expire within the next 36 months.

- People who visited a shopping center at least once in the previous month could be the focus of a study used to evaluate expansion plans.

- A hotel would ask area businesses if they would use the new banquet hall being planned or ask frequent visitors whether changes are needed in services or physical spaces.

- Commuters who use a train station could be asked about the types of stores they patronize during, before, or after work, as well as what new shops and services they would be likely to use.

- A developer of retirement housing with assisted living and nursing care components will want to focus on people age 75 and older who live within 10 miles of the proposed site. In addition, it may be helpful to survey younger households in the area, because a high percentage of residents in retirement housing move to be closer to their children and grandchildren. Active adult retirement communities will target younger seniors to assess their interest in age-restricted living.

Using Quantitative Research

Quantitative research is conducted when it is necessary to predict the target group's behavior with a degree of statistical accuracy. An example of what can be learned is either the percentage of people who are likely to shop at a certain store or shopping center or the share of office tenants in older buildings who are likely to move rather than renew their leases. Quantitative research (statistically valid and reliable) usually requires a large sample size. Typically, a minimum of 200 or more completed surveys from targeted respondents will be needed; requirements will be much higher if the client wants to know about the characteristics, preferences, and perceptions of particular subgroups.

Although online surveying has gained popularity, some surveys are still performed by mail, telephone, or in person, depending on the resources provided by the organization commissioning the research. In all cases, the survey instrument must be designed for easy data entry and analysis. Questions must be simply worded, unambiguous, and easy to answer. The survey company should have the capability to tabulate raw results and generate cross-tabulations as requested by the client. For example, a shopping center manager will want to know about the age of her shoppers, but she also needs to know if the frequency of visits and purpose for visiting varies by age or income.

Each survey method has its own strengths and weaknesses. Consistent administration, cost, and timing are the most important considerations. Market researchers must select the methodology that best fits their needs and budgets.

Mail Surveys

Mail surveys are fairly easy to administer. Once the firm conducting the survey has identified the target respondents, it should obtain a list of potential recipients and select a sample for mailing. Sources include current customer or tenant lists, municipal mailing lists, business address lists, membership rosters, and other commercially available lists—all of which the market analyst or survey firm can purchase from reputable marketing companies. To increase response rates, surveys can offer targets a nominal incentive to participate. A public agency conducting or sponsoring a survey might use a letter from the mayor to appeal to recipients' civic pride.

Response rates for mail surveys conducted for private projects are usually low, but a short survey will probably draw more responses than a lengthy questionnaire will. A major drawback of mail surveys is that respondents may not represent the population at large. Older recipients are more likely to participate than young adults. Those with strong opinions (pro or con) will send back their questionnaires; those who are uninformed or apathetic will not. Another concern may be the length of time needed to obtain the required number of responses.

Telephone Surveys

Telephone surveys are another way to gauge consumer opinions. Potential respondents can be reached using random-digit dialing within particular exchanges or using purchased phone number lists. However, phone surveys are increasingly difficult to administer:

- Many consumers—especially younger ones—no longer have fixed telephone landlines. A sample needs to reach households with both landlines and cellphones, or the opinions it generates will not represent the population as a whole.

- Cellphone numbers are portable; their area codes are no longer tied to particular locations. A telephone survey targeting residents of particular suburbs or zip codes must ask respondents if they still live in the target area; if they do not, their answers cannot be counted. In

response to this issue, technology has been developed to better geo-track cellphone users on the basis of data gleaned from their social media and web browsing habits.

- Many households have put their names on "do not call" lists, which makes telephone surveys impossible without the cooperation of a local government agency or nonprofit sponsor. Response rates for phone surveys are usually higher than for those sent by mail but are still relatively low. With caller ID allowing people to screen their calls, telephone surveying is becoming much more difficult.

- Although telephone surveys can be completed more quickly than mail surveys, processing them still takes a few weeks. Surveyors may have to call respondents multiple times before a qualified interview is completed. Refusal rates are high, and many of the sampled phone numbers will not be usable. In multiethnic trade areas, bilingual interviewers will be needed to ensure that a representative group of households is reached. As a result, most survey sponsors find that telephone surveys are too expensive.

Online Surveys

Online surveys are growing in popularity because households can answer them on their cellphones, tablets, or desktops. They are relatively inexpensive and fast to administer (popular programs such as Surveymonkey.com are helpful). Even so, the audience is limited to online respondents who know about the survey because they have received an email or text message asking them to click on a link that takes them to the survey. For example, existing tenants in an apartment

Improving the Accuracy of Online Survey Results

One way to address the problems associated with underrepresented population subgroups is to use a survey research company that maintains large panels—sets of respondents who agree in advance to participate in repeated online interviews over time. The Pew Research Center,[16] a respected opinion research company, now uses this method. Pew is able to learn the demographic characteristics of willing respondents and use subsamples to minimize biases that often result from undersampling some groups and oversampling others. Results are weighted on the basis of demographic data from the Census Bureau's ACS and CPS. Pew also gives tablets to panelists who do not have regular access to the internet. Others take their surveys on smartphones, on their own tablets, on a laptop, or on a desktop computer.

Constructing panels is time-consuming and costly but efficient for national surveys. However, getting a sufficiently large and representative sample in a *local* housing market or retail trade area may not be feasible.

building, office building, or business park are likely to have their email addresses on file with management, allowing staff to send an email blast notifying tenants that a survey is underway and encouraging them to participate.

Retail stores also have a captive audience—credit card holders or online shoppers who have made purchases in the past. Community groups can reach out to members to learn how they feel about a proposed development. Hotels commonly send opinion survey links to recent guests.

Although it can be easy to put a consumer survey online, the results can suffer from the same limitations intrinsic to mail questionnaires—respondents may not represent the target market as a whole. In other words, these are "surveys of the willing." Low-income households tend to be underrepresented. Also, surveys must be optimized for viewing and responding on different devices. Mobile phones are the instrument of choice for younger participants, but older respondents may prefer to answer questions on a desktop, laptop, or tablet. The market analyst will have to retain the services of a survey research firm to set up the questionnaire in different formats for multiple devices, reach out to respondents, and tabulate results.

Intercept Surveys

In-person intercept surveys are conducted at high-traffic locations, such as shopping malls, transit stations, arenas, or pedestrian-oriented urban business districts. Surveyors approach potential respondents and ask whether they would be willing to answer a brief series of questions, or surveyors may invite shoppers to use a tablet or kiosk to answer the questions. Some organizations offer respondents a printed survey form; staff members then scan the forms or enter the collected data by hand.

Intercepts are inexpensive and easy to administer. However, they cannot ensure that respondents meet specific demographic or psychographic criteria (although the interviewer can screen participants who meet age or gender requirements). Intercept surveys must be shorter than questionnaires that participants complete at work or at home (no more than five minutes is recommended). Despite the limitations, intercepts can provide a reasonably reliable portrait of shopping center and business district patrons and their purchasing habits. The key is to structure the survey properly:

- Interviewers will have to work at various times of day, on both weekdays and weekends.

- They should wear name tags that clearly identify them, and they should dress in a casual but professional manner to blend in with customers.

- Potential respondents should be approached in a nonthreatening, friendly manner.

- Surveyors should make it clear to potential respondents that they are not selling anything and should provide

an honest estimate of how long it will take to answer the questions.

- Both weather and season can affect whether an intercept survey's results truly represent typical shopping patterns.

Using Qualitative Research

Qualitative research is usually conducted with a small number of respondents. Although this type of research is not statistically projectable, it allows perceptions to be probed in depth. As with quantitative surveys, the client's objectives and budget will determine how to conduct the research.

The focus group is the most common type of qualitative research because it provides a good balance between accuracy and cost. Respondents are screened for specific demographic and psychographic criteria. Groups usually comprise no more than 10 to 12 participants. Multiple focus groups can be used to see variations in the perceptions and reactions of different targets. A professionally trained facilitator is usually hired to conduct the discussion. Clients can observe the proceedings either on site or at a remote location using video- or audio-conferencing technology. Recorded sessions are also possible, provided that participants agree. After all the focus group sessions have been conducted, the moderator reviews the comments and prepares a report.

One-on-one interviews are the most expensive type of qualitative research to conduct because they are time-consuming to administer. However, personal interviews allow control over respondent targeting and provide the greatest amount of time to probe issues in depth. After identifying potential respondents by demographic and psychographic criteria, the market analyst should hire a professional firm to recruit the respondents. A trained moderator conducts each interview and reports his or her observations.

Intercept interviews, like intercept surveys, are conducted at high-traffic locations such as shopping malls; they are the least expensive form of qualitative research. However, like intercept surveys, they allow the least amount of control over targeting and selecting respondents, and they must be much shorter than focus group sessions. Using a topic outline, interviewers approach potential respondents and ask whether they would be willing to sit down for an informal discussion. To speed up the process, multiple interviewers might be needed. However, using more than one interviewer risks inconsistency because the method of questioning is conversational.

Here are some examples of how qualitative research can be applied to specific real estate projects:

- A residential builder can conduct focus groups with consumers who are potential buyers or renters, asking them about their space requirements or getting their reactions to possible architectural elevations, building materials, interior finishes, appliances, or color schemes.

A blend of modern and historic office buildings in Washington, D.C.'s Chinatown.

- A retail developer can conduct intercept interviews with consumers (shoppers) and one-on-one interviews with potential tenants (retailers).

- An office and industrial real estate agent might use focus groups with potential tenants. The agent may have access to information on leases that will expire in the next 12 to 18 months, allowing him or her to zero in on businesses that represent potential tenants for a new or renovated building.

- A hotel can use focus groups with both business and pleasure travelers and then conduct one-on-one interviews with business travel managers regarding corporate accounts.

- A developer of a master-planned community can benefit by using focus groups with retail and office tenants, one-on-one interviews with homebuilders, and intercept interviews with homebuyers as they leave a sales center.

It is important to remember that any survey research, whether quantitative or qualitative, is a single component of a comprehensive market study and cannot replace the vital information that is gathered through other market analysis techniques.

Documentation of Historical Supply Trends and Current Conditions

The supply section of a market study looks at current conditions in light of past performance trends. In addition, key indicators for the local market area are compared with metropolitan area or countywide data. The greatest detail is presented for those properties deemed to be most competitive with the subject site. The study assesses the strengths and limitations of competitive buildings objectively, and it presents the findings in tables or property data sheets. It also discusses known additions to future supply (under construction or approved) as well as other potential competitors not yet underway. The amount of space in the planning pipeline should be compared with historical data to determine whether future construction levels are sustainable.

The types of data to be presented in the supply analysis will vary depending on the land use being studied. In general, the following indicators are important in looking at metropolitan submarkets:

- The size of the current inventory (number of housing units; square feet of office, industrial, or retail space; number of hotel rooms).

- How much the inventory has increased over time.

Luxury hotels in Las Vegas. (Leonard Zhukovsky/Shutterstock.com)

Beachfront condominiums in Rehoboth Beach, Delaware. (Khairil Azhar Junos/Shutterstock.com)

- Inventory quality (often expressed as class A, class B, or class C), based on property age, amenities, special features, and visual appeal.

- Anticipated near-term new construction.

- Number of units or square feet or space yet to be absorbed in projects already completed or under construction.

- Current vacancy rates (including available sublet space for multitenant office and warehouse properties).

- Sales prices, rent levels, or hotel room rates over time.

- Long-term supply of land that is zoned for the land use being examined (if known).

Historical trends in inventory size, average rents, and average vacancy rates should also be presented. The narrative should discuss changes in rents and vacancies over time, average annual additions to the inventory, leasing activity (number of units or amount of space leased each year), and annual net absorption (change in number of occupied units or amount of leased commercial space). Data limitations (and the cost of acquiring data) will dictate exactly which supply indicators receive the greatest emphasis.

To the extent possible, trends in the local submarket or trade area should be contrasted with those in the larger citywide or metropolitan market. Steady absorption, rising rents, or lower vacancies can occur in a hot submarket (a cluster or sector within the region) even when areawide indicators are negative. The opposite can also be true. An underperforming submarket could be the victim of localized overbuilding, or it may be affected by the relocation of one or more major tenants. The analyst must explain the reasons for any significant deviation from areawide norms.

Breaking Down the Numbers: Property Types, Location, and Class

For rental apartments and commercial properties, three factors affect how performance trends are analyzed: the type of property, its location and proximity to similar properties, and its quality. To understand how a proposed development or an existing building is likely to perform in the future, the competitive supply must be examined in terms of all three factors:

- *Property type:* Residential properties are classified by tenure (for sale or for rent) and physical characteristics (single-family detached, townhouse, or condominium; walk-up or elevator buildings). Industrial property types include manufacturing, warehouse and distribution, flex space (containing office space as well as showrooms or inventory storage areas), and research and development (space that can include both offices and laboratories). In recent years, big-box warehouses have dominated industrial construction activity, but smaller facilities (both single tenant and multitenant) are still being built. It is important to note that office space and industrial/warehouse inventories often ignore single-user buildings if they are owner-occupied. Hotels are classified as luxury, upscale, limited-service, budget, or all-suite. For the many types of retail centers, space is classified by design (enclosed or open-air), size, or tenant mix. Chapters 5 through 8 provide additional information on commercial real estate classifications.

- *Geographic submarkets:* Office buildings tend to cluster in or near downtowns, near transit stations, or at highway-oriented suburban nodes. Some airports have nearby concentrations of office space; in many markets, multitenant office buildings are located near major universities or hospitals. Hotel rooms will be found near convention centers or tourist attractions, at major office or industrial nodes, and at airports. Industrial users often seek space near interstate highway interchanges, alongside major water ports, or near cargo airports. The market study should present data on the share of the metropolitan area–wide supply that exists in the submarket being studied, and it should examine how its other performance characteristics compare with those of the metropolitan area as a whole.

- *Class:* Office, industrial, and apartment buildings are categorized as class A, B, or C, depending on the property's age, quality, and amenities. A property does not have to be less than five years old to be deemed class A, but it needs to be well maintained and retrofitted with the amenities desired by today's tenants. Hotels are classified by their amenities, services, and price points (luxury, upscale, budget). Market studies should break down the inventory by class whenever possible, focusing the analysis on buildings in the submarket that are most comparable to the subject property.

Analyzing Rents and Prices

Rent trends are a key part of the metropolitan area or county market overview. Data on rents in the submarket can be compared with broader trends, providing the context for evaluating the performance of the subject property and its nearby competitors. Price information for recent property sales and historical sales price trends can be found online or from private data vendors. It is important to note, however, that real estate market studies are not property appraisals, although they are often used as input in estimates of property value.

A report analyzing trends in the metropolitan area or one of its submarkets should provide data on average and median rents (or sales prices for homes and condominiums) and how they have changed over the past five years or more. It is desirable to disaggregate prices or rents for new product from those for existing property if possible. For commercial properties, rent trend data can be purchased, but a given property type in a specific submarket may have only a few sales transactions (or none at all) in any given year.

Each property type has unique aspects that should be noted in a price or rent analysis. For example,

- Prices for condominiums should be displayed separately from those for single-family homes, if possible. Note whether new home prices include the value of buyer upgrades.

- If possible, data for multitenant office or warehouse buildings should be distinguished from information on buildings with a single occupant.

- Hotel room rates fluctuate: weekdays versus weekends, high season versus other times of the year, group rates versus individual rates. Hotel systems use sophisticated algorithms to set room rates for any given date, and these rates will change as rooms are reserved over time. As a result, hotel studies quote not only average room rates but also RevPAR (average revenue per available room). RevPAR is calculated by dividing total room revenue in a given time period (net of discounts, taxes, and other charges) by the number of available rooms. (See chapter 8.)

- Rents for office, industrial, and retail properties are typically expressed as annual rate per square foot of leasable area.[17] Measurable space varies by type of property. Office rents are typically calculated on the basis of net rentable area, while shopping centers report gross leasable area. Apartment rents are usually shown on a per-month basis.

- For rental apartments, the market study should show the range of monthly rent by unit type and should indicate which utility charges, if any, are included in the rent. Rent ranges should be shown by type of unit (studio, one-, two-, or three-bedroom). To account for variation in unit sizes in any given submarket, data should also be presented on a per-square-foot basis.

  As is the case with hotels, apartment landlords with multiple properties also use algorithms to adjust rents as new units are absorbed, as prospective tenants' available choices become more limited, or as vacancies occur. As a result, the asking rents can change daily or weekly. When asking about the rents for particular unit types or sizes in comparable properties, the market analyst should be specific. For example, the analyst should ask what the rent will be for a 12-month lease starting March 1.

When one compares rents for individual competitors within a submarket, it is important to note what utilities and other costs, if any, are included in the quoted rent per square foot. Newer commercial buildings will usually write leases with triple-net rents: units are metered separately and tenants pay for their own utilities. They also pay a proportional share of real estate taxes, janitorial costs, and (in some cases) security. Older commercial buildings may quote gross rents, perhaps including all utilities except electricity.

Apartment buildings rarely use the terms "net" and "gross" in their advertising, but the Census Bureau uses them to report rent levels in a given geographic area. In the newest apartment properties, tenants may pay separately for all utilities and for garbage collection, parking, and even the use of recreation facilities. In others, renters pay separately only for electricity, internet, and cable television. Enclosed shopping malls typically charge tenants for common area maintenance (CAM) on a proportional basis relative to the amount of space each store occupies. Retail leases may also require tenants to pay percentage rent, which is based on a share of sales above a certain base level. (Chapter 5 provides more detail on rent charges in shopping malls.)

Using Sources of Supply Information and Knowing Their Limitations

Numerous information sources are available to help market analysts get started in examining the supply side. They may cover area or submarket trends and provide little information on individual properties or may focus on property-level information without looking at the entire market or submarket. Data vendors will offer both types of information for a fee. Some firms may provide current information only, while others keep historical records and have sophisticated models that allow them to forecast demand and supply inputs, as well as performance indicators.

Brokerage Reports

Summaries of current and historical market conditions (inventory, rents, occupancy rates, leasing activity, net absorption) are available for many larger metropolitan areas and their submarkets. National brokerage and investment advisory firms—such as Cushman & Wakefield, CBRE, Colliers International, JLL, Marcus & Millichap, NAI, Newmark Knight Frank, and others—provide these data for the biggest markets in the United States and around the world.[18] Some firms focus on office and industrial properties, while others provide information on shopping centers and rental apartments as well.

National and global brokerage firms have sizable research staffs that are responsible for monitoring inventory and performance trends. They update information quarterly and typically present year-end summaries and forecasts online. Brokerages use this information in their marketing packages when they represent properties offered for sale. Researchers can find a great deal of information about conditions in a metropolitan area free of charge when they use brokerage reports available on the internet, but detailed submarket reports and history may require paying a fee. Online brokerage reports do not offer performance information on individual properties, although they may report recent building sales and new property completions.

Definitions of the sizes and types of properties included in commercial broker inventories vary among the many firms that provide this type of data. Some firms count only buildings with at least 50,000 square feet or with multiple tenants, but others count single-tenant office and warehouse buildings in their inventories if they are not owner-occupied. Firms may count small office buildings but focus their industrial data on large warehouses with at least 100,000 square feet. Also, property class definitions are often inconsistent among sources and across markets. Because inventories that include only multitenant buildings or focus on structures over a certain minimum size undercount total supply, an analyst's report must specify the sizes and types of properties included in the databases.

For smaller markets, local brokers often provide important information, either in reports or through press releases sent to local newspapers and real estate trade publications. Local consulting or appraisal firms may sell more detailed project-by-project inventories, which provide rent, apartment unit mix, occupancy rates, and project amenities. They may also report occupancy and rent averages by metropolitan area and submarket, while providing commentary on market trends. Individual commercial and industrial properties currently available for sale or lease can be identified using LoopNet.com or Showcase.com by entering the location and property characteristics that are of interest to the analyst. These sources also sell information; they may provide some listings free of charge but require payment for full coverage.

Local firms will be very familiar with individual properties as well as marketwide conditions. However, relying solely on local brokers poses problems for analysts who must prepare reports for properties located in numerous metropolitan areas because methodologies and definitions among brokers will be inconsistent.

Property Types Covered by Reis

- Affordable housing
- Apartments
- Land
- Office
- Research and development
- Retail
- Self-storage
- Senior housing
- Student housing
- Warehouse/distribution

Consultants, Associations, and Trade Media

Organizations that represent real estate professionals can be useful sources of information on supply trends, both at the national level and in individual metropolitan areas. These groups include the International Council of Shopping Centers; National Association of Home Builders; NAIOP, the Commercial Real Estate Development Association; National Association of Realtors; National Multifamily Housing Council; and hotel associations, tourism trade groups, and other organizations representing property niches ranging from manufactured housing to timeshare resorts. Some trade associations conduct surveys and sponsor research efforts that help market analysts better understand consumer preferences. The Urban Land Institute also commissions research on market conditions, location trends, product design, consumer preferences, and investment results.[19]

A new warehouse with a row of loading docks.

Private Vendors

Since the late 1990s, data vendors such as CoStar and Reis[20] have greatly expanded the availability of information on apartments, commercial and retail projects, and multitenant industrial space.[21] For a onetime fee or through a subscription, analysts can buy current and historical data on area and submarket performance or can purchase data on individual buildings within a particular submarket or with specified criteria such as size and age.

Investment advisory firms such as Real Capital Analytics offer databases on transactions.[22] These reports are available to clients on a subscription basis.

Like brokerage firms, each private data vendor uses different criteria to define the submarkets, property classes, and types and sizes of properties it covers. For example, in its retail reports, Reis does not include regional malls or freestanding big-box stores but focuses on neighborhood and community centers with at least 10,000 square feet of multitenant space.

The products available from data vendors and economic consultants vary in their accuracy over time and across land uses. No two methodologies are identical. When a market analyst uses a particular source for projections, he or she should understand how that source develops its forecasts. The market analyst should purchase a report covering a single metropolitan area for a given property type and then see whether interviews and field observations concur with the report's findings. And before ordering an expensive subscription from a vendor, an analyst should also ask for information on the accuracy of its inventory data and forecasts over time.

Government Sources, Directories, and Lists

Directories of apartment complexes, office buildings, or industrial parks (available online or published as magazines) provide an inexpensive way to get started, because they contain basic information about individual buildings. Economic development agencies and utility companies often keep lists of available blocks of space in privately owned industrial buildings, office buildings, or both. They may also have lists of improved, available development sites in office or industrial parks. (However, government lists are not updated as frequently as listings on commercial websites are.) Agencies charged with promoting tourism or booking conventions and meetings will have lists of hotels in their jurisdiction and descriptions of those facilities, as well as information on publicly operated convention venues. (These inventories may not include hotels in locations far from a convention center.) To find affordable housing for families or seniors in a market area, market analysts should consult lists published by HUD, state and local housing agencies, and advocacy groups (see chapter 4). These sources should list the names, addresses, and phone numbers of affordable rental buildings. State housing or community development agencies have websites where landlords can post available affordable apartments and provide information on unit sizes, features, and rents.

Such lists can provide a road map for the market analyst, but more complete information usually has to be obtained through field visits or telephone interviews. None of the aforementioned directories of affordable housing resources include all of the properties where tenants must meet maximum income guidelines. For example, many online directories include only public housing or privately owned and managed Section 8 properties (some include both), but not those built using low-income housing tax credits (LIHTCs).

Importance of Fieldwork

Although the quantity and quality of statistical information on competitive supply is continually improving, even the best inventory reports cannot substitute for field observations. Seeing the subject property and its competition firsthand results in a more precise definition of the trade area. Preparing a thorough market analysis also requires "kicking the bricks"—determining how a competitor's location, surrounding uses, design, amenities, and other features compare with the subject property.

A competitor's curb appeal—its architecture, building materials, landscaping, exterior signage, and surrounding uses—draws potential tenants into the leasing office. For an office building, lobby appearance, interior signage, lighting, elevator systems, security, and other design elements also influence whether an older building can effectively compete with a new project. In a community shopping center, frontage visibility from the street, access and turn lanes from nearby arterial roads, exterior signage, parking lot layouts, and physical attributes (such as store signage and maintenance) can make or break a project. Even with color photos, none of these things can be clearly understood without a site visit.

When time and budget permit, the market analyst should visit model apartments to observe room or floor layouts, natural light, quality of built-ins, and storage space. Inspecting older properties may have limitations. Some properties will have no vacant units to show. Others may not have floor plans or measurements readily available. However, seeing

model kitchens and baths tells the analyst whether the property has been maintained and renovated to be competitive with new units. Looking at photographs posted on the property's website or on third-party apartment rental sites (such as apartments.com) is an acceptable alternative when model units are not available or when a property does not have an on-site leasing office. If a model unit in an older apartment complex has been recently upgraded, the market analyst should ask whether all of the units have been renovated in a similar manner and, if they have not, when those upgrades will be completed.

The market analyst should look at the tenant directory in an office building, shopping center, or business park to determine whether the property is leased by a few large space users or by numerous small businesses. The directory provides insight into occupancy in those situations where data are unavailable. Note the types of tenants present. Are they national chain retailers or Fortune 500 businesses, or is the space occupied by individual entrepreneurs? When an analyst still has questions, follow-up telephone calls to building managers are a good option. Business lists available from sources such as InfoUSA can also help; the market analyst will have to sort businesses by street address to identify occupants of competitive buildings.

Interviews with building managers or leasing staff members can enhance an analyst's understanding of an area's market dynamics, especially when published data are limited in scope, are too expensive, or are unavailable. These conversations yield insight into what types of households are attracted to an apartment complex (young singles and couples versus empty nesters and seniors, or a mix of both), whether children are present, what attracts tenants to this complex, and where prospective tenants are coming from and why. Such knowledge helps an analyst accurately define the market area from which tenants will be drawn to a new apartment community.[23] However, turnover in leasing staff can be problematic; new staff may not know a property's history. And in a big multibuilding complex, junior leasing staff members may not know much about the tenants, and senior staff members may decline to answer questions about tenant characteristics in residential buildings.[24] Commercial real estate agents and building managers know about their own tenants and the types of businesses that are looking for office or industrial space—their spatial needs, technical requirements, and parking requirements.

Analysts will not be able to interview every building manager in the field. Time and budget constraints will intervene and building staff members will not always cooperate. Some building owners refuse to permit their personnel to show model homes or apartments (or vacant units) to researchers. They may be unwilling to divulge project-specific information to market analysts—especially if the analyst is working for a current competitor or a future new building. Vacancy rates and lease expiration information

---

"Barriers to Entry" Limit Future Competition"

Limits on the amount of new construction that can occur in a submarket will lift occupancy rates for existing properties and hasten absorption for those already under construction. As availability tightens, rents are also likely to rise. Reasons for constrained supply can include

- Zoning and other land use controls that limit the location or pace of development for certain product types;

- Wetlands or protected farmland where development is prohibited;

- Insufficient utility service capacity; growth management programs that limit utility service extensions; and

- Political opposition to new construction, which can delay projects or result in modifications that render them no longer feasible.

are especially sensitive, although owners are usually willing to disclose asking rents. Analysts often "shop" competitive properties by posing as prospective tenants, either in person or over the phone.

Documentation of Historical and Future Construction Activity

Accurately gauging the demand and supply balance requires careful consideration of the future construction pipeline and of how it will differ from development activity in the recent past. For housing market reports, the analyst should tabulate the average annual number of single-family and multifamily building permits issued over the past five to 10 years. (It is important to remember that permitted units could be for sale or for rent.) The analyst should then discuss any dramatic shifts in permit volume or structure type. In most instances, the shifts will result from national economic cycles and changing consumer preferences. However, local zoning, land availability, and price and rent trends can also influence the type of housing being built. The local market area's capture of housing development activity throughout the county or metropolitan area should be highlighted.

Commercial and industrial properties already under construction will be among the most important competitors for a proposed development that has yet to line up financing and break ground. In areas with many visible construction projects, the analyst must determine the size of these competitors at full buildout and how much of the space has been preleased or presold. Asking rents for space yet to be leased should also be included in the supply analysis.

Some local government agencies, such as economic development authorities or planning departments, periodically update lists of projects that have received planning approvals but have not yet been started. Where no such reports exist, conversations with planning officials are needed to clarify the size of the development pipeline and determine if and when planned projects will begin construction. This research can be time-consuming in a trade area or submarket with numerous small jurisdictions.

Analysts should consider the amount of well-located, properly zoned, undeveloped land that could be competitive with the subject building in the future. A new project located in a mature community with little or no vacant land will face less competitive pressure than will one surrounded by sites where similar or identical buildings might be constructed three years hence.

Suburban market areas often cross municipal boundaries. In such cases, the analyst will be required to assemble permit data from state or county agencies or from Census Bureau reports. It is important to keep in mind that residential builders take out permits shortly before construction begins. However, permits provide no indication of when construction will be completed, and not all units for which permits are issued are actually completed. Also, permits for townhouse or apartment projects typically do not state whether the housing units are expected to be sold or rented, and plans can change with shifts in demand or competitive supply. Chapter 4 includes a discussion about the growing share of single-family homes that investors build as rentals.

Local building permit data are less useful for tracking commercial and industrial construction. Nonresidential building permits provide little detail about the type or timing of a development. In the past, real estate magazines, newspaper supplements, and economic development agencies tracked construction announcements and project openings. These sources can provide useful information, but they are time-consuming to find and assemble so the resulting reports can be spotty.

Construction pipeline data can be purchased through private vendors such as Reis and Dodge Data and Analytics (formerly known as the F.W. Dodge Co.). These data include projects of all sizes, both single user and multitenant. Dodge MarketShare provides 10-year historical information on construction starts and five-year forecasts by building type for metropolitan areas and counties.

Presentation of Findings

The art and science of market analysis require judgment and vision as well as facts. Once market analysts have completed fieldwork, collected data, and prepared maps and tables, they must synthesize the findings and reach conclusions about a proposed project's marketability or the future performance of an existing property.

Market studies are more easily understood when they are accompanied by summary tables that highlight the key characteristics of the competition, both existing and under construction. Such tables should provide the following:

- Name and address of competitive properties,
- Age (or year built),
- Overall size (units or square feet),
- Size of units, spaces, or lots offered,
- Asking rents and concessions (discounts such as a month of free rent in an apartment building or an allowance for moving expenses offered to commercial tenants),
- Whether utilities are included (for apartments),
- Whether asking rents are gross or net (for commercial and industrial properties), and
- Occupancy or vacancy rate.

The analyst may include other observations, such as location advantages and tenant mix. The table of competitive projects should be keyed to a map that shows the locations of the subject property and its competitors.

As mentioned earlier, some analysts prefer to use individual project sheets for each of the most competitive developments. This format allows them to include one or more digital photos of each building (and its surroundings, if space permits) alongside its pertinent data. However, a summary table will still be needed to facilitate comparisons between the subject property and others in the market area.

If the subject property is planned but not yet built, a color rendering of the building(s) will allow readers of the report to compare its visual appeal with that of its competitors. Aerial photographs can provide the reader with a sense of the site's surroundings and access to major roads, as well as its proximity to competitors and nearby services such as shopping, restaurants, transit stations, parks, trails, and public buildings.

Notes

1. Labor statistics count persons with either full-time or part-time employment as "employed." A person holding two part-time positions counts as having two jobs. Thus, the total number of employed persons can be overstated.

2. Employment & Earnings (a longtime source of BLS data) is no longer published in print form, but tables with annual averages for larger metropolitan areas and divisions are online in PDF format. Monthly labor force numbers, unemployment rates, and employment by industry are also available for smaller metropolitan areas. See www.bls.gov/opub/ee/home/htm.

3. Moody's Analytics offers detailed employment forecasts, with 20 years of history and long-range projections for two- and three-digit NAICS codes. These data are available for counties and metropolitan areas. www.economy.com.

4. The U.S. Census Bureau's CBP counts employment at government-operated hospitals but not at the U.S. Postal Service, pension funds, or trusts. For more information on coverage and data availability, see www.census.gov/epcd/cbp/view/intro.html.

5. Information on location quotients can be found at the following BLS web page: https://data.bls.gov/cew/doc/info/location_quotients.htm.

6. Labor force statistics do not count military personnel on active duty or residents of nursing homes. They count people age 16 through 64, who are then classified as employed or unemployed. Labor force participation rates include all persons 16 and older, with data available by age and gender. The data are taken from household surveys.

7. www.bls.gov/lau.home.html. A person is classified as unemployed if he or she was not working during the week of the survey, was available for work (except for temporary illness), and had made specific efforts to find employment some time during the four-week period ending with the reference week. Conversely, a person is considered employed if he or she worked for compensation during the week in question, even if it was only part-time work.

8. Such conversions include shuttered factories, warehouses, office buildings, hotels, schools, and hospitals in urban neighborhoods. Locations or structures no longer considered desirable for commercial or institutional uses have been transformed into successful loft apartments.

9. Average household income is the total reported income from all sources for the entire trade area, divided by the number of households. Median income is the point at which half the households are earning less and half are earning more.

10. Household income statistics include single people living alone and unrelated people living together. Their average and median household incomes tend to be lower than those of families (which consist of two or more related people living together).

11. The BLS's home page for its Consumer Expenditure Survey can be found at www.bls.gov/cex. Standard data tables that show income and expenditures by different demographic groups are published annually.

12. The decennial census does not ask questions about household income. Information on incomes is available from the Census Bureau's ACS sample surveys. For small communities, data are summarized on the basis of responses over a five-year period. In larger cities and suburbs, these estimates are available annually. Estimates for custom-defined market areas can be purchased from private demographic data companies on either a subscription or a single-use basis.

13. Examples of Claritas cluster names include "Kids and Cul-de-Sacs" and "Second City Startups." Esri has segments labeled "American Dreamers" and "Up and Coming Families."

14. See the Census Bureau's home page for Housing Vacancies and Homeownership statistics, https://www.census.gov/housing/hvs/index.html.

15. https://www.census.gov/programs-surveys/acs/guidance/handbooks/general.html.

16. The Pew Research Center is a nonpartisan fact tank that informs the public about the issues, attitudes, and trends shaping the world. Pew conducts public opinion polling, demographic research, content analysis, and other data-driven social science research. For more details on how Pew conducts national research panels in the United States, see Scott Keeter, "Growing and Improving Pew Research Center's American Trends Panel," February 27, 2019. https://www.pewresearch.org/methods/2019/02/27/growing-and-improving-pew-research-centers-american-trends-panel/.

17. In California, rents are often expressed as dollars per square foot per month rather than on an annual basis.

18. www.cushwake.com, www.cbre.com, www.colliers.com, www.marcusmillichap.com/research, www.naiglobal.com, www.ngkf.com.

19. ULI and PwC publish *Emerging Trends in Real Estate®,* an annual trends and forecast publication that provides an outlook for real estate investment and development trends, real estate finance and capital markets, property sectors, metropolitan areas, and other real estate issues.

20. Reis started issuing reports on a subscription basis in 1980, covering four sectors: apartments, office buildings, retail space, and industrial buildings. In the mid-1990s, it provided data to customers on CD-ROM or dial-up connections. Online subscription services began in 2001. In 2018, the company was acquired by Moody's Analytics, combining Reis's supply-side information with Moody's economic and demographic trend data and forecasting capabilities on the demand side.

21. www.costar.com, www.reis.com.

22. www.ppr.info, www.rcanalytics.com.

23. The analyst should be aware that fair housing laws limit how much information apartment leasing staff members or home sales agents can share about tenant or buyer characteristics. Visual observations of toys, bicycles, or playground use will indicate the presence of children, but the prevalence of families with children (or not), young singles and couples, empty nesters, or seniors cannot be determined from fieldwork alone.

24. Answering questions about tenant demographics can be viewed as a violation of fair housing laws. Market analysts can ask the questions, but property staff will often decline to answer them.

CHAPTER 4

CHAPTER 4

HOUSING

The objectives of a housing market analysis include the following:

- Identify and evaluate potential development sites.

- Provide input for site planning lot sizes, layouts, road access, and amenities.

- Recommend an appropriate mix and size of units to be offered.

- Suggest unit and project amenities and optional upgrades needed to be competitive.

- Determine appropriate pricing and likely absorption.

- Conduct a due diligence review for a loan application, acquisition, or equity investment.

- Provide documentation in support of a grant application submitted to a public-sector agency.

- Monitor the market performance of a completed project relative to its competition.

- Reposition an asset that is not performing up to expectations.

- Guide public-sector housing policy, determine whether incentive programs are needed to produce more units, and decide how to target the incentives if adopted.

Demand is calculated from an understanding of population and household demographics, which are driven by employment, location preferences, and lifestyle choices. Supply analysis includes surveying existing and planned projects in terms of building styles and community types, density, unit layouts, amenities, pricing, and occupancy or absorption. When assessing the for-sale market, mortgage terms and credit standards also play important roles in determining whether consumers will be able to buy what the market offers.

A developer may start with a product type (especially one that has been successful for the company in the recent past) and may ask the market analyst to determine whether

a sufficient number of income-qualified households are likely to be interested in this product. The analyst then needs to match demand with competitive supply by studying existing homes or apartments, projects currently being marketed, and the future development pipeline.

Housing Stock Overview: Products and Community Types

As listed in the sidebar on the following page, the U.S. housing market encompasses a wide range of product types in terms of physical structure, tenure, and location. Each housing type can be found in a variety of sizes, floor plans, elevations, and price or rent ranges.

Single-Family Subdivisions

Conventional single-family subdivisions have accounted for the largest percentage of new home construction since World War II, stimulated by Federal Housing Administration (FHA), U.S. Department of Veterans Affairs (VA), and other mortgage programs that were designed to encourage homeownership. Project sizes vary, but what distinguishes the traditional subdivision is the placement of homes on individual lots; their density (number of units per acre); and the size of front, rear, and side yards—sizes that are controlled by local subdivision and zoning codes. Most single-family developments are constructed on greenfield sites, but there are many examples of small single-family infill projects in cities and older suburbs.

In moderate- to middle-priced subdivisions, a single homebuilder will construct all the units. A given neighborhood can contain both homes built "on spec"—constructed before a buyer is signed—and semi-custom units selected by the homebuyer from plans or models, often with a choice of different exterior elevations for each model. Prices will vary according to the size of the unit, its features, and the range of upgrades selected by the purchaser. New homes are marketed directly by the builder or developer or through local real estate agents.

Housing Product Types

Community Types

- Master-planned communities (MPCs) with a mix of housing types and ancillary amenities such as golf courses, trails, water features, shopping areas, clubhouses (often with restaurants), and exercise facilities.

- Single-family subdivisions, typically in "greenfield" locations at the urban fringe.

- Infill—urban and suburban projects involving redevelopment or adaptive use of nonresidential structures or vacant parcels in mature communities.

- Market-rate rental apartment complexes with shared community spaces.

- Age-restricted rental, entry-fee, and for-sale retirement communities.

- Affordable housing (with income restrictions for prospective buyers or renters) and mixed-income projects (serving a range of incomes).

- Niche products, such as college housing, urban live/work spaces, golf course communities, water-oriented developments, and units designed for persons with disabilities or health issues.

- Seasonal or second-home communities.

Housing Types and Construction Methods

- Single-family detached houses.

- Attached duplexes, triplexes, coach houses, and townhouses.

- Multifamily buildings (walkup, mid-rise, and high-rise).

- Stick-built or factory-built structures.

- Mobile homes or modular construction.

Tenure of Residents

- Fee-simple, condominium, and cooperative (co-op) ownership.

- Rentals.

- Timeshare or fractional ownership.

- Condo-hotels, where hotel rooms or suites are individually owned and where management provides short-term rentals and hotel services for owners.

- Homes and units built on ground leases.

Luxury communities cater to a small cohort of affluent consumers, either as primary or secondary residences. These custom home developments will have fewer units and larger lots than will middle-priced projects. Multiple builders often buy lots within a single luxury home project and market their design and construction expertise directly to prospective buyers.

Although the Census Bureau and private data vendors now provide an estimate of the number of households with incomes greater than $200,000, this upper limit may be insufficiently detailed to provide a true picture of affordability for custom homes. And as indicated in chapter 3, income estimates alone do not paint a complete portrait of household wealth. Analysis of the market potential for a luxury development requires a clear understanding of target households and their preferences. Moreover, direct consumer research may be needed, along with in-person interviews with residential brokers who cater to this demographic segment.

Master-Planned Communities

In parts of the United States, primarily in the West and South, master-planned communities (MPCs) are a common development type. These developments usually include a range of housing types along with recreational amenities, supporting retail and service businesses, and other commercial development (such as medical offices). Many feature gated entries providing 24-hour security to residents and convey exclusivity. Monthly owner assessments or fees and community association management are needed to support the amenities, common areas, and security features of the project.

Master-planned communities often encompass several thousand acres and include schools, libraries, and other public facilities, as well as a substantial amount of office or retail development. Many have grown to the extent of becoming recognized as cities in their own right. Irvine, California; Reston, Virginia; and Summerlin outside Las Vegas, Nevada, are examples of MPCs that sold new homes for decades. In fact, Summerlin still ranked number three in sales of new homes in 2018.

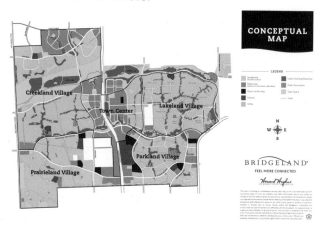

A conceptual map of the 11,400-acre Bridgeland master-planned community in Cypress, Texas. (Howard Hughes Corporation)

Master-Planned Communities

The consulting firm RCLCO Real Estate Advisors provides the following definition of an MPC:

> True MPCs are developed from a comprehensive plan by a master developer, and they incorporate a variety of housing types, sizes, and prices along with shared common space, amenities, and a vital public realm. The best examples of MPCs are developed with a strong vision and comprehensive plan that guide development and unify the community through distinctive signage, wayfinding, entry features, landscaping, and architectural or design standards. Beyond the built environment, MPCs differentiate themselves from typical suburban subdivisions in that they provide a means for interaction among neighbors in the sense of the word "community."
>
> RCLCO reported that, in 2018, communities in Texas, Florida, and California accounted for 34 of the top 50 MPCs in sales and for 68 percent of total U.S. MPC home sales. The other 16 MPCs in the top 50 are in Arizona, Nevada, and Colorado, with a small number in Utah, Washington state, the Carolinas, and Virginia.

Source: Greg Logan and Karl Pischke, "Top-Selling Master-Planned Communities 2018," RCLCO Real Estate Advisors, January 3, 2019, www.rclco.com.

In these communities, the amenities package is important in attracting buyers, so the market analyst needs to identify the right mix of amenities along with lot sizes, home sizes and features, and association fees.

New urbanist communities are a specific type of MPC that emphasizes compact, mixed-use, pedestrian-oriented site plans. Residents trade larger lots for a more community-centered lifestyle. Streets are usually narrow and arranged in grids. Short blocks contain a mix of housing types and supporting commercial and institutional uses in street-facing buildings. Parking is provided at the rear of structures.

Infill Development: Urban and Suburban

As prime developable land became scarce, developers turned to infill sites for new residential construction. Infill parcels may have been skipped over during previous waves of development because they were physically difficult to develop, were environmentally contaminated, lacked access to utilities, had delinquent tax obligations, or had ownership that could not be clearly traced or could not be convinced to sell. Such properties may be totally vacant or have derelict buildings or environmental issues that need to be addressed and cleared before redevelopment can proceed.

The advantages of infill development include the ability to tap into existing infrastructure and community services, as well as an established market—the residents of the surrounding neighborhoods. Infill locations are typically much smaller than suburban greenfield sites, so absorption periods will usually be shorter. However, infill development can be difficult. Often developers are challenged by the need to assemble small parcels with multiple owners, obtain approvals for higher densities or unfamiliar designs, remove contaminants, or demolish existing structures.

NIMBY ("not in my backyard") opposition from nearby residents may be a stumbling block to redevelopment activity that increases neighborhood density, generates additional traffic, or reduces availability of on-street parking. Nevertheless, many developers find that the rewards outweigh the difficulties. In recent years, consumers have shown a preference for living in established, walkable, or transit-served communities where shopping and services are nearby, especially if infill development can reduce commuting times.

Second-Home Communities

Second-home markets depend on discretionary buyers. Property types include luxury single-family homes, condominiums in beachfront or ski communities, lakefront and oceanfront properties with boat slips, golf course communities, and modest cabins in rural locations.

Second-home demand can be regional, national, or even international in scope. Buyers are typically in their 40s and early 50s with household incomes in the top 10 percent. However, only a small portion of affluent middle-aged households buy second homes. Accessibility can be a major factor in the purchase decision. At the high end of the market, access by air and even proximity to small airports that serve private planes are important considerations. For most of the market, however, driving time from the owner's primary residence is a pivotal consideration. The 200-mile typical distance should be a key consideration when determining the market area and potential demand for a second-home development.

Second Homes or Vacation Homes

The NAR reported in 2016 that vacation home sales accounted for 12 percent of all home sales, a decline from the 16 percent share seen in 2015. The median sales price for vacation homes sold in 2016 was $200,000. The most popular locations for vacation properties were beaches (36 percent), lakefronts (21 percent), and country sites (20 percent). The median distance from a primary home to a vacation home was 200 miles. Median interior size was 1,460 square feet—considerably smaller than primary residences. Single-family detached homes account for most vacation home purchases; 22 percent were condominiums and 21 percent were townhomes.

Source: Amanda Riggs, "Vacation and Investment Home Sales: A Breakdown for 2017," Economists' Outlook blog, Realtor.com, posted April 26, 2017, http://economistsoutlook.blogs.realtor.org/author/ariggs.

Affordable housing in suburban Baltimore. *(Deborah L. Brett & Associates)*

Affordable housing in Philadelphia. *(Deborah L. Brett & Associates)*

Even among the target age and income groups, the motivation for buying a second home varies:

- Buyers are drawn from large metropolitan areas where the stress of everyday life is an additional motivation to own property in a different environment.

- Families with children may buy a second home to pursue outdoor sports or hobbies and to have an opportunity for interaction that is lacking during the work week. These households will use their second home on weekends and during vacations.

- Some buyers expect to use their second home as an eventual retirement location.

- A portion of the second-home market buys a lot in anticipation of building sometime in the future. Lot buyers are attracted by the quality of a golf course, associated club facilities, or other amenities in a private community; they may purchase the lot primarily to secure access to the community's recreation facilities. Some of these lot buyers may never build a home; rather, they sell the lot when their interests change.

- Pre-retirees are attracted by a community's recreational amenities but are also concerned about its social fabric. Climate, the quality of the area's medical facilities, convenience of shopping and services, cultural opportunities, cost of living, and learning opportunities are also important to younger buyers who may decide to eventually make their second home a permanent residence.

- International buyers are a major source of demand in coastal markets such as Miami, Orlando, and Southern California. They often see their second home as an investment; they can rent out their units when they are not using them. This type of buyer looks for multifamily condominiums and purpose-built resort residential

properties where visitors can rent units by the week, month, or season. Note that demand from outside the United States is particularly vulnerable to national economic downturns, political changes, and currency fluctuations in the buyers' home countries.

Although resort-home markets generally track closely with the economic cycle, their swings are often more severe and therefore pose significant risks for developers. Careful research—including an understanding of cyclical performance during economic downturns—is required.

Identifying the sources of demand for second homes, as well as the comparables, can be a daunting task. Sales managers at newer projects as well as real estate agents serving destination locations can be helpful in identifying locations that generate potential buyers. When one conducts market studies in resort areas that are popular with second-home buyers, it is important to distinguish owner or user demand from investor buyers who are more interested in the revenue from rentals than in personal or family use. Because second-home market analysis requires unique expertise, developers tend to hire consultants who specialize in assessing demand for these projects.

Affordable Housing

In virtually all markets, the need for affordable housing exceeds the supply of sound units available to low-income renters. The federal LIHTC program produces the largest number of new and substantially rehabilitated rental units. Tax credits are allocated by state housing agencies on a competitive basis; a market study is typically required when developers submit an application. Housing agencies may also award other credits for properties financed by state revenue bonds, subject to bonding limits (known as "volume caps"). For both types of credits, however, competition is intense in many locations.

Market studies for properties with affordable units must define the eligible population on the basis of criteria dictated by government funding sources:

- Federal regulations used to prohibit renting LIHTC units to tenants whose incomes are higher than 60 percent of the area's median income (AMI), adjusted for household size. As a result of changes in the tax law in late 2017, households with incomes as high as 80 percent of AMI are now permitted to live in new LIHTC units. However, the average income targeting for all units in an LIHTC development cannot exceed 60 percent of AMI.

- States can require that a share of units within an LIHTC project be restricted to households with extremely low incomes—below 20 or 30 percent of AMI.

- States can also encourage mixed-income developments by favoring projects that include both market-rate and LIHTC units.

- Some jurisdictions have "workforce" rental housing programs, which are targeted to households with incomes higher than those permitted for LIHTC properties (generally between 60 and 100 percent of AMI or (in high-rent areas) up to 120 percent of AMI.

- Many LIHTC properties are targeted to households age 55 or older and others to age 62 and older. States can also have "setasides" for development projects that target households with special needs as well as veterans or others who require supportive living services.

Housing finance agencies want to be sure that local markets are not saturated with affordable units serving the same target groups. The agencies may be issuing bonds for a project (and worry about defaults), and they want to avoid the neighborhood issues that can result from overconcentration of low-income families. In addition, market analyses for LIHTC properties must demonstrate that rents for the proposed affordable units will save money when compared with units in the unsubsidized inventory. Quality differences between new LIHTC units and existing low-rent stock must also be addressed.

State and local governments also have their own affordable or workforce housing programs for prospective homeowners, oriented almost exclusively to first-time buyers. Projects vary in scale and can include a mix of housing types. Generally, buyers must have incomes that fall between 80 and 120 percent of AMI. The nature of incentives for both developers and buyers is determined by state and local policies and programs.

Some jurisdictions have requirements specifying that 10 percent or more of the units in market-rate projects be designated for low- to moderate-income households. Cities prefer these units to be provided on site, but they may allow developers of small projects to make a per unit contribution to a low- to moderate-income housing fund that helps produce units in other locations. Municipalities also have financial incentive programs that help developers with upfront costs—such as TIF for infrastructure improvements or environmental remediation. When determining project feasibility in urban areas, the market analyst should investigate the existence of low and moderate housing requirements as well as special funding mechanisms that might be available to help defray the cost of creating affordable units.

Age-Restricted Housing

Many types of housing exist for seniors. Those who can live independently have a range of choices, both rental and for sale.

Market-rate senior rentals generally offer one or two bedrooms and full kitchens in buildings that include lounges, libraries, and activity rooms. Properties that target wealthier residents also offer a limited number of three-bedroom units. Services range from scheduled transportation to social and recreational activities, wellness programs, and (sometimes) meals and housekeeping, either optional or included in the rent. This product is targeted primarily to middle- and upper-income households age 65 and older, although most residents are at least age 70 and in good health. Properties that have affordable rents for seniors and that were developed using LIHTC or other government programs have income as well as age restrictions.

In the for-sale segment of the senior market, active adult communities offer traditional homeownership (in single-family detached homes, townhouses, or elevator condominiums) without maintenance responsibilities for households that have at least one member who is age 55 or older. These communities often have extensive recreation amenities, such as tennis courts, trails, and clubhouses with a pool, gym, and space for social events. Some have golf courses as well.

Seniors age 75 and older may be drawn to congregate housing or continuing care retirement communities (CCRCs) that include a variety of housing types and the same recreation facilities found in active adult rentals or ownership communities. There are differences, however:

- Congregate properties usually offer personal care options, laundry services, housekeeping, emergency call systems, and at least one daily meal at an additional cost. They may require an entry fee (in many cases, partially

A market-rate, age-restricted rental complex in Mercer County, New Jersey. Some units have garages; all have elevator access. *(Deborah L. Brett & Associates)*

New for-sale housing styles in an active adult community.
(Deborah L. Brett & Associates)

refundable depending on how long the resident lives in the community) in addition to a monthly maintenance charge. As in independent living buildings for seniors, the resident furnishes the apartment, which is equipped with a full kitchen. Many congregate buildings are affiliated with local hospitals and nursing homes. The typical resident of congregate housing is a single woman, age 75 to 85, who is generally in good health and able to live independently. Market studies for these property types must focus on the demographic and income characteristics of older seniors, because the units will draw relatively few prospects from the 65 to 74 age cohort.

- Within a CCRC, independent living, assisted living, and skilled nursing are available in a campus setting. Residents can move within the community as they need more supportive services. CCRCs usually require payment of an entrance fee or endowment, as well as monthly charges. Some facilities provide life-care commitments; most provide only a guarantee of admission to buildings or units that offer more personal assistance or medical care as needs change. (Fewer life-care communities are being built than in the past; as the population ages, it is more difficult for developers or nonprofit sponsors to assure residents that monthly charges will be stable.) CCRCs appeal both to couples and to singles who are still in good health but are concerned about their future needs. Most CCRCs are sponsored by nonprofit religious denominations or fraternal groups. Universities have sponsored such projects to attract alumni who want to take advantage of classes and cultural offerings.

Assisted-living residences are smaller buildings (typically fewer than 80 residents); they offer 24-hour supervision and assistance for frail elderly persons who need help with bathing, dressing, medication administration, mobility, or other activities of daily living. The mix of units can include apartments with separate bedrooms or single-occupancy and shared rooms, either furnished or unfurnished. Rents are charged on a daily or monthly basis, and cost varies according to the extent of personal assistance the resident

needs. Three meals a day are usually included, along with scheduled transportation to medical appointments, organized outings, church services, housekeeping, and activities. Units may have small kitchenettes with a refrigerator and microwave oven, as well as cabinets. Bathrooms are designed for persons with limited mobility.

Assisted living is proving to be an acceptable—and more affordable—alternative to nursing homes for seniors who do not need skilled nursing care. Increasingly, assisted-living facilities offer specialized floors or wings for people with Alzheimer's disease or similar illnesses. A relatively small but growing proportion of assisted-living facilities serve *only* patients with dementia.

In most cases, assisted-living residents or their families must have sufficient resources (income or assets) to afford the monthly cost, which is significantly higher than that of more standard housing without supportive services. A relatively new initiative in several states uses the LIHTC program to build affordable supportive-living facilities for very-low-income seniors, with Medicaid paying for needed personal care services while tax credits keep housing costs lower. States find this arrangement a more affordable option than paying for skilled nursing through Medicaid when that high level of care is not needed by the resident.

It is easy to overestimate the demand for senior housing of all types. However, it is important to understand this age cohort, rather than to rely on generalizations:

- Most seniors prefer to age in place (living as long as they can in the homes they owned or rented when they were younger). As a result, they are less mobile than younger households. According to the Census Bureau's CPS, only 3.5 percent of people age 65 and older moved between March 2017 and 2018. (The mobility rate for the total population was 10.1 percent during this period.)

- For a person in good health, the decision to move to a retirement community is a lifestyle choice, not a necessity.

- Some seniors who are willing to move to a smaller home or a maintenance-free situation do not like age-restricted communities. Other choices are available to them.

Skilled nursing and rehab building in a continuing care retirement community.
(Deborah L. Brett & Associates)

A freestanding assisted-living building in Essex County, New Jersey.
(Deborah L Brett & Associates)

Increasingly, homebuilders incorporate universal design principles in their floor plans and built-in features, making their products physically accessible to all households, regardless of age. Homeowners can hire caregivers on a part-time basis to assist with personal needs; depending on income, Medicaid may pay for all or part of the cost.

■ Other seniors move in with relatives when their health deteriorates and they can no longer live independently. This alternative may be a family preference or a financial reality, because senior housing can cost thousands of dollars a month depending on the extent of services provided.

Absorption periods (the length of time it takes to reach stabilized occupancy—generally 95 percent or better—during initial lease-up) for rental retirement housing are longer than for conventional new apartment complexes. Studies have shown that seniors make far more visits to retirement buildings before making a decision to rent or buy than do typical apartment tenants or condominium buyers. Because seniors tend to be homeowners in most markets, they must sell their existing homes before moving, which can be a problem when the for-sale market is weak. Moving can be a very emotional decision that takes a great deal of time, possibly involving other family members. As a result, the pace of lease-up or sales in market-rate senior housing can be slow.

In 2017, 26 percent of new single-family housing units completed were age-restricted; for multifamily units, the share was 24 percent. These shares represent a significant increase when compared with those seen in 2010, when only 11 percent of new single-family homes and 12 percent of multifamily units were designed for occupancy by seniors. (The low shares seen in 2010 reflected the effects of the housing recession, which made it more difficult for seniors to sell their existing homes so they could move to new age-restricted communities.) As a result, absorption of market-rate senior housing was slow during and after the Great Recession.

In some suburban markets, local governments encourage construction of senior housing, thereby limiting the number of additional children that would have to be accommodated in already overburdened schools. As a result, it is relatively easy for market-rate age-restricted housing to be overbuilt.

Determining effective demand for senior housing requires looking not only at the number of seniors in the market area and their current incomes, but also at their assets and the value of the homes they must sell before moving (see discussion on household assets in chapter 3). The diversity of product, services provided, and pricing plans also pose challenges when examining the strengths and weaknesses of competitive properties in a given area. For example, per-square-foot rents must be adjusted to account for variations in meal plans; some facilities include housekeeping services in the rent and others do not. As is the case with second-home communities, developers and sponsors often call upon specialists in senior housing to prepare their market studies.

Market-Rate Rental Developments

Conventional rental apartments take many forms, ranging from two-story walkups to mid-rise and high-rise buildings. They are located in cities, suburban downtowns, and outlying locations. Because of the high cost associated with installing elevators, mid- and high-rise products tend to dominate in areas where multifamily sites are scarce, land prices are high, and rents can justify the costs. The rental apartment inventory includes older complexes that are rated as class B or C, which would not be truly competitive with new product. Renovating an older B property can, however, improve it to the point that it can be fairly competitive with A or A– buildings. Units in the newest communities tend to be smaller than those in class B complexes; class B properties can draw tenants who want more space but do not need the amenities and features seen in brand-new buildings.

An outdoor swimming pool and a clubhouse (often with exercise equipment, party room, kitchen, fireplace, business center, and media room) are typical of the newest suburban rental complexes. Organized social gatherings such as movies or happy hours take place at the clubhouse. In more upscale apartment communities, covered parking (single-car garages tucked under the units, freestanding garage buildings, or underground spaces) or carports are frequently provided at an additional cost to the tenant. Unreserved outdoor parking spaces are usually free of charge in both new and older complexes.

In urban areas, parking is typically provided in garages that are either underground, on lower floors, or occasionally in a separate building. In very dense downtowns with strong public transit service (as in Manhattan), no parking may be provided at all, even in high-end buildings. Many cities are now offering density bonuses and other incentives to encourage the development of multifamily housing (both rental and for sale) adjacent to transportation stations or hubs. Transit-oriented development (TOD) is becoming increasingly popular in both dense urban locations and suburban station areas. The ability to increase densities at these locations can be a powerful economic advantage for both the developers and end users. In communities without rail access, TOD projects can be attractive if adjacent to or within walking distance of park-and-ride lots with express bus service to employment centers.

College Student Housing

Privately owned and managed campus housing is a product distinct from university-owned dormitories or conventional apartments in college towns. Although new student-oriented apartments may look like conventional rentals from the outside, the properties are often leased in a very different way—by the bed rather than by the unit. Utilities, including cable television and high-speed internet service—are typically included in the rent. Managers will arrange for furniture rental at a fixed monthly cost. These projects have amenities—full kitchens in the units, exercise rooms, social spaces, and even swimming pools—not found in dormitories or older rentals found near campus. Most units are shared by multiple roommates; the proportion of units with three or four bedrooms is far higher than in most apartment complexes, and the rents per square foot are higher because of the amenities and services included.

Demand for campus housing depends on a number of factors:

- Enrollment trends at nearby universities;

- Availability of beds in university-owned dormitories (which can cost less than a bed in privately owned student housing);

- The college's housing policies (first- and second-year students are often required to live in university housing);

- Availability, quality, and cost of older private housing options in the community; and

- Willingness of parents to pay for upscale accommodations for their children.

Note that distance from campus is an important factor in determining both the attractiveness of new student rental buildings and the continued strong occupancy of stabilized properties. As the supply of student housing increases—and students have more choices—properties located less than a half mile from campus will do better. These sites are not easy to find, but they will command higher rents per bed.

The private campus housing business now attracts large management and development firms as well as institutional investors. Many of these firms now manage tens of thousands of units.[1] Student housing real estate investment trusts (REITs) are publicly traded on the New York Stock Exchange. However, despite rising enrollments and the shortage of dormitory beds at some universities, demand for college housing is not recession-proof. Although college enrollments tend to rise during the early stages of recessions as young people without jobs decide to continue their educations, parents who are facing financial constraints may be unwilling to pay the extra cost associated with better-quality housing. Even as the economy begins to recover, this sector's performance can suffer as students and parents exhaust financial resources in a weak economy.

Preparing a market study for privately owned student housing will require important data inputs from the university: information about off-campus housing policies, occupancy in existing dormitories (and plans for renovation or replacement of older structures), on-campus housing costs, and enrollment trends and projections. Publications and websites that focus on this segment of the apartment market should also be consulted to identify and track upcoming developments.

New two-bedroom, two-bath apartments with a den and a one-car garage. *(Deborah L. Brett & Associates)*

New rental apartments adjacent to a commuter-rail station in Orange, New Jersey. *(Deborah L. Brett & Associates)*

Single-Family and Multifamily Stock: Size and Age

According to the Census Bureau's 2017 American Housing Survey (AHS), single-family detached units make up 63.2 percent of the total occupied U.S. housing stock; for renter-occupied units, the single-family detached share is 28.3 percent (see figures 4-1a and 4-1b).[2]

The 2017 AHS reported that most of the U.S. occupied housing stock is more than 50 years old—51.6 percent for owner units and 58.5 percent for rented homes and apartments, as seen in figure 4-2. The aging of the housing stock creates opportunities for renovation and replacement, which leads to demand beyond what is generated through new household formation. For local market areas, information about the age of the housing stock can be found in the Census Bureau's ACS or through data vendors such as Claritas or Esri.

Figure 4-1a
All Occupied U.S. Housing Stock, by Units in Structure
2017

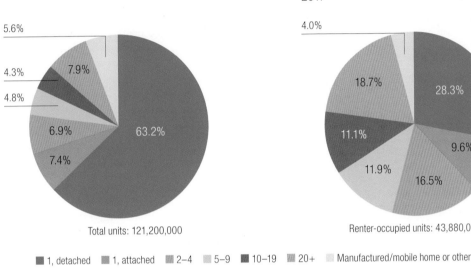

Total units: 121,200,000

Figure 4-1b
Renter-Occupied U.S. Housing Stock, by Units in Structure
2017

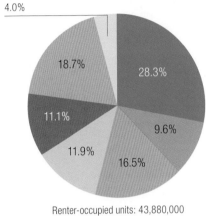

Renter-occupied units: 43,880,000

■ 1, detached ■ 1, attached ■ 2–4 ■ 5–9 ■ 10–19 ■ 20+ ■ Manufactured/mobile home or other

Source: U.S. Census Bureau and U.S. Department of Housing and Urban Development, American Housing Survey, *2017.*

Figure 4-2
Occupied Housing Units by Year Built and Tenure

Year built	Owner-occupied		Renter-occupied	
	Number (000s)	Share (%)	Number (000s)	Share (%)
2010–2017	3,726	4.8	2,227	5.1
2000–2009	11,770	15.2	5,579	12.7
1990–1999	11,340	14.7	4,334	9.9
1980–1989	10,570	13.7	6,067	13.8
1970–1979	11,050	14.3	6,822	15.6
1960–1969	8,145	10.5	4,499	10.3
1950–1959	8,392	10.9	4,380	10.0
1940–1949	3,477	4.5	2,246	5.1
Pre-1940	8,844	11.4	7,730	17.6
Total	**77,314**	**100.0**	**43,884**	**100.0**

Source: U.S. Census Bureau and U.S. Department of Housing and Urban Development, American Housing Survey, *2017.*

Cyclical Nature of New Housing Construction

Changes in the general economy and the housing sector specifically affect the ability of builders to successfully market new housing. From the perspective of the builder or developer, the pace of development is governed by availability of land at a reasonable price, local government regulations affecting permitted uses and densities, funds for upfront expenses, and access to construction financing and permanent mortgages with acceptable terms. Some locations have limited land availability and strictly regulate the types of housing units that can be built, while others have relatively few controls on what is built or where. Developers may find it relatively easily to raise capital—or not. When supply and demand are imbalanced or when the cost of building is too high, construction activity will slow. If the general economy weakens, unemployment rises, and household incomes stagnate, consumers will not look for better-quality apartments, will defer buying a home for the first time, or will delay a move to a bigger residence. As the economy improves, developers, lenders, and investors will be more willing to take risks. Figure 4-3 illustrates how new housing construction plummeted during the most recent economic cycle.

In the mid-2000s, the number of new single-family homes completed exceeded historical averages. Mortgage money was plentiful, and credit standards were relaxed. Households eager to become homeowners for the first time, trade up, or buy a second home encouraged construction activity, especially for single-family dwellings. In most markets, the first signs of a contraction appeared in 2007 when the number of completions nationally dropped to 1.5 million, down from nearly 2 million the previous year.

Figure 4-3

Total New Privately Owned Housing Units Completed in the United States
2000–2017

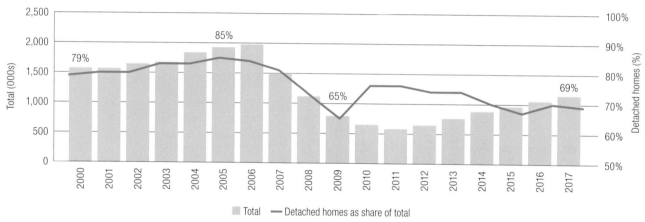

Source: U.S. Census Bureau, https://www.census.gov/construction/nrc/historical_data/index.html.

Figure 4-4

Median Square Feet of New Single-Family Homes Completed in the United States
United States and Regions, 1987–2017

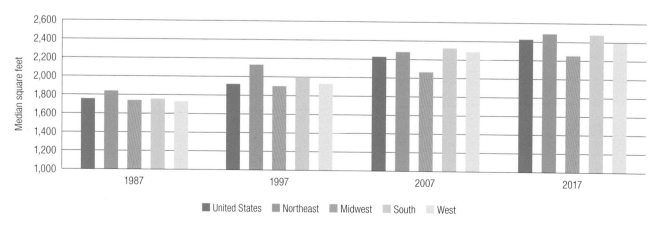

Source: U.S. Department of Commerce and U.S. Department of Housing and Urban Development, 2017 Characteristics of New Housing, https://www.census.gov/construction/chars/pdf/c25ann2017.pdf.

The number of single-family detached units as a share of new housing completions has declined as rental apartment construction increased after the housing downturn that began in 2007. Detached homes accounted for 81 percent of new housing units completed between 2000 and 2008. Between 2009 and 2017, the detached home share dropped to only 69 percent.

Although single-family construction still dominates the new housing market, its share of total residential building activity is unlikely to return to pre-recession levels any time soon. Even if many millennials still want to own a home someday, young consumers (especially singles and couples without children) are interested in urban living or seek suburban nodes near transit stations or highway interchanges. Reducing commuting time has taken on greater importance than in previous decades. Young households also want to live near shopping, dining, and entertainment choices (as do many empty nesters and seniors). These amenities are more concentrated in cities and older suburbs, where land for building new single-family detached homes is less available and more expensive than in outlying suburbs.

Whether these trends will continue has yet to be determined. As millennial households get older and have children, they may want more space. At the same time, baby boomer households with no children living at home have been less willing to downsize than was previously predicted, preferring to remain in their homes near friends, children, and grandchildren. These demographic trends suggest continued interest in suburban living.

Characteristics of New Single-Family Homes

Figure 4-4 shows trends in the median size of new single-family homes built from 1987 to 2017 in the United States. New single-family home sizes have continued to increase over time despite concerns about affordability. The median size of new homes built nationwide was 1,755 square feet in 1987; 30 years later, it had grown by more than 38 percent to 2,426. Although the median size trended downward after 2007 (when the median was 2,277 square feet) in response to the economic recession, by 2011 new home sizes had

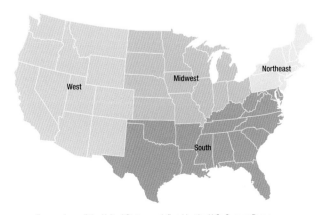

Four regions of the United States as defined by the U.S. Census Bureau.

returned to pre-recession levels. Smaller unit sizes were seen in new multifamily rental buildings post-recession but not in the single-family market. (See discussion of trends in multifamily construction later in this chapter.) However, escalating materials costs and labor shortages in the construction trades put pressure on builders to reduce the median size of new detached homes in 2018.

Recognizing Signs of a Downturn in the For-Sale Market

Many indicators provide evidence of a housing market slowdown. Analysts will be able to easily find publicly available (free) data for some indicators, but not for others, especially for submarkets. Local Realtors can be helpful in tracking trends at the microlevel.

It is important to remember that not all evidence of market contraction will be observable simultaneously, even if the analyst has access to a wide range of current statistics and recent consumer surveys. Clues include:

- Slowdown in the pace of home sales relative to the previous quarter and the same time a year ago.

- Fewer resale home listings: when consumers have fewer choices, sales activity drops.

- Changes in the difference between listing prices and actual sales prices. In a strong market, there can be bidding wars: prospective buyers compete for a property by making offers above listing price. In a weak market, sellers reduce asking prices more than once to generate offers.

- Changes in the median sales price of new and existing homes: the rate of price increases will slow or prices will decline.

- Listings take longer to sell (more time on the market).

- Rising interest rates, especially if rates have been relatively low for a long time. First-time buyers get discouraged; move-up buyers decide to stay where they are.

- Increasing number of mortgage delinquencies and foreclosures.

- Slowdown in new home starts because of shortages of suitable sites, higher production costs, or construction labor shortages, or any combination of the three.

- Declining stock share prices for publicly traded homebuilder companies.

- Changes in reported buyer traffic (shopper visits to new home sales offices) that cannot be explained by seasonal variations.

- Declining affordability in areas where prices have gone up faster than incomes.

Factory-Built Housing

According to the Manufactured Housing Institute (MHI), which is a trade organization representing the factory-built housing industry, manufactured homes—shipped as a completed unit for on-site installation or built with modular components—accounted for 9 percent of new single-family home starts in 2017.[3] It is important to note that manufactured home shipments (completed units) have been declining in recent decades. Between 1988 and 1997, shipments averaged more than 260,000 per year. From 2008 through 2017, this figure was only 58,742. In areas where affordable homes are needed, resistance to factory-built units may be found in local building codes and from unions in the building trades. Zoning requirements—minimum lot sizes, side yard or setback requirements, or other site design standards—can also make it difficult for new manufactured home communities to be built because their lots tend to be smaller than average.

At 1,446 square feet in 2016, the average manufactured home was considerably smaller than the average "stick-built" home. Manufactured housing advocates cite the affordability of these units for moderate-income households. Factory-built homes must meet standards that are set by HUD that cover safety and energy efficiency. Those homes remain popular in rural counties and in warm-weather locations. Long thought to attract transient population groups, manufactured homes gained respectability when their unit sizes grew larger and they provided more amenities. According to MHI, the per-square-foot cost of manufactured homes is less than half the cost of stick-built units.

Increasingly, manufactured single-family homes are found in professionally managed projects where the resident buys the unit but rents the land (often referred to as a "pad") from the community operator. Management provides security, common area maintenance, lighting, and playgrounds. Owner-occupied homes can be financed as personal property (similar to automobile financing) or as real estate if the sale also includes the lot or pad.

Modular components are being used in multifamily construction, in affordable single-family homes, and even in some upscale homes. Prefabricated modules built with wood or steel have been used in infill multifamily buildings in the San Francisco Bay area, Washington state, and Denver. Firms are also experimenting with reusing steel shipping containers in apartment construction.

Source: Will Macht, "Steel Modules Speed Construction," Urban Land online, January 28, 2019.

Although new home sizes in the Midwest trail those seen in other regions, the differences are not dramatic. Preliminary data on single-family homes completed in 2018 indicate that the U.S. median size dropped to 2,390 square feet from 2,436 a year earlier and 2,467 in 2015. Some industry observers believe that the long-term trend toward larger median and average home sizes will slowly shift downward as millennial buyers who postponed purchasing decisions are entering the new home market and are looking for affordable starter homes rather than a move-up product.

Home size is one of the major determinants of price. When comparing competitive projects, the market analyst examines not only the base sales price (plus extra charges for upgrades and options) but also the price per square foot.

In contrast to the trend toward more indoor space, median lot sizes of new single-family homes built for sale have declined in recent years, from 8,638 square feet in 2009 to 8,369 in 2017. Lot sizes are largest in the Northeast and smallest in the West.

Single-family homes are changing in other ways as well. Builders use an ever-evolving mix of building materials, heating systems, interior designs, kitchen appliances, bathroom amenities, and energy-saving or environmentally friendly features. Figure 4-5 compares selected characteristics of new single-family homes completed between 1987 and 2017. The data show that, over time, new houses have tended to include more bedrooms, baths, and attached garage spaces. Another feature that is increasingly popular is having the laundry area on an upper floor of a multistory home rather than in the basement or on the first floor. Air conditioning is now a virtually standard feature. In contrast, the share

Figure 4-5

Selected Characteristics of New Single-Family Homes
1987–2017

	Percentage of new homes			
	1987	1997	2007	2017
Central air conditioning	71	82	90	93
Four or more bedrooms	23	31	38	46
Two and a half or more baths	38	50	59	66
One or more fireplaces	62	61	51	45
Two or more stories	34	33	43	55
2,400 sq ft or more	21	31	45	51
Gas heat	52	69	60	59
Heat pump system	27	23	34	41
Two-car or more garage	65	78	82	85

Sources: U.S. Department of Commerce and U.S. Department of Housing and Urban Development, 2017 Characteristics of New Housing, *https://www.census.gov/construction/chars/completed.html. Some data from 2007 and earlier from https://www.census.gov/construction/chars/historical_data.*

A four-story steel module building with 22 studio apartments, under construction in Berkeley, California. *(Panoramic Interests)*

samples. Model homes are used to showcase different floor plans and features. The buyer might be able to choose an open loft or an enclosed bedroom, a screened porch, or a fireplace. Depending on climate and subsurface conditions, a finished basement might be yet another option. Buyers can also select flooring, countertops, and cabinetry. A market study need not provide the details on every option offered by competitive properties in the market area. Rather, the analyst should get a sense of what choices are available and, if possible, how the average sales price (after options and upgrades) compares with the base price.

It is important to stress that national and regional trends in single-family home and lot sizes, unit characteristics, and amenities may not be reflected in local housing markets. Analysts must obtain information from marketing materials for comparable projects, local homebuilder publications, data vendors, or marketing consultants to determine whether a proposed development's mix of housing characteristics and lot sizes will be competitive. Understanding the features of base models and available options offered by nearby competitors will help in formulating recommendations.

New Multifamily Buildings: Styles, Sizes, and Features

Multifamily building styles include a two- to four-flat building on a single lot, rowhouses with six or eight units, suburban garden apartment complexes with multiple buildings, and urban mid-rises or high-rises. The owner of a duplex or a two- or three-flat building may occupy one of the units and rent out the other(s), thus providing an income stream to help pay the mortgage. Infill development of this type is common in older cities in the Northeast but is seen less frequently elsewhere.

Garden apartment buildings typically have two or three floors; their lack of elevators keeps construction costs down. They may have double-loaded interior corridors or (in milder climates) exterior walkways and staircases. High-rise apartment buildings and some mid-rise buildings have lobbies on the first floor, often with on-site management and package delivery rooms. They may have multilevel garages below or above ground. Laundry rooms and storage space can be found on each floor or only on the lower levels, but newer apartment buildings have in-unit laundries, either full size or stacked.

Figure 4-6 shows that most new apartment buildings designed for rent have fewer than 20 units. However, the share of larger buildings is growing as available sites in good locations become more difficult to find and expensive to develop, and as demand for new rental units has increased since the recession. Multifamily buildings designed for sale are typically duplexes, townhouses, or multistory condominiums. Throughout the United States, only 20 percent of new multiunit buildings built for sale had more than 10 units, and this share did not increase between 2007 and 2017.

of homes being built with a fireplace is declining. Not all luxury features remain popular over time.

Although the Census Bureau does not collect statistics on home office spaces, having a den or private office is an increasingly popular feature in new units. Formal living rooms have given way to open family rooms with a view of the kitchen. New technologies allow households to control heating systems and turn on lights or air conditioning remotely by using a phone app. Green features—energy- and water-conserving appliances; windows; heating, ventilation, and air-conditioning (HVAC) systems; and environmentally friendly building materials—are increasingly popular with homebuyers, especially if the extra costs of those features have relatively short payback periods. An analysis of price trends should consider the extent to which new properties have advanced technology and energy-efficient features not found in older homes.

New home features vary by region and location. In the Northeast, two-story homes dominate, but they are less common in Florida. In the Midwest, most new homes have basements, which is atypical in other parts of the country. Stucco covers 55 percent of home exteriors in the West; vinyl siding is most typical in the Northeast and Midwest, while brick is used most frequently in the South. Many homes use more than one exterior material (for example, brick and reinforced fiber-cement siding that looks like wood, or a combination of face brick and vinyl). Homebuilders in larger subdivisions often give buyers a choice of exterior materials as well as elevations; some choices will be upgrades.

In new single-family subdivisions, home models typically have a base price and a wide range of options available at additional cost. A choice of exterior designs, materials, and trim colors is usually offered; the sales office will have

New multifamily dwellings intended for sale (typically duplexes, townhouses, and condominium units) have increased in size, but the median size of new rental apartments has been fairly stable since 2000—as seen in figure 4-7. The median new multifamily rental unit completed in 2000 had 1,014 square feet; in 2017, the median size was 1,088 square feet. Townhouses and condominiums built for sale are usually larger than rental units with the same number of bedrooms.

Typical sizes for new suburban garden units for rent are 600 to 825 square feet for one-bedroom and one-bath apartments and 875 to 1,050 square feet for two-bedroom and two-bath units. A two-bedroom condominium with

two baths is more likely to have 1,200 square feet or more. As figures 4-7 and 4-8 show, the features of new units in multifamily buildings can be very different depending on whether the buildings are intended for rent or for sale. Units built for sale tend to have more bedrooms and baths.

Views can be a primary consideration in designing and pricing high-rise units, with upper-level units commanding higher prices. An outstanding view can add a substantial premium to the rents or sale prices of units. Desirable features on or adjacent to the property can also boost price points. In a golf course community, units with views of the course are priced higher than those without views. The same is true for waterfront buildings, especially in projects with boat docks or beaches.

Unique to multifamily development is that all major design decisions must be made upfront, usually at least 12 to 18 months before marketing and leasing begins, depending on the height of the building. The timeline for high-rise buildings is even longer. In contrast, single-family homebuilders have the opportunity to adjust their product according to which models are selling best and which upgrades are purchased most often.

Before the 2008 housing recession, upscale rental buildings were designed—and the units were amply sized—to be attractive candidates for eventual conversion to condominiums as an exit strategy for a project's original investors. With more institutional investors buying class A rental properties in response to their strong performance post-recession, designing rentals with large units because they might be suitable candidates for condominium conversion "someday" became less important to developers. Also, the growing number of jurisdictions that adopted tenant protections, thereby limiting the ability to convert

Figure 4-6
**New Multifamily Buildings Completed,
by Units per Building and Intended Tenure**
2007 and 2017

Number of units per building	% of buildings for rent		% of buildings for sale	
	2007	2017	2007	2017
2	19	9	33	42
3–4	16	8	30	25
5–9	23	17	17	14
10–19	18	20	12	12
20–49	21	34	5	5
50+	4	13	3	3

Source: U.S. Department of Commerce and U.S. Department of Housing and Urban Development, 2017 Characteristics of New Housing, *https://www.census.gov/construction/chars/pdf/c25ann2017.pdf.*

Figure 4-7
Median Size of New Multifamily Units Completed, by Planned Tenure
2000–2017

Source: U.S. Department of Commerce and U.S. Department of Housing and Urban Development, 2017 Characteristics of New Housing, *https://www.census.gov/construction/chars/pdf/c25ann2017.pdf.*

from rental to ownership, was also a consideration in project planning. As the economy improved, building a condominium product from scratch seemed to make more sense than converting rentals.

Housing Tenure

The share of U.S. households who owned a home peaked at 69 percent in 2004, up from 64 percent a decade earlier. By 2010, the rate had fallen below 67 percent, and it continued to drop through 2016 to a low of 63.4 percent. Only in 2017 did the share of households owning homes begin to tick higher, as millennials became more receptive to the idea of homeownership and more able to afford it.[4]

Strong demand in the early to mid-2000s was fueled by escalating home prices. Potential buyers expected that prices would continue to rise and were determined to buy before they were priced out. Lax credit review standards, low (or no) downpayment loans, and rapid growth of residential mortgage-backed securities (often lacking sound underwriting and investor scrutiny) contributed to the problem. Teaser adjustable-rate loans made ownership feasible for many more households, at least for a few years. But the market euphoria did not last.

Many factors propelled the downward trend at the end of that decade:

- The supply of new homes and condominiums, resale listings, or both exceeded demand in many areas, pushing home values down. New construction exceeded historic levels in fast-growing markets, especially vacation and resort locations in Florida, Arizona, and Nevada. Construction levels exceeded what was needed to accommodate household growth and replacement demand.

- After the economic downturn became evident in 2008, potential owners were skittish about buying for the first time, moving to a bigger home, or downsizing as their needs changed.

- Households adversely affected by the economic recession had trouble making their mortgage payments.[5] Interest rates rose on adjustable mortgages. Lenders resisted modifying mortgage terms. Owners were under water—they owed more on their mortgages than their homes were worth.

- The rising number of foreclosures was well publicized in the news media, further discouraging possible buyers.

- Lenders with an inventory of foreclosed homes struggled to maintain them and ultimately sold units to investors who shifted the formerly owned homes to rentals.

- Mortgage lending standards were tightened. Even those households who still were employed and hoped to find a "bargain" in the midst of the downturn found it difficult to qualify for a loan.

Figure 4-8
Selected Characteristics of New Multifamily Homes, by Intended Tenure
2007 and 2017

	Percentage	
	2007	2017
Design type		
Built for rent		
Townhouses	5	1
Conventional apartments	95	99
Built for sale		
Townhouses	5	1
Conventional apartments	95	99
Number of bedrooms		
Built for rent		
Efficiency	2	6
One bedroom	37	44
Two bedrooms	46	40
Three or more bedrooms	15	9
Built for sale		
Efficiency	2	3
One bedroom	16	19
Two bedrooms	52	42
Three or more bedrooms	30	36
Number of bathrooms		
Built for rent		
One bathroom	45	53
1.5 bathrooms	4	4
Two or more bathrooms	50	43
Built for sale		
One bathroom	18	22
1.5 bathrooms	6	3
Two or more bathrooms	76	74

Source: U.S. Department of Commerce and U.S. Department of Housing and Urban Development, 2017 Characteristics of New Housing, https://www.census.gov/construction/chars/completed.html.

Figure 4-9
Homeownership Rates by Age of Householder
1987–2017

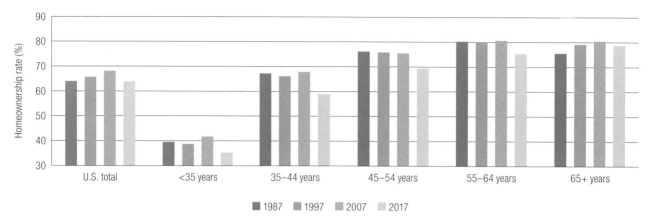

Source: U.S. Census Bureau, Current Population Survey: Housing Vacancy Survey, February 27, 2018, https://www.census.gov/housing/hvs/data/ann17ind.html.

Shrinking Size of Rental Apartments

In high-density urban locations, apartments are getting smaller, but amenities and common areas are using more space. Small units in amenity-laden buildings are becoming the norm in new rental construction. Parking ratios are also dropping; a minimum of one space per unit used to be standard (depending on the mix of units in the building, and hence the number of vehicles likely to need parking spots). Today, it is increasingly common to see only 0.5 spaces per unit if most of the apartments have fewer than two bedrooms; millennial tenants are unlikely to have more than one vehicle per household. Where good transit access to employment centers is available, some apartment buildings will have no on-site parking—if the developer can get local officials to agree.

RENT Café, a searchable database of apartment and home rental listings, analyzed trends in apartment unit sizes by number of bedrooms. It used data from Yardi Matrix, an affiliated company that provides property management software for multifamily buildings. The analysis covers only rental buildings with 50 or more units in 133 market areas.[6] Note that the results use average sizes, as opposed to the median-size trends reported in figure 4-7. The author confirms that although average rent in newly built units increased by 28 percent between 2008 and 2018, average unit sizes were 5 percent smaller. One of the study's most surprising findings is that Seattle (not New York City) now has the smallest rental units (new and existing) in the country, as shown in the graphic. The young workforce at Seattle-based companies (Amazon, Costco, Microsoft, Starbucks) is a key reason.

Source: Nadia Ballint, "As Apartments Are Shrinking, Seattle Tops New York with the Smallest Rentals in the U.S.," RENTCafe.com/blog, November 30, 2018.

Top 20 Cities with Smallest Apartments in the United States

	City	Average size (sq ft)
1	Seattle	711
2	Manhattan	733
	Chicago	733
4	Washington, DC	736
5	San Francisco	737
6	Tucson	738
7	Los Angeles	771
8	Glendale, AZ	781
9	Phoenix	783
10	Minneapolis	785
11	Wichita	787
12	Detroit	791
13	Cleveland	796
14	Mesa, AZ	801
	Philadelphia	801
16	Portland, OR	802
17	Albuquerque	804
18	Pittsburgh	811
	Toledo	811
20	El Paso	812

Source: RENT Café, using data from Yardi Matrix.

The decline in homeownership rates continued even after the economy began to recover, despite low mortgage interest rates. Many young households lacked the funds for a downpayment or were burdened with student loan debt, which rendered them unable to qualify for a home loan. As a result of lingering insecurity about job prospects, young households were reluctant to make a commitment to buy and felt that they needed to remain flexible to follow the best career opportunities. Although figure 4-9 shows that homeownership rates dropped between 2007 and 2017 in all age cohorts, the impact of the recession on households under age 44 was more dramatic than for households age 55 and older; those families had been homeowners for a long time and had substantial equity in their homes.

The decision to buy a home reflects many factors that are related to both finances and lifestyle:

- The supply and characteristics of available homes, both new and existing.

- Asking prices and price trends.

- Availability of mortgage funds and mortgage loan terms (required downpayment, mortgage duration, interest rate, differences between interest rates on fixed versus adjustable loans, whether the lender requires mortgage insurance).

- Whether the household has the required downpayment, funds to cover closing costs (fees for title search, appraisal, attorney), and sources of income sufficient to carry the mortgage.

- A household's willingness to take on responsibility for maintenance and repairs.

- Expectations regarding job security and mobility and whether more than one adult in a household must be employed in order to afford the costs associated with ownership.

- Expectations regarding the potential for price appreciation over time.

Typically, when stricter residential lending standards are in place, households that would like to buy are unable to do so and tend to remain longer in rental apartments. At the same time, homeowners who cannot keep up their payments will lose their homes or have to sell, adding to the demand for rentals. A large inventory of unsold new homes and foreclosed properties not only weakens the for-sale market but also creates a "shadow rental market" in which lenders try to rent out their foreclosed holdings. The supply overhang (builder inventory, investor-owned units, and foreclosed homes of all types) competes with units in rental apartment

Features Found in New Multifamily Communities

Community amenities	Techology amenities	Unit features
Basketball, tennis, or sand volleyball courts	In-unit alarm systems with closed-circuit television and internet monitoring	Private unit entries in low-rise buildings
Pool(s)	Community-wide wi-fi	Direct-entry garage parking in low-rise buildings
Playgrounds (in communities with children)	In-wall speaker systems with theater-quality sound	Nine-foot ceilings with crown moldings
Media rooms with large wall-mounted screens	Units prewired for multiple telephone lines, cable or satellite television, smartphone-based HVAC controls	Bay windows and skylights
Billiard tables		Better soundproofing
Business centers[a]		Two-level units in selected models
Roof gardens and decks	High-speed internet service	Hardwood or simulated wood floors (rather than wall-to-wall carpeting)
Dog runs or dog parks	Smartcard systems for entry to units and common spaces	Granite, quartz, or other high-end, durable countertops
Concierge services, such as plant watering, dog walking, dry cleaning pickup and delivery, and grocery pickup	Smartphone apps to control heat and air conditioning	High-end appliances that can be controlled with cellphone apps
Package delivery rooms or lockers	Web-based communication with management, including online rent payment and maintenance requests	In-unit, full-size laundry facilities
		Patios and balconies with secure storage areas
		Keyless entry systems
		Package delivery rooms or pickup lockers

a. Less popular than 10 to 15 years ago, but many communities still have a computer, printer, fax machine, or combination of these in their clubhouse for tenant use.

buildings. When the inventory of unsold new homes or the number of foreclosed units is unusually large, the shadow rental market must be considered as researchers conduct an apartment market analysis.

Softening demand for homeownership creates a tighter rental market with fewer vacancies in the short run. Eventually the supply of rental units catches up with demand. As rents increase, developers are attracted to building more apartments, and investors buy up excess inventory of single-family homes, make improvements, and rent out the homes.

The five main types of rental housing consumers are the following:

- Young adults moving away from their parents' home.
- Lifelong renters—households that never earn enough or save sufficient funds to buy a home.
- Lifestyle renters—including many affluent adults who do not want the responsibilities of homeownership or whose career paths require frequent moves.
- Households in transition, including recent immigrants and people moving because of job relocation, divorce, or a return to school.
- Seasonal renters of second homes.

Larger Unit Sizes and Higher Prices for New Homes Make Them Less Affordable for Young Buyers

Even with a stronger economy and low unemployment, a disconnect exists between the demographics of young households in the prime homebuying years and the types, sizes, and prices of new homes being produced. Household sizes have been declining, as is demonstrated later in this chapter, with more singles and couples and with fewer children per family. Yet home sizes increased (adding to construction costs) post-recession, with prices rising more quickly than did salaries and wages.

Research by Logan and Waldman at RCLCO indicates that this disconnect is contributing to the affordability crisis in new housing. The authors note that "compared to the years leading up to the Great Recession, the share of newly constructed homes larger than 3,000 square feet increased from 19% to 30%. The share of new homes priced below $300,000 has dropped from over 55% to just over 40% in just the past five years . . . the share of newly constructed homes smaller than 1,400 square feet decreased from a prerecession high of 13% to only about 7% today."[7]

The authors also point out that potential future demand for homeownership is tempered by the racial or ethnic diversity of young households; with the exception of non-Hispanic Asians, minority households have lower homeownership rates—a result of lower incomes and less access to credit. RCLCO suggests that there is more demand for smaller homes than available product.

Figure 4-10 demonstrates that homeownership rates can vary by many demographic and geographic characteristics. Not surprisingly, homeownership rates are highest in the Midwest and South, where homes are more affordable than they are in many Northeast or West markets. In many of the nation's largest cities, most units are rented. In the suburbs of metropolitan areas, nearly 71 percent of units are owned. The highest homeownership rates are seen in nonmetropolitan areas, where prices are low and rental options are limited.

The propensity to rent differs by race and ethnicity. On average, minority households have lower incomes, historically higher unemployment, and shorter workplace longevity, which have made it relatively difficult to qualify for a mortgage. Patterns of discrimination (redlining, subprime loans with onerous terms) have also held down homeownership rates for African American and Hispanic households.

As discussed earlier, new for-sale housing typically offers many options for customization, ranging from alternative facade styles and exterior materials to finished basements, upper-level lofts, upgraded flooring, bonus rooms, and high-tech wiring. Rental apartment buildings tend to offer fewer choices.

Single-Family Homes: A Growing Share of the Rental Market

Single-family homes were always a significant share of the rental housing inventory in outlying suburbs, small towns, and rural areas where large apartment complexes were uncommon. The housing market downturn that began in 2007 increased the number of individual homes for rent in big cities and mature suburbs, largely as a result of lender-owned inventory. Investors purchased much of this inventory, renovated the homes (to varying degrees), and made them available to renters—many of whom were former owners who had lost their homes. In 2017, the Joint Center for Housing Studies reported that single-family homes (both detached and attached) accounted for 39 percent of the nation's rental stock.[8]

Growth in demand for single-family rentals generated new companies that specialize in this product, including publicly traded REITs. Investors were initially skeptical, given the difficulty in locating, buying, renovating, and managing large numbers of units in scattered locations. Their opinions changed as the REITs generated strong returns.[9] Buy-to-rent firms are now building new single-family homes specifically for the rental market and are seeking investments in more metropolitan areas by acquiring existing homes. Millennials who prefer renting to owning (or cannot qualify for a mortgage) will be attracted to professionally managed detached homes, especially when their households include children. The key challenge for firms specializing in renting single-family homes is efficiently managing and maintaining scattered locations.

- Studio units are uncommon in the suburbs and are typically seen only in the densest urban neighborhoods, despite growth in the number of single-person households.

- Developers may offer one-bedroom units of different sizes or offer a one-bedroom-plus-den style. The majority of units in new urban high-rise projects are now studio and one-bedroom units—and many new buildings that cater to millennials have these smaller unit types only.

- "Micro-apartments" with hotel room–style features and sizes are a trend in dense cities with demand from millennial and generation Z employees (those age 23 and younger in 2019) who are just entering the workforce. Tiny apartments are an extension of the "small unit/large amenity base" trend. Studios often have only 325 square feet, and one-bedroom units can have under 550 square feet. Smaller sizes result in more affordable rents.

- Two-bedroom units with two baths command higher rents than do those with only one bath, especially if they are designed as split masters, with a bedroom and bath on each side of a common living area. This floor plan allows roommates to share a unit while maintaining privacy. For renters no longer enchanted with having a roommate, well-designed studio apartments are an increasingly attractive option.

- Three-bedroom rentals typically account for less than 15 percent of units in new rental apartment projects, although the proportion can be higher in affordable housing that caters to low- and moderate-income families.

- Historic properties and nonresidential buildings adapted for apartments can have many sizes and unit layouts. Accessing federal tax credits for historic renovations makes these projects economically feasible. Their vintage elements—brick walls, exposed beams or pipes, high ceilings, ornate window styles, etc.— can create rent premiums.

Another distinction between owner-occupied and rental units is how utility costs and property taxes are treated. In evaluating a homeowner's ability to buy a home, one must consider the monthly cost of utilities, real estate taxes, and insurance that are extra expenses. Many rental properties (especially newer, individually metered buildings) require tenants to pay directly for all utility costs in addition to their monthly rent. In older buildings, however, the situation is less predictable. Tenants might pay separately for electricity, cooking gas, telephone, internet, and cable television services, but water, sewer, and trash collection are included in the rent. Some multiunit rental buildings (especially older ones) include heat, water heating, and cooking gas; others do not.

Because of these distinctions, analytic methods for rental apartments are somewhat different from those used for product designed for sale. In fact, some market analysts specialize only in one or the other. Also, complex regulations

Figure 4-10

U.S. Homeownership Rates by Location and Race/Ethnicity 2017

By region	%
Northeast	60.5
Midwest	68.3
South	65.5
West	59.2
By location	
Inside MSAs	62.3
In principal MSA cities	49.2
Not in principal cities	70.9
Outside MSAs	73.0
By race	
White	68.5
African American	42.3
Asian or Pacific Islander	57.2
American Indian or Alaska Native	50.8
By Hispanic ethnicity	
Hispanic	46.2
Non-Hispanic	66.6
Non-Hispanic white	72.3

Source: U.S. Census Bureau, Current Population Survey: Housing Vacancy Survey and Homeownership, February 27, 2018, https://www.census.gov/housing/hvs/data/ann17ind.html.

Note: A principal city is the largest incorporated place with a population of at least 10,000 in a core-based statistical area (CBSA), or if no incorporated place of least 10,000 population is present, the largest incorporated place or census-designated place. Both metropolitan and micropolitan areas are included in the definition of CBSAs.

affecting affordable housing properties (built using tax credits or other government incentive programs) dictate that developers hire market analysts who are familiar with this segment of the rental market.

Demographic Trends Affecting U.S. Housing Markets

Housing market analysts must be familiar with the broad national demographic trends that affect demand so that they can understand how individual metropolitan areas and the local markets within them are similar to or different from the norm. Housing demand in the United States is influenced not only by growth in population and households but also by the ever-changing characteristics of consumers.

Population and Household Growth

Population growth and the resulting formation of new households are the most important determinants of demand for new housing. Census Bureau population projections for the United States released in September 2018 indicate that the nation's population will exceed 344 million in 2025 and grow to nearly 389 million by 2050.[10] As figure 4-11 shows, the rate of population growth has slowed considerably since 1995 and is projected to continue doing so.

Harvard University's Joint Center for Housing Studies prepares household growth projections and analyzes trends that affect housing demand. The Joint Center publishes insights into housing demand, supply, and affordability—and how they are changing—in its annual *State of the Nation's Housing* report.

Demographic Changes Affect Housing Demand

"The size and age structure of the adult population, together with the rates at which people form households, determine how much new housing is needed to meet increased demand. In 2016, the Joint Center projected robust growth of 13.6 million households over the next decade, assuming a pickup in household formations among the millennial generation, . . . longer periods of independent living among the baby boom generation . . . and moderate growth in foreign immigration. However, based on the Census Bureau's new lower population estimates and additional declines in household formation among young adults, the latest Joint Center projections put household growth in 2017–2027 significantly lower at 12.0 million. This total is more in line with the 1.1 million average annual increase over the last three years.

"Most of this new outlook reflects lower net foreign immigration and higher mortality rates among native-born whites. In combination, these changes mean slower growth in the number of older white households as well as of Hispanic and Asian households of most ages. Although lower than the 1.3 million per year previously projected, net immigration is still expected to average 1.0 million over the next decade as growth of the native-born population continues to slow. As a result, immigrants will increasingly drive household growth, especially after 2020 when native-born population growth decelerates further. As it is, the foreign-born share of household growth has already climbed from 15 percent in the 1980s . . . to nearly half so far this decade.

"Relatively low headship rates among millennials also contribute to lower projected household growth. Despite the recent pickup in incomes, adults under age 35 are still not forming households at rates as high as previous generations at that age. This suggests that other forces are at play, including higher rates of college and graduate school attendance and lower rates of marriage and childbearing. High housing costs may also be a factor, given the smaller share of young adults heading up households in expensive housing markets."

Source: Joint Center for Housing Studies, The State of the Nation's Housing 2018, *p. 2.*

Market analysts looking at local population and household growth data must consider the impact of the demographic trends identified by the Joint Center and others. Lower net foreign immigration and the possibility of deportations of undocumented U.S. residents are two areas where political decision-making could have an impact on future housing demand.

Aging

In 2008, seniors (people age 65 and older) accounted for 12.7 percent of the total U.S. population. By 2016, this share increased to 15.2 percent as the large baby boomer cohort began reaching retirement age. The Census Bureau projects that by 2030, seniors will make up more than 20 percent of all Americans, as shown in figure 4-12. Although the future housing choices of people who have yet to retire are not precisely known, a wide range of development types (described earlier) have already emerged to meet the lifestyle preferences and needs of active older adults. At the same time, increased longevity will require supportive-living facilities (including dementia care) and nursing homes to provide assistance for frail elderly persons. For those who want to age in place and are able to do so, the growing older population means greater demand for home renovation services. In surveys, seniors voice a preference for staying in their homes (perhaps making modifications to improve safety) rather than moving to smaller units.

Impact of Immigration and Racial or Ethnic Diversity

Foreign-born persons, their families, and descendants have accounted for an increasing share of household growth (and, therefore, housing demand) in the United States. In 2017, 13.7 percent of U.S. residents were foreign-born, according to the ACS. As recently as 1970, only 5 percent of U.S. residents were born in another country. Although relatively recent immigrants tend to rent by a wide margin, homeownership rates for foreign-born households increase dramatically with their length of residence in the United States.

The American population is increasingly diverse. Figure 4-13 shows that Hispanics are projected to account for 21 percent of the total U.S. population in 2030, up from an estimated 18 percent in 2016. The number of Hispanic residents will grow by 17.3 million. The Asian population is also projected to show significant gains (an increase of nearly 6.1 million).[11] Growth in the number of non-Hispanic whites will be very small; their share of total U.S. population will shrink from 61 percent in 2016 to 56 percent by 2030. The African American population will increase by 6 million (14 percent), but its overall percentage among American residents will increase only slightly. Note the 49 percent uptick in Americans who identify themselves as biracial or multiracial.

As discussed earlier, homeownership rates vary by race and ethnicity, which is a result of income differences and historical discrimination. Diversity is becoming more accepted in residential neighborhoods and rental apartment complexes, which reflects changing attitudes, better enforcement of fair housing laws, and improved training for real estate agents and property managers. Market studies should not assume any biases on the basis of race or ethnicity when calculating the number of age-and-income-qualified households that might be interested in renting or buying in a proposed development project.

Smaller Households

Household sizes (reported by the Census Bureau as the average number of persons per household) dropped steadily during the past 50 years as marriage was delayed, families had fewer children, and more persons chose to live alone. In 1970, American households had 3.14 persons on average, a significant drop from 3.33 persons just a decade earlier. By 2017, average household size had dropped to 2.54, but

Figure 4-11
Historical and Projected U.S. Population Growth
1970–2050

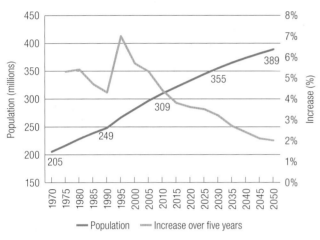

Source: U.S. Census Bureau, Population Division, Projected Population Size and Births, Deaths, and Migration: Main Projections Series for the United States, 2017–2060. Revised release date: September 2018. https://www.census.gov/data/tables/2017/demo/popproj/2017-summary-tables.html.

Figure 4-12
U.S. Population Projections by Age Group, 2016–2050

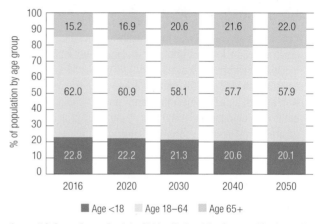

Source: U.S. Census Bureau, Population Division, "Projected Age Groups and Sex Composition of the Population: Main Projections Series for the United States, 2017–2060." Revised release date: September 2018. https://www.census.gov/data/tables/2017/demo/popproj/2017-summary-tables.html.

Figure 4-13
Projected Population Growth by Race and Hispanic Ethnicity
2016–2030

	2016 population estimate		2030 population projection		Change 2016–2030	
	(000s)	% of total	(000s)	% of total	(000s)	% growth
Total	323,128	100	355,101	100	31,973	10
One race	314,648	97	342,432	96	27,784	9
White	248,503	77	263,453	74	14,950	6
White non-Hispanic	197,970	61	197,992	56	22	0
Black/African American	43,001	13	49,009	14	6,008	14
Asian	18,319	6	24,394	7	6,075	33
Other[a]	4,826	1	5,576	2	750	16
Two or more races	8,480	3	12,669	4	4,189	49
Hispanic or Latino	57,470	18	74,807	21	17,337	30

Source: U.S. Census Bureau, Population Division, "Projected Race and Hispanic Origin: Main Projections Series for the United States, 2017–2060." https://www.census.gov/data/tables/2017/demo/popproj/2017-summary-tables.html.

a. Includes American Indian, Alaska Native, Native Hawaiian, and Other Pacific Islander.

the downward trend has stabilized over the past decade. As figure 4-14 also shows, the number of single-person households as a percentage of total housing demand has grown dramatically, from 13.1 percent in 1960 to 28.0 percent in 2017.

It would be incorrect to conclude that smaller households always prefer smaller homes. As noted earlier, despite declines in average household size, the size of new housing units continued to increase in recent decades.

In a given market area or neighborhood, the rate of household growth can outpace population growth. This means neighborhoods that attract small households—

Co-Living in San Jose

"The latest trendy new apartment building coming to downtown San Jose will offer plenty of luxury amenities, including cleaning services, laundry, and dog-walking. The catch? Each resident will share a kitchen and living room with at least a dozen other strangers. The 800-unit building, set to break ground early next year, is the latest project to embrace 'co-living'—a dorm-like setup where residents sleep in small private bedrooms and share common spaces, as a way to pack more people into a building and keep rents down. It's a lifestyle that's becoming increasingly popular as Bay Area residents, grappling with sky-high housing costs, are forced to find ever more creative ways to stay afloat and developers are encouraged to come up with innovative methods to house more people faster. . . . Entrepreneurs are finding a range of innovative solutions to the region's housing shortage—from turning shipping containers into tiny homes to building micro-houses in people's backyards."

Source: Marisa Kendall, "World's Largest Dorm-Style 'Co-Living' Apartment Building Coming to San Jose," San Jose Mercury-News, November 5, 2018.

young singles, couples and roommates without children, empty nesters, and seniors—can demonstrate demand for additional housing units even in the absence of absolute growth in population.

Fewer Child-Oriented Households

As seen in figure 4-15, families (two or more related persons living together) accounted for more than eight of every 10 American households in 1970. Married couples (with or without children) accounted for most of these families (70.5 percent). In 2018, the Census Bureau reported that fewer than two-thirds of households are families, and less than half of all households are married couples. Other family types and nonfamily households—singles and unrelated persons living together (otherwise known as roommates)—influence housing demand more than ever before.

Among families, fewer than three of every 10 have children under age 18. This finding means that school quality is not as important for most households when they are deciding where to buy or rent. To a large extent, suburbanization was propelled by child-oriented families looking for good schools and spacious homes with private yards. Today, new housing construction occurs in downtowns and other city neighborhoods despite negative opinions about urban schools. As mentioned earlier, this trend could change as the large millennial generation, which has delayed childbearing until well into their 30s, decides that having children is important to them.

The Census Bureau reported that in 2017, 26 percent of adults ages 25 to 34 lived with parents or other family members, and another 9 percent lived with roommates. For some, this arrangement is a lifestyle choice. For those who live in high-rent areas and have limited earning power or student loans to repay, such a choice can be an economic necessity. The most important reason for the seemingly high

Figure 4-14
Trends in Household Size
1960–2017

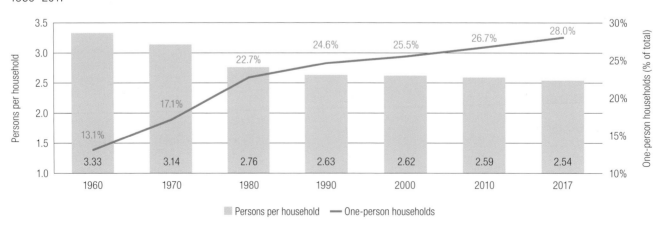

Persons per household — One-person households

Source: U.S. Census Bureau, Current Population Survey, March and Annual Social and Economic Supplements. Historical Households Tables: 1960 to Present, Table HH4. Released November 2018. https://www.census.gov/data/tables/time-series/demo/families/households.html.

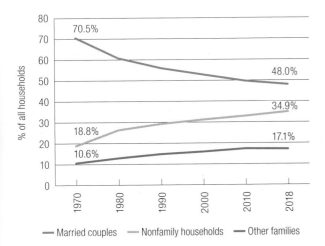

Figure 4-15
U.S. Households by Type
1970–2018

Source: U.S. Census Bureau, Current Population Survey, March and Annual Social and Economic Supplements: 1960–Present, Table HH-1. Released November 2018. https://www.census.gov/data/tables/time-series/demo/families/households.html.

Note: Before 2007, Census Bureau definitions of family groups were restricted to married couples and single-parent families. In 2007, unmarried two-parent family groups with opposite-sex partners were added to the data.

share of young adults who are not living independently is that fewer young adults are getting married; if they do, they are much older than was the case decades ago.

Older married couples are living long after their millennial children have grown. Those who live in the suburbs often decide to remain there—at least for a while—because their friends are nearby. In contrast, young adults—couples and singles—are choosing lifestyles on the basis of location criteria different from those their parents chose. For such households, quality schools, lots of bedrooms, and spacious yards are often less important than is convenient access to work, restaurants, and entertainment, as well as maintenance services provided by a condominium board, landlord, or community association.

The Census Bureau also finds a declining share of child-oriented families living with two parents: 87 percent in 1970 but only 70 percent in 2018. Single-parent families with children often have more financial constraints on their ability to pay for housing than do two-parent families.

Migration and Mobility

Between 2017 and 2018, just over 10 percent of persons age one year and older moved to a different residence, but most did not go very far. More than six in 10 persons who moved stayed in the same county. Only 15 percent moved across state lines. As a group, renters are much more mobile than owners. Between 2007–2008 and 2017–2018, the share of renters who moved averaged 25.1 percent each year, while the share of homeowners who moved in any given year

averaged only 5.1 percent during the same period. Mobility rates have been declining for both owners and renters, a trend that began during the post-2007 housing recession.[12]

Household inflow and outflow from county to county within states and between regions of the country can help forecast larger trends and enhance the accuracy of housing demand numbers. As the nation's moving companies will attest, household movement can be an indicator of the strength or weakness of state and county residential markets.

States in the Northeast and the Midwest are experiencing net domestic outmigration, but some states and metropolitan areas in those regions have been able to stem population losses by attracting immigrants from other countries. It is important to note, however, that the settlement patterns of newcomers to the United States have changed. Previous waves of immigrants settled in the nation's largest central cities, but today's newcomers frequently move directly to the suburbs. Others are going to smaller metropolitan areas and rural counties, essentially replacing native-born Americans who have left in search of better jobs or a more appealing climate.

Many large cities have gained population in recent years, spurred by renewed interest in urban living, an influx of millennials, and immigration. Population increases were registered between 2010 and 2017 in all of the nation's 20 largest cities. A few cities (Philadelphia, Memphis, Tulsa) that lost residents between 2000 and 2007 experienced

More Nontraditional Households

In 2008, the Harvard Joint Center for Housing Studies commented on the changing profile of American households—changes that continued over the ensuing decade:

"Married couples are a shrinking share of American households. Several trends have contributed to this shift, including higher labor force participation rates for women, delayed marriage, high divorce rates, low remarriage rates, and greater acceptance of unmarried partners living together. The resulting growth in unmarried-partner, single-parent, and single-person households has increased the share of adults in all age groups heading independent households.

"Two trends in particular have lifted the number of nontraditional households. First, fewer marriages survive. And second, remarriage rates have reached historic lows. In addition, more people defer their first marriage. The never-married share has also climbed sharply. Another noteworthy change is that a larger share of each succeeding generation is choosing to live with a partner without marrying. This is true for households with and without children. In 2007, fully 29 percent of heads of households with children were unmarried. Within this group, about 18 percent lived with partners, and another 21 percent lived with nonpartner adults."

Source: Joint Center for Housing Studies of Harvard University, The State of the Nation's Housing: 2008, p. 12.

Using Data from Tax Returns to Understand Migration Patterns

Another source of U.S. migration information is Internal Revenue Service (IRS) tracking of household tax filings. IRS migration data for the United States are based on year-to-year address changes reported on individual income tax returns. Information by state or by county is available for inflows—how many new residents moved to a different state or county and where they moved from—and outflows—how many residents left each jurisdiction and where they went. As of early 2019, data were available for tax filing years 1991 through 2016 and included the following:

- Number of returns filed, which approximates the number of households that migrated.

- Number of personal exemptions claimed, which approximates the number of individuals.

- Total adjusted gross income (AGI), starting with filing year 1995.

- Aggregate migration flows at the state level, by the size of AGI and the age of the primary taxpayer, starting with filing year 2011.[13]

IRS data are useful for tracking multiyear movement trends. However, because of time lags in collecting and processing returns and in creating the mobility data files, the data are less helpful when analyzing recent changes in origins or destinations.

Out of Reach

The National Low Income Housing Coalition (NLIHC) publishes annual research on the gap between wages and rents across the United States. Using its concept of a housing wage, the NLIHC calculates the hourly wage that a full-time worker must earn to afford a modest home or apartment and what he or she can expect to pay for a one- or two-bedroom rental unit. The NLIHC uses HUD's Fair Market Rents (FMRs) for individual metropolitan areas or counties in its estimates. FMRs are not the median or average rents; rather, they are calculated at the 40th percentile of gross rents (including utilities) in each area.[15]

Nationally, the housing wage is calculated to be $22.10 per hour for a two-bedroom home and $17.90 for a one-bedroom home. A full-time worker earning the federal minimum wage would need to work 122 hours per week (the equivalent of three full-time jobs), 52 weeks a year, to afford the two-bedroom FMR. In no state, county, or metropolitan area could a minimum wage earner afford the local FMR by working only the standard 40-hour week.[16] In 2018, eight of the 10 metropolitan counties with the highest housing wage were in California, six of those in the Greater San Francisco region.

Source: National Low Income Housing Coalition, Out of Reach: The High Cost of Housing, *2018, https://reports.nlihc.org/oor.*

modest growth a decade later, but others (Baltimore, Cleveland, and Detroit) continued to decline.[14] Aggressive job recruitment efforts and economic development programs have stemmed the tide in some locations, so these trends must be carefully monitored.

Affordability Gap

In many parts of the United States, typical rents or home prices are unaffordable for households earning the area's median income. Despite a still-improving economy in 2018, years after the recession, millions of tenants were unable to find shelter costing less than the recommended standard measure of rental affordability (paying less than 30 percent of household income for rent and utilities). Millions of homeowners can afford their mortgage payments or rents only if two members of the household are full-time workers; when there is another economic downturn, they will struggle to keep their homes and pay their other bills if one worker loses his or her job.

Data from the 2017 ACS show that 27.5 percent of homeowners with a mortgage and 49.5 percent of renter households were spending more than 30 percent of income on shelter. For renters, the proportions have increased since 2007 despite completion of nearly 2.5 million multifamily units between 2008 and 2017. Most new units target young professionals, some of whom cope with rising rents by sharing their apartments. Sharing is usually impractical for families or seniors on fixed incomes.

Changing Attitudes toward Long Commutes

Post-1950s suburbanization created a mismatch between place of work and place of residence, resulting in longer commuting distances and more time spent going to and from work. To some extent, recent population increases in core cities and mature suburbs (where new housing construction is occurring in downtowns and close to suburban transit stations) reflect employees' resistance to spending more time and money commuting to their jobs.

More employees are working from home—at least part time—and are taking mass transit (where available), walking, bicycling, or moving closer to work. Headquarters offices formerly located in outlying suburbs are shifting a portion of their workforces, especially executives and tech staff members, to more convenient locations. Transit-oriented residential projects located near commuter-rail, city subway, and light-rail stops are benefiting from this trend, which can be especially helpful in reducing auto usage for members of two-worker households who travel in different directions.

Resistance to long commutes has also led to growth in demand for flexible office space in convenient locations, as is discussed further in chapter 6. It is important to remember, however, that most metropolitan areas lack rail lines of any type and have infrequent bus service; transit is even more limited in small towns and rural areas. Not surprisingly, three of every four employed Americans drove to work alone in 2017; less than 5 percent used public transportation.[17] Moreover, many households choose to live in the distant suburbs, consciously opting for a longer commute time in exchange for lower housing prices or more space. Market analysts should not assume that greenfield suburban sites—even those near the edges of metropolitan areas—will be at a disadvantage in competing for demand from future homeowners. In some metro areas, exurban locations are performing better than are closer-in suburban communities as vehicles achieve better fuel economy, provide more safety technology, and offer greater driving comfort. With autonomous vehicles on the horizon, consumer location preferences will be affected if the new technology proves to be safe and economical.

Preparing a Housing Market Study

As with other real estate product types, a residential market study generally begins with an examination of the regional setting, including population and household trends, recent or anticipated changes in the economic base, and employment patterns. The focus then narrows to the county or municipality for more specific information. Analysts should provide data on population characteristics, household growth, household types, and incomes.

If a particular site has been proposed for development, the market study evaluates the suitability of the site with respect to accessibility, surrounding land uses, school quality, proximity to shopping and health care, and recreational opportunities. Other topics that might be addressed include zoning and other land use controls, environmental issues, special site features, and compatibility with adjacent or nearby uses. The report should contain an analysis of competitive properties (existing and planned). It concludes with recommendations for action and an assessment of how well the property is likely to perform.

The introduction to the market report should clearly define its objectives and the scope of services it covers. The report may provide only a regional overview (for purposes of monitoring area conditions), or it may include an analysis of specified submarket areas and a detailed review of competitive projects within the submarket. If a specific development proposal is being examined, the report will usually give an opinion about marketability, demand, pricing, and absorption. It may also suggest changes to the plan that, in the opinion of the analyst, would improve the project's chances of success.

It is important to stress again that national and regional trends in home and lot sizes, unit features, and building or community amenities may not be reflected in local housing markets. Analysts may need to obtain information from local homebuilder organizations, data vendors, or consultants to determine whether a proposed development's mix of housing characteristics and lot sizes will be marketable. Relying on the characteristics of nearby competitors will help in formulating recommendations.

Identifying the Market Area

A project's primary market area is usually defined as the area from which 60 percent to 80 percent of the buyers or renters in a new development are drawn. But many exceptions to this standard exist. For example,

- A project in a rapidly growing metropolitan area that attracts corporate transfers or retirees might draw most of its residents from outside the local area.

- An infill project that offers attractive new units with modern features and off-street parking might attract nearly all of its residents from the immediate neighborhood or a small number of zip codes.

- A second-home community is likely to draw most of its residents from outside the local area.

Model Content Standards for Rental Housing Market Studies

The National Council of Housing Market Analysts (NCHMA) is a professional organization whose membership includes consultants, appraisers, government housing agency staff members, lenders, and others involved in underwriting rental residential properties. NCHMA publishes a directory of member housing market analysts who meet its standards for professional designation.[18] It also created Model Content Standards for Rental Housing Market Studies, a resource last revised in 2013. NCHMA originally developed the standards to encourage thorough analysis of proposals submitted for low-income housing tax credits but has since adapted them for market-rate housing proposals. The standards include a detailed content outline for market study reports. The NCHMA standards encourage critical thinking; they require the analyst to look at both positive and negative factors affecting marketability. They also ask the analyst to consider the impact of the proposed project on the existing rental market. Details are available on the NCHMA website, www.housingonline.com.

Senior citizens will move away from their former community to live close to adult children and grandchildren. Unfortunately, no reliable data sources match the place of residence for young families with that of their parents and grandparents.

ULI's *Real Estate Development: Principles and Process* defines the residential market area as follows:

For the marketability study, the market area where the subject project is located receives the most attention, but competitive supply almost always exists in other locations. As a result, residential market areas are often noncontiguous areas in the same labor market or metropolitan area. Residential developments in different sections of the metropolitan area often compete to attract the same in-migrants or local homebuyers and renters who are moving up.[19]

The market area for a primary-home residential project usually centers on a major employment node, a transportation corridor, or a desirable neighborhood or natural amenity. Physical barriers, either natural or built, or political considerations—such as a county line or school district boundary—usually determine the borders. Working households often focus their housing search on the basis of commuting times and distances as well as neighborhood affordability. Community image or perceived status can also be important in determining where consumers will look for alternative housing choices.

Consider a new downtown high-rise condominium project in a big city. The primary competition would include newer condominium properties within a few blocks of the proposed site; similar-quality buildings in large mature suburbs with comparable amenities and good transportation access would be secondary competitors. Potential buyers would come from other downtown buildings (both condominium and rental) but may also include suburban empty nesters who are considering a move downtown, as well as young professionals moving from another metro area to take a new job. These buyer segments should be identified in the market study, but it may be difficult to quantify them with available data. Once the developer expects to go ahead with the project, focus groups can be helpful in determining customer interest from different market segments.

In a sparsely populated, semirural community with few competitive projects, the market area for a new single-family subdivision could comprise the entire county or even several adjacent counties. The market area for a large master-planned community on the outskirts of a rapidly expanding metropolitan area might encompass the entire metropolitan area and even areas out of state.

Further, a distinctive project with little or no competition will draw from a larger market area than will a conventional property with a large pool of similar competitive projects. Relatively standard projects of moderate size usually have a primary market area with no more than a four- or five-mile radius, but their secondary market area would be much larger.

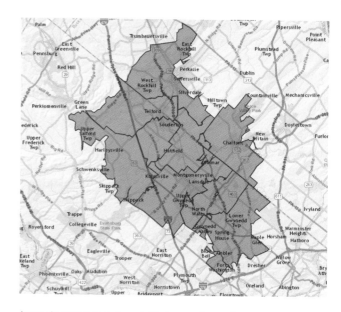

A map of a primary market area in Montgomery County, Pennsylvania, defined with municipal boundaries. *(Real Estate Strategies Inc./RES Advisors)*

In many cases, the market areas for supply and demand are identical, although competitive projects can exist outside the target market area. In some instances, the two market areas are very far apart, as is usually the case for second-home developments. Most market areas for year-round shelter, however, are within a reasonable commute of major employment centers or other key destinations. Some factors to consider in delineating the market area include the following:

- *Travel time from major employment centers.* By identifying major employment centers, analyzing transportation modes, and determining acceptable commuting time, market analysts can define a target market area.

- *Socioeconomic status and community character.* An area's income, age, household types, and other demographic characteristics influence housing choice and location. Although discrimination based on race, ethnicity, or religion is illegal in the United States, consumers often chose to locate near others of similar background.[20] In some locations, housing developments that exclude children are politically attractive because they generate positive fiscal benefits for the local school district. Age-restricted housing brings in property tax dollars without generating the need for more classrooms or school staff members.

- *Political subdivisions.* Municipal boundaries can be especially important when adjoining jurisdictions differ markedly in political climate, tax policies, or status or when different attitudes about growth exist. School district boundaries can be critical if households with school-age children represent a major market segment.

- *Data availability.* For practical reasons, market analysts will often define their local market areas according to Census Bureau geography and will use combinations of counties, municipalities, census tracts, zip codes, or block groups. This practice is not always ideal; standard geographic combinations might not truly match the boundaries of the probable market area. Mapping programs provided by private data vendors allow the analyst to create demographic reports for custom-defined geographies—polygons, corridors along a highway, etc.

Analyzing Market Area Demand

Demographic trends and projections underlie the analysis of housing demand. Several demographic factors are of primary importance in analyzing the market potential for a project:

- *Employment* opportunities usually drive population growth. If an area has an expanding employment base, new workers will be moving to the market area, and existing households will stay in the area to take advantage of opportunities for advancement.

- *Households* are the unit of measure most relevant for assessing the housing market, because it is households that buy or rent a unit of housing. The perceived strength or weakness of national and local economic conditions influences whether a recently employed high school or college graduate will rent an apartment or stay in her parent's house. A sense of financial security, among other things, will influence whether a senior citizen will continue to live independently or move in with family members. Economics also determine, in part, whether couples will marry or live together.

- *Household income* is key to determining the pricing structure for a proposed development. As discussed earlier, the federal government's standard for determining housing affordability suggests that households should pay no more than 30 percent of income for mortgage amortization, utilities, and property taxes; the same standard applies to monthly rent plus utility payments. This standard is less valid for a senior housing development, where homes are being sold to buyers with substantial equity in an existing home or with other assets that can be used to pay for shelter costs. If meals and other services are included in the monthly cost of senior housing, residents may be able to spend 45 to 50 percent of income on rent. Some younger households will consciously choose to pay more for shelter if they can live close to family, friends, school, or work (especially if they can avoid the cost of owning, maintaining, and parking a car).

- *Other demographic statistics* may be relevant for evaluating the project's potential, such as household size, ages of householders, and family composition. Educational attainment can also influence housing preferences.

Employment

Because employment throughout a region determines population growth, employment statistics for the metropolitan area should be gathered. Chapter 3 provides details on how to use metropolitan, county, and local employment data in preparing market studies.

In large metropolitan areas, workers commonly will commute fairly long distances. Only a small proportion of people work in the same suburb or zip code in which they reside, which suggests that housing market areas could be large. It is important to know where jobs are locating within the metropolitan area and to use this information in forecasting housing demand. When labor markets are tight, however, new housing that attracts well-educated workers or skilled blue-collar tradespeople can encourage employers to move a portion of their workforce to new locations.

Demographers use projections of employment growth as one of the bases for determining future population growth. Some analysts—especially those studying multifamily housing—prefer to base demand scenarios on employment rather than on household projections, because in most metropolitan areas, demand for new housing is closely tied to new workers who move into an area. These workers often rent before they decide to buy. Thus, being able to forecast both the total housing demand and the share of demand likely to be captured by rental apartments is critical to understanding aggregate housing demand at the metropolitan level.

Population and Households

Population and household data are critical in forecasting the demand for new housing in the market area. Trend analysis should begin with the population count dating from, at a minimum, the preceding decennial census. As time passes from the decennial census year, it is increasingly important for the analyst to find accurate current estimates. A good market analysis undertaken in 2019 will not rely solely on 2010 census numbers. The smaller the local market area, the more it is likely to have changed since the most recent census. Although the Census Bureau publishes population estimates for incorporated places and minor civil divisions every two years, these geographic definitions often do not correspond to a market area that is defined according to zip codes, streets and highways, natural features, or other identifiers. Because projections must be updated regularly, market analysts are increasingly turning to private data vendors for current estimates and five-year projections of population and households by age, especially if their market areas contain multiple jurisdictions or are based on combinations of census tracts, zip codes, or other complex geographies. These estimates and five-year projections are updated annually.

The market analyst also needs to get a sense of the types of households currently living in the local market area. To some extent, this information can be gleaned from looking at

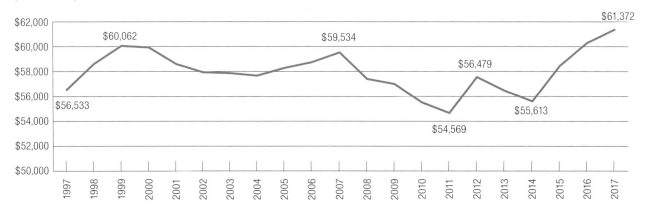

Figure 4-16

U.S. Real Median Household Income, 1997–2017

(2017 dollars)

Source: U.S. Census Bureau, Current Population Survey, Annual Social and Economic Supplements,
https://www.census.gov/data/tables/time-series/demo/income-poverty/historical-income-households.html.

estimates of the age distribution, median age, and education levels for adults (age 25 and older), as well as household sizes. As part of their standard demographic reports, most vendors sell estimates of the number of households by type, but these numbers may simply represent trend line extrapolations from decennial census findings. They may not take into account the changing composition of households living in particular neighborhoods.

Each household type has specific housing needs, which provide opportunities in a variety of market niches. Studying local trends in household size and type can help shape a concept and influence the design of a new development and its housing units. Researchers must also remember that the same product can appeal to more than one type of household. Witness the number of successful downtown rental or condominium properties in large cities that are occupied by a mix of young singles, childless young couples, households with preschoolers (but few school-age children), empty nesters, and retirees.

Income and Assets

As introduced in chapter 3, analysis of household incomes in the metropolitan area, the county, and the target market area provides a sense of the region's economic vitality as well as valuable insight into the scope and magnitude of available purchasing power. The market analyst has to look at the distribution of households by income bracket as well as the median and average household incomes for the target market area. If a secondary market area is defined, the market study must show the same information for this geographic area and provide comparisons with the county or metropolitan area data.

Figure 4-16 shows how median household incomes in the United States have changed since 1997. The graph shows the prolonged effects of the 2008 economic downturn

after adjusting for inflation. The loss of jobs, earnings, and purchasing power lasted more than five years; not until 2016 did households see real gains in income when compared with 2007.

It is important to note that not every part of the United States suffers equally during a recession. And even when the economy is strong, regional differences in income persist. Figure 4-17 compares 2017 median household incomes by region. Incomes in the South and Midwest are lower than those in the Northeast and West regions.

Mortgage lenders have their own standards for determining whether they think a borrower's income will be sufficient to make his or her monthly payments. At mid-2018, borrowers seeking a conventional mortgage loan with a 15- or 30-year term needed a credit score of at least 620. The ratio of debt to income (including housing-related debt) could not exceed 43 percent. If the homebuyer could not put down 20 percent of the purchase price, he or she would need private mortgage insurance (costing 0.15 to 1.95 percent of the outstanding loan balance). Over the past 10 years, underwriting has been conservative to avoid the excesses seen before the last housing downturn—when mortgage applications were approved without employment or income verification. However, if banks have funds to lend, they will loosen some standards to generate business.

The market analyst should look at the proposed purchase price range for a for-sale development, consider the cost of typical upgrades, and then calculate income that will be needed to afford the homes or condominiums. Ongoing costs should also be considered, including taxes, utilities, maintenance, and homeowners association fees if applicable. The analyst can then determine the minimum income range needed to afford the home. Lending institutions and housing organizations have online mortgage calculators that can help determine the minimum income needed to buy homes available for sale in a particular development or neighborhood.

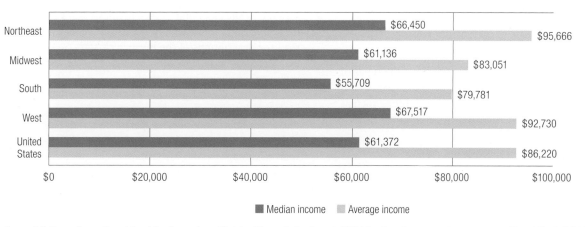

Figure 4-17
Median and Average Household Income by Region
2017

Source: U.S. Census Bureau, Current Population Survey, Annual Social and Economic Supplement, 2017, https://www2.census.gov/programs-surveys/demo/tables/p60/263/tableA1.xls.

Income information is invaluable in determining the price ranges that a significant portion of the population can afford. But as chapter 3 suggested, income alone cannot be used as a precise indicator of the ability to pay for housing. Wealth (assets minus liabilities) is a more precise measure when looking at move-up for-sale communities (those that are targeted to existing homeowners, not first-time buyers) or market-rate housing for seniors. Looking only at current income will underestimate the ability of consumers to afford the planned project.

Understanding household assets is especially important when analyzing the marketability of housing for seniors. The annual income of senior citizens will usually fall well below the overall average, but many retirees have substantial savings and investment assets, as well as little debt. Counting a portion of assets (especially the potential investment earnings from equity realized upon sale of long-owned homes) is important in determining whether seniors in the market area can afford the monthly payments. However, low- and moderate-income seniors often must draw on their assets to purchase goods and services, whether for luxuries (such as travel) or necessities (prescription drugs and food).

Because the decennial census and the ACS do not measure wealth, some private data vendors provide their own estimates; but methodologies vary and accuracy can be questionable, even for larger areas. The Federal Reserve Board publishes its triennial national Survey of Consumer Finances, which provides indicators of wealth by selected demographic characteristics.[21] However, the survey's sample is too small to provide any metropolitan or local data. Information on equity in (and sales prices for) existing homes within the local market area can serve as a partial proxy for wealth.

Replacement Demand

An area with relatively few new units may have replacement demand that would not be evident from household growth statistics alone. In markets where most housing units are more than 50 years old, a long-established rule of thumb is that 1 percent of existing units should be replaced in any given year. The percentage could be lower if older stock has been renovated or has appealing features that could make rehabilitation worthwhile. Conversely, replacement could be higher if units constructed decades ago do not have amenities sought by today's consumers and have not been maintained or updated. Replacement demand can be considerable if the market area has lost units as a result of fire, flooding, or other disasters. A market study should include a factor for replacement demand.

Estimating Demand for Housing Replacement

Information from the Census Bureau's American Housing Survey suggests another way to look at housing replacement needs. For example, the 2017 survey in the Birmingham-Hoover (Alabama) MSA found that 3.1 percent of occupied units in the MSA's central cities were deemed severely inadequate. In the MSA as a whole, only 1.2 percent were categorized this way. The AHS reports deficiencies in plumbing, heating and electrical systems, wiring, and upkeep and maintenance on the basis of reported problems and frequency of breakdowns. In the United States overall, the 2017 survey found 1.5 percent of occupied units to be severely inadequate and 4.2 percent moderately inadequate. Note that not every metro area is covered by the AHS; for those that are, MSA data are collected only once every six years.

Households are changing and so must their communities. As discussed earlier, singles, childless couples, and so-called nontraditional households now form a larger share of households than do married couples with children. More people work out of their homes, at least part of the time, so unit designs must reflect the need for quiet office space. These are just two of the trends that will affect the types of homes and neighborhoods people will choose in the coming decades. At the same time, child-focused amenities such as playgrounds and ball fields may decline in importance in some locations.

Both the product and the consumer must be understood in terms of choices people make, evolving lifestyles, personal tastes, and many other considerations that cannot be easily quantified. In today's competitive environment, understanding the local market and targeting specific household segments can help to set a development apart from its competition. However, the analyst must be careful not to overgeneralize about the target customers' needs. Not all young families want a suburban backyard, and not all wealthy retirees want to play golf. Within age or income cohorts, markets can be quite diverse; if one is to reach potential consumers, their preferences must be understood.

As discussed in chapter 3, many private companies that sell current demographic estimates and projections have developed psychographic or socioeconomic profiling systems that tell the market analyst about lifestyles of market area residents. These systems divide national and local households

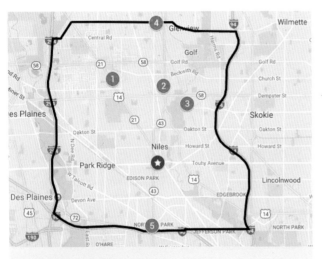

1   Huntington Apartments
2   Morton Grove Senior Residences
3   The Homestead at Morton Grove
4   Patten House of Glenview
5   Senior Suites of Norwood Park

A market area and competition map for a suburban Chicago senior housing study. The market-area boundaries are defined using interstate highways and major arterials. *(Valerie S. Kretchmer Associates Inc.)*

into groups on the basis of many factors, which typically include age, income, ethnicity, marital status, education, urban or suburban residence, presence of children, and propensity to own or rent. Once the analyst defines a market area, he or she can obtain household estimates for each lifestyle group represented in the area. The analyst must read the descriptions of the lifestyle clusters present in the area and determine which of these groups are likely to be interested in the proposed product.

Traditional techniques for learning about housing preferences include focus groups, interviews, and surveys of current home shoppers or apartment rental office visitors. (For more information on types of consumer research and their advantages and drawbacks, see chapter 3.) Ideally, direct consumer research and psychographic analysis can be combined to provide a nuanced portrait of potential buyers or renters. Surveys and focus groups can yield a wealth of information about the potential residents of a new project if the right questions are posed and the data are interpreted correctly. Consumer research should be designed by experienced firms.

Examining Competitive Supply

The current and likely future housing stock in the competitive market area forms the supply side of the market analysis equation. The analyst must first examine the number of units and the general characteristics of the existing housing stock (tenure, age, density, current prices or rents, and vacancies) in the market area and then supplement the data with trend information (new construction activity, rent or price growth or decline, changing vacancy rates, and status of planned projects) in the larger area and the local competitive market. Then the analyst decides which projects are the most competitive (sometimes referred to as the "competitive set") by virtue of age, location, or quality. Absorption information should be collected from newer properties if it is available. As indicated in chapter 3, sales or leasing agents may lack familiarity with the historical experience of a large project that has been marketing units for a long period of time.

Studying Existing Competition

In most housing market studies, the analysis of existing competitive projects is the most detailed part of the report. The competitive project inventory—presented in table form or in separate information sheets for each project—provides a wealth of information about project characteristics (project size, unit mix, unit sizes, project and unit amenities, prices or rents, available inventory and vacancy rates, and sales and absorption history). In the report text, the narrative should highlight each project's advantages and drawbacks relative to the proposed development, and a map should identify their locations.

Figure 4-18 is an example of information presented in a market study for a proposed rental development in an urban location. Because the purpose of the report was to study

Figure 4-18

Example: Apartments for Rent in the Primary Market Area

Spring 2017

Property type	Age	Bedrooms/ baths	Size (sq ft)	Rent	Comments
Rental buildings					
High-rise 1	Opened 3/2017	Studio/1 1/1 Large 1/1 2/2 3/2	400–573 654–728 827 1,048–1,083 1,241	$2,065–2,270 $2,365–2,680 $2,580 $3,500–3,670 $4,595–4,775 $550 annual amenity fee, $150–250 pet fee + $25–50/mo. Parking: $275/mo.	53-story building with 538 units to the east of a commuter-rail station. Seven floors of parking. Rooftop lounge with stadium seating, 86" TV screening room, 24-hr concierge, business center, pool, catering kitchen with cooking classes, fitness center with virtual classes, yoga studio, children's playroom. Amenities are on the ninth floor. Units have hardwood floors and stainless-steel GE appliances including a microwave and an in-unit washer/dryer. 153 parking spaces. Offering one free month w/13-month lease on some models. About 33% are studios; 50% are one bedroom. 65% leased; 45% occupied.
High-rise 2	Opened 5/2017	Studio (89) 1/1 (114) 2/2 (32) 3/2 (5)	496 689–794 1,052–1,207 1,260	$2,015–2,080 $1,995–2,535 $3,110–3,390 $4,300–4,350 $250 amenity fee, $500 + $50/mo pet fee.	13 stories with 240 units, distributed as shown in parentheses. Lounge, roof deck, fire pit, fitness center with virtual classes, yoga studio, BBQ, concierge, club/party room, dog run. Units have granite and quartz countertops, stainless-steel kitchens, and full-size washer/dryers. Some units have city skyline views. Tenant pays all utilities excluding trash. >80% leased, 67% occupied.
Mid-rise 1	Opened 11/2015	Studio/1 1/1 2/2	506–609 658–838 965	$1,656+ $2,026+ $2,580 Garage: $175/mo. Pet fee: $50/mo or $500 per yr. No amenity fee.	Five-story building with 265 units. Rents shown are net after one month of free rent on a 13-month lease. 24-hr concierge, shuttle to train every 15 minutes during peak hours, game room, lounge, fitness room, dog run, outdoor courtyard, adjacent to park and across from arts center. Some retail spaces still vacant. Units have hardwood floors, white appliances, washer/dryers, granite countertops, and terraces. 92% occupied.
Mid-rise 2	Opened 8/2014	Studio (9) 1/1 (39) 2/1 (8)	422–501 661–713 941	$1,800 $1,900 $2,375–2,500 No amenity fee.	56 units in a converted former eight-story office building. Rents include cold water and sewer. Roof deck, fitness center, game room, lounge with flat-screen TV, bicycle storage, lockers (+$). No off-street parking. Quartz countertops, hardwood floors. Limited availability. Rents shown for available units only.
Mid-rise 3	Opened 12/2014	Studio 1/1 2/2 (5)	618–644 769–926 1,113	$1,500–1,550 $1,850–1,950 $2,300+	56 units in a six-story building. Bamboo floors, stacked washer/dryers, stainless-steel kitchens with microwaves, granite countertops, and dishwashers. Garage parking (+$), gym, outdoor courtyard. Majority of units are one bedroom. Rent includes cold water and sewer. No availability at present.
Mid-rise 4	Opened 2009	Studio (5) 2/2 (15)	508 995–1,030	NA $2,095	20 units in a six-story building originally planned as a condo. Unit mix shown in parentheses. Stainless-steel kitchens, granite countertops, hardwood floors, stacked washer/dryers. Covered parking: $100.

Source: Compiled by Deborah L. Brett & Associates from broker listings, rental websites, Zillow, Trulia, and Realtor.com.
Note: NA = not available.

(continued on next page)

Figure 4-18 (continued)

Property type	Age	Bedrooms/ baths	Size (sq ft)	Rent	Comments
Rental buildings					
Low-rise 1	Opened 2017	2/1	675	$1,450	New small building, only six units, two per floor. First five units leased in two weeks. Small bedrooms. Rent includes heat, cold water, and sewer.
Low-rise 2	Opened 7/2017	1/1 2/2	NA 1,050	$1,900–1,925 $2,550	Eight units. Narrow infill building. No pets. Units have stainless-steel kitchens with microwaves, stacked washer/dryers, hardwood floors, and terraces. No parking. Three units available.
Low-rise 3	Opened 2016	1/1	750–805	$2,100–2,300	11 units in a four-story building with ground-floor commercial space still vacant. Full-size washer/dryers, hardwood floors, stainless-steel kitchens with granite countertops, microwaves, and white cabinets. Elevator. No dogs.
Low-rise 4	Opened 2017	1/1	NA	$1,850–1,995	Small infill building. Hardwood floors, stacked washer/dryers, and stainless-steel kitchens with microwaves and white cabinets. City skyline views.

Note: NA = not available.

whether there would be demand for another rental apartment building in the same neighborhood, the focus was on properties built or renovated in the past 10 years. Note that the analyst could not find the same level of detail for every property, especially with respect to utilities included in the rent.

A grid that examines prices or rents for the subject property along with its comparables while adjusting for property age, unit size, amenities, location, and utilities can be helpful when comparing "apples and oranges," given that no two properties are exactly the same. Figure 4-19 shows how the proposed rent ($1,818) for a two-bedroom/ one-bath apartment in a planned mid-rise building would compare with the rents for its competitors. All five comparables are mid- or high-rise buildings with elevators, but only two are within the same neighborhood. However, the locations of all five are similar with respect to access to transit and shopping. One is an adaptive use of a former warehouse building; the others involved new construction. Rents for the competitive properties are adjusted for differences in condition, location, unit sizes, number of bathrooms, and tenant-paid utilities.[22] The analysis shows that the subject property's two-bedroom units would be slightly more expensive than are those in other apartment projects in the area.

When one plans a new for-sale development, a more detailed comparison of amenities and optional upgrades will be in order. For rental projects, only the newest projects (preferably less than 10 years old) in the market should be included. (In figure 4-19, only three of the five comparable properties were less than 10 years old, but these were the best examples available.) Older properties that have been renovated to class A standards can also be considered.

Figure 4-20 shows how to summarize amenities offered in seven moderately priced active adult communities located in the outlying suburbs of a large metropolitan area. Not all features are shown. The market analyst should describe those features that are most important in marketing the properties and the features that are clearly different among projects in the competitive set. Figure 4-20 shows that some amenities were standard in all seven communities, but variations were seen in flooring and countertop materials, cabinet heights, kitchen appliance brands, and recreation facilities. One project did not have a clubhouse, and only two of the seven had gated entryways.

Ideally, the market area contains a sufficient number of comparable projects. If the proposed project is a new high-rise rental apartment building, only other rental buildings with elevators (if they exist) should be included in the inventory. If no similar properties exist in the market area,

Figure 4-19
Example: Comparing Rents for Two-Bedroom/One-Bath Units

Building type	Subject property	Comparable #1		Comparable #2		Comparable #3		Comparable #4		Comparable #5	
	Elevator	Elevator		Elevator		Elevator		Elevator		Elevator	
Avg. sq ft	900	919	−$5	900	$0	955	−$14	1,075	−$44	1,037	−$34
Net rent		$1,875		$1,500		$1,272		$1,800		$1,675	
Rent per sq ft		$2.04		$1.67		$1.33		$1.67		$1.62	
Rent adjusted for size		$1,870		$1,500		$1,258		$1,756		$1,641	
Age	New	1 year	$0	50+ yrs	$50	12 years	$20	1 year	$0	8 years	$0
Power & AC	Tenant	Tenant	$80	Tenant	$80	Tenant	$80	Tenant	$80	Tenant	$80
Heat	Gas	Gas	$39	Included	−$39	Gas	$39	Gas	$39	Electric	$55
Cooking gas/electric	Gas	Gas	$9	Gas	$9	Gas	$9	Gas	$9	Gas	$9
Hot water	Gas	Gas	$12	Gas	$12	Gas	$12	Included	−$12	Electric	$24
Cold water & sewer	Included	Included	$0	Included	$0	Included	$0	Included	$0	Included	$0
Parking	Included	Included	$0	Included	$0	Included	$0	Reserved	$50	Reserved	$75
Bathroom adjustment	1 bath	1 bath	$0	1 bath	$0	1 bath		1 bath	$0	2 baths	−$50
Condition/curb appeal	Excellent	Excellent	$0	Fair	$50	Excellent	$0	Excellent	$0	Excellent	$0
Location	Excellent	Excellent	$0	Fair	$50	Excellent	$0	Excellent	$0	Excellent	$0
In-unit washer/dryer	Yes	Yes	$0	No	$25	No	$25	Yes	$0	Yes	$0
Dishwasher	Yes	Yes	$0	Yes	$0	Yes	$0	Yes	$0	Yes	$0
Estimated gross rents, 5 comparables		$2,010		$1,737		$1,443		$1,922		$1,834	
Average gross rent, 5 comparable properties	**$1,789**										
Proposed subject rent	**$1,818**										

Source: RES Advisors.

the analyst will have to find examples in other locations in the metro area with similar demographics, perceived neighborhood quality, access to employment centers, and proposed rents. A master-planned community with amenities relies only on this type of project for its competitive survey. Small subdivisions without similar features would not be competitive.

Whenever possible, it is useful to benchmark the characteristics and performance of comparable properties against market area averages with respect to prices or rents, unit sizes, and prices or rents per square foot. Although consumers tend to think about total selling price or monthly rent plus utilities when making their choices, presenting data on a per-square-foot basis is important to prevent consumers from drawing conclusions based on comparisons of dissimilar products. In addition, per-square-foot data are useful for developers when comparing achievable rents or prices with estimated construction costs.

For rental projects, vacancy rates in a market area reveal that area's strength. A high overall vacancy rate should be seen as a sign of limited current development potential. However, renovating existing product to gain a competitive edge might well make sense, especially in neighborhoods where nearby homeowners are investing in upgrades. A vacancy rate of 5 percent or lower can indicate a strong market for a particular type of product, but the analyst must view vacancy rates qualitatively. Older rental projects that lack modern amenities may skew the market's vacancy rate upward and not accurately capture demand for a new project. Moreover, projects in the initial lease-up phase will have an artificially low occupancy rate as units are being absorbed. These projects must be considered when the analyst estimates absorption for a new project, but not when considering the market area's vacancy statistics. The latter should focus on occupancy in stabilized properties.

All other factors being equal, projects with the lowest average prices or rents—or the lowest average prices or rents per square foot—should report the fastest absorption. If the analyst finds that consumers are not responding consistently to value, then less-tangible factors must be examined. For example, home features that are standard in one project may be upgrades in another. One development may be more aesthetically pleasing than another. Locations can have small differences that matter a great deal to buyers. A particular builder's reputation or experience may add perceived value. These intangibles can often be ascertained only through discussions with sales agents or surveys of prospective buyers. The analyst's own judgment is crucial in these evaluations.

When analysts identify and analyze competitive projects, nothing substitutes for fieldwork. Visiting each project and talking with a sales manager or leasing agent is the only way to determine whether an existing property is truly competitive with a planned development. Although data vendors may offer detailed information on many projects, discussions with staff members at active projects are the most effective way to learn about the characteristics of households being drawn to the area (if respondents are willing to share this information), where they come from, what they like (or do not like) about current offerings, what the most desirable product features are for each consumer type, and how competing projects are performing.

Identifying Future Competitors

Projects in the development pipeline must be identified, and relevant data, similar to that for existing projects, should be provided: (a) the project name and location; (b) the number of units planned; (c) the type of units planned, (d) preliminary estimates of rent or base price ranges (if available), and (e) expected opening dates. It is likely that many details will be missing in the early planning

Figure 4-20

Example: Features and Amenities Provided at For-Sale Active Adult Communities

	Project 1	Project 2	Project 3	Project 4	Project 5	Project 6	Project 7
Number of models[a]	4	3	4	2 in Phase I 2 in Phase II	7	6	4 TH, 7 SF
Interior features							
1st-floor master bedroom	All models	All models	All models	Not in Phase I	All models	5 of 6 models	All models

Master bath
   Jacuzzi or soaking tub
   Separate shower
   Double-bowl vanity
   Bathroom flooring
	All models
	All models
	All models
	Ceramic tile
		Option
		All models
		All models
		Ceramic tile
			Option
			No
			All models
			Vinyl
				Option
				All models
				All models
				Vinyl
					Some models
					All models
					All models
					Ceramic tile
						Some models
						All models
						All models
						Ceramic tile
							Some models
							All models
							All models
							Ceramic tile

Garages	2 car	2 car	1 and 2 car	1 car	2 car	1 and 2 car	2 car
Finished basement	No	Option	Option in some models	Optional walkout	Option	Optional walkout	Option
Breakfast nook	All models	No	No	No	All models	3 models	3 models
Patio/deck/porch	All models	Option	All models	All models	All models	All models	Not shown
Family room/ great room	In 2 larger models	1 model	No	No	4 models	1 model	1 TH model; 4 SF models
Sunroom/ garden room	Option	Option	Option in some villas	Std in larger model	Option	Std in 1 model; option in 4	Option in 2 models
Fireplace	Option	Option	Option	Std	Option	Std in 1 model; option in 4	Std in some
Finished loft	All models	Option	Option in 3 largest models	Option as 3rd floor	4 models	All models	Option in SF models; std in TH

Source: Deborah L. Brett & Associates.

Note: MBR=master bedroom/bath; SF=single family; std=standard; TH=townhouse; NS=not specified; — = not applicable.

a. All models are single-family homes unless otherwise noted.

stages. By talking to local planning and zoning officials, the analyst should be able to determine how many units are being proposed, what the type of project is (detached homes, elevator apartments), what approvals have been obtained from local government, and (usually) whether the units will be offered for sale or for rent.[23] Additional information may be available in the local real estate press or in newspaper coverage of planning board hearings. Some private data vendors monitor announced additions to supply, but not all metro areas are covered in these reports, and coverage within metro areas can be spotty.

Occasionally, a developer may be unwilling to provide any details regarding a proposed development. Also, some planned projects may never actually get off the ground. During a market slowdown, later phases of a large project may be delayed well beyond the developer's initial schedule. Units that have been sold may reappear on the market if transactions fail to close. Unsuccessful condominium projects may be converted to rental units.

Any local inventory of proposed projects will fail to identify some developments or will include others that are never started or completed. Nevertheless, it is important to compile as complete an inventory as possible. This can be a time-consuming task, especially if the market area includes multiple jurisdictions and requires numerous calls to individual developers and government jurisdictions.

Municipalities tabulate residential building permit counts and share these data with state agencies and the Census Bureau. Although a market area's boundaries may not precisely conform to municipal borders, the market analyst should examine historical building activity patterns, going back at least five years, for all of the municipalities in the market area. Single-family permits should be distinguished from units in small multifamily structures and buildings with 10 or more units. The analyst will want to see what proportion of demand in the county or metropolitan area has occurred in municipalities within the local market area. Three cautions: (a) multifamily permits reported at the local

Figure 4-20 (continued)

	Project 1	Project 2	Project 3	Project 4	Project 5	Project 6	Project 7
Number of models[a]	4	3	4	2 in Phase I 2 in Phase II	7	6	4 TH, 7 SF
Kitchen—standard features							
Standard kitchen flooring	Vinyl	Vinyl	Vinyl	Vinyl	Hardwood	Vinyl	Vinyl
Standard appliances	Whirlpool	Kenmore	Not known	GE	GE	Whirlpool	Whirlpool
Standard kitchen cabinets	42"	42"	36"	42"	42"	36"	42"
Standard countertops	Granite	Granite	Laminate	Laminate	Corian	Laminate	Laminate
Recreation							
Clubhouse	Yes	Yes	Planned	None planned	Yes	Yes	Yes
Kitchen	Yes	Yes	NS	—	Yes	Yes	Yes
Fitness center	Yes	Yes	NS	—	Yes	Yes	Yes
Party room	Yes	Yes	NS	—	Yes	Yes	Yes
Activity rooms	Yes	Yes	NS	—	Yes	Yes	Yes
Outdoor pool	Yes	Yes	NS	—	Yes	Yes	Yes
Indoor pool	No	No	NS	—	Yes	No	Yes
Library	Yes	No	NS	—	Yes	No	No
Billiard room	Yes	No	NS	—	No	No	Yes
Tennis	Yes	No	No	No	Yes	Yes	Yes
Golf	Yes	No	No	No	Putting green	No	No
Trails/paths	Yes	Yes	No	No	Yes	Yes	Yes
Security							
Gated entry	Yes	No	No	No	Yes	No	No

A renovated two-bedroom condominium in an older elevator building. *(Deborah L. Brett & Associates)*

level do not indicate whether the units are intended for rent or for sale; (b) some municipalities do not report multifamily units accurately, even though fieldwork indicates their presence; and (c) most, but not all, permitted units are actually built.[24]

Calculating Capture and Penetration Rates

Once the market analyst has determined total housing demand (household growth plus replacement needs), the next step is to calculate a project capture rate. The *capture rate* is the percentage of qualified consumers who would have to be attracted to the proposed development if it is to reach stabilized occupancy (usually 95 percent of total units in a rental property) or to sell out a for-sale project. For family housing (not age-restricted), total demand can be narrowed down on the basis of owners versus renters, depending on whether the target market is first-time buyers or move-up owners. (For age-restricted housing, the target market can include both owners and renters, provided that the capture analysis focuses on the appropriate age and income cohorts.)

For affordable housing targeted to families, narrowing the target market by household size in addition to age and income would yield more precise results. The market analyst should recognize that projects that are not age-restricted (or

age-targeted) may appeal to a variety of age or psychographic groups. For example, urban condominiums often attract both young first-time buyers and empty nesters, provided that they have unit layouts and amenities that appeal to both groups.

Many factors determine the size of the demand pool used to calculate a capture rate, and these factors may vary over the lease and sales period. If house prices are appreciating and if mortgage funds are available with attractive terms, renters may decide to buy, and the share of future demand that will be captured by for-sale projects will increase beyond the current homeownership rate. Conversely, if for-sale markets weaken, prices decline, or mortgage terms are restrictive, prospective owners will think twice about leaving the rental market.

The pool of likely buyers or renters in a local market area will be expanded by households coming from outside the area for job relocations or in response to an effective advertising campaign. This external demand can account for as much as 20 percent or more of the total units sold or rented. In a project oriented to seniors, an even higher percentage of renters or buyers is likely to come from outside the primary market area; those prospects will move to be closer to family members or to return to a familiar location. For second-home communities, the boundaries of the market area might be based on drive time from the nearest large population centers; households will then be qualified by age and income. Capture rates will be much lower than for a primary residence. However, an attractive second-home community with unique amenities (for example, waterfront access or nearby skiing) can draw purchasers from a much larger distance (even though they will probably use their second home infrequently). In these circumstances, households living beyond a four- to five-hour drive could outnumber those from the local market.

Once total demand has been quantified, calculating the capture rate is simple: use the number of units in the project (with an allowance for normal vacancy) divided by total qualified demand (including a factor for replacement and outsiders). It is important not to overestimate the market potential of the subject property; a single development project will rarely capture more than 5 to 10 percent of total market area demand. But this standard can vary. In an area that is growing slowly, if at all, and where no new product has been built in many years, a higher capture rate could

make sense. Examples would be in a rural county with little projected population growth or a mature urban community with a scarcity of developable sites. A good understanding of competitive projects is critical for accurately evaluating the capture rate.

For affordable housing developments, market analysts are often asked to calculate a *penetration rate*. This rate indicates the extent to which the total supply of housing that serves a particular age and income group is at risk of overbuilding. The penetration rate is expressed as the total number of existing and approved units that are in the market area and that serve the age- and income-qualified market divided by the total number of households in the target group. (The proposed project is counted, even though it may not yet have all approvals.) Generally, government agencies prefer that penetration rates not exceed 15 to 20 percent of target households.

Figure 4-21 is an example of how to analyze demand and calculate capture or penetration rates for a proposed new market-rate rental building to be built in the downtown of a

Figure 4-21

Example: Demand and Capture Calculations for New Market-Rate Apartments

Downtown Submarket, Medium-Sized City

Citywide demand	2018	2023	Change
City households under age 65—total	35,140	33,285	−1,855
With incomes:			
$35,000–49,999	4,581	4,223	−358
$50,000–74,999	5,569	5,043	−526
$75,000–99,999	4,284	4,135	−149
$100,000–149,999	5,028	5,157	129
Subtotal with incomes $35,000–149,999[a]	19,462	18,558	−904
Renter household share	36%	39%	
Estimated renter households under 65 with incomes $35,000–149,999	7,006	7,238	231
City households age 65+ by income—total	12,286	13,335	1,049
With incomes:			
$35,000–49,999	1,749	1,893	144
$50,000–74,999	1,868	1,982	114
$75,000–99,999	1,137	1,259	122
$100,000–149,999	1,095	1,309	214
Subtotal with incomes $35,000–149,999[a]	5,849	6,443	594
Renter household share	18%	21%	
Estimated renter households over 65 with incomes $35,000–149,999	1,053	1,353	300
Demand for new apartments from all city renter households with incomes $35,000–149,999			
Total renter households with incomes $35,000–149,999	8,059	8,591	
Demand for *new* rental units for households with incomes $35,000–149,999, assuming 95% occupancy			559

Source: Valerie S. Kretchmer Associates Inc., based on estimates and projections from Esri and the American Community Survey 2012–2016.

a. Income target for market-rate units, based on proposed rents and utility costs.

b. Units in market-rate buildings downtown and their share of citywide units with monthly rents over $800.

(continued on next page)

medium-sized midwestern city. The city made a considerable investment in public improvements downtown, which generated interest in the conversion of older warehouse buildings into apartments, restaurants, and entertainment venues. Although young renters had shown interest in living in these buildings (which now achieve higher rents than better-quality apartments elsewhere in the city), no new apartments had been built downtown for decades. Older households were also looking for more maintenance-free housing options and would find downtown cultural attractions and walkable environments appealing.

The market analyst concluded that there was a deficit of new rental housing in the city and in the downtown submarket and therefore calculated demand assuming a higher share of renter households in the next five years than in the past.[25] Although a new 132-unit building would need to capture a high share (18 to 20 percent) of downtown demand, only 38 other units were planned in the submarket. The overall penetration rate would be 23 percent of income-qualified renter demand in 2023.

Estimating Absorption Rates for Apartments

In a given apartment market area, net absorption is the difference between total units (including any new supply) and occupied units during a given time period. When market conditions are strong, net absorption will be positive: the number of new leases signed will exceed the number of apartments vacated because of turnover. (This term is also used in market studies for commercial space, as later chapters will explain.) Projecting a new property's future absorption rate must take into account the number of units in competing projects that will be coming online during the marketing period. The absorption rate is typically stated as the number of signed leases divided by the number of months elapsed since leasing began or since the property opened. A similar concept in a new for-sale project is usually expressed as the sales pace (the number of units placed under contract each month). Some analysts look only at closings as a more precise estimate of actual sales.

Figure 4-21 (continued)

Downtown demand	2018	2023	Change
Downtown demand for new apartments from renter households with incomes $35,000–149,999			
Existing downtown market-rate units targeted to households with incomes $35,000–149,999 (9.2% of city units > $800/month)[b]	369		
Downtown's *potential* capture of existing city renter households with incomes $35,000–149,999 (11–12% of city units)	887–967		
2018 unmet demand for downtown units for households with incomes $35,000–149,999 (potential demand less existing units)	518–598		
Downtown's potential share of city demand for new rental units for households with incomes $35,000–149,999 between 2018 and 2023 (25%)			140
Total 2023 demand for downtown units for renters with incomes $35,000–149,999 (2018 unmet demand + share of new demand between 2018 and 2023)		657–738	
Average annual demand for downtown units for renters with incomes $35,000–149,999		131–148	

Capture and penetration for downtown units	2023 range	
Total 2018–2023 demand for downtown units for renters with incomes $35,000–149,999 (2018 unmet demand + share of new demand between 2018 and 2023)	657	738
Proposed units, subject property Capture rate of total 2018–2023 demand	132 20.1%	132 17.9%
Additional planned market-rate units	38	38
Total—subject property and additional planned units Penetration rate of total 2018–2023 demand	170 25.9%	170 23.0%

Source: Valerie S. Kretchmer Associates Inc., based on estimates and projections from Esri and the American Community Survey 2012–2016.
a. Income target for market-rate units, based on proposed rents and utility costs.
b. Units in market-rate buildings downtown and their share of citywide units with monthly rents over $800.

An aerial view of a single-family subdivision in Charlotte, North Carolina.

Comparable projects currently being leased or sold provide the best sources for estimating absorption. If there are no other new developments, the experience of properties leased or sold within the past two years is a reasonable proxy. Calling newer apartment buildings or homebuilders outside the local market area may be necessary if no recently built competitors exist in the local market area.

It is important to use a consistent definition of how absorption is calculated—whether the pace of leasing or sales is based on the date when the property began taking deposits or reservations or on when the apartment lease is signed or the new home sale closes. Several private real estate market data sources collect historical sales and absorption information, although not in all locales. Access to this information can save the analyst a lot of time; information from a given data vendor is likely to be consistent across properties. The market analyst must use judgment in adjusting the experience of other properties to reflect current market conditions, as well as the relative advantages and drawbacks of the planned development.

Recommendations and Monitoring

A good developer will welcome suggestions from the market analyst that would enhance marketability, improve the projected capture rate, or speed up absorption. Market analysts should tell the client if economic conditions are not positive, if vacancy rates are trending upward, if rents are flat or declining, if an adjustment to unit mix or unit sizes would make the property more competitive, or whether amenities and standard finishes should be upgraded. The analyst may conclude that the project is too big and advise that it be built in phases—or even postponed entirely. Lenders and government agencies often ask the analyst to state if, in his or her opinion, the project should be built as planned or if adjustments should be made to the developer's plans.

Although a market study is one of the first elements in the development process, market research does not end with a project's completion: it often continues after sales begin, with the builder fine-tuning prices and even changing designs, features, and options. In a rental project, research is part of an ongoing effort during leasing and management to keep tabs on competitors' vacancies, rents, and incentive programs. This monitoring continues after the

Figure 4-22

Median Sales Price of Existing Single-Family Homes

United States and 10 Selected Metropolitan Areas

	Median price (000s)				Change, 3rd quarter 2017–2018 (%)
	2015	2016	2017	3rd quarter 2018[a]	
United States	**$223.9**	**$235.5**	**$248.1**	**$266.9**	**4.8**
Atlanta-Sandy Springs-Marietta, GA	$173.6	$184.5	$198.5	$224.1	9.7
Cleveland-Elyria, OH	$125.1	$132.2	$140.4	$159.8	9.5
Fayetteville, NC	$116.9	$126.9	$130.8	$141.0	5.0
Houston-the Woodlands-Sugar Land, TX	$213.4	$217.4	$231.1	$240.2	2.7
Los Angeles-Long Beach-Glendale, CA	$480.1	$509.0	$550.8	$628.9	5.7
Minneapolis-St. Paul-Bloomington, MN	$223.7	$237.0	$252.1	$274.5	6.5
Peoria, IL	$120.7	$118.0	$122.6	$131.3	2.0
Philadelphia-Camden-Wilmington, PA-NJ-DE-MD	$223.7	$225.4	$230.0	$240.6	0.7
Salem, OR	$210.3	$237.2	$265.5	$307.3	12.1
Salt Lake City, UT	$255.0	$272.5	$308.9	$323.3	9.4

new apartment complex has reached stabilized occupancy; moreover, keeping an eye on the market is critical to maintaining a property's competitiveness over time. Sophisticated computer programs using big data from a range of comparables in the broader market will help leasing agents make frequent adjustments to asking rents for different unit types.

Data Sources

Chapter 3 provides a thorough discussion of information sources that can be used in analyzing employment trends and demand demographics. Those sources include the Census Bureau; state, county, and municipal planning agencies; and private demographic data vendors that provide basic information on population and households and their characteristics (including current-year estimates and five-year projections).

For analysts working with affordable housing proposals, background information for the metropolitan area or county can be obtained from the National Low Income Housing Coalition, as discussed earlier.[26] Additional information sources are discussed later.

Supply-Side Data from Trade Associations, Real Estate Brokers, and Government Sources

At the national level, the NAR regularly updates housing sales price data and trends on its website (www.realtor.org/research), which provides annual and quarterly data on

the median sales price of existing single-family homes in metropolitan areas large and small. A sample of recent data for 10 metropolitan areas is shown in figure 4-22. (Note the wide range of prices.) In a smaller number of metropolitan areas, NAR also provides median sales prices for condominium and cooperative dwellings. Its publicly available data go back three years, which allows the analyst to examine recent price trends. However, no submarket information is shown, which is a key limitation in larger markets. Also, analysts who want to examine historical trends going back beyond three years will have to purchase this information from NAR.

Local or state Realtor associations also collect statistics on home sales that help analysts take the pulse of the home resale market at the county and municipal levels. Available information varies from state to state and among Realtor organizations within states. Historical data can include the number of homes listed and sold, the median or average sales prices, and the average number of days it takes for a house to sell. Local Realtor organizations may also have summary statistics on the characteristics of all homes currently listed for sale. Note that sales information from Realtor groups or individual Realtor firms does not cover existing homes offered for sale by owner and may not cover new homes being marketed directly by builders without the services of an agent.

If the market area being studied is fairly small, the analyst can examine information (and photos) of individual homes and condominiums listed for sale on Realtor.com, zillow.com, or trulia.com; the listings can be searched by municipality or zip code. Users can filter the listings in a variety of ways (for example, by number of bedrooms) and can focus their search on new versus existing homes. The market analyst should note that listing prices are not a good indicator of sales prices when market conditions are weak.

Home sale price trend data are also available from the Federal Housing Finance Agency (FHFA) and, in a small number of markets, from the CoreLogic Case-Shiller Index.[27] Both of these sources have limitations: they do not include all sales and their methodologies differ.

- The FHFA index provides one- and five-year estimates of the percentage change in home prices for the four census regions, nine multistate census divisions, individual states, and selected metropolitan areas on a quarterly basis.[28] The indices are based on repeat sales or refinancings of conventional mortgages. They do not include homes with jumbo loans,[29] nor do they include sales with subprime financing. FHFA indices do not show actual prices, only changes over time (one quarter, one year, five years, and since 1991).

- The Case-Shiller indices, published monthly, cover 10 or 20 metropolitan areas. They use a three-month moving average and are published with a two-month time lag. Like the FHFA index, Case-Shiller uses repeat sales that are weighted to account for major remodeling or neglect. Case-Shiller also provides a regional and national index each quarter. Unlike the NAR data, neither the FHFA nor the Case-Shiller publications provide the actual median or average prices, only the change in price levels over time.

In addition to reporting sales price trends, NAR commissions consumer research on the characteristics of homebuyers (including second-home buyers) and their housing preferences; copies of these reports can be purchased for a fee. Results of these surveys are widely studied and publicized in the press. NAR economists issue national forecasts of market performance and construction activity for both residential and nonresidential properties.

The NAHB focuses its research on new home construction. It publishes Eye on Housing, a blog covering housing-related economic trends, and uses data from a variety of sources on new home sales, mortgage interest rates, builder confidence, mortgage delinquencies, and barriers to affordability. NAHB also aggregates data from the Census Bureau on new home construction (permits and starts) for metro areas, and it forecasts housing starts (both single-family and multifamily) for the nation, regions, and metro areas. Much of its data is publicly available, but some series (especially forecasts) require paid subscriptions. NAHB's special surveys of new homebuyer characteristics and consumer preferences are widely studied and publicized in the press.[30]

Additional insights can be found through research conducted by other specialized trade and advocacy organizations such as the American Seniors Housing Association (ASHA), the Manufactured Housing Institute (which represents mobile home and modular housing manufacturers and dealers), the National Apartment Association (NAA), and the National Multifamily Housing Council (which represents owners of large, professionally managed apartment complexes). Generally, their surveys are national in scope; however, some of these organizations have state and local affiliates that can provide area-specific insight into buyer or renter characteristics.

To get a better sense of local submarkets, market analysts should contact local brokers, especially when dealing with for-sale projects. National brokerage firms that specialize in apartment transactions regularly publish metropolitan market updates and can be a source of useful background statistics and insights.

Private Data Providers

For-sale housing has its own unique information sources. For new or recently completed projects, Hanley Wood's Metrostudy allows researchers to buy detailed information about individual development projects, including number of lots or units, model characteristics, base prices, and absorption on a per property basis. However, its geographic coverage is limited to 40-plus markets, mostly in California as well as the Middle Atlantic, Southeast, and Southwest states.[31] The same company publishes reports covering permitting trends and housing market indicators, newsletters, and magazines that cater to homebuilders. Local firms throughout the United States produce similar data that are widely used by real estate appraisers who focus on single-family homes.

Numerous free local apartment guides that are available in metropolitan areas (both online and in print) can direct the market analyst to competitive properties in a given submarket. Apartment owners and managers pay to showcase their properties in these publications, which provide photos and information about the types of units offered, rents, and amenities. They do not provide any information on historical trends. With more information now available on the internet, print publications (which are more expensive to produce and distribute) are disappearing. However, chambers of commerce and other local business organizations frequently maintain apartment lists that help transferees and workers with temporary assignments to find housing in the area.

Web-only sources (such as apartments.com) have search capabilities and can sort listed properties by submarket or zip code. It is important to verify information provided in apartment guides, because listed rents may not be current. Not all properties will pay to be listed in these guides. When vacancy rates are very low, properties may not want to pay the cost of online listings or print advertising.

Private vendors such as Axiometrics, CoStar, RealPage (formerly MPF Research), and Reis sell information on inventory, rent, and vacancy trends. They also provide details on individual competitive projects in a local area. The number of private data vendors has expanded in the past decade. Some firms cover metropolitan areas across the country. Others are regional or local in geographic scope.

Housing analysts should carefully examine the breadth and depth of the information they obtain from private vendors and should consider the cost of onetime data purchases versus annual subscriptions. For a large consulting firm, a development company, or an investment firm that works nationwide or in a multistate region, a subscription

How to Evaluate Apartment Data Provided by Private Vendors: Questions to Ask When Considering a Subscription Service

- How does the vendor collect information (by phone, mail, or fax)? In what ways does the vendor encourage properties to cooperate?

- How often is information updated? Are follow-up calls made to properties that do not respond? Large apartment management companies are likely to use sophisticated computer programs that help them adjust rents on a weekly or monthly basis according to demand in the area for particular unit types and sizes. How does the data firm deal with this?

- How detailed are the data? For example, if an apartment complex offers four models, each with two bedrooms, are size and rent data collected for each model? Or are only rent ranges provided?

- In a high-rise building, where premium rents are charged for units with attractive views, is information on premiums by floor or view available?

- For older properties where some—but not all—units have been renovated, does the rent range distinguish between units that have been upgraded and those that have not?

- Which utilities are included in the rent, and which are paid by the tenant?

- What about extra fees for storage lockers, parking, or use of recreation amenities?

- In calculating average rents, does the vendor consider the impact of concessions (discounts offered when occupancy is soft or when a particular unit type is not renting quickly)?

- What information does the vendor provide on projects under construction but not yet occupied?

can be cost-effective. In other situations (where the user is looking for information to make preliminary decisions or works in only one city), making a onetime purchase or buying data for a single metro area may be more affordable.

No survey gets cooperation from every competitive property. Inventories compiled by private companies, consultants, or brokerages may not offer complete coverage within a market. Also, turnover in a property's leasing staff may mean that the person answering questions has little historical knowledge. Busy staff members may not be willing to take the time to answer all questions, regardless of whether they are reached by phone, through an online survey from a data vendor, or during a visit by a market analyst. Owners or developers may tell staff members not to cooperate with surveys, and it is easy to miss a new or recently completed project. For these reasons, it is critical that the analyst drive the market to identify and visit competitive projects.

In lieu of—or to supplement—available information, the analyst should search online rental information sites, local housing magazines, and newspaper real estate sections for additional comparables. The analyst should visit these properties and ask leasing staff members about the location of their competitors. (Fieldwork helps the market analyst determine which comparables are most important and how their locations compare with that of the subject property.) A comprehensive market study should also include photographs of the subject property and its competitors.

As an example, figure 4-23 summarizes the types of apartment supply data that can be purchased from Reis.

To provide supply information for senior housing, the National Investment Center (NIC) for the Seniors Housing and Care Industry developed the NIC MAP Data Service system. This resource allows analysts to compare key market indicators (number of properties, average occupancy, market penetration as a percentage of households age 75 and older, and construction activity-to-inventory ratios) for 100 metropolitan areas, their constituent counties, and customized geographies. Data are available for independent living, assisted living, nursing home, and dementia care segments. Single reports or subscriptions are available for purchase.

Most information on the supply of subsidized housing comes from government sources (discussed in the next section). Novogradac & Co., a firm of certified public accountants who specialize in affordable housing, provides information on income and rent limits for low-income housing tax credit properties in all states and metro areas on its website, and explains how the program works.[32]

Government Sources

As indicated earlier, the Census Bureau publishes many statistical series on housing construction:

- Census building permit tabulations are the only uniform, nationwide source of information on recent construction for individual counties or municipalities.[33]

Figure 4-23
Apartment Supply Data Available for Purchase from Reis

Geographic coverage	Metro area Submarkets Comparable group (specified)
Property class	Class A Class B and C
Time series	Quarterly and annual
Supply size indicators	Inventory (units) Completions
Supply characteristics	Unit mix by number of bedrooms Unit sizes

Supply performance indicators	Inventory age
	Occupied and vacant stock
	Vacancy rate (%)
	Net absorption
	Asking rent ($/sq ft or per unit) by number
	    of bedrooms
	Rent change (%)
	Construction/absorption (ratio)
	Performance variation by class
	Comparisons with metro area, region, and nation
	New construction status and estimated
	    completion date

Demographic indicators	Population, households, employment, and average household income estimates
Forecasts	Five-year

Note: Obtaining all information shown in this table for a single submarket will require purchasing multiple reports.

They offer data on the number of units permitted (broken out by number of units per building). As discussed previously, the Bureau's building permit statistics for local jurisdictions do not indicate whether multifamily units are intended for sale or for rent. No information is provided about unit mix, size, or pricing and rents.

- The Census Bureau also tabulates housing starts and unit completions in the United States and its four major regions but not at the metropolitan, county, or municipal level. (Data on completions have been featured in figures 4-3 through 4-8 used earlier in this chapter.) Reports on completions distinguish between new units built for rent and those built for sale. A separate Census Bureau report provides benchmarks for gauging recent absorption rates in new multifamily buildings.[34]

- Annual owner and rental unit vacancy rates and homeownership rate estimates for the nation's 75 largest metropolitan areas are also available from the Census Bureau, but they do not include details on occupancy or tenure in individual counties, municipalities, or submarkets.[35]

HUD issues periodic market overviews for larger metropolitan areas; the overviews are available on HUD's U.S. Housing Market Conditions webpage.[36] These reports include submarket or county-level data depending on the size of the metro area. In 2018, the web page posted 45 different reports. The methodology applied by HUD is consistent between markets and can provide a useful starting point for a more detailed analysis. HUD also provides national and regional housing market summary statistics quarterly.[37] The quarterly reports posted on the HUD website provide a narrative overview of supply and demand and other key indicators nationally.

In the past, HUD had an online database that generated lists of federally subsidized affordable rental properties.[38] This website listed properties by state, county, municipality, or zip code; by number of bedrooms; and by whom the property serves: families, senior citizens, or persons with disabilities. The information was designed for consumers, not researchers. It did not offer information on the type of subsidy, but it did give users an address and a contact phone number for each property. The HUD database did not include properties made affordable through LIHTCs or state and local subsidy programs. Its focus was on privately owned and managed Section 8 buildings, not public housing. As of May 2019, the information was being revised.

State housing finance agencies will have information on affordable rental properties, but the coverage and formats they offer will vary widely. Some state housing sources provide information only on properties for which they have supplied tax credits, mortgage financing, or other forms of assistance; they may not list older HUD-assisted affordable buildings and public housing properties. Like the HUD database, state sources offer limited details but usually provide contact information.

Local governments may have databases on existing market-rate rental apartments and affordable housing options. To identify future properties in the planning pipeline, the analyst must contact municipal planning or construction staff members to determine how many units are planned and approved. Lists of approved development projects may not contain sufficient detail on unit mix or tenure, and they do not include anticipated rents. Follow-up calls to developers and leasing staff members will be necessary.

Notes

1. For current information about the top managers and developers in this field, a useful resource is *Student Housing Business* magazine, which publishes regular directories and rankings of the largest players.

2. Analysts can create interactive tables from the American Housing Survey and can focus on owner-occupied or renter-occupied units as well as on overall housing stock characteristics. https://www.census.gov/programs-surveys/ahs/data.html.

3. www.manufacturedhousing.org.

4. By the end of the third quarter 2018, the homeownership rate improved to 64.4 percent but still remained well below the pre-recession peak of 69.2 percent in the second quarter 2004.

5. In past decades, a homebuyer typically had to make a downpayment of 10 to 20 percent of the sales price to obtain a 30-year mortgage with a fixed rate of interest through a local bank or mortgage broker. (A buyer who could put down only 10 percent of the purchase price had to obtain private mortgage insurance or take out a loan insured by the FHA.)

6. Yardi Matrix's definition of markets often means areas smaller than a metropolitan area—in reality a submarket (Manhattan), major city (Atlanta), or large suburb (Marietta, Georgia).

7. Gregg Logan and Rachel Waldman, "Disruptive Demographics: Housing Production and Demographic Reality Are Moving in Different Directions," The Advisory, RCLCO, March 14, 2019.

8. Joint Center for Housing Studies of Harvard University, *America's Rental Housing 2017*, p. 14.

9. Invitation Homes's portfolio included more than 80,000 rental homes in 2018. See Bendix Anderson, "SFR Investors Are Filling the Pipeline with New Development," *National Real Estate Investor* online, May 14, 2018. Overall, developers built more than 36,000 new single-family homes for the rental market in 2017.

10. The projections, originally issued in 2017 and later revised, assume that net international migration will range between 1.0 million and 1.1 million persons per year. Changes in federal immigration policy could result in fewer persons moving to the United States from other countries. The projections also show a slowdown in net natural increase (births minus deaths)—from 1.37 million persons in 2019 to a low of just 392,000 in 2049—before increasing again.

11. U.S. Census Bureau, Population Division, *Projected Race and Hispanic Origin: Main Projection Series for the United States*, 2017–2060.

12. Based on tabulations from the Census Bureau's Current Population Surveys conducted between 2000–2001 and 2017–2018.

13. The IRS office that produces Statistics of Income also compiles mobility information. For assistance in accessing IRS mobility files, see https://www.irs.gov/statistics/soi-tax-stats-migration-data.

14. U.S. Census Bureau, Population Division, *Cumulative Estimates of Population Change for Incorporated Places over 100,000*, April 1, 2000, to July 1, 2007, table 2, www.census.gov/popest/cities/SUB-EST2007.html.

15. HUD uses FMRs to calculate payment standards for rent subsidies in Section 8 buildings and for housing choice vouchers.

16. Some states and local jurisdictions have minimum wage rates higher than the federal rate, but even in these places, the minimum wage is insufficient to afford FMRs.

17. U.S. Census Bureau, *American Community Survey*: 2017.

18. To qualify for designation, market analysts must have a bachelor's degree and a minimum of three years of experience or 10 years of experience in the absence of a degree. Applicants must submit a résumé and examples of their work for peer review. They must meet continuing education requirements and adhere to a code of ethics.

19. Mike E. Miles, Gayle L. Berens, Marc Eppli, and Marc A. Weiss, *Real Estate Development: Principles and Process*, 4th ed. (Washington, DC: ULI–the Urban Land Institute, 2007), p. 425.

20. In some states, it is also illegal to discriminate in the sale or rental of housing on the basis of sexual orientation.

21. Jesse Bricker et al., "Changes in U.S. Family Finances from 2013 to 2016: Evidence from the Survey of Consumer Finances," *Federal Reserve Bulletin*, vol. 103, no. 3, September 2017, https://www.federalreserve.gov/publications/files/scf17.pdf. This article discusses changes in household net worth that occurred between 2013 and 2016. For homeowners, median net worth in 2016 was $231,400, an increase of 15 percent in inflation-adjusted dollars since 2013. In contrast, median net worth for renters was only $5,200 and declined by 5 percent in the previous three years.

22. Adjustment factors can be arbitrary because researchers may not agree on the contribution of a half-bath, a balcony, or other unit and building features in setting rents.

23. When market conditions are in flux, projects originally intended for sale may be converted to rental before they are completed. Permit-issuing jurisdictions usually do not have the legal authority to challenge such shifts as long as the built project conforms to the approved site plan and zoning provisions.

24. Census Bureau research indicates that 2.5 percent of permitted units nationwide are not started and 4 percent of starts are not completed. Note that the Census Bureau counts townhouse units as single-family homes, but local jurisdictions may consider them to be multifamily homes.

25. The calculations in figure 4-21 do not show a factor for replacement demand.

26. National Low Income Housing Coalition, *Out of Reach 2018: The High Cost of Housing*, 2018, www.nlihc.org.

27. CoreLogic Case-Shiller index measures housing markets in 20 metropolitan regions across the United States. It is published monthly.

28. https://www.fhfa.gov/DataTools/Downloads/Pages/House-Price-Index-Datasets.aspx#qpo. Data can be downloaded in Excel.

29. "Jumbo mortgages" refers to loans that exceed the limits set by the government-sponsored enterprises (Freddie Mac and Fannie Mae), which buy most home loans and package them for investors. Because they exceed the maximum dollar limits, jumbo mortgages are referred to as nonconforming loans. As of 2018, the maximum conforming mortgage limit is $453,100 in all states except for Alaska, Guam, Hawaii, and the U.S. Virgin Islands, where the limit is $679,650. The conforming limit can be higher in counties with higher home prices. A jumbo loan will typically have a higher interest rate, will have stricter underwriting rules, and will require a larger downpayment than will a standard mortgage.

30. Using the results of the 2017 American Housing Survey, NAHB reported on the characteristics of homebuyers during the previous two-year period. The results: 37 percent were first-time buyers with a median age of 32; 63 percent of buyers were trading up; and 37 percent of first-time buyers were racial or ethnic minorities.

31. www.metrostudy.com. Only three markets in the Midwest (Chicago, Indianapolis, and the Twin Cities) are covered.

32. www.novoco.com.

33. www.census.gov/const/www/permitsindex.html.

34. Survey of Market Absorption of New Multifamily Units, https://www.census.gov/programs-surveys/soma.html.

35. www.census.gov/hhes/www/housing/hvs/hvs.html.

36. https://www.huduser.gov/portal/ushmc/chma_archive.html.

37. https://www.huduser.gov/portal/ushmc/quarterly_commentary.html.

38. https://apps.hud.gov/apps/section8/index.cfm.

CHAPTER 5

CHAPTER 5

RETAIL SPACE

The retail market analyst must understand the retailing business and its customers as well as the real estate. Retail properties include shopping centers (open air and enclosed), pedestrian-oriented business districts, and freestanding stores. The International Council of Shopping Centers defines a shopping center as "a group of retail and other commercial establishments that is planned, developed, owned, and managed as a single property." Store space—whether in malls, in strip centers, or on Main Street—is most commonly tabulated as gross leasable area, the total floor area that a tenant occupies exclusively, including any space used for storage or offices.[1] GLA does not include any common area, management office space, or other space that is not leased to individual tenants. Shopping centers of all sizes account for an estimated 42 percent of the total inventory of retail space in the United States, as shown in figure 5-5 later in this chapter. Freestanding stores, ground-floor shops in apartment buildings, and business strips that lack central management account for the majority of retail square footage,[2] especially in urban neighborhoods, older suburbs, or small towns.

Why Do a Retail Market Study?

Adding new retail space cannot generate new consumers or enhance purchasing power. It can only attract customers away from existing stores within or beyond the trade area; fulfill a need that has not been met within the market area; draw consumers who would otherwise shop online (by bringing exciting new offerings to the area); or capture the increase in potential expenditures that results from population, household, employment, or income growth. A new, renovated, or expanded center can, however, alter consumer shopping habits. Each new center must be justified by gauging the purchasing power available to it in light of its competition, both physical stores and online offerings. In any market study, assumptions should be conservative and clearly described.

A retail market study can provide valuable input for a variety of real estate decision-makers—developers, potential tenants, investors, and government agencies:

- Shopping center developers use market studies to shape the nature of their proposed projects, attract the interest of prospective tenants, win needed approvals from the community, and secure financing.

- Real estate departments at chain retailers and franchisers use market data to create profiles of top store performers, thereby providing guidance for future location decisions. They also study demand demographics and competitive store inventory when deciding whether to enter a market where they have not yet been represented.

- Tenants conduct their own market studies because their decision-making criteria are different from a developer's. A developer's profit is based on achievable rents, occupancy, and operating expenses for the entire center. A store is most concerned with whether it can draw its target customer base and generate the sales levels that will make the location a good performer, while being careful not to cannibalize sales at their other nearby locations.

- Local governments and economic development agencies use retail market studies when preparing redevelopment plans for business districts or older shopping centers and in determining the feasibility of tax increment financing programs. (See the Glossary for a brief summary of how TIF programs work.)

- Market studies are prepared as part of the due diligence process for lenders, purchasers, and investors in construction of new retail space, and by investors in New Markets Tax Credits for commercial revitalization projects.

Trends in Shopping and Spending

When the general U.S. economy is healthy and household incomes are growing, retail sales will increase each year. Even in years with weak economic growth, an expanding population creates new demand for goods and services. The U.S. Census Bureau collects monthly sales data from a sample of retailers representing all types of stores and online businesses; annual reports are prepared (and periodically revised), allowing market analysts to see how sales have changed over time by type of store. At the present time, trend data available online go back to 1992.[3]

Retail analysts—and the Census Bureau—group store types into two major classifications: *GAFO* and *convenience*. GAFO is an acronym for stores selling *g*eneral merchandise (discount and conventional department stores, warehouse clubs, supercenters), *a*pparel and accessories (including shoes and jewelry), *f*urniture and home furnishings (including electronics), and *o*ther goods (specialty shops selling toys, luggage, jewelry, books, sporting goods, and other items).[4]

Convenience stores include supermarkets and other food stores (such as bakeries or fruit and vegetable markets) and drugstores. Home improvement, hardware, and building supply stores are classified as convenience stores. However, the increasingly varied array of merchandise sold at stores such as Lowe's or Home Depot (appliances, floor coverings, kitchen cabinets) make this classification questionable.

Restaurants and bars (NAICS code 722) are also considered to be convenience establishments. The Census Bureau identifies two main types of restaurants: NAICS code 7221 (full-service eateries where patrons are served by wait staff and pay after they finish their meals) and 7222 (limited service, where patrons order and pay before eating).[5]

Entertainment activities can be important in drawing customers to retail venues. Movie theaters are most closely associated with malls and other commercial business districts, but many shopping center operators are adding such recreation venues as gyms, exercise studios, skating rinks, children's museums, and music or theatrical performance spaces. Revenues for these businesses are not counted as retail sales, but their presence can help draw more customers to shopping centers and mixed-use developments.

Figure 5-1 compares U.S. retail sales for 2007 (before the past recession) and 2017 (the most recent annual data available as of 2019), indicating how sales have changed over time on both a total and a per capita basis. The per capita statistics adjust for growth in the number of consumers over the 10-year period. Past changes can be tracked using the annual reports, but the data are not adjusted for changes in the prices of goods sold.[6]

Sales data presented in figure 5-1 illustrate the dramatic changes underway in retailing and, by implication, retail real estate. Although total sales (excluding motor vehicles and parts) grew by 25.5 percent during this 10-year period (in spite of the long economic downturn) and per capita sales by 16.3 percent, GAFO sales (which are critically important to enclosed malls, power centers, and large community centers) increased only 11.0 percent overall and just 2.8 percent on a per capita basis. GAFO stores accounted for 37.1 percent of total sales in 2007, but only 32.8 percent in 2017. Double-digit declines in electronics stores, book stores, and department stores account for most of the losses. On a per capita basis, furniture and home furnishings also lost ground. The emergence of e-commerce (especially Amazon) accounted for much of this decline, but store closings were also an important factor.

Analysts should note the strong sales gains for apparel and sporting goods, as well as for warehouse clubs and supercenters. Specialty apparel did well, drawing sales away from department stores. Sporting goods benefited from increased interest in fitness and outdoor activities. Warehouse clubs compete well on price and selection, as do supercenters run by Target and Walmart, and regional chains Meijer (in the Midwest) and Fred Meyer (in the West). (Supercenters sell apparel, jewelry, sporting goods, baby items, linens, housewares, and small electrics in addition to groceries.)

Stores selling everyday needs (grocery stores, dollar stores,[7] drugstores, home improvement and hardware stores) have staying power, even during troubled economic times. Even so, e-commerce is making inroads into store sales in these categories. Although consumers are willing to buy paper goods, laundry and cleaning supplies, canned goods, dry groceries, and other nonperishables online, shoppers say they want to see meat, fish, and produce before buying it. Grocery delivery logistics are still problematic. Despite increased availability of delivery services, older apartment buildings lack refrigerated lockers to hold food items, and scheduling deliveries when homeowners can receive them can be inefficient in low-density residential neighborhoods. For now, supermarkets retain sales by offering special parking areas or curbside pickup for customers placing orders online. Walmart is also advertising curbside pickup for all types of purchases, as are many casual restaurants.

E-Commerce: A Game-Changer

The Census Bureau groups online sales with other forms of nonstore retailing (mainly catalog orders, which used to be handled primarily by phone or by mail but are now mostly online). As figure 5-1 indicates, e-commerce and mail order/catalog orders (NAICS code 4541) are shown in the Census Bureau's annual sales statistics. However, census reporting of e-commerce in the annual retail sales report focuses on sales from establishments that have *no* physical store presence (often called "pure play" online vendors). The report does not account separately for the growing importance of "omni-channel" retailers who sell goods both in store and online. Both types of businesses fulfill orders from warehouses (which has contributed to the dramatic growth in demand for fulfillment centers, as noted in chapter 7).

To better report on the growing importance of e-commerce, the Census Bureau now tracks it on a quarterly basis, with data released more quickly than for the annual

Figure 5-1
Estimated Annual U.S. Retail Sales by Type of Business, 2007 and 2017

NAICS code	Store type	Total sales 2007 ($, millions)	Total sales 2017 ($, millions)	Change 2007–2017 (%)	Per capita sales[a] 2007 ($)	Per capita sales[a] 2017 ($)	Change 2007–2017 (%)
	Total retail sales, excluding motor vehicle and parts dealers	3,085,043	3,872,477	25.5	10,241	11,910	16.3
	GAFO[b]	1,143,426	1,269,077	11.0	3,796	3,903	2.8
	GAFO share of sales (%)	37.1%	32.8%	−11.6			
442	Furniture and home furnishings stores	111,144	113,783	2.4	369	350	−5.2
4421	Furniture stores	59,288	59,898	1.0	197	184	−6.4
4422	Home furnishings stores	51,856	53,885	3.9	172	166	−3.7
443	Electronics and appliance stores	110,341	99,401	−9.9	366	306	−16.5
443141	Household appliance stores	17,799	16,506	−7.3	59	51	−14.1
443142	Electronics stores	92,542	82,895	−10.4	307	255	−17.0
448	Clothing and clothing accessories stores	221,205	258,472	16.8	734	795	8.3
4481	Clothing stores	161,622	189,056	17.0	537	581	8.4
4482	Shoe stores	26,811	35,498	32.4	89	109	22.7
4483	Jewelry, luggage, and leather stores	32,772	33,918	3.5	109	104	−4.1
451	Sporting goods, hobby, musical instrument, and book stores	80,909	84,264	4.1	269	259	−3.5
4511	Sporting goods, hobby, and musical instrument stores	62,457	72,797	16.6	207	224	8.0
45111	Sporting goods stores	35,804	45,193	26.2	119	139	16.9
45112	Hobby, toy and game stores	16,344	18,952	16.0	54	58	7.4
45121	Book stores and news dealers	18,452	11,467	−37.9	61	35	−42.4
452	General merchandise stores	578,582	683,854	18.2	1,921	2,103	9.5
452111	Department stores[c]	76,887	50,265	−34.6	255	155	−39.4
452112	Discount department stores	132,505	94,402	−28.8	440	290	−34.0
45291	Warehouse clubs and supercenters	324,963	461,712	42.1	1,079	1,420	31.6
45299	All other general merchandise stores	44,227	77,475	75.2	147	238	62.3
453	Miscellaneous store retailers[d]	116,418	125,500	7.8	386	386	−0.1
444	Building materials, garden equipment and supplies dealers[e]	320,854	365,651	14.0	1,065	1,125	5.6
445	Food and beverage stores	547,837	725,915	32.5	1,819	2,233	22.8
4451	Grocery stores[f]	491,360	648,504	32.0	1,631	1,994	22.3
	Specialty food stores	18,349	22,228	21.1	61	68	12.2
	Beer, wine, and liquor stores	38,128	55,183	44.7	127	170	34.1
446	Health and personal care stores[g]	237,164	333,219	40.5	787	1,025	30.2
447	Gasoline stations	451,822	452,856	0.2	1,500	1,393	−7.1
454	Nonstore retailers (exc. fuel dealers)	271,331	629,562	132.0	901	1,936	115.0
4541	Electronic shopping and mail order sales	223,681	552,214	146.9	743	1,698	128.7

Source: U.S. Census Bureau, "Estimated Annual Sales of U.S. Retail Firms by Kind of Business," 1992–2017.

a. Based on Census Bureau midyear population estimates of 304.094 million in 2007 and 325.147 million in 2017.

b. Includes NAICS codes 442, 443, 448, 451, 452, and 4532.

c. Includes leased departments.

d. Includes florists, office supply stores, pet shops, gift shops, stationery, gift stores, and used merchandise.

e. Includes home centers, paint and wallpaper stores, hardware stores.

f. Includes supermarkets and convenience stores.

g. Includes drugstores, cosmetic stores, optical goods.

Top 10 Online Retailers: Estimated Share of Total U.S. E-Commerce Sales, 2018

The following figure illustrates the extent to which Amazon dominates online retail sales in the United States. None of the other companies in the top 10, either pure-play or omni-channel, captures more than 10 percent of e-commerce activity.

1	Amazon[a]	49.1%
2	eBay	6.6%
3	Apple	3.9%
4	Walmart	3.7%
5	Home Depot	1.5%
6	Best Buy	1.3%
7	Qurate Retail Group[b]	1.2%
8	Macy's	1.2%
9	Costco	1.1%
10	Wayfair	1.1%

Source: eMarketer Retail, www.emarketer.com.

a. Includes both Amazon Marketplace (third-party vendors selling through Amazon) and Amazon direct sales.

b. E-commerce sales for QVC, HSN, and Zulily.

Figure 5-2

Trends in E-Commerce: Nonstore vs. Omni-Channel Sales
Share of Sales Fulfilled Directly from Stores and Warehouses, 2011–2016

	Nonstore retailers (%)	Omni-channel retailers (%)[a]
2011	50.9	49.1
2012	51.4	48.6
2013	52.4	47.6
2014	53.1	46.9
2015	55.6	44.4
2016	58.1	41.9

Sources: John Connolly, "New Census Dataset Breaks Out Warehouse-Fulfilled Online Sales," Industry Insights, ICSC, April 13, 2018. Based on data from the U.S. Census Bureau.

a. Retailers who sell in stores and online; figure includes orders fulfilled from in-store inventory.

retail trade report. However, the quarterly report does not provide sales for omni-channel retailers by NAICS code. In the third quarter of 2018, e-commerce was estimated at $130.9 billion, accounting for 9.8 percent of total retail sales (adjusted for seasonal variations). This figure compares with 9.0 percent just a year earlier.[8] Clearly, online shopping is growing much faster than are retail sales overall. Also, Census Bureau estimates of e-commerce do not include online orders fulfilled from in-store inventory maintained by omni-channel retailers. Thus, at the end of 2018, e-commerce likely captured well over 10 percent of total retail sales.

Research conducted by the ICSC gives a clearer picture of online sales from all sources. ICSC estimated that, in 2016, Amazon accounted for 24 percent of e-commerce sales ($79.8 billion) fulfilled through warehouses, while other pure-play online retailers sold $146.3 billion (44 percent). Omni-channel vendors accounted for $106.2 billion (32 percent). When orders shipped from stores were included (a better measure of how brick-and-mortar stores are capturing online commerce), omni-channel retailers accounted for 42 percent of online sales. However, the share of online sales generated by omni-channel retailers has dropped as more pure-play online vendors enter the business.[9] (See figure 5-2.)

Amazon's capture of online sales continues to grow. According to eMarketer.com, Amazon's share of online sales was 43.5 percent in 2017 and an estimated 49.1 percent in 2018 (as shown in the sidebar); it now accounts for nearly 5 percent of *all* U.S. retail sales. (The differences between the market shares calculated by ICSC and eMarketer.com result from how Amazon's sales from third-party vendors are counted.)

Computers and consumer electronics accounted for more than a quarter of Amazon's retail e-commerce business in 2018.[10] With its acquisition of Whole Foods, Amazon will be moving more aggressively into selling grocery items online, while using Whole Foods locations as pickup points for Amazon's nonfood package deliveries.

Declining sales at department stores cannot be totally blamed on the growth of e-commerce. Although internet sales were reaching—and probably exceeding—10 percent of total retail sales in 2018, department stores were already losing market share in the 1980s as big-box stores captured consumer spending in categories as diverse as pet supplies, sporting goods, consumer electronics, linens, toys, and shoes. Online sales as a share of total retail spending are expected to reach 15 percent by 2022.

Omni-channel retailers can compete with purely online stores such as Amazon—but only if they have easy-to-use software, an extensive merchandise assortment, and stock depth that goes beyond what is available in their stores. Shopper-savvy customer service and secure payment systems are also important. The cost of shipping—and the time needed to get orders to customers—often favors Amazon Prime from the consumer's perspective, but delivery is a big expense for both pure-play and omni-channel stores. Some omni-channel retailers offer free shipping to their credit card holders or frequent shoppers, but they do not deliver the merchandise within a day or two. Improving the delivery experience will be very costly for conventional retailers Despite the difficulties, more retailers are promising next-day or two-day deliveries.

Measuring Store Performance: Sales per Square Foot

Retail leases in shopping centers are based on the number of square feet occupied.[11] In addition, common area charges in malls (for real estate taxes, maintenance, security, utilities, marketing, and special events) are allocated proportionally according to the amount of space in a given store as a proportion of total center size. As a result, store chain management tracks the performance efficiency of individual locations on the basis of sales generated per square foot. Publicly held retailers will provide information on sales performance per square foot or per store; similar information may not be available for privately held chains.

Note that retailers calculate sales per square foot of *selling space*; space used for inventory storage or other back-room needs is not typically counted when determining sales per square foot, although such space is part of the lease. Corporate annual reports often include this metric, but it can be time-consuming for market analysts to assemble these statistics for multiple chains.

Not surprisingly, Apple stores generate the highest sales (close to $6,000 per square foot) because they sell big-ticket items and occupy space in the best super-regional malls and upscale shopping streets. Other strong performers according

Boxes stacked at the Amazon fulfillment center in Whitestown, Indiana. *(Russ Vance/Shutterstock.com)*

to sales per square foot include high-end jewelry store Tiffany and warehouse club Costco. According to the Food Marketing Institute, supermarket sales averaged $618 per square foot in 2016.[12]

Figure 5-3 presents per-square-foot sales data for selected store types, as tabulated by ICSC. Note that it does not break out department stores (or discount department stores) separately. The figure shows the dramatic variation in performance among different types of stores. It also provides information on sales for restaurants, food courts, and other fast-food operations in shopping centers.

Measuring Store Performance: Same-Store Sales

For retail chains, another key measure of store performance is annual growth in "comparable store" or "same store" sales—at locations open at least a year. (New stores, even those that are part of a well-established retail chain, could post higher-than-expected revenue as a result of "grand opening" and other promotions or could experience lower-than-expected performance because the store needed time to build a clientele. This is the rationale for excluding sales from a brand-new location when computing overall chain performance.) Long-term downward movement in same-store sales during a period of overall economic growth can indicate

Figure 5-3
Sales per Square Foot: Selected Store Groups and Categories
July 2017–2018

Category	Per sq ft
Apparel overall	$369
Women's ready-to-wear	$275
Family apparel	$423
Family shoe stores	$330
Athletic shoe stores	$476
Home furniture and furnishings	$407
Home entertainment & electronics	$2,931
Other GAFO	$663
Food services overall	$615
Fast food	$635
Food court	$1,031
Restaurants	$541
Personal services	$365

Source: International Council of Shopping Centers, Industry Insights: Performance Series, October 23, 2018.

Changes in Store Performance Metrics

With growth in omni-channel retailing, sales and expenses per square foot may no longer be the best way of measuring a chain's productivity across stores or an accurate way to compare the performance of individual locations. Chains that are successful selling their goods both online and in store will instead look at their overall bottom line. Brick-and-mortar locations will be reviewed based not only on sales but also on whether or not customers are using in-store pickup and return options for their online purchases, make repeat purchases, and give positive feedback on the overall shopping experience.

problems with the chain's appeal to customers or an inability to compete with online offerings. Declining sales productivity can also show that the chain expanded too fast (with new stores drawing sales from established locations).

Publicly held store chains report same-store sales on both a quarterly and an annual basis. These statistics are widely cited by stock analysts and retail market observers as an indicator of how consumers view stores. For example, off-price retailer TJX Companies (parent of HomeGoods, Homesense, Marshalls, Sierra Trading Post, and T.J. Maxx) reported 23 consecutive years of comparable-store sales growth as of 2018. In fourth quarter 2018, same-store sales grew 6 percent overall. In March 2019, news reports stated that Target's same-store sales for 2018 were up by 15 percent over 2017, a very strong performance, attributed in part to its capture of sales formerly generated by the now-closed Toys "R" Us and Babies "R" Us chains.

As with the sales-per-square-foot metric, no single source of information exists on trends in same-store sales for all chains, and even less information is available for privately owned stores. Tracking changes in same-store sales over time may be less important in an era when online purchases account for an ever-increasing share of sales.

Store Closings and Store Openings

News media reports highlight store closings. These announcements can reflect an ongoing process stretching over multiple years (as with Sears and Kmart), result from chain mergers and acquisitions (Walgreens/Rite Aid), or occur quickly after bankruptcies and liquidation of entire chains (Bon Ton department store brands, Sports Authority, Toys "R" Us and Babies "R" Us, Gymboree, A&P supermarkets).

Coresight Research reported more than 8,000 store closings in 2017 and 5,524 in 2018. Apparel stores constituted the majority of reported closings. As of the end of March 2019, Coresight counted 5,399 planned store closings and 2,396 openings for the year.[13] This finding suggests that closings are outpacing 2018 levels. Chains with plans to shutter more than two dozen locations each nationwide include Abercrombie & Fitch, Chico's, Family Dollar, Footlocker, Sears, Shopko, and Stage Stores. Not all of these stores will close in 2019; some may not be shuttered at all. However, Charlotte Russe, Gymboree, Payless Shoe Source, and Things Remembered announced going-out-of-business sales in early 2019. As in previous years, some closures could be attributed to merger activity that made many store locations redundant. Dollar Tree's acquisition of Family Dollar is one example.

Is Same-Store Sales Growth Still a Relevant Metric?

"While it remains to be seen whether retail traffic declines will last forever, most traditional retailers will struggle to grow physical store sales in the face of the significant and inexorable shift to online shopping. With few exceptions, so-called 'omni-channel' retailers are experiencing flat to slightly down brick-and-mortar revenues while their e-commerce business continues to grow 10–20%. The mostly moribund department store sector points to this new reality. While overall revenues are basically going nowhere, online sales now account for over 30% of total revenue at Neiman Marcus, over 20% at Nordstrom and Saks, and some 18% at Macy's (according to eMarketer), with the percentage growing every quarter. . . .

"What we do know, and what's important to grasp and appreciate, is that physical stores are critical drivers of e-commerce success—and vice versa. For most retailers, a brick-and-mortar location sits at the heart of a brand's ecosystem for a given trade area. Any retailer with a decent level of channel integration employs stores to acquire new customers, to serve, buy online, pickup in-store orders (and returns) and to convert shoppers that start their shopping online but need to touch, feel or try on a product before buying. . . . [L]egacy retailers must be careful to avoid closing too many stores or they risk damaging the overall brand, slowing e-commerce growth and accelerating a downward spiral.

"With this understanding, same-store sales performance may still have some utility, but 'same trade area' performance—which accounts for all sales regardless of purchase channel within the influence area of a store— becomes a far more interesting and useful metric . . . without a broader view of how digital commerce and the in-store shopping experience work together, an obsession with same-store sales performance will inevitably lead to some very dumb decisions indeed."

Source: Steve Dennis, "'Same-Store Sales' Is Retail's Increasingly Irrelevant Metric," Forbes online, April 3, 2017, www.forbes.com.

A CVS Pharmacy inside a Target store in Bloomington, Minnesota. *(Jeff Bukowski/ Shutterstock.com)*

An Amazon Go store in San Francisco. *(MariaX/Shutterstock.com)*

Regardless of the reason, frequent announcements of store closings contribute to the perception that traditional shopping habits have irreversibly changed, stores are a dying breed, and, by implication, shopping centers are a bad investment. Yet retail analysts and brokers who buy and sell shopping centers on behalf of investors argue as follows:

■ The number of shuttered stores is less than 1 percent of the total number of establishments tracked by the Census Bureau.

■ High-performing shopping centers are very much a focus of interest by institutional investors; single-tenant net-lease properties and small centers attract capital from private individuals.

■ Value-oriented brands, such as Aldi and Lidl supermarkets and dollar store chains (Dollar Tree, Dollar General, Five Below), are in expansion mode. Dollar stores are bringing in new merchandise lines, especially in fresh and frozen foods.

■ Off-price retailers (Burlington, Marshalls, Ross, T.J. Maxx), are seeking more locations that match their customer profiles. They provide name-brand apparel and household goods at attractive prices, with quick merchandise turnover; because they turn over merchandise quickly, online sales are not their focus. Customers are drawn to the stores by the chance to find something special at a good price; some analysts refer to this as "treasure hunting."

■ Innovative reuse of vacated retail space (as community facilities, entertainment spaces, restaurants) is bringing new energy to shopping centers.

Clicks to Bricks

Retailers that started in catalog sales (by phone or mail order) or sold merchandise only online are now looking for brick-and-mortar locations to showcase their goods. They might start with "pop-up" or temporary locations in malls or open-air centers and then move to permanent locations. Test marketing often takes place in high-density locations (Manhattan or San Francisco). Examples of digital-native brands now taking store space include Bonobos (menswear), Casper (mattresses), Peloton (exercise equipment), Untuckit (shirts), Warby Parker (eyewear), Rent the Runway (designer clothing rentals), and various shoe brands. They view retail storefronts as showrooms; often, shoppers can see, feel, and try the merchandise and then order online from the store. This approach can increase sales not only for apparel but also for furniture.

As indicated earlier, Amazon ventured into brick-and-mortar commerce through its acquisition of the Whole Foods supermarket chain, which surprised many industry observers. Amazon is trying other conventional retail ventures that can enhance its primary business:

■ Amazon can test whether it can grow its online businesses using the "buy online and pick up in store" concept at its Whole Foods locations.

■ It is also said to be considering other supermarket retailing ventures with more affordable prices than Whole Foods.

■ A new prototype is Amazon Go, a fully automated convenience store that uses cameras and artificial intelligence to track shopper purchases and automatically bill their Amazon accounts. Industry insiders say that this concept could have 3,000 locations by 2021.[14]

Vacant in-line storefronts in a well-maintained regional mall.
(Deborah L. Brett & Associates)

Reuse of Vacated Store Spaces

More than 800 Toys "R" Us and Babies "R" Us spaces became available in 2018, ranging in size from 20,000 to 65,000 square feet (averaging 40,000) in freestanding locations, power centers, or large community centers. Interest in these spaces came from supermarkets, discount retailers (Big Lots and Ollie's), off-price stores (TJX formats—HomeGoods, Homesense, Marshalls, T.J. Maxx—or Ross and Burlington), and furniture stores. However, many locations have yet to find new tenants or buyers.

New uses for vacated store space have included the following:

- Entertainment venues, ranging from children's indoor play spaces to bowling alleys to mini-golf to axe throwing.

- Medical facilities—cancer treatment centers, dialysis centers, urgent care clinics.

- Coworking office space. Brokerage firm JLL says that the amount of coworking space at retail centers will increase 25 percent per year through 2023. Mall owners are forming partnerships with coworking operators, such as Industrious and Serendipity Labs. (See chapter 6 for an in-depth discussion of the coworking trend.)

- Retail incubator space for new entrepreneurs to showcase their goods.

- Fulfillment centers for "last mile" e-commerce deliveries (see chapter 7 on the need for large spaces in densely populated areas). In some locations, the need to rezone properties from commercial to industrial use could delay these conversions.

- Seasonal temporary stores for Halloween or Christmas.

- Churches.

- Call centers.

- Amazon has opened a small number of bookstores (books were its first online success story). These stores stock relatively few titles but could generate impulse purchases. Customers can order additional choices online while in the store. They can also buy Kindles and other Amazon tech.

- Pop-up (temporary) Amazon locations were tried in malls and in Kohl's stores, but they will be discontinued.

- Amazon 4-star stores focus on best-selling, highly rated items from its huge online assortment.

- All of Amazon's brick-and-mortar spaces offer an opportunity to sign up more Prime members, building customer loyalty.

Despite store closings, size shrinkage, and nonretail reuse of vacated space, most industry experts agree that the United States is still "overstored"—especially when compared with Canada and western European countries. In shopping centers alone, the United States has an estimated 23 square feet of space per capita—and this number does not count freestanding store space. Canada has approximately 17 square feet of space in centers for every resident. In Europe, less than five square feet per capita is the norm.

Store Size Shrinkage

Rather than close stores with subpar performance, some chains are downsizing these locations (by walling off entire sections or floors) or changing their merchandise mix. For example, a 200,000-square-foot Macy's store in Stamford, Connecticut, reduced its footprint by about 8 percent after closing off part of the first floor and moving the departments once housed there to the third floor. Common checkout stations on each floor replaced scattered customer service locations, and the number of on-floor staff members was reduced.[15] At other locations, Macy's installed its Backstage store-within-a-store, which provides a mix of discounted goods from various departments designed to compete with off-price chains. Macy's also converted several upper floors in its downtown Chicago flagship to office space.

In some cases, new tenants take over the excess space. A central New Jersey Petco took over more than 15,000 square feet from a large Staples location, gaining entry into an area that lacked a large pet store.

Types of Shopping Centers

The ICSC describes 10 types of shopping centers, as summarized in figure 5-4. Most, but not all, shopping centers have a mix of *anchor tenants*[16]—and *in-line* or *mall shop* space (small tenants, usually a mix of national, regional, and local stores and service businesses). A shopping center's classification is based on its tenant mix and the size of the trade area it serves, not solely on the square footage of the structure.

Shopping center types include the following:

Super-regional malls have at least 800,000 square feet of GLA, three or more department stores, and a range of entertainment and food offerings. Centers with more than 1.5 million square feet are not unusual. Each department store has at least 75,000 square feet of space. Many super regionals need more than 100 acres of land to accommodate parking demand; anchor tenants may want even more parking than is required by local authorities. In densely populated areas, trade areas for super-regional malls can be as small as five miles, but in typical suburban locations, they can extend eight to 10 miles or more, depending on density and proximity to other large centers.

Regional malls also focus on general merchandise, apparel, furniture, and home furnishings. They are usually enclosed, with two or three department stores. They may have movie theaters and a food court or restaurants. Sizes range from 400,000 to 800,000 square feet. Anchor stores are usually at least 50,000 square feet each, except in rural centers where they may be smaller. Regional malls typically serve a trade area of five to eight miles, depending on population density, but trade areas in smaller cities can cover a much larger area.

Community centers are open-air single-story buildings typically laid out in "L" or "U"-shaped configuration. They do not include traditional full-line department stores; rather, other general merchandise stores (discount department stores such as Walmart, Target, and Kohl's; Stage Stores [Bealls, Peebles, and Goody's]; and Stein Mart) are typical anchors. Community centers often contain large supermarkets (say 45,000 square feet or more) and (depending on size) may also include a home improvement center (Home Depot, Lowe's, or a local chain) and an off-price family apparel, home decor, or housewares chain. Community centers serve a smaller trade area than does an enclosed regional or super-regional mall, generally a three- to six-mile area depending on household density.

A typical community center contains smaller retailers and service businesses located in storefronts between the anchor stores and on freestanding "pad" sites in the parking lot. Small tenants might be dollar stores, nail or hair salons, a florist, and specialty foods (bakeries, sandwich shops, ice cream or yogurt shops). In communities with few office buildings, the mix of in-line tenants often includes attorneys, accountants, financial services, real estate agents, and medical or dental offices. Fast-food franchises, banks, and drugstores with drive-up windows; quick-casual restaurants; card and gift shops; small offices; and larger restaurants with table service will be found on pad sites. Community centers usually range from 100,000 to 400,000 square feet and can occupy 30 or more acres.

Neighborhood centers sell convenience goods (food, drugs, toiletries, cards and gifts, flowers) and provide personal services (dry cleaning, banking, package shipping, hair and nail care) that meet the day-to-day living needs of the immediate area. They typically serve a trade area with a radius of two to three miles or less. Take-out food and small

Enclosed Malls Face Challenges

Changes in retailing and consumer shopping preferences have affected super-regional and regional malls more than neighborhood and community-scale centers. High-performing super-regional malls in upper-middle to upscale trade areas continue to do well; they are able to find new concepts to fill space if vacancies occur. If they lose a department store, they can split the space among smaller users—off-price retailers, small supermarkets, specialty food stores, restaurants, and nonstore uses—and renovate the interiors. Some former department stores have been demolished and replaced by a mix of uses: apartments, hotels, movie theaters, or civic space. Their sea of surface parking can be used more intensively.

Regional malls with only two anchors have more trouble filling the space formerly occupied by their third anchor, especially in trade areas with modest household incomes. Entire malls have shuttered over the past 10 years, without serious attempts at renovation and retenanting. Some sit as eyesores, while others have been demolished for other uses.

sit-down restaurants are also common in neighborhood centers, which are typically less than 100,000 square feet in size. Usually anchored by a supermarket, larger neighborhood centers serve a two- to three-mile radius and need 10 to 15 acres of land, including parking.

A *convenience or strip center*, with less than 30,000 square feet, serves the same purposes but does not have a full-size grocery store. Instead, it will be anchored by a mini-mart or convenience store (under 3,000 square feet) with a limited assortment of snacks, beverages, prepared foods, canned goods, deli items, refrigerated and frozen foods, and cleaning and laundry products. As is discussed later in this chapter, these stores are facing stiff competition from dollar stores (Dollar General, Dollar Tree, Family Dollar) that are expanding their selection of refrigerated, frozen, and prepared foods and that plan to sell more fresh produce than in the past. Many larger convenience centers now have their own gasoline service stations.

Power centers, developed in large numbers between the mid-1980s and early 2000s, are also known as super community centers. They range in size from 250,000 to (in rare instances) more than 1 million square feet. Power centers contain at least four big-box stores (at one time called "category killers"), each having a minimum of 20,000 square feet of space. Such stores offer in-depth merchandise selection at attractive prices. Less than 20 percent of power center space consists of small stores; some have no in-line space at all. These open-air centers tend to be in locations near large malls; they draw shoppers from a radius of five miles or more.

In recent years, power centers have experienced increased vacancies that they struggle to fill. In most instances, the problems have little to do with the centers or their locations. Rather, some tenant chains expanded too quickly or were

Figure 5-4
U.S. Shopping Center Classification and Typical Characteristics

Type of shopping center	Description	Typical GLA range (sq ft)	Number of anchors	Anchor % of GLA	Types of anchors	Size of trade area (miles)
General-purpose centers						
Super-regional mall	Similar in concept to regional malls, but offering more variety and assortment.	800,000+	3+	50–70	Full-line department store, mass merchant, discount department store, fashion apparel store, mini-anchor, cineplex or other large-scale entertainment attraction, or food/beverage service cluster	5–25
Regional mall	General merchandise or fashion-oriented offerings. Typically enclosed, with inward-facing stores connected by a common walkway. Parking surrounds the outside perimeter.	400,000–800,000	2+	50–70	Same as a super-regional mall	5–15
Community center/large neighborhood center	General merchandise or convenience-oriented offerings. Offers a wider range of apparel and other soft goods than neighborhood centers. The center is usually configured in a straight line as a strip, or it may be laid out in an "L" or "U" shape, depending on the site and design.	125,000–400,000	2+	40–60	Discount department store, supermarket, drug store, large specialty store	3–6
Neighborhood center	Convenience-oriented.	30,000–125,000	1+	30–50	Supermarket	3
Strip/convenience	Attached row of stores or service outlets managed as a coherent retail entity, with on-site parking (usually located in front of the stores). Open-air canopies may connect the storefronts, but there are no enclosed walkways linking the stores. A strip center may be configured in a straight line or have an "L" or "U" shape.	<30,000	Anchorless or a small convenience store anchor		Convenience store/mini-mart	<1

Source: International Council of Shopping Centers, www.icsc.org.

Note: NA = not applicable.

Figure 5-4 *(continued)*

Type of shopping center	Description	Typical GLA range (sq ft)	Number of anchors	Anchor % of GLA	Types of anchors	Size of trade area (miles)
Special-purpose center						
Power center	Category-dominant anchors, including discount department stores, off-price stores, and wholesale clubs, with only a few small tenants.	250,000–600,000	3+	70–90	"Category killers" such as home improvement stores, discount department stores, warehouse clubs, and off-price stores	5–10
Lifestyle center	Upscale national chain specialty stores with dining and entertainment in an outdoor setting.	150,000–500,000	0–2	0–50	Large-format upscale specialty stores	8–12
Factory outlet	Manufacturers' and retailers' outlet stores selling brand-name goods at a discount.	50,000–400,000	NA	NA	Manufacturers' and retailers' outlet stores	25–75
Theme/festival	Leisure, tourist, retail, and service-oriented offerings with entertainment as a unifying theme. Often in urban areas, may be adapted from older/historic buildings and part of a mixed-use project.	80,000–250,000	NA	NA	Restaurants, entertainment	25–75
Limited-purpose property						
Airport retail	Concentration of retail stores within a commercial airport.	75,000–300,000	NA	NA	No anchors; retail includes specialty stores and restaurants	NA

overburdened by debt; others were left with unneeded space in the same trade area after two chains selling the same merchandise merged (for example, Office Max and Office Depot). In 2019, few expanding store types need 20,000 to 30,000 square feet, and they have many possible locations to consider.

Specialized centers include *factory outlets*—collections of discount stores directly operated by brand manufacturers or store chains. They sell out-of-season items and production overruns. Many apparel manufacturers produce goods especially for their outlet stores. Most outlet centers are single-story, open-air strips, but a few occupy renovated older buildings. They usually have less than 400,000 square feet and no traditional anchor tenants. Most tenants occupy less than 10,000 square feet. An outlet mall may have a food court or a collection of restaurants in its tenant roster.

Originally, factory outlets were limited to tourist destinations and busy highway locations far from regional malls. (Full-line department stores prohibited their manufacturers from selling directly to consumers in the same trade area.) Today, outlet centers can also be found at the fringe of large metropolitan areas and in big cities. Nearly 400 operate in the United States. In the aggregate, they have few vacancies. However, not many new outlet centers are being built: only one opened in 2018 (15 miles north of downtown Denver), with another scheduled for 2019 (at the Staten Island waterfront in New York City).

Factory outlet stores serve a very large trade area. Shoppers drive from metropolitan areas an hour or more away; as a result, they stay longer than they would at a super-regional mall. Other patrons are visiting nearby tourist attractions (amusement parks or theme parks, historic sites) or passing through on the way to more distant destinations.

Hybrid outlet centers, combining large discount and off-price anchors with smaller factory outlet stores, were popular formats in the 1990s and early 2000s. Pioneered by the Mills Corporation, these centers (now part of Simon Property Group) were as large as 2 million square feet, but

A suburban main street shopping district in Tarrytown, New York. *(quiggyt4/Shutterstock.com)*

Three new stores now use part of a 200,000-square-foot Macy's store in Burlington County, New Jersey, vacated in 2017. The stores open directly to the parking lot; only the store on the far left has an exit into the mall. *(Deborah L. Brett & Associates)*

most were much smaller. The better hybrid malls (generally enclosed) draw shoppers from an hour away, but the primary trade area is typically within a half-hour's drive. These centers often combine stores with sports or entertainment spaces (go-karts, golf simulators, virtual ski slopes, etc.). Because of their sheer size, few new centers of this type are being built today.

Lifestyle centers are tenanted with the upscale-branded apparel, housewares, and gift shops often found in regional malls, as well as restaurants, specialty food stores, and entertainment (movie theaters, music venues, and community gathering spaces). They do not have a traditional department store anchor. Lifestyle centers appeal to time-strapped shoppers who do not want to walk through a large mall to reach one or two stores and to those who prefer an outdoor environment. Many of the centers are designed to mimic a pedestrian-oriented neighborhood business district, which is also appealing. They are often part of mixed-use developments.

According to the ICSC, lifestyle centers range in size from 150,000 to 500,000 square feet and need at least 10 acres of land. Their primary trade areas can stretch for eight to 12 miles; secondary trade area patronage can be significant if no similarly tenanted centers are within 20 miles or more.

Town centers are open-air, walkable neighborhood business districts, suburban downtowns, and small-town retail cores that contain many of the store types found in lifestyle centers. They may also include pharmacies, dry cleaners, florists, banks, post offices, and other civic space. In cities that have extensive subway systems or suburban commuter-rail lines, town centers can be found near transit stations. Professional offices (medical practices, attorneys, insurance agents, stock brokers, real estate agents) may occupy a significant share of the ground-floor space.[17] In some cases, upper-level office or residential uses complement the retail space.

In the past, clear tenant distinctions existed among shopping center types. Today, the definitions are blurring.

- Urban street retail—once the province of independent entrepreneurs or small regional or local chains—now draws national retailers that used to locate only inside regional malls.

- As stores go out of business or vacate spaces they no longer need in enclosed malls, new tenant types have taken some of the surplus square footage. Big-box stores that once located only in power centers are leasing empty department store space. So are off-price retailers. An empty Sears, JCPenney, or Macy's is big enough to house three or four such stores along with restaurants and service businesses. The photograph above shows how a portion of a former Macy's store was partially redeveloped with three expanding store chains.

- Some supermarkets see an advantage in a regional mall location, allowing them to provide a one-stop-shopping environment for time-pressed consumers. An empty department store space will have lots of parking already in place.

- Even high-performing super-regional malls are changing their physical layouts to accommodate new tenant types. Some malls have added open-air lifestyle tenants at their perimeters, thus bringing in new apparel shops, home furnishings, restaurants, and recreation activities not found inside.

Stand-alone retail (in individual buildings or streetfront business districts) provides competition for shopping centers. Well-capitalized retail chains are often able to build their own stores—and attract customers—without being in a shopping center.[18]

Shopping Center Space Trends

Shopping center space continues to grow, as measured by number of centers and total GLA. That being said, the pace of new construction is far below that seen decades ago. Cushman & Wakefield reports that 15.5 million square feet of retail space was under construction in the first quarter of 2018, compared with 22.0 million during the same period a year earlier.

Figure 5-5 shows that the vast majority of centers and the bulk of square footage are found in smaller properties—convenience centers, small strips, and neighborhood centers. These property types, which serve primarily local consumers, accounted for nearly nine of every 10 shopping centers but, because of their small average size, only 43 percent of square footage. There were 590 super-regional malls at the end of 2018 and 602 regional malls. Together, these two shopping center types accounted for only 1 percent of all centers and just under 15 percent of total space in retail centers.

Store Mix in Shopping Centers

In a regional or super-regional mall, the full-line department stores are referred to as the *anchors*. Anchors might also be entertainment centers (multiplex movie theater, indoor recreation center) or big-box specialty stores. As indicated previously, most enclosed malls (especially in large metro areas) have three or more anchor tenants. The anchor chain stores typically design and build their own buildings, executing a ground lease with the mall owner. Some anchor stores own their land and a portion of the parking lot. The arrangements can be different for each anchor in a given center.[19] As a result, understanding whether reported mall sales include the department stores and/or other anchors is important. Some mall managers report sales for an entire center; others report sales only for space owned by the mall, thereby covering only in-line or mall shops.

Community centers also have anchor stores. Typical anchors are discount department stores, home improvement centers, off-price stores, crafts and sporting goods stores, and drugstores. These centers may also have a supermarket anchor, depending on the proximity of neighborhood centers with popular grocery chains.

Anchor tenants determine the competitive strengths of any shopping center. Without firm commitments from popular chain stores that have a proven track record of success, a developer may not be able to find debt financing or attract equity investors. When contemplating construction of a new center, developers will try to attract the dominant retailer in a particular category—for example, the top-volume supermarket chain—if it is not already represented in the trade area. If the best performers already have stores nearby, leaving only less-successful operators available for the proposed site, the proposed center's chances of success will be evaluated differently. Historically, centers lacking the top retailers in their categories experienced problems if new competition entered the market.

Figure 5-5

U.S. Shopping Center Space by Type of Center
2018

Center type	Number of centers	Share of all centers (%)	Aggregate GLA, sq ft (millions)	Share of total center GLA (%)
Super-regional malls	590	0.5	758.6	9.9
Regional malls	602	0.5	347.1	4.5
Subtotal, malls	1,192	1.0	1,105.7	14.5
Community centers	9,809	8.4	1,934.9	25.3
Neighborhood centers	32,725	28.2	2,352.4	30.8
Strip/convenience centers	68,933	59.4	921.3	12.1
Power centers	2,288	2.0	1,011.6	13.2
Lifestyle centers	541	0.5	182.5	2.4
Outlet/value centers	394	0.3	92.4	1.2
Theme/festival centers	150	0.1	21.8	0.3
Subtotal, open-air centers	114,840	98.9	6,516.9	85.3
Airport retail	77	0.1	16.3	0.2
Total, centers (including airport)	**116,109**	**100.0**	**7,638.9**	**100.0**
Freestanding retail			10,664.9	
Total retail space			**18,303.8**	
Shopping center space as a percentage of total retail space				**41.7**

Source: International Council of Shopping Centers, www.icsc.org; based on data from CoStar.
Note: Figures as of the fourth quarter.

An in-store package pickup locker. Customers enter a code provided when an online purchase is confirmed. Packages can be collected after store hours. *(Deborah L. Brett & Associates)*

Figure 5-6
U.S. Shopping Center Performance Measures

	2016	2017	2018[a]
All centers			
Base rent (per sq ft)	$19.14	$19.54	$19.94
Change from previous year (%)	4.3	2.1	2.0
Occupancy rate (%)[a]	93.2	93.1	92.8
Open-air centers[b]			
Base rent (per sq ft)	$17.42	$17.70	$18.04
Change from previous year (%)	5.4	1.5	1.9
Occupancy rate (%)[a]	93.2	93.1	93.1
Enclosed malls			
Base rent (per sq ft)	$27.30	$28.37	$29.07
Change from previous year (%)	1.3	3.9	2.5
Occupancy rate (%)[a]	93.6	93.5	91.0

Source: ICSC, Industry Insights: Performance Series, November 13, 2018, and February 20, 2019; National Council of Real Estate Investment Fiduciaries.

a. At year end.

b. Includes neighborhood, community, and power centers.

National and regional commercial brokerages may have exclusive representation agreements with key potential anchors or in-line store chains. Therefore, shopping center developers need to establish relationships with these firms as well as the real estate decision-makers at the store chains.

A combination of operating economics and shifting consumer preferences dictates a shopping center's desired tenant mix. In newer super-regional malls (or those that have been recently renovated), anchor tenants account for 50 to 70 percent of total GLA. Although in-line mall shops pay higher rents per square foot than anchor tenants do, leasing agents may have increasing difficulty finding creditworthy tenants for smaller store spaces. It is becoming more common to find discount department stores or big-box formats taking over vacant anchor space in enclosed malls or (as discussed previously) to see these spaces divided up among multiple stores or civic uses.

Stores that sell clothing for teens and preteens dominate the mix of apparel stores in many enclosed malls. Increasingly, older women shop for clothing online, at department stores, and at specialty shops in pedestrian-oriented areas or open-air lifestyle centers. Among non-GAFO tenant types, food service and entertainment—food courts, restaurants, coffee bars, and multiscreen movie theaters—have become more important in enclosed malls.

Drugstore chains (CVS, Walgreens) changed their location preferences more than a decade ago; they moved out of enclosed malls and in-line spaces in community shopping centers in favor of freestanding pad sites that allow drive-up prescription dropoff and pickup windows. These stores, typically 13,000 to 15,000 square feet, have expanded their nonprescription personal care merchandise and food items, while also focusing more on overall wellness. With CVS's recent merger with Aetna, its Minute Clinics will expand health care services with the goal of pulling more visitors to CVS stores. This merger will help maintain CVS's position at a time when Amazon is likely to branch out into selling prescription medications online. Walgreens has opened cafés in some of its downtown stores.

Shopping Center Performance Measures

Shopping centers—not just individual stores—look at trends in total sales, sales by store type, overall sales per square foot, and occupancy over time to determine how a property is performing and where areas of weakness might be. For example, women's apparel stores might be losing sales, while athletic footwear is getting stronger. A wing in an enclosed mall might be experiencing problems after a popular store closed. Management keeps a careful watch on sales performance lest it be caught unaware when a store closing is announced. Note that because department store anchors in enclosed malls often own their stores, vacant department store space would not be counted in reported mall vacancy rates.

Figure 5-6 shows that base rent in enclosed malls is much higher than in open-air centers. Although occupancy in open-air centers has been stable over the past three years, mall occupancy showed slippage between 2017 and 2018. Base rents in both types of properties have increased but at a slower rate than in previous years.

Not included in base rent trends are pass-through expenses paid by retail tenants with triple-net leases—a share of common area maintenance costs, utilities, and property taxes based on the amount of space leased. These additional costs are billed to tenants along with the base rent and can be a very significant expense for stores. When a mall or community center has significant vacancies, the terms of the lease may permit management to reallocate common costs to the remaining tenants depending on the precise terms of their leases. This practice could lead to more vacancy as marginally performing stores are hit with even higher costs.

Tenants in any center will look at the share of sales spent on occupancy costs. A general rule is that rent and other charges should require no more than 15 percent of sales. If extra charges are higher than in competitive locations, the tenant will want a lower base rent. This situation helps explain why enclosed malls, with their higher base rents and occupancy costs, can be at a competitive disadvantage when compared with open-air properties for tenants that do not need to be indoors.

Staying Competitive

To survive—and thrive—in an increasingly risky environment, stores and shopping centers are focusing on ways to draw shoppers away from their phones and laptops even if they enjoy shopping online:

- Stores are encouraging customers to buy online but pick up their shipments at a store (BOPUS [buy online, pick up in store], or "click and collect" in the parlance of retailers). This strategy allows customers to get their goods faster. Stores also benefit by lowering last-mile delivery costs; multiple shoppers can collect their purchases at the same location. As an extra bonus for the retailer, the customer might look at other items while in the store.

- Drawing online shoppers into stores for returns or exchanges can also boost in-store sales, while saving customers the cost of return shipping.

- Customer loyalty programs—discounts, coupons, points programs, emails, or text messages announcing special in-store flash sales—also bring longtime patrons inside stores.

- Working with partners, as Best Buy has done with cellphone service providers and computer companies, allows these suppliers to showcase their goods and services and answer questions from customers. Best Buy's Geek Squad tech support services are also a draw.

- In-store tech features not available to online customers can improve the shopping experience. Smartphone apps can help shoppers find items in stores. Printed shelf labels with prices are being replaced with digital screens that show not only prices but product information.

- Omni-channel retailers need to be vigilant in maintaining in-store inventory. Lack of sufficient stock and a full range of sizes and colors pushes store customers out the door. Many retailers have online order kiosks in their stores to keep customers from going elsewhere.

- Mall management companies are sponsoring more special events—not just photos with Santa, but all year round. The focus might be gardening in the spring, harvest and fall holidays in September and October, and beach items and water sports in the summer. Malls also host cooking classes or cake decorating; these events can be done in cooperation with stores that sell housewares. Stores selling fitness apparel offer yoga classes.

- Vacant storefronts can be used for wellness programs and exercise classes. Converting surplus store space to medical or dental offices or lab space can bring patients to the center but will not compete with existing tenants.

- Chains are developing small-format stores suitable for dense urban locations. They can take space on the ground floor of apartment or office buildings. The merchandise mix might be food-oriented (grab and go) or highlight small and lightweight items that do not have to be carried in a car. Small stores are also popular near college campuses.

- Small-format stores are also taking infill locations; these more compact footprints are expected to appeal to time-pressed shoppers who prefer to patronize stores close to home. Examples include a scaled-down A.C. Moore Essentials craft store with 12,000 square feet, compared to their full-size stores having as much as 20,000 square feet, and small-format Target stores under 50,000 square feet (compared to their typical 145,000-square-foot full-sized spaces).

A small-format Kohl's store in a community shopping center.
(Deborah L. Brett & Associates)

Revival Food Hall in downtown Chicago. *(Valerie S. Kretchmer Associates Inc.)*

Single-Tenant Net-Lease Retail Spaces

Retail real estate investors that do not want to be involved with the day-to-day operations of shopping centers are drawn to buying or building single-tenant net-lease properties. Net-lease investments are most commonly used with freestanding stores. They appeal to wealthy individuals and institutional investors alike, although private buyers are still the majority. For new or renovated spaces, building owners can obtain construction loans on the basis of the credit-worthiness of the tenants.

Buying existing net-lease buildings is especially useful to investors who need to do 1031 tax-deferred exchanges to avoid capital gains; under federal tax law, they have limited time to buy and close on a new property after selling a property they already own.[20] Negotiations and closings for single-tenant net-leased buildings can occur more quickly than for a multitenant community or neighborhood center.

Tenants pay the real estate taxes and insurance on the building, as well as all utilities and maintenance costs. Net-lease tenants tend to be well-known, stable operators with less exposure to economic downturns and less risk from e-commerce competition. The advantage for tenant stores or restaurants is that they do not have to borrow funds or otherwise raise capital to do site work and construction for a new store. Convenience stores, dollar stores, freestanding supermarkets, fitness centers, pharmacies, restaurants, fast-food chains, quick-serve eateries, banks, furniture stores, auto parts stores, urgent care centers, and other medical specialties have all used net leases.

Greater Focus on Restaurants

Decades ago, large enclosed malls had food courts, and fast food could also be found at scattered locations inside a mall or on pad sites along the perimeter. Food court tenants were mainly national fast-food franchises, with a few regional or local chains added to the mix. Sit-down restaurants, which have high turnover rates, were also primarily national names. Ownership opted to play it safe with established names and known cuisine.

Shopping centers of all sizes now see restaurants as a way to draw new (or more frequent) patrons, to reuse space in vacated in-line stores or big boxes, and to make parking-lot acreage more productive. Malls, open-air centers, downtowns, and neighborhood business districts have added all types and sizes of restaurants since the 2008 recession. Some focus on locally sourced ingredients (farm to table), others on ethnic cuisine, regional specialties (seafood, southern cooking), craft beer, or comfort food.

"Quick-casual" (also known as "fast-casual") restaurant concepts have proliferated in recent years. Examples include established brands (Five Guys, Panera, Potbelly, Qdoba, Zaxby's) and more recent additions (El Pollo Loco, Habit Burger Grill, Zoe's Kitchen). As is the case at fast-food establishments, patrons at quick-casual eateries order meals at the counter. Paper plates and plasticware are common. However, quick-casual establishments promote fresh ingredients and the ability to customize an order to eat in or take out. Because of their recent successes, new fast-casual concepts are emerging every year. Few quick-casual restaurants have drive-up windows—another contrast with fast food.

Many casual or family restaurant chains (Applebee's, Chili's, Olive Garden, Ruby Tuesday) have been in business for decades, but a smaller number of new chains are joining this category. Patrons order at their tables, and their meals are brought to them. Newer chains specialize in steaks, seafood, or barbecue. Fine-dining establishments are less likely to be part of a chain, but Del Frisco's and Ruth's Chris are exceptions. Chefs are professionally trained, and tables are set with linen and glassware. Fixed-price multicourse meals may be offered. These establishments offer extensive wine lists.

Observers are concerned that greater dependence on restaurants—be they fine dining or fast casual—is risky, because consumer tastes change and restaurant turnover has always been high. Also, the demand for carryout and delivered meals is growing: restaurants need more kitchen space and (possibly) fewer seats. The market analyst should look at the types of eateries that are already represented or lacking in the trade area and the staying power of longtime operators. Using the services of a market analyst who specializes in restaurants can save time and money.

In the past 10 to 15 years, malls have been seeking more unique local fare and ethnically diverse eateries—proprietors that could not be found elsewhere in the trade area. As Cushman and Wakefield pointed out in a 2016 report,[21] property owners are increasingly drawn to food as an anchor. Hence the growth in food halls—which are quite different from old-style mall food courts. Food halls focus on freshly prepared foods featuring locally grown ingredients and local chefs. They are not a new concept; in fact, they combine aspects of traditional farmers markets (with vendors selling produce, poultry, meats, dairy products, and baked goods) with fast-casual dining (order at the counter, carry out or eat in). Long-established examples include Chelsea Market in Manhattan, Pike Place Market in Seattle, Ponce City Market in Atlanta, Reading Terminal Market in Philadelphia, Quincy Market in Boston, and Union Market in Washington, D.C. Food halls can be very successful draws in upper-income trade areas, in locations with tourist activity, and in areas with a large daytime workforce. However, turnover rates for stall operators can be high. Entrepreneurs are creating new training facilities as incubators for food-related businesses and are teaching business skills to potential food hall tenants and food truck operators.

Adding Entertainment

"Experiential retail" covers a broad range of tenant types now taking spaces in shopping centers. Going beyond the multiplex movie theater, malls and open-air centers now house bowling alleys, private party space, laser tag, children's museums, virtual reality games, trampolines, and escape rooms. To attract families, these spaces have to offer activities not available at home at a reasonable cost and provide high-quality food and beverage choices as well.

Fitness tenants (broadly defined) are another way to fill empty space, especially if centers are offering rents more attractive than those found at freestanding locations. The possibilities range from large gyms offering exercise equipment, pools, spas, and group classes to specialized studios (karate, kickboxing, spinning, yoga), shops selling fitness apparel, and physical therapy or massage practices. Aside from exercise, entertainment uses can also include crafts (in designated studio spaces or as special events), exhibits, and musical or theatrical performances. Lifestyle centers are well suited to these diverse attractions.

As with restaurants, using specialists with experience in entertainment retailing will result in a more reliable market analysis and less likelihood of costly mistakes.

Prospects for New Construction

Virtually no new enclosed regional or super-regional malls are underway or in the planning stages. They take too long to plan, get approved, and construct. General economic conditions, as well as the financial stability of key tenants, can change dramatically during a multiyear time frame.[22] And owing to mergers, consolidation, and bankruptcies, there are simply not enough department store chains available to fill anchor spaces in an enclosed mall. A mall developer might or might not be able to attract nontraditional anchors—supermarkets, big-box stores, off-price retailers, or movie theaters—to take large spaces in new enclosed malls, no matter how strong the location. And small in-line tenants can find space in open-air locations at lower costs than in enclosed centers.

A new section of the Ala Moana super-regional mall in Honolulu. (Theodore Trimmer/Shutterstock.com)

New power-center development is focused on metro areas experiencing population growth. Where new power centers are still being built, competition to land the strongest anchors is still keen.

Rather than focus on new construction, owners and managers of enclosed regional and super-regional malls in the United States are renovating their properties to keep them fresh and competitive and looking for successful store chains and new concepts to fill vacant spaces. Increasingly, they subdivide and retenant former department stores with home furnishings, movie theaters, children's play areas, and other store or entertainment uses—often with entrances that are directly accessible from parking lots.

These trends suggest that market analysts who specialize in enclosed malls will be monitoring the performance of existing properties and suggesting how they might be expanded, redesigned, or retenanted. Such studies will be conducted on behalf of property owners and investors, rather than developers. Lenders will be requesting market studies for malls that are experiencing financial problems. New construction will be focused primarily on neighborhood, community, and lifestyle centers, with increasing attention given to retail and entertainment tenants as part of mixed-use projects.

Preparing a Retail Market Study

With the growth of online shopping and the emergence of new tenant types, the retail market study is more complicated than it used to be. However, the key issues that must be addressed remain unchanged:

- A developer who is contemplating construction of a new center, regardless of size or concept, must be sure the market can absorb the increase in retail space that is being proposed. The new center must be able to achieve rents that will be sufficient to cover operating expenses and debt service and still provide an acceptable return on investment.

- The owner of an existing center with vacant space or one that is not showing year-to-year sales growth needs to rethink its merchandise mix, enhance the appearance of the center, and create more "buzz." Changes may be necessary in the mall's advertising strategy and its promotional events as well as its store mix. The changes needed to improve the center's competitive position could range from cosmetic improvements (new flooring, lighting, signage, entranceways) to a total or partial "de-malling."

In a retail market study, the analyst may be asked to come up with a specific list of tenant prospects that make sense for the project, given current store chain requirements (space size, street frontage, population density, access, median household income). The analyst must answer the following questions:

- What tenant types and which successful store chains are not already represented in the market area?

- Which ones are looking to expand in the area?

- Which ones would be appropriate for the proposed center (given the size of the center, its available spaces, and the socioeconomic characteristics of trade area households)?

A good location for one type of retailer may not be a good location for another. For example,

- A community center located on a busy highway is appropriate for a destination-type tenant such as a home improvement store. The store's site location staff will be interested in the center's visibility, its entrance and egress, the ease of vehicular movement, and the availability of space for loading bulky or heavy items.

- An upscale fashion-oriented store wants to be located near other shops that cater to an affluent clientele. It will be attracted to malls in high-income suburbs or to urban business districts near upscale apartments and condominiums and close to attractions that draw international visitors. Upscale retailers are very concerned about a mall's lighting, signage, architecture, layout, and finishes. Valet parking is an attractive amenity.

- A supermarket needs ample parking; because it draws large numbers of frequent shoppers, the ability to get in and out of the parking lot quickly and easily is very important.

- Because many shoppers visit after dark, security is also important. Many older regional malls experience negative publicity because of inadequate security. Some malls are now requiring teenage patrons to be accompanied by adults during evening hours, with security personnel assigned to entrances to check identification.

- Many store chains have preferred cotenants; it will be easier to persuade them to sign a lease if other stores that cater to the same demographic profile have already committed to a proposed center or have been successful at an existing center. The downside of cotenancy provisions in shopping center leases: small tenants can try to get out of their lease commitments when an anchor store shuts its doors.

The experienced retail analyst will be familiar with the expansion plans of national and regional chains and understands what they look for in trade area demographics, which other tenants they like to be near, and what their space requirements are. Several trade publications and directories listed in the webliography provide useful information. Retailers' websites often have pages with information on their store location standards, as suggested in figure 5-7.

Defining the Trade Area

For retail studies, analysts typically refer to "trade areas" rather than "market areas." For a large center, the analyst is likely to identify a primary trade area (from which 50 to 65 percent of the patronage and sales will be drawn) and a secondary trade area that might account for another 20 to 30 percent. However, these shares can vary. All retail concentrations will draw at least some patronage from people who live outside the area but drive past it on their way to or from work or while on vacation or visiting friends and relatives.

The primary trade area provides the majority of the steady customers necessary to support a retail center or district. Although figure 5-4 suggests typical sizes (in miles) for trade areas covered by different types of centers, no uniform standard exists for defining their size or shape. In general, retail trade areas are limited by road, transit, and (in some cases) pedestrian access. Distance, road networks, and travel time help define the boundaries. But ease of travel is not the sole determinant of where consumers will shop. They may drive a considerable distance to patronize a unique mix of stores, reach a retail concentration with many shopping choices, find affordable prices or luxury brands, or simply

Figure 5-7
Examples: Store Location Criteria

Store name and type	Size criteria	Location criteria	Trade area criteria
Aldi (discount grocery)	+/− 17,000-square-foot store; minimum 85 dedicated parking spaces; 2.5-acre pad or in-line	End-cap or in-line space with minimum of 100 feet of frontage; daily traffic count >20,000 vehicles per day	Dense population within 3 miles
Lidl (discount grocery)	Originally sought minimum 4 acres, for 36,000-square-foot stand-alone store; now considering leased spaces with 15,000–25,000 square feet	Site zoned for retail use; daily traffic count >20,000 vehicles per day; high visibility, signalized intersection	Dense population within 3 miles
Family Dollar (dollar store)	8,000–9,100 square feet; 30+ dedicated parking spaces; 35,000-square-foot pad for freestanding stores	Freestanding or in-line in grocery-anchored center	Median household income below $60,000
Longhorn Steakhouse (sit-down restaurant)	5,627 square feet; 1.1- to 2-acre site; 120 parking spaces	Minimum 30,000 average daily traffic count on major frontage	Minimum 125,000 people within 15- to 20-minute drive
CVS (pharmacy)	14,600 square feet; freestanding location; 1.5- to 2-acre site that can accommodate a drive-thru; parking for 60 cars	High visibility, with pylon sign; high traffic, signalized intersection	"Sufficient population" in the trade area
Walgreens (pharmacy)	14,820 square feet; freestanding location; 75,000-square-foot site that can accommodate 70 cars and drive-thru	Signalized intersection of two main streets; will consider central business district locations, outlots (pad sites) in shopping centers, or anchor space in strip centers	Trade area population: 20,000+
Burlington (off-price store)	40,000- to 50,000-square-foot store, with 120 feet of frontage; 4.5 parking spaces per 1,000 square feet	Power centers, strip centers, freestanding or downtown locations; prefer cotenancy with other off-price stores	Trade area population 200,000+; middle income
Wawa (convenience store)	4,000- to 6,000-square-foot building with parking for 50–60 cars; 2 acres	Minimum traffic count of 25,000 vehicles per day; corner location with signalized access and good visibility; outparcel or pad in shopping center; zoning for 24-hour operation and gasoline sales, but will consider special exception, variance, or rezoning	Not specified

Sources: Store websites; broker representative websites.

enjoy an attractive physical environment. A center's visibility and perceived safety can also be factors in determining how a consumer chooses a shopping destination. Competition from similarly tenanted centers with the same mix of stores is certainly a factor as well.

Distance and travel time to competitive retail agglomerations influence the size of the trade area. Retail chains do not want to locate a new store too close to an existing one, lest they find that the new store cannibalizes the older store's sales. Having too many similar stores nearby merely divides up a relatively fixed pool of sales dollars. Yet recommended distances between shopping centers cannot be precisely established, either for centers that are the same type or for different types of centers. Distance is only one factor in determining a trade area; population density, customer convenience, accessibility, and diversity of merchandise should be considered.

Multiple convenience and neighborhood centers can operate successfully within the trade area of a super-regional or regional center or even be located next to or across the road from it. Likewise, power centers and other types of community centers often are developed across from or next to super-regional malls to tap the area's established identity as a shopping destination. Such coexistence is possible because the two types of centers offer distinct store chains and types of merchandise. A group of retail centers can complement each other and create synergies that add to their attraction.

When considering a new store or shopping center, retail analysts often start with a preliminary "ring" analysis, looking at population density, household counts, and income characteristics at a distance from a site being considered. (Many retail stores indicate that they look for sites where the population count is, say, 50,000 people within three miles and where the median household income is $75,000.) If the location looks promising, a more sophisticated analysis would then be undertaken.

One indicator of whether or not a trade area has a sufficient—or an excess—amount of retail space is shopping center square footage per capita. To use this indicator effectively, an accurate estimate of retail space in the metropolitan area as well as in the primary trade area is important, as is a reliable population estimate. Obtaining a tally of total retail space for a large metropolitan area can require considerable effort but is easier to do for a local trade area. In general, metropolitan areas in the Northeast that have viable downtowns, neighborhood business districts, and freestanding stores have a lower share of total retail space in shopping centers than do tourist-oriented locations or fast-growing Sunbelt markets.

For larger centers, the market analyst will often define primary, secondary, and even tertiary trade areas. The primary trade area will include households that live closest to the site or have the most convenient access. It is the geographical area from which the center will derive its largest share of repeat sales. As suggested in Figure 5-4, primary trade areas typically extend as far as two to three miles for a neighborhood center, three to five miles for a traditional community center, five to eight miles for a power center, and eight to 10 miles (or more) for a super-regional mall or lifestyle center. However, a shopping center's trade area may extend farther in one direction than in another. Natural features (lakes, rivers, hills, parks and other preserved open space, or undevelopable land) and built barriers (railroads, freeways, and large institutional or industrial uses) can act as boundaries. The shape of the trade area is not likely to be uniform in every direction.

Secondary trade areas account for 20 to 30 percent of sales; their residents will be drawn to the subject property because it offers a mix of stores, price points, or ambience not available closer to home. The tertiary market includes persons who live outside the primary and secondary areas, including tourists and business visitors. Rather than precisely define a tertiary trade area, some studies simply assume that a proportion of center sales comes from outsiders.

The size of the primary trade area will also depend on population and household density and the extent to which the center offers a unique shopping experience:

- A large center with strong entertainment offerings in a small metropolitan area could draw from the entire area, with secondary patronage coming from the rural hinterland.

- In larger metropolitan areas, a suburban primary trade area will rarely extend beyond a 10- to 15-minute drive for a neighborhood or community center, or a 30-minute drive for a super-regional center.

- In densely developed cities, primary trade area distances will be shorter, but travel times may be similar because of local road congestion or reliance on mass transit to reach shopping destinations.

- Trade areas for specialty centers or downtown locations can differ from those for a traditional neighborhood, community, or regional center. Consumer segments for downtown retailing include residents of nearby buildings and neighborhoods, office building workers, and hotel guests, as well as day visitors (especially on weekends). The trade area for a downtown coffee bar or sandwich shop might extend for only a few blocks. For unique retailers with very few locations, the trade area could encompass an entire metro area, with a significant draw from out-of-towners. Convention and visitors bureaus (agencies that promote local tourism) often have data on nonlodging spending by visitors.

- In the past, sales at downtown retailers or shopping centers depended on lunchtime or after-work patronage by workers and business visitors. As new downtown housing is built, stores have adjusted their merchandise mix and their hours of operation to accommodate the newly expanding neighborhood population. Increasingly, downtown centers also benefit from proximity to visitor draws such as museums, sports facilities, concert halls, theaters, and historic sites.

- A well-located outlet mall—visible from a heavily traveled tourist route—may derive more sales from occasional visitors than from nearby residents. These centers create patronage by accommodating tour buses, church groups, and other day-trippers.

As was discussed in chapter 4, trade areas can be defined using a combination of municipalities, census tracts, or zip codes. However, today's digital geographic information systems also allow the market analyst to create a customized trade area that may reflect local conditions better than municipal boundaries or zip codes. Demographic data vendors can map boundaries defined by the market analyst and then pull demographic and retail trade data. These companies also can create drive-time mapping that helps in refining trade areas. The availability of geographic information system (GIS) technology and proprietary demographic databases allows the market analyst to easily test different trade area configurations. Trying different configurations is not expensive when analysts have subscriptions to the demographic databases. Sophisticated retailers have been using GIS as a tool for site selection strategies for more than 30 years.

GIS programs that define a trade area according to drive-times use information on roadway characteristics, speed limits, and traffic capacity to show areas that can be reached within a five-, 10-, or 15-minute drive of an existing or proposed shopping center. However, accurate drive-time data may not be available for every potential trade area. Retailers evaluating possible locations for new stores can augment drive-time mapping by plotting the place of residence of a store's regular or occasional customers. This can be done by (a) analyzing credit card purchaser data (online or in store), (b) tracking cellphone users who come into a store, and (c) learning the location of potential patrons who search the store's website without making a purchase. Store chains can see how many of their loyal shoppers live within a certain distance of a possible new store location. Such models also help them see how a new store might cannibalize sales at existing locations.

Trade Area Demand Demographics and Purchasing Power

Analyzing the demand for new retail space involves many of the same techniques—and data sources—that are used in housing market analysis, with the added component of spending: estimating household expenditure patterns; adding spending by trade area workers, tourists, or other visitors; and then determining the share of each type of spending that might be captured in a new or retenanted retail space.

Key steps in the demand analysis are summarized here. The analyst should also review the general discussion of demand in chapter 3 and the specific demographic data sources cited in chapter 4. Demand analysis includes the following elements:

- A review of metropolitan area economic conditions, including overall trends in employment growth, key sources of economic activity, planned expansions and contractions, and household growth patterns within the region.

- Examination of population, household, and employment growth trends and projections for the primary and secondary trade areas. For retail analysis, household growth and composition are more important than population growth. The household is the consumer unit, even though individuals will make their own spending decisions on items such as apparel or meals and will make their clothing purchases online or in different locations. Household composition (families with or without children, roommates, singles), tenure, age, and ethnicity also influence how money is spent.

- Analysis of household, family, and per capita income, as well as the percentage of after-tax income available to spend on consumer goods. Five-year income projections are also important; they can be obtained from the demographic data vendors previously cited in chapter 4.

- Demographic data vendors use proprietary models to calculate the number of trade area households in different lifestyle segments on the basis of their psychographic or lifestyle profiles. (See chapter 3 for more details on use of psychographics in trade area analysis.) These data are combined with information from the Department of Labor's BLS Consumer Expenditure Survey (CEX, discussed later in this chapter) to determine household spending for different types of goods and services.

- An examination of sources of shopper spending other than the resident population, such as tourists, convention and business travelers, college students,[23] and workers employed near the subject site. These nonresident sources can be significant in the analysis of demand for retail space in downtowns, near hospitals, or on university campuses.

In trade areas with few nonresidential sources of demand (little office employment, no visitor attractions or hotels), the analyst need not devote much time to analyzing nonresident demand. Obviously, the need to explore these sources will differ when looking at space within walking distance of a large university or city blocks with high-rise office buildings. Demand from workers at medical centers is not likely to be significant because workers do not get much time for lunch and have access to subsidized meals at hospital cafeterias.

Determining a trade area's potential spending on retail goods and services (and how these dollars are allocated) requires data on household income, disposable income (after taxes), and demographics or lifestyle characteristics. Household characteristics determine how families spend their discretionary dollars—the money they can spend in stores after paying taxes, mortgage or rent, utilities, insurance, transportation, health care costs, and other obligations. In addition, to the extent that households save or invest a portion of their earnings, these funds are not available for retail spending.

The Commerce Department's Bureau of Economic Analysis (BEA) publishes annual and quarterly estimates of disposable (after-tax) per capita income, and it adjusts them for inflation, as seen in figure 5-8. Because the methodology is very different and the BEA's base year is 2012, the results are not comparable to those seen in the Census Bureau's household surveys. The BEA numbers suggest that real disposable incomes increased at a very modest pace between 2008 and 2018.

The percentage of disposable income spent on retail purchases varies by income. Other factors that influence spending include household size, ages of people living in the household, education, ethnicity, and place of residence (urban, suburban, or rural). The BLS's Consumer Expenditure Survey indicates how much households (the BLS calls them consumer units) spend for each major category of goods and services sold in stores, depending on income and other characteristics (see sidebar). Market analysts can take the per household spending estimates in the latest BLS survey, update them for inflation, and then multiply them by the number of households in the trade area.

Using national CEX results to estimate spending in any category can be misleading, because the lifestyles and shopping habits of households in the trade area may not match the national averages calculated by the BLS. In addition, spending by type of merchandise or service needs to be translated into spending by store type if the data are

Data from the Consumer Expenditure Survey

Households that are part of the CEX panel keep detailed diaries on their income and spending. It is the only federal government survey that provides information on the complete range of household spending. Twelve-month estimates are published twice a year. Because of the large number of participants, the BLS is able to cross-tabulate the findings by a number of important household demographic and location characteristics. Tables showing how consumer unit spending patterns vary by the following demographic criteria are available on the CEX website:

- Pretax income (quintiles, deciles);

- Age of reference person (eight categories, ranging from under age 25 to age 75 and older);

- Household or family type (married couples with children in three age groups), single-parent households, married couples without children, single persons, and other household types;

- Owner or renter tenure;

- Race;

- Hispanic or Latino origin;

- Highest level of education (for any household member);

- Number of people in the consumer unit;

- Number of earners in the consumer unit;

- Occupation (self-employed, five categories of wage and salary earners, retired, other);

- Census region;

- Type of area (urban central city, other urban, rural); and

- Population size of urban areas (six categories).

Source: Bureau of Labor Statistics, www.bls.gov/cex.

Figure 5-8

U.S. Disposable Income per Capita

Current dollars and adjusted for inflation

Source: Bureau of Economic Analysis, National Income and Product Accounts, Table 2.1; as of October 26, 2018.

Note: Data are as of 3rd quarter 2018.

Figure 5-9
Example: Expenditure Potential, Selected Items
2018

Estimated total and per household expenditures, 2018	Three-mile radius	Primary trade area
Total households	**16,002**	**52,726**
Apparel & services:[a] total	$39,199,816	$127,393,135
Average spent per household	$2,450	$2,416
Spending potential index	113	111
Entertainment/recreation:[b] total	$58,328,752	$189,933,656
Average spent per household	$3,645	$3,602
Spending potential index	113	112
Food at home: total	$88,353,745	$290,010,723
Average spent per household	$5,521	$5,500
Spending potential index	110	110
Food away from home: total	$62,905,118	$205,158,655
Average spent per household	$3,931	$3,891
Spending potential index	112	111
Household furnishings and equipment:[c] total	$38,027,771	$123,529,983
Average spent per household	$2,376	$2,343
Spending potential index	114	112
Personal care products and services: total	$15,074,242	$49,058,886
Average spent per household	$942	$930
Spending potential index	114	112

Source: Real Estate Strategies, Inc./RES Advisors, using data obtained from Esri; derived from the 2015 and 2016 Consumer Expenditure Surveys from the Bureau of Labor Statistics.

Note: Categories are not mutually exclusive. The spending potential index represents the amount spent in the area relative to a national average of 100.

a. Includes footwear, watches and jewelry, and dry cleaning, alterations, and repair services.

b. Includes membership fees, tickets and admissions, lessons, cable/satellite TV service, video game software, DVDs, streaming services, hardware purchases (TVs, DVD players, video equipment, game players, etc., and their installation/repair), toys and hobbies, camping and RV fees, sporting goods and exercise equipment, and reading materials.

c. Includes linens, curtains, drapes, furniture, rugs, major appliances, housewares, small appliances, luggage, and telephones.

to be useful in determining store mix at a new or revitalized center. For example, a household that spends $5,000 per year on clothing will make purchases at a number of different store types—full-line and discount department stores, family apparel stores, specialty shops, and even warehouse clubs and superstores—as well as at online-only and omni-channel merchants. How that $5,000 is spent will also vary according to the age of consumers, where they live, and the extent to which they are brand-conscious or value-conscious.

To make the task easier, some demographic data vendors calculate expenditure potential by type of merchandise, type of store, or both, reflecting their household demographic estimates, consumer psychographics, and the results of the BLS surveys. Some sources allow comparison of trade area spending potential with national averages. Figure 5-9 shows an example of total and per household expenditure potential for two geographies—an area within three miles of the property being studied and the larger primary trade area. The index is based on a national average of 100. For all of the expenditure categories shown, the primary trade area's potential exceeds the national average.

Data vendors have sophisticated models that estimate actual trade area sales by store type and compare them with sales potential calculated to reflect household characteristics. A comparison of the total *potential* retail sales and the estimated actual sales (as shown in figure 5-10) provides an estimate of *leakage*—whether purchasing power is being spent outside the trade area because the store mix is inadequate or unappealing.

Where leakage is significant, it can indicate unmet potential for new retail development within the trade area. The opposite situation (known as *inflow*) can exist in locations that have a large inventory of successful retail centers that draw above-average sales from secondary or tertiary trade areas or from tourists.

Analysts must recognize that up-to-date and accurate information on actual sales is much more difficult to obtain than estimates of potential expenditures. States that collect retail sales tax revenue on the basis of point of purchase are more likely to have good information on where sales are generated. In states where sales tax rates are uniform for all locations, information on taxable sales by store type might

Figure 5-10
Example: Sales Potential and Estimated Sales, 2018
Primary Trade Area

Selected store types	Sales potential (demand, 000s)	Estimated sales (supply, 000s)	Leakage/inflow (000s)	Number of businesses
Auto parts, accessories & tire stores	$34,647	$33,173	$1,475	28
Furniture stores	$39,473	$65,220	−$25,746	15
Home furnishings	$38,538	$7,067	$31,470	11
Electronics and appliance stores	$75,280	$35,771	$39,509	27
Lawn & garden equipment & supply stores	$10,738	$5,065	$5,673	9
Grocery stores	$286,987	$322,974	−$35,987	61
Specialty food stores	$15,047	$20,805	−$5,758	21
Beer, wine & liquor stores	$39,571	$38,933	$638	23
Health & personal care stores	$140,322	$111,625	$28,697	54
Clothing, shoes, and accessories stores	$142,503	$30,893	$111,610	48
Sporting goods, hobbies, book & music stores	$59,185	$32,284	$26,902	38
Department stores (ex. leased departments)	$172,841	$193,519	−$20,678	11
Other general merchandise stores	$112,689	$34,441	$78,248	27
Office supplies, stationery & gift stores	$20,549	$8,047	$12,402	26
Other miscellaneous store retailers	$43,434	$13,441	$29,993	32
Electronic shopping & mail-order houses	$23,323	$1,549	$21,774	4
Drinking places	$6,031	$2,061	$3,970	10
Restaurants & other eating places	$194,412	$135,639	$58,773	247

Sources: Esri; RES Advisors.

Note: Negative numbers indicate inflow—estimated sales that exceed trade area demand. Positive numbers indicate that potential sales dollars are not being captured by trade area establishments (leakage): shoppers are going elsewhere.

be reported only statewide or countywide rather than by place of sale. Even then, trade area boundaries often do not match tax jurisdiction boundaries. As a result, data vendors model sales, but their data inputs may not be as current as would be desirable.

One source used in modeling trade area sales is the Economic Census for NAICS sectors 44-45, which covers retail trade. Conducted every five years, this census includes information on the number of establishments and reported sales by type of store and provides information for metro areas, counties, and places.Although the last survey was completed in 2017, data had not yet been released as of spring 2019.[24] As a result, sales estimates from private data vendors are still based on 2012 information. The primary trade area analyzed in figure 5-10 appears to have a surplus of furniture stores, grocery stores, department stores, and specialty food stores. This conclusion is questionable in 2019, in that the trade area lost more than one department store and a supermarket in recent years. (However, the trade area has numerous other full-line and discount supermarkets.)

Changing buying habits, including growth in online sales, complicate the analyst's task. Even if the numbers show leakage, development opportunities may be weak. The dollars flowing out of the primary trade area may not be sufficient to support the array of stores needed for a successful new center or individual store types. However, a trade area with a large stock of older retail space may be able to stem the outflow of sales dollars if centers are renovated and more exciting tenants are recruited.

In growing communities, developers will be tempted to build new community or neighborhood centers that, in the aggregate, exceed the amount of space needed to meet current demand. Using reliable population and household projections for growth areas is important in determining when a center might be able to achieve success. The full sales potential of large centers that rely heavily on future trade area household growth may not be reached for a decade, as the market matures around them. The risk increases if a planned center is located at the edge of an urban area where its success is dependent on new homebuilding. A national or regional economic downturn can slow the number of new consumers coming to an area for years, as occurred during the last recession. At the same time, builders will have difficulty selling new homes if their buyers have no convenient place to shop for necessities.

Retail developers must also consider the incomes of households in growing trade areas. If average incomes are low, the proportion of total household income spent in nonfood stores is typically less than in an area of middle- or high-income households. Conversely, low-income families spend a higher percentage of income on food. Ethnicity influences spending patterns in low-income neighborhoods. Some groups are more "brand loyal," while others are price-oriented. As a result, new retail centers need to be carefully tenanted.

Significant purchasing power exists even in the poorest neighborhoods, particularly those in dense urban settings. Because demand may not be fully met, sales (and jobs) leak into surrounding, wealthier trade areas. In recent years, retailers have begun to better understand the significant potential of untapped markets in lower-income urban areas.

Using Shopper Data Analytics

Chapter 3 introduced the various ways in which consumer opinion can be solicited when preparing real estate market analyses. Customer research is widely used by shopping center developers, center management, and retail chains, as well as government agencies that are involved in business district revitalization. As indicated in chapter 3, telephone surveys are being used less frequently because of problems with reaching a representative population sample. Mail surveys are too expensive, and response rates are low. As a result, customer satisfaction surveys are now conducted primarily online with email links sent to recent shoppers, with follow-up contacts to generate greater participation.

Shopping center management wants to know which stores are being patronized, how much is being spent, whether shoppers are also visiting restaurants and food courts, and how visitors feel about signage, parking, hours of operation, safety, and store mix. In the past, these short surveys were done on paper by paid interviewers at various locations within a center and at different times. Today, trained interviewers can give shoppers a tablet, so that responses can be immediately recorded and quickly tabulated.

Marketing staff members can also see shopping patterns within a center while using mobile phone tracking (geospatial analysis) and an analysis of credit card receipts. Visitation and spending in a store's brick-and-mortar locations can be compared with online purchases. Store credit card holders may be asked to participate in surveys, with questions regarding items typically purchased, locations most frequently visited, satisfaction with merchandise (selection, quality, sizing), ease of online ordering, on-time delivery, and customer service.

A shuttered supermarket.

Food and Pharmacy Deserts

Despite sizable numbers of households, many urban neighborhoods are "food deserts"—areas with few grocery shopping choices other than small corner stores. The U.S. Department of Agriculture (USDA) defines food deserts as parts of the country lacking fresh fruit, vegetables, fresh dairy products, whole grains, and other healthful foods; food deserts are usually found in impoverished areas. This lack of access is worsened by a lack of transportation. The USDA's Economic Research Service has been tracking food deserts since the late 2000s. It provides mapping programs and analysis, but the most recent data are for 2015.[25]

Many food desert neighborhoods also lack pharmacies. Getting to a supermarket or pharmacy location can mean walking one to two miles or transferring between two bus lines. Although the absence of supermarkets in any neighborhood limits consumer choice, researchers from the National Bureau of Economic Research say that merely opening a supermarket will not necessarily result in healthy eating habits in low-income neighborhoods.

Decisions to close grocery or pharmacy locations are said to be based on below-average sales, but operational problems (staffing shortages, security issues) may also influence management decisions. Food deserts are found in sparsely populated rural areas as well as in low-income urban neighborhoods. As mentioned earlier, dollar stores in communities lacking supermarkets are adding more fresh, refrigerated, and frozen food items to their merchandise mix when renovating or opening new locations. Community groups and government agencies are looking for ways to encourage greater availability of healthy food and medicine in underserved neighborhoods. Deliveries are one option, but many urban customers lack a secure place where packages can be dropped off, and items needing refrigeration would be even more difficult to store. Lyft has teamed up with a nonprofit group to offer low-priced rides to supermarkets in Washington, D.C.

Sources: Else Olumhense and Nausheen Hussain, "Pharmacy Deserts a Growing Health Concern in Chicago, Experts, Residents Say," Chicago Tribune online, January 22, 2018; Bob Curley, "How to Combat 'Food Deserts' and 'Food Swamps,'" Healthline, January 18, 2018; Kori Hale, "Food Deserts Get a Lyft with Low Cost Rides," Forbes online, December 27, 2018.

Using Artificial Intelligence in Retail Decision-Making

"Placer.ai allows you to see where customers are coming from, what do they do before and after going to a store, how much is being spent there, and where they live and work—essentially it provides stats in the real world. . . . The learning model technology also allows users to gain insight into other nearby stores in order to predict how a particular store might perform, or to project opening new locations."

Source: Noam Ben-Zvi, chief executive officer of Placer.ai, as quoted in the January/ February 2019 issue of Real Estate Forum.

Analyzing the place of residence for both in-store and online shoppers can help store chains decide where to open new locations and where to close existing ones. Data mining provides more input for better decision-making; store location staff members no longer have to base their decisions only on forecasts of sales and operating expenses per square foot or on changes in same-store sales.

Artificial intelligence and machine-learning programs are now available to retailers and shopping centers. Some companies focus on consumer demographics, others on housing stock characteristics and values in user-specified geographic areas. Placer.ai (see sidebar) provides foot traffic analysis for retailers, using mobile phone tracking. Space Jam Data surveys shoppers at retail centers using social media and crowdsourcing. The tool can ask patrons what they like and dislike about a center, and what new stores or services they would like to see. If a center is losing tenants or if an expansion is planned, owners may use focus groups to get opinions on what changes should be made and what new store types should be sought.

In downtown or neighborhood business districts with pedestrian-oriented "street retail," economic development agencies or merchant associations with limited research budgets can conduct intercept surveys with people on the street, using tablets to record responses. They learn which businesses are visited, if visitors are happy with their shopping experience, whether the merchants are doing a good job, and what improvements should be made to the tenant mix or the physical environment.

When conducting surveys, the analyst should use professionals who have experience in questionnaire design. To provide meaningful input, the survey company must cross-tabulate answers with consumer characteristics— place of residence (town, zip code, neighborhood), age, sex, household size, and income. It is also important to know whether the respondent has children (which affects interest in child-oriented stores or entertainment) and whether the respondent rents or owns (which affects demand for home

improvement and home furnishings categories). A general rule of thumb is that intercept surveys need a minimum of 300 completed responses to allow for meaningful analysis. A much larger number of respondents is needed if results are to be cross-tabulated by age, race, ethnicity, household characteristics, or income. The same would be true of a web-based survey.

If focus groups are the method of choice, it may be necessary to convene multiple groups living within a trade area to learn whether opinions differ. For example, having a group of older adults meet separately from a group of young singles and couples may be helpful. The venues used for the focus group may influence willingness to participate. Incentives—coupons, gift cards, etc.—as well as refreshments will be needed. The experience of the moderator, carefully selected discussion topics, and the availability of on-screen and printed visual aids help ensure the success of this approach to consumer research.

Understanding the Supply Side

Although numerous distressed shopping centers and freestanding locations have closed since the recession that began in late 2007 and the pace of new retail construction has clearly slowed, the supply of retail space still exceeds what can be supported by American households if online shopping continues to grow as expected. As indicated earlier in this chapter, a first step in evaluating the extent of competition is to estimate total retail space in a trade area, divide the results by a current estimate of the population, and then review the results to see if the trade area is overstored or could support new space.

However, an accurate analysis of the strength of the competitive supply inventory requires field research (visits to the most competitive centers and freestanding stores); interviews with leasing managers, property owners, or both; and contacts with local brokers who specialize in retail real estate. The analyst will need to provide the following information in the market study report:

- Provide background on retail market conditions in the county or metropolitan area, while looking at trends in total space inventory, rents, vacancy, and net absorption.

- Identify the location of similar properties within the primary trade area and near its perimeter.

- Describe the characteristics of competitive centers and relevant freestanding retailing, including the amount of space (square feet of GLA), anchor tenants, types of in-line tenants, property age and remodeling activity, vacancy rate, sizes of available spaces, and ease of accessibility.

- Research the characteristics and status of planned and approved retail developments in the trade areas, as well as identify other vacant, zoned sites that could become competitive in the future.

- Estimate the share of potential sales that could be captured by the proposed development given its planned mix of spaces and store types, and the strength of its location.

- Compare projected sales per square foot with recent performance experience of retail chains at comparable projects, while recognizing the limitations of this approach as online purchases increase.

A second approach is more qualitative. It involves looking at other markets with similar demographics and purchasing power to see if any store types and service businesses are missing in the trade area being studied. This approach is the most time- and cost-efficient strategy if the market study is being conducted for an institutional investor, shopping center REIT, or retail property management company that has existing centers in areas with similar demographics and shopping patterns. In-house market analysts frequently use this method, which has been enhanced by innovations in retail data mining.

As mentioned earlier, a traditional way to measure supply and demand balance is to see whether sales per square foot of space continue to grow despite additions to supply over time. However, information on recent sales for individual shopping centers or stores is not readily available. Center managers may not be willing or able to share sales data with analysts who represent existing or potential competitors.

The increasing complexity of the retail business, combined with a multiplicity of overlapping trade areas, requires that the analyst consider multiple methods to estimate potential sales. Depending on time and budget available for preparing a market study, the analyst may have to rely on estimates prepared by data vendors, as were shown in figure 5-10, despite their limitations in a rapidly changing environment.[26] If a new center or store location is being proposed by a REIT that owns multiple centers in market areas or a chain that has stores in areas with similar household demographics, information will be shared with the team preparing the market study. If no such information is available, the analyst can use average sales per square foot for other stores in the chain and can assume a similar productivity per square foot for a new store, adjusted for variations in trade area characteristics. Or a retailer may estimate the volume achieved by its competitors in the trade area and then redistribute these sales after considering the impact of a new entry into the market. Retailers also estimate a new store's market share according to shares achieved in other comparable locations. The latter methods work well for supermarkets, where a limited number of chains with established positions compete in a trade area.

Construction Activity and Future Competition

Unlike residential building permit statistics collected by the Census Bureau, no comprehensive source of government data exists on retail construction. Even where state or metropolitan agencies collect data, its scope varies among jurisdictions.[27]

Current construction and announced projects are monitored by private sources, who sell their information for a fee.

Analysts can compile their own lists of projects in the development pipeline, thereby avoiding paying fees charged by private vendors. Analysts will usually need to contact municipal planners or other public officials in multiple trade area jurisdictions and review minutes of public hearings or planning department files, which can be time-consuming activities. Site plans and building permit applications for a proposed center may not tell the market analyst which tenant stores or restaurants have already committed to a center.

Putting It All Together

When looking at a proposed new retail facility, the analyst will be asked to provide an opinion of how many square feet of space can be supported, using estimates of expenditure potential and sales levels that will meet the expectations of developers, equity investors, lenders, and prospective tenants. The analyst will need to estimate a *capture rate*—the percentage of expenditure potential in the trade area that is likely to be captured at the site, given the competition, the planned mix of stores, and the likely anchor tenants.

The analyst may need to adjust center or store sales norms on the basis of the proposed center's location and the likelihood of getting the best-performing tenants. For example, if a typical family apparel store generates sales that average $423 per square foot (as shown in figure 5-3), a top performer will expect to do much better and will want to see that there is sufficient purchasing power to achieve its target sales. The analyst will make recommendations regarding the mix of stores and anchor tenants (retailers, service businesses, restaurants), and provide an opinion on rents that could be achieved for in-line (nonanchor) spaces, given asking rents elsewhere in the primary market area. Suggestions on design elements, parking, signage, or traffic signalization, can be offered.

In contrast to market studies for residential properties, retail analysts will probably not be asked to estimate monthly absorption. As a practical matter, large new projects cannot proceed without significant pre-leasing or sales of store sites. Lenders will expect firm commitments for at least half the space, especially anchors. (Smaller in-line stores will be reluctant to sign until they know the "draws" that will bring shoppers to the center.) At the same time, it is important to remember that small shops pay higher rents per square foot and thus may contribute more to the bottom line in the aggregate. In an uncertain retail environment, lenders will want to see pre-leasing for the bulk of the space.

Data Sources

Demographic and psychographic data used to provide vital information on a trade area's population, households, household characteristics, lifestyles, housing tenure, and income are discussed in chapter 3. Retail market analysts can save time by purchasing reports from reliable sources

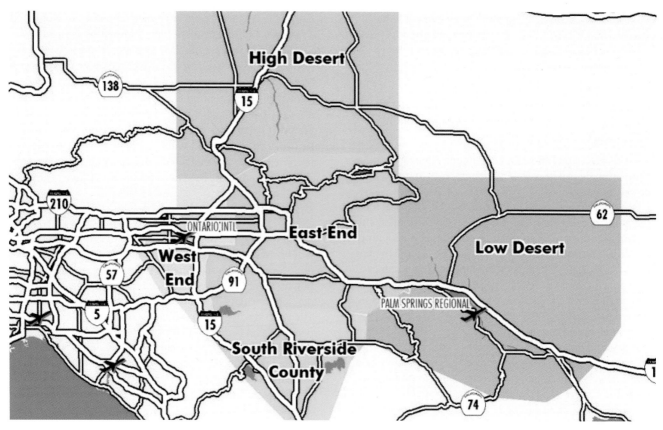

A map showing retail submarkets in the Inland Empire region of California. *(CBRE. Reprinted with permission.)*

that translate demographics into purchasing power and estimates of supportable sales. Their proprietary models will use inputs from the BLS's Consumer Expenditure Survey.[28] In some cases, the market analyst will want to use local population and household estimates and projections, applying them to estimates of per household spending from other sources. As was illustrated in figure 5-10, private data vendors also prepare sales estimates and calculate inflow or leakage by store type.

Additional sources are necessary to estimate demand from nonresident sources: nearby workers, tourists, or college students living in dorms or privately owned student apartments. The ICSC conducted surveys of office worker spending (downtown and suburban) for meals and other purchases; results were last published in 2012 and need to be updated.[29] Similarly, the National Association of College Stores (www.nacs.org) conducts periodic surveys of retail spending by college students. Rough estimates of tourist and business visitor spending may be available from local convention and visitors bureaus. Although these sources of demand could be significant in certain locations (in downtowns with a large daytime worker base, in neighborhoods with college campuses, or in areas with significant visitor demand—for example, along the Las Vegas strip or near one of the many theme parks in metro Orlando), they will not generate much in the way of sales inflow in typical residential areas. Market analysts should focus their time and resources on the key sources of demand and then add an "order of magnitude" estimate for other spending on the basis of the attractiveness of the location and its likely mix of stores. This demand can be expressed as a percentage of total sales from residents and added to sales generated by primary and secondary trade area household spending.

On the supply side, statistics on the physical characteristics and market performance of shopping centers are more widely available than for freestanding space or streetfront retailing. The market analyst will not be able to find published sales data for individual centers, except (possibly) in annual reports for centers owned by public companies or when a center's sale, expansion, or renovation is announced in the press.

Background information on shopping centers and retail stores can be obtained from many sources.

■ The ICSC (www.icsc.org) reports sales by store type for larger shopping centers, but these data are available only to members. Information on individual centers is not released. The ICSC also publishes a monthly news magazine (*Shopping Centers Today*) with feature stories on center tenanting, construction, and operations, and *Value Retail News* (covering factory outlet centers) as well as special research reports.

- The Census Bureau publishes an Economic Census every five years for retail trade (NAICS codes 44 and 45) and the food service industry (NAICS code 722). Data from these surveys can be accessed through the Census Bureau's online interactive database (data.census.gov). Statistics include the number of retail and restaurant establishments, sales, and employment for states, counties, and zip codes, but sales data are not available for small areas (such as census tracts) to protect respondent confidentiality. As of this writing, the most recent available numbers were for 2012[30]—too dated to be of much use in 2019 in light of the growth in e-commerce. As noted earlier, results from the 2017 Economic Censuses will not be available until 2020.

- States and local governments that collect sales taxes may have information on receipts by municipality. This information is especially likely to be available in areas where counties or cities levy their own sales taxes, or where a portion of state sales taxes is shared with municipalities according to the jurisdictions where sales occur.

- The National Retail Federation (www.nrf.com) represents all types of retail stores as well as catalog and internet merchants. It publishes *Stores* magazine and periodically ranks top retailers in terms of revenues and store growth. The NRF also issues occasional special reports on holiday spending and online purchasing.

- Main Street America (www.mainstreet.org), a program of the National Main Street Center, offers technical assistance and publications designed to help communities revitalize their traditional, pedestrian-oriented business districts. Many states have similar programs for older downtowns and for transit-oriented development projects.

- The *Directory of Major Malls* (www.shoppingcenters.com) covers centers with at least 250,000 square feet.

- Similar searchable directories are available for retail and restaurant chain tenants. Sources include the *Retail Tenant Directory* (www.retailtenants.com) and *Chain Store Guide* (www.csgis.com), which also provide information on store expansion plans.

- Information on shopping centers and retail market conditions and trends can be purchased for metropolitan markets and selected submarkets from such sources as Reis and CoStar.

- National brokerages such as CBRE, Cushman & Wakefield, JLL, and Marcus & Millichap have reports on national retail market conditions and provide greater detail for larger metropolitan markets. Figure 5-11 shows information on retail real estate conditions in the Inland Empire area of California (generally defined as Riverside and San Bernardino counties) for the fourth quarter of 2018 from CBRE Research. It covers only those shopping centers and freestanding properties with at least 50,000 square feet. CBRE reported nearly 1 million square feet of new space added in 2018, with even more space still under construction. Two submarkets experienced negative net absorption for the year. The West End and South Riverside County submarkets were the best performers.

Figure 5-11
Example: Retail Market Supply Snapshot
Inland Empire Metro Area and Submarkets

	Inventory (sq ft GLA, 000s)[a]	Overall vacancy (%)	Year-to-date net absorption (sq ft)[b]	Under construction (sq ft)	Average asking rents (per sq ft per month)[c]
East End	39,978	8.3	−140,110	178,268	$2.07
High Desert	9,295	10.5	−33,920	0	$1.63
Low Desert	16,464	11.3	−155,139	0	$2.02
South Riverside County	18,416	6.0	153,848	81,618	$2.31
West End	28,020	7.2	436,782	0	$2.12
Total Inland Empire	**112,173**	**8.3**	**261,461**	**259,886**	**$2.03**

Source: CBRE.

a. In centers with 50,000 sq ft or more.

b. Change in occupied shop space as of the date when a lease is signed.

c. In California, retail rents are quoted per month, not per year.

As discussed earlier, it is important for analysts who use brokerage data to verify the minimum size of properties included in their reports. (If the analyst is looking at a neighborhood center, the data source should include centers over 100,000 square feet.) Also, some data sources do not include store-owned anchor space in their vacancy rates, which can understate the amount of surplus space in a market area that has seen department store and big-box closings.

- Local or county economic development departments, chambers of commerce, newspapers, and business journals often prepare lists of the larger shopping centers and may have information on available space. Brokers' online listings of available space can be useful in gathering information on asking rents. A conversation with one or more local retail brokers can also be helpful to get a sense of rent, expenses, and vacancy trends, as well as store chains looking for space in a particular trade area. Some brokers specialize in representing store and restaurant chains, helping them to find new sites (or dispose of closed locations).

- Sales information for individual chains can be found by perusing corporate annual reports or searching retail trade websites and magazines. Business newspapers will also carry articles on changes in same-store sales.

Online directories are updated at least once a year, but the tenant mix in shopping centers changes frequently and new competition is always being added. The expansion and contraction plans of chain stores and restaurants can also change, as dictated by general economic conditions or store performance. Shopping center or tenant directory listings should be checked in the field; online announcements in the real estate and general business press can be helpful. Follow-up telephone contacts with center managers or leasing agents are necessary to learn about future expansion or renovation plans and anticipated changes in tenancy, as well as current rents, real estate taxes, and common area maintenance charges. Some managers may be willing to share data on sales per square foot.

Data on retail space and other commercial construction activity are available for a fee from Dodge Data & Analytics. Dodge customers can purchase reports on historical and projected construction value and square feet of space for individual metropolitan areas, but no submarkets are delineated. As discussed in chapter 3, construction project databases are designed to serve the needs of contractors looking for bidding opportunities (and not real estate market analysts). Reis and CoStar, as well as local brokerages that specialize in selling shopping center properties or finding locations for stores they represent, will be well informed about planned shopping center construction.

Notes

1. GLA is measured from the centerline of joint partitions and outside wall faces.

2. Space separately owned by anchor tenants in large centers may not be counted as part of center GLA.

3. Monthly sales data are reported by NAICS code for each type of store. Monthly sales are cited both with and without seasonal adjustments. Year-end totals take seasonal variations into account and are revised periodically.

4. GAFO includes stores in the following NAICS codes: 442, 443, 448, 451, 452, and 4532.

5. Some limited-service restaurants cook food to order and bring it to the table (NAICS code 72221) and make deliveries. NAICS code 722 also includes self-service restaurants (cafeterias and buffets), specialty food and beverage establishments (ice cream and yogurt shops, juice bars, coffee bars), caterers, food-service contractors at business establishments, and mobile food trucks.

6. Other retail sectors also report sales to the Census Bureau: motor vehicle and parts dealers (including new- and used-car showrooms); establishments that sell boats, recreational vehicles, and auto parts; home heating fuel providers; and gasoline stations. These numbers are generally not part of a local retail market study.

7. Dollar stores are classified as "other general merchandise" stores.

8. U.S. Department of Commerce and U.S. Census Bureau, "Quarterly Retail E-commerce Sales, 3rd Quarter 2018," press release and tables.

9. John Connolly, "New Census Dataset Breaks Out Warehouse-Fulfilled Online Sales: Assessing the Impact of Pure-Play and Omni-Channel Retailers," *Industry Insights*, International Council of Shopping Centers, April 13, 2018.

10. "Amazon Now Has Nearly 50% of US Ecommerce Market," July 13, 2018, www.emarketer.com.

11. Rents for streetfront retail spaces are often quoted on a monthly basis, regardless of the size of the space.

12. According to the Food Marketing Institute, median supermarket store size grew from 35,100 square feet in 1995 to 48,058 10 years later. By 2015, the median dropped to 42,800 square feet. Supermarkets do not generate high profit margins, which helps explain why sizes are smaller. Growth in discount groceries (such as Aldi) and specialized grocery purveyors also contribute to smaller median grocery sizes.

13. Coresight Research, "US and UK Store Opening & Closures Tracker," 2019 Week 13, March 29, 2019.

14. In early 2019, there were 10 Amazon Go stores, which were located in Seattle, Chicago, and San Francisco.

15. Suzanne Kapner, "Macy's Plans to Grow by Shrinking Its Stores," *Wall Street Journal*, November 13, 2018, p. 1.

16. Anchors are traditionally department stores but increasingly can be other large stores or entertainment uses.

17. Many communities are concerned about the amount of ground-floor office space in town centers and neighborhood business districts; they would prefer that storefronts be occupied by retail shops and restaurants, with office space users on the upper floors.

18. Although they can benefit from being close to other shopping attractions, freestanding stores usually enjoy lower occupancy costs. Freestanding retailers do not have to pay for common area maintenance and mall marketing. Furthermore, some chains want exclusive control over store siting, design, and parking, which is not always possible in a multitenant shopping center.

19. Over time, the percentage of department stores that own their buildings has increased.

20. Like-kind exchanges—in which real property used for business or held as an investment can be exchanged solely for other business or investment property that is the same type or "like kind"—have long been permitted under the Internal Revenue Code. Generally, if the property owners make a like-kind exchange, they are not required to recognize a gain or loss under Internal Revenue Code Section 1031.

21. Cushman & Wakefield, *Food Halls of America*, 2016 edition. The report lists the top U.S. food halls and lists projects still under construction or in planning. As of the third quarter 2016, there were 96 major food halls totaling 2.4 million square feet, www.cushmanwakefield.us/en/research-and-insight/2016/food-halls/.

22. American Dream, a new 3 million-square-foot center, was slated to open in northern New Jersey in late 2019. The project was started in 2003, went through an ownership change, and then stalled during the recession. More than half the space will be entertainment related, including a Nickelodeon theme park, two roller coasters, movie theaters, an aquarium, a Ferris wheel, a water park, an indoor ski slope, and an ice rink. Mall shops will be a mix of upscale and midmarket stores. Half the visitors are expected to be from the greater New York City area, with 30 percent from other parts of the United States and 20 percent from other countries.

23. College students who reside in dormitories are part of census population counts but are not considered to be living in households. Although they may spend considerable amounts of money at stores near campus, their buying power is not typically included in estimates of expenditure potential for trade areas.

24. Economic Census reports for 2017 for Accommodation and Food Services (sector 72) will also be available.

25. U.S. Department of Agriculture, Economic Research Service, *Go to the Atlas*, https://www.ers.usda.gov/data-products/food-access-research-atlas/go-to-the-atlas/.

26. Data vendors' sales estimating models are based on the Census Bureau's economic censuses for retail store types and eating and drinking establishment types. The 2012 data do not reflect the growth of e-commerce and its effect on store sales; quick-casual restaurants have expanded rapidly since 2012, while older casual restaurants have not seen the same sales growth.

27. Some sources focus on the dollar value of commercial construction permits and do not provide data on GLA. In a mixed-use project, retail space may not be distinguishable from office space in permit data.

28. www.bls.gov/cex. Results from the Consumer Expenditure Survey include information on spending by age, education, Hispanic origin, race, and occupation of the reference person (similar to head of household), as well as the consumer unit's region of residence, size, number of wage earners, and housing tenure.

29. Michael P. Niemira and John Connolly, *Office-Worker Retail Spending in a Digital Age* (New York: International Council of Shopping Centers, 2012).

30. U.S. Census Bureau, 2012 Retail Trade (NAICS Sector 44-45), Geographic Area Series, EC1244A1 – "Retail Trade: Geographic Area Series: Summary Statistics for the U.S., States, Metro Areas, Counties, and Places: 2012," https://www.census.gov/data/tables/2012/econ/census/retail-trade.html.

CHAPTER 6

CHAPTER 6

OFFICE SPACE

As with retail properties, office buildings exhibit a wide range of sizes and styles, from modest low-rise structures with a single tenant (or just a few), to mid-rise suburban campuses, to high-rise multitenant buildings with top-quality finishes and amenities. "Flex" buildings—which combine office space with storage and light assembly—can be counted in inventories of either office or industrial space, depending on the extent of the office finishes in the space. Potential office tenants would not necessarily limit their search to a single type of building; they would consider a variety of available locations, depending on their space requirements, labor needs, and location preferences.

According to Colliers International, the 57 U.S. office markets that the firm monitors provided nearly 6.2 billion square feet of office space as of mid-2018.[1] When compared with Colliers's 2007 inventory, the 2018 report shows that more than 1.4 billion square feet of new space were added since 2007, an increase of 30 percent in less than 11 years, despite the recession.[2] Demand for office space is changing, dramatically affecting the need for new construction. Flexible arrangements for office workers (more home offices, rapid expansion in coworking locations for corporate staff as well as individual entrepreneurs and startup businesses) result in less space per employee. These changes dictate the need for careful analysis of market conditions.

Characteristics of Office Buildings

Office buildings can range from less than 10,000 square feet to millions of square feet of space. Downtown construction projects often consist of only one very large building; but in the suburbs, developers or property owners offer multiple buildings in landscaped office parks with common amenities. However, the distinctions between downtown and suburban office development patterns are blurring. Increasingly, in both locations, office space is part of mixed-use developments that may include retail, residential, hotel, entertainment, and civic uses. (Mixed-use projects—and the synergies among uses—are discussed in chapter 9.)

Office space can be categorized according to several factors:

- Class,
- Location,
- Size and flexibility,
- Use and ownership, and
- Features and amenities.

Class

Class is measured by evaluating the space's age, location, quality of finishes, building systems, amenities, lease rates, and tenant profile. Office space inventories generally segment buildings into classes A, B, or C. Class A space includes professionally managed buildings that have an excellent location and access, as well as prestigious corporate and professional tenants. Increasingly, they are characterized by environmentally sensitive or "green" building materials and operational systems that save on energy and water costs; these systems also provide a healthy work environment for employees. Exercise facilities may be available solely for the

The One Workplace headquarters office/showroom/warehouse in Santa Clara, California. *(Bruce Damonte)*

A renovated suburban office building in the Forrestal Center in Princeton, New Jersey. *(Deborah L. Brett & Associates)*

High-rise office towers in downtown Boston. *(Alexander Rodas/Shutterstock.com)*

tenants' use, or at a discounted rate at health clubs open to the public. Amenities such as coffee bars, takeout food, restaurants, and other services help attract businesses. Buildings are also installing shared conference room spaces that all tenants can reserve; individual tenants are pleased not to have to provide this infrequently used (but costly) feature.

Most, but not all, class A buildings are less than 10 years old or have been extensively renovated to bring them up to current high standards. (Rockefeller Center in Manhattan is an example of a decades-old office complex with perpetual class A status.) Building materials and amenities are top quality, and the property conveys a high-status image for its tenants.

Class B buildings have good locations, professional management, and high-quality construction. Although they are not new, these properties show very little physical deterioration, but they may lack state-of-the-art HVAC, lighting, mechanical systems, or tech capabilities. Class C buildings are substantially older than class A or class B buildings, with inferior locations, lack of design appeal, or signs of deferred maintenance.

Tenants "filter up" from class B to class A and from class C to class B as their businesses prosper or their space needs change. In some cases, class B properties can be renovated to class A standards, if they can provide the environmental and tech features found in new buildings, and if their layouts can be reconfigured to be more efficient. However, extensive renovations are often not cost-effective for either the landlord or the tenant.

Most large new buildings are class A, but new small structures with few amenities can be class B from the outset. Definitions vary, but age, size, rent level, location, building materials, tech capabilities, operating systems, and amenities are all considered when classifying office properties. Security is an increasingly important factor when choosing a building.

Location

Downtowns or central business districts (CBDs) are usually characterized by tall office buildings and high rents. Major business and professional services providers in law, accounting, architecture, engineering, and consulting find downtown locations attractive, as do many corporate headquarters and regional offices. Government offices are often concentrated in CBDs, but rarely in class A space.

Although downtown locations once dominated the office market, high volumes of suburban construction from the 1970s through the 1990s changed the location profile of multitenant office space. Spacious suburban office parks, with a variety of building styles and heights, captured a growing share of demand from both large corporations and small businesses. Suburban rents and other operating costs were lower, and parking was ample and free. However, the shift to the suburbs has slowed. Colliers International indicates that the amount of office space in downtowns grew by nearly 28 percent, while the suburban inventory grew 31 percent between 2007 and 2018. The suburban share of total office square footage accounted for 65 percent in 2000, 67 percent in 2007, and 68 percent in 2018. (See figure 6-1.)

Inside big cities but beyond traditional downtowns are secondary office nodes that cluster near hospitals, universities, or other business magnets. Many mature suburban communities, especially those located near transit, have their own concentrated "downtown" office cores that can compete with the CBD. Other suburban office districts are more linear, typically lining a major highway corridor, with larger concentrations at interchanges. As an example, the Los Angeles CBD is just one of many large office nodes that include Pasadena, Santa Monica, Universal City, and West Los Angeles.

The inventory of quality office space has expanded in suburban downtowns over the past 25 years. New space has been added as part of mixed-use, transit-oriented projects along commuter-rail lines. In more typical car-oriented suburbs, much of the office space inventory is located in centrally managed office parks or in mixed-use business parks that combine office, light industrial, hotel, and restaurant space.

Small suburban office buildings can be found along major arterials and adjacent to retail centers and multifamily residential complexes. These properties appeal to a diverse group of users. Some tenants are branch offices of corporations, whereas others (insurance agents, real estate agents, banks, medical practitioners, small law offices, mortgage companies) provide services to households in nearby communities. Startup businesses may also prefer the convenience and lower costs associated with suburban locations. Storefront space in neighborhood or community shopping centers can compete with small office buildings for these tenant types.

Size and Layout

Office buildings generally fall into three size categories: high-rise (16 stories or more), mid-rise (four to 15 stories), and low-rise (one to three stories). Floor plate size is an important consideration, with some tenants requiring large floor plates so they can occupy fewer levels. Of late, tenants seem to prefer smaller floor plates so that workers have more natural light. Floor space flexibility is important as more tenants opt for open-floor layouts and more efficient use of space. Interior columns or odd angles that make it difficult to lay out space will make a building less desirable. Office floor plates in new class A buildings generally range from 18,000 to 30,000 square feet. Some older office buildings that are no longer competitive can be converted to residential use or hotels if their floor plates are not too large.

Use and Ownership

A majority of office buildings are occupied by multiple tenants who lease their space. However, a relatively small number of office condominiums also exist, primarily in low-rise, multibuilding properties in outlying suburbs. Office condominium tenants tend to be professional practices (physicians, attorneys, accountants) and other locally owned or franchise businesses. Office condominiums capture a relatively small share of total space.

Some office buildings are configured to appeal to distinct market niches: medical and laboratory space, university-affiliated institutes, nonprofits, financial services, or back-office functions (for example, data processing or customer service). Multitenant office buildings are owned by real estate investment trusts, pension funds, limited partnerships, family businesses, and individuals. An office building constructed for a specific tenant is called *built to suit*, whereas a building constructed for unknown tenants is a *speculative* or *spec* building. Lenders typically require that a significant portion of a building's total space be pre-leased (with signed commitments from one or more creditworthy tenants) before construction begins.

Corporations often occupy an entire office building; they may own it or lease it from an investor-owner. However, owner-occupied single-user buildings are generally excluded from a market's office space inventory until vacated and marketed for multitenant occupancy. Documenting the extent of owner occupancy is difficult because of the widespread use of sale-leasebacks, whereby a corporation sells one or more real estate assets (usually to an institutional investor, such as a pension fund, or a private investor group) and then leases them back from the new owner. The corporation frees up capital by removing expensive assets from its balance sheet, even though it must still pay real estate taxes, insurance, and maintenance costs. A major reason to lease is the tax benefit of being able to take the rent paid as a business expense. The new owner gets a quality property leased to a credit tenant, usually for a period of at least 10 years.

Features and Amenities

A building's architecture and the style and quality of finishes in public areas will be important in the selection of a location by image-sensitive tenants. Corporations want to strike a balance between high quality and cost consciousness, but the balance depends on the kind of image they are trying to convey.

Some prospective tenants will be looking for on-site health clubs, restaurants, and retail outlets as features that can be used in attracting and retaining employees; these prospects will look only at spaces that have such facilities in the building or nearby. Yet others value proximity to daycare centers, which makes it possible for employees to visit their young children during lunch or breaks, thereby helping to reduce commuting time and stress.

During recent real estate market downturns, companies were interested in reducing costs. As the worker head count declined, tenants tried to sublet excess space—often without success. That situation led to a temporary increase in the amount of office space per worker. With an improving economy, the labor market tightened. Employers began to respond to the growing millennial workforce by creating

Figure 6-1

U.S. Office Space Inventory by Location, 2007–2018

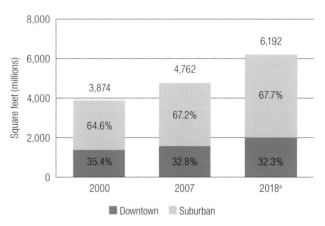

Sources: Colliers International, U.S. Real Estate Review, *2008;* U.S. Research Report: Office Market Outlook, *Q2 2018, www.colliers.com.*

Note: Percentages are share of total inventory.

a. As of June 30, 2018.

MoZaic, a mixed-use office building in Minneapolis adjacent to the Midtown Greenway, offers an array of transportation options. *(Saari Photography)*

amenities that make working enjoyable and by finding locations accessible for staff members who did not want to drive.[3] With the ability to store information in the cloud, space formerly used for storage was repurposed as group meeting rooms of varying sizes, or for lounges and recreation activities that fostered social interaction among staff members.

Office developers added roof decks, bike rooms, shared conference centers, and expanded health/fitness options in their buildings, and owners of older properties retrofitted space with these amenities in order to remain competitive. Cafeterias once installed by a single tenant for the sole use of its employees were renovated and opened to an entire building. Some buildings even installed quiet rooms where workers could take a nap. New amenities included dry cleaning dropoff and pet care; hair and nail salons or medical/dental professionals were recruited for ground-floor retail space; and discounts were arranged with other nearby providers. Office building management companies now offer their own apps, allowing employees to order and schedule services.[4] Installing storage space for delivered packages helps workers without secure places for home delivery during the business day.

Allocating Space for Office Amenities

"In the past, approximately 3 percent of portfolio space was committed to features like gyms and on-site dining. Today, owners should expect to allocate 10 percent, and those who are trying to attract highly sought-after tenants should look to reserve 12 percent or more."

Source: Colliers International, "Amenities: A Hot Commodity," white paper, Summer 2015.

Security and Technology

Security is paramount for government agencies and private tenants, both in the lobby and at the entrance to individual office spaces. Post 9/11, a staffed security desk in the lobby is common, even in relatively small properties and in suburban locations. Visitors must be cleared before entering the elevator area, and their belongings subjected to X-ray screening. Newer buildings are equipped with key-card entry systems or coded keypads for individual offices. Companies needing the most up-to-date security features are moving to fingerprint or retina recognition systems.

High-capacity electrical systems (with backup) are another requirement. All professional and business service firms want high-speed internet, flexible telecommunications systems, and both on- and off-site data storage capabilities. Call centers and other customer service operations have their own unique needs. Entire buildings have been converted to handle and store data generated by office-using businesses.

Energy-Saving and Environmentally Friendly Features

Energy-saving and environmentally sensitive "green" features are considered essential in a class A office building. Tenants are attracted to building features that reduce water and electricity use (thereby lowering the utility bills that are passed through to them) and create a healthy workplace for their employees. Indoor air quality, temperature and noise controls, and use of nontoxic building materials are as important as lavish lobbies, if not more so. Tenants expect their landlords to provide recycling services.

Developers of new buildings are seeking Leadership in Energy and Environmental Design (LEED) ratings, paying attention to site planning that maximizes natural light, installing windows that actually open, using recycled carpet, and devising under-floor heating and air-conditioning systems. Existing buildings are being retrofitted with conservation in mind. Improvements include use of nontoxic paint, replacing traditional lighting with energy-efficient types, and installing better controls for HVAC and interior lighting systems.

Studies have shown that these improvements enhance worker productivity and reduce illness-related absenteeism. Such changes can be achieved with little additional cost to building developers and owners, particularly if the building is relatively new. Some suburban properties are assigning close-in parking spaces to employees who drive hybrid or all-electric vehicles and are installing charging stations. Carpooling is still being rewarded with more convenient parking locations.

Parking and Transit

The availability and cost of parking and accessibility to mass transit in urban cores are important features when marketing office buildings. Auto-oriented suburban locations generally provide surface parking lots; spaces are usually available at no cost to users. In big-city downtowns, workers are expected to take mass transit. With the development of more housing in downtowns or nearby neighborhoods, walking or biking to work became more common, and some buildings installed secure bike parking areas. In smaller cities, transit service is often inadequate, so most workers will still have to drive to downtown jobs and will need parking.

Parking ratios that worked for suburban office parks built in the 1980s—three spaces per 1,000 square feet of office use—were deemed insufficient by tenants looking for new locations two decades later. As floor space per worker declined and more employees were using a given amount of floor space, suburban tenants wanted five or six parking spaces per 1,000 square feet of rentable area. Businesses that operated multiple shifts needed to feel comfortable that the available parking was sufficient to accommodate cars coming in and going out when shifts changed.

In mature suburbs with high demand for office space, new or upgraded office projects began to include decked parking. As a result of more intensive suburban space use, shuttles to nearby transit stations became increasingly common in large cities in the Northeast (and in other markets with commuter rail), making it easier for employees (especially reverse commuters) to leave their cars at home.

In dense downtowns in transit-friendly cities, many new buildings now provide no on-site parking at all,[5] or only an underground garage with a limited number of spaces at a high monthly cost. Instead, employer-subsidized transit cards encourage workers to use buses and trains. When employees need to drive, they park in public or privately operated garages that may not be on the same block as their offices. Market studies for downtown office buildings need to note available parking options for employees and visitors.

Greater use of ride-sharing services such as Uber and Lyft have affected how office building developers determine parking demand. And although the widespread use of driverless vehicles is still years away, this technology will also reduce the number of on-site parking spaces needed in suburban office parks and will require site plans to include safe pickup/dropoff areas. Market analysts need to monitor trends in ride sharing and use of driverless vehicles when evaluating whether a development's proposed parking ratios are appropriate.

Shared Spaces, Flexible Commitments

As more employees are permitted to work remotely one or more days a week or work as independent contractors, a growing trend is to use professionally managed flexible office arrangements, often referred to as "coworking" space. Coworking originally catered to the needs of freelancers, sole proprietors (consultants, attorneys, accountants, manufacturers' reps), or branch offices of larger businesses needing a presence in a small market. Tenants leased a small private office from a service provider, often for a year.

In contrast to conventional office-leasing situations where small businesses had to design, furnish, and equip their own spaces, shared office spaces in the 1990s and 2000s provided desktop computers and telephone lines, along with shared printers, copy machines, a receptionist, and conference rooms that their users could reserve. New businesses and self-employed professionals could show prospective clients or customers a permanent mailing address, an advantage for firms that were just getting started.[6]

Today's coworking spaces provide opportunities for collaboration among both entrepreneurs and established professionals. Multiple users might share a single large worktable rather than a private office (although coworking operators often include a limited number of private spaces, small-group meeting areas, and "booths" where phone calls can be made in private). Users drop in as needed, bringing their own laptops and cellphones. The operator provides

Coworking Gains Traction

Cushman & Wakefield estimates that over 200 coworking companies across the country are operating at least one location of more than 5,000 square feet. Nearly 20 companies have at least 10 locations in the United States. Half the inventory of coworking space at the end of 2017 had been added in the previous three years alone.

The company states: "In our view, the market currently seems to be comfortable with 15%–30% of a building/asset being allocated to a coworking provider with relatively strong credit. Anything above that may currently be viewed adversely. However, we expect that the range of comfort will increase over time as investors and lenders have more experience trading assets with significant coworking occupancy."

Source: Cushman & Wakefield Research, Coworking and Flexible Office Space, Additive or Disruptive to the Office Market?, August 2018.

wi-fi, high-speed internet access, and shared printers. Leases run for a year or less, in contrast to traditional office lease lengths of five to 10 years. Some operators allow users to pay by the day, the week, or the month, with no lease at all.

Other small shared office providers also emerged as the popularity of coworking was demonstrated by WeWork's fast growth after the recession. Although no REITs appear to be overexposed to this type of tenant, there is concern that coworking operators could lose members—and revenue— during an economic downturn, ultimately affecting occupancy in these buildings. The performance of coworking space during a future economic downturn is untested. Of the bigger players in the coworking business, only Regus/IWG was an established operator during the two real estate downturns in the 2000s.[7]

Initially, most coworking space users were independent contractors. Today, the user mix is more varied, including startup businesses using multiple desks. Large corporations are also leasing coworking space to quickly house an expanding workforce, move into new markets, experiment with new operations, and bring interdisciplinary talent together to brainstorm special projects.

For many startup firms, coworking is a way to save money on rent until their operations are well established. Flexible layouts allow businesses to add workers as their business picks up without adding space. Some users like the "cool factor"—using trendy office designs favored by tech companies. Management may believe that contemporary design and amenities such as lounges and exercise space would help attract young talent.

It is important to note that coworking spaces are being created in locations other than office buildings—in vacant retail stores, in excess space in office supply stores,[8] and in clubhouses of large apartment complexes. This factor contributes to an overall decline in demand for office space in traditional locations.

A coworking office space.

Not all workers are enamored with offices that have no privacy and long tables in lieu of individual desks. Some observers argue that open offices are noisy and distracting (not that "cubicle farms" had many fans). As stated in a 2018 *Harvard Business Review* article: "Despite optimistic assertions about the benefits of open office space, outcomes are mixed. In some cases, open-plan office designs are reported to increase collaboration, employee satisfaction, and communication, but in others these new spaces are criticized for creating distractions, reducing privacy and autonomy, and undermining employee motivation and satisfaction."[9]

Using Office Market Studies

As with other property types, office market studies can serve a variety of needs:

■ Developers want insight into whether current conditions justify new construction, advice on amenities and services to include, and assistance in determining the types of spaces to build. They need input on recent rent trends, likely vacancy rates, and future space absorption for their financial models. Developers also use market studies to convince local officials that modifications in zoning or site planning requirements are needed.

■ Owners of office buildings may commission a market study before embarking on a major renovation program or deciding whether the asset should be sold and, if so, how to price it.

■ Asset managers monitor markets to see how they respond to major additions to supply or to changes in demand (as when a major corporation vacates its space).

■ Potential buyers use studies to assist in making purchase decisions, soliciting equity investors, and obtaining financing.

■ Corporations that are considering moving their national or regional headquarters conduct office market screenings to identify suitable locations.

Big Management Firms Offer Coworking Spaces

Brokerage and property management firms that represent institutional landlords are beginning to take a more direct role in creating and managing coworking spaces (rather than simply leasing space to third-party operators). With more prospective tenants looking for lease terms that are shorter than the traditional 10 years, landlords are protecting their interests by jumping on the coworking bandwagon. CBRE created a new coworking brand of its own (Hana) as a wholly owned subsidiary that will build out and manage coworking spaces in partnership with owners. Its first venture will be in Dallas (opening in 2019), with plans for locations in 25 markets within three to four years.

Source: Peter Grant, "CBRE Launches New Co-Working Business, Taking on WeWork," Wall Street Journal (online), February 19, 2019.

How WeWork Works

In 2018, WeWork was leasing over 12 million square feet of space from building owners in 4,000 locations. The company states that its mission is to "build a community," not just a place to work.

WeWork's tenants are called members. Commitments run month to month, with four possible packages of services at different base prices. The least expensive membership entitles the user to a "hot desk" in a common area with no advance reservation needed; beyond one day per month, members pay for what they use. A "dedicated desk," also in an open area, reserves a personal space and adds a lockable cabinet. "Private" offices are glass enclosed, lockable spaces for one to 10 people; rooms can be created for larger teams if space is available.

Monthly fees include an allocation of credits that can be used to book conference rooms. Additional credits can be purchased. Members can also buy health insurance for themselves and their employees at WeWork's group rates. (This feature encourages members to continue to rent space.) WeWork can also arrange for members to receive accounting services for an extra charge. The following services are included in the monthly fee at a typical WeWork location:

- Offices designed to maximize natural light;
- Free wi-fi and ethernet connections;
- Desks, chairs, lamps, and filing cabinets;
- Use of a copier/scanner/printer on each floor;
- Coffee, tea, and fruit water;
- Common area lounges;
- A nine-to-five on-site manager;
- Daily cleaning;
- Special events, including catered lunches where members share experiences and solutions to problems;
- Networking gatherings with established professionals and business leaders in the community;
- Wellness programs; and
- Bike storage.

Many locations are pet friendly.

Source: WeWork, www.wework.com, January 2019.

- Tenants use market data to compare the terms offered by different landlords.
- Economic development officials commission market studies to determine competitiveness, identify potential development sites, evaluate untested office locations, and help them decide whether to offer incentives to prospective developers.

Preparing an Office Market Study

Market studies for office properties follow a format similar to that used in residential or retail reports, with a few notable exceptions. For office space, demand is more closely related to employment growth and the need to replace obsolete buildings than it is to household demographics—although household growth does create the need for local-serving office businesses. Net absorption is the key indicator of effective demand. As with all property types, attention must be given to supply trends, including construction activity, occupancy rates, and rent growth.

Defining the Market Area

Identification of the market area for commercial real estate is less subjective than for residential or retail development. In many cases, generally accepted development corridors or nodes can be used as the market area for the study. These local submarkets are commonly used by brokerage companies that report on market conditions, although those firms often have somewhat different geographic boundaries for the areas.

The exact extent of the competitive market area for a proposed office project depends on many factors:

- The location of buildings of similar size, age, and quality;
- Street and road patterns in the area surrounding the building;
- Proximity to mass transit, major metropolitan highways, and (at times) airports;
- Commute times from residential areas;
- Proximity to other facilities relevant to target businesses, such as universities, medical centers, research laboratories, or other institutions;
- Jurisdictional boundaries (and associated real estate tax rates);
- Physical barriers to access; or
- The image and quality of nearby land uses.

Office users tend to cluster in downtowns and along suburban highways, although smaller, specialized submarkets may blossom around universities or major medical centers. The market area for a downtown office building may encompass only a few blocks surrounding a proposed development site or an existing property, whereas the market area for a suburban office project may encompass several nearby nodes. In a large metropolitan area, a suburban submarket usually includes more than one highway interchange.

Submarkets can serve distinct tenant niches. For example,

■ In Manhattan, market analysts generally refer to the Downtown, Midtown South, and Midtown submarkets. In the past, these areas catered to different types of tenants: Downtown buildings were oriented to financial services firms and government offices; Midtown South buildings to creative, knowledge-based industries and companies engaged in the apparel industry; and Midtown buildings to law firms, accountants, public relations, and real estate companies. These distinctions began to blur in the 1990s, a trend that has continued.

Although the geographic definitions of these three submarkets remain largely unchanged, market analysts are now more likely to consider comparable properties in all three locations, depending on their tenant mix. New Manhattan submarkets are emerging with the development of Hudson Yards on Midtown's west side. Recent rezoning near Grand Central Station is encouraging sizable new office towers in Midtown East.

■ An office submarket can usually be found near an airport; it appeals to companies with a "frequent flyer" workforce.

■ An office building located next to a transit station might be more competitive with buildings located at other stations than with buildings in the same submarket that are well beyond walking distance from the station. A definition of the market area for such a building would need to take that possibility into account.

Site Evaluation

A parcel proposed for a stand-alone office—or for an office campus—will need to be carefully examined for its suitability. A team of engineering and environmental consultants must determine the site's physical suitability for the proposed development, evaluating utility capacity (and expansion potential), soil conditions, and groundwater issues early in the development process.

Land planners determine site and lot layout requirements, then prepare preliminary designs to see whether any variances will be needed. A site's topography plays an important role in project feasibility. For example, hilly sites may require extensive grading, which increases construction costs, but they may also provide excellent opportunities for tucked-under parking, which requires less excavation on a hilly site.

The market analyst gets involved at different points in the planning process. A developer who is unfamiliar with local market conditions may commission a preliminary market overview before hiring site planners and engineers, then proceed with detailed site studies only if market support for the project is likely. The market analyst is often asked to look at preliminary site plans and building designs to see whether they will be attractive to potential space users. Successful projects benefit from give-and-take between market analysts and the design team.

A market study should include a thorough evaluation of the site's advantages and drawbacks. The project's location directly affects the rent and occupancy levels it can achieve. Even office buildings located relatively near each other can experience significant location-based differences in rent and occupancy levels. As noted, a building within walking distance of a mass transit station, for example, may be able to obtain substantially higher rents than buildings a half mile away. Buildings with highway visibility can command higher rents than those without it. Land prices can reflect these location differences. Developers who choose sites based on price alone can find themselves unable to successfully compete in the market, even at lower rents.

Suburban office buildings gain a marketing edge when they are located close to freeways or roads that feed into the regional traffic system. Good access to adjacent roads is critical. Parcels located on key highways may have great visibility, but they may be inaccessible from those highways. Access for parcels located along major highways or frontage roads may be limited to side streets or even rear streets. The location, number, and arrangement of curb cuts and traffic lights for left turns into the parking lot can significantly affect the ease of access to a suburban office building.

However, good road access is not the sole determinant of success for a suburban property. Proximity to restaurants, shopping areas, and both outdoor and indoor recreation generates higher rents and faster leasing. These amenities are common in downtown submarkets; freestanding buildings in suburban markets may not be so fortunate. However, suburban locations are increasingly able to provide urban-style amenities, as more town centers and other types of mixed-use developments come on line.[10]

Demand for Office Space

In the past, the need for additional office space was primarily a result of employment growth in industries and occupations that use offices. Growth can occur when new businesses enter the market or when existing businesses expand. As discussed below, space allocation standards determine how many square feet of office space are needed. Although these standards are changing, this approach is still valid; however, the market analyst must take into account growth in the number of freelancers, independent contractors, and self-employed people, many of whom work from home or use nontraditional office locations.

Identification of Office-Prone Employment

Employment growth is considered to be the best indicator of demand for office space. However, the character and composition of the local economy greatly influence the share of total employment that is "office prone" or "office using." All sectors of the economy have some employees who use office space—even if they are just a few executives and senior managers in national or regional headquarters locations. However, office requirements for these high-level personnel can be quite different from those for entry-level or clerical employees. A high percentage of workers at individual businesses may spend most of their time in the field, traveling or working remotely. They need a permanent base of operations but not much space.

The ideal method for examining the extent to which employees of particular industries use office space would be to cross-reference employment by industry with occupation categories in a particular metropolitan area. But this analysis can be very time-consuming (and beyond the scope of work typically requested in a market study for a new or renovated office building). For example, NAICS code 51 (information) includes the motion picture industry, where only about one in four employees work in office occupations; however, this NAICS designation also includes the software development industry, where 95 percent of employees work in offices. Similarly, fewer than half of all workers in health care and

Estimating Office-Prone Employment

Moody's Analytics provides estimates and projections of office employment for a fee. Its "Employment in Office-Using Industries" indicator has historical data going back as far as 1970 and projections 30 years into the future. The numbers— provided at the national level and for states, metropolitan areas, and counties—are frequently updated. They are based on data from the Bureau of Economic Analysis, and the Current Employment Statistics (CES) and Quarterly Census of Employment and Wages (QCEW) from the BLS. The QCEW is the key source for county estimates because the CES's smallest geography is a metropolitan area.

Moody's definition of "office-using industries" has changed over time as the NAICS has been revised. In 2019, the NAICS categories for 2017 will be used. Because of differences among industries in the extent to which their workforce is office-using, Moody's relies on three- and four-digit NAICS codes. Only in the case of NAICS codes 52 (finance and insurance), 53 (real estate and rental and leasing), and 55 (management of companies and enterprises) are two-digit codes deemed sufficiently detailed, as shown in figure 6-2.

Analyzing employment at the three- and four-digit NAICS level zeroes in more precisely on job growth at potential tenant businesses. To see why, consider NAICS 53 (real estate and rental and leasing). The real estate segment (531) is a significant user of office space. However, NAICS 532 (rental and leasing services) is composed primarily of businesses that do not typically occupy space in multitenant office buildings—auto and truck rental, heavy equipment leasing, and formal-wear rental.

social assistance (NAICS 62) are in office occupations; the ratios are even lower for workers in nursing homes, home health, or child care agencies.

The concentration of jobs in specific industries can vary dramatically from national averages, and even within individual states or metropolitan areas. Market analysts need a good understanding of metropolitan area economies to determine how projected job growth translates into possible demand for new office space. Although economic trends are positive in the past few years, net absorption of office space is not growing at the same pace as job growth.

Figure 6-2
NAICS 2017 Office-Using Industries

Code	Description
5112	Software publishers
512	Motion picture and sound recording studios
513	Broadcasting (except internet)
5173	Wired and wireless telecommunication carriers
5179	Other telecommunications
518	Internet service providers, web search portals, and data processing services
52	Finance and insurance
53	Real estate and rental and leasing
5411	Legal services
5412	Accounting, tax preparation, bookkeeping, and payroll services
5413	Architecture, engineering, and related services
5415	Computer systems design and related services
5416	Management, scientific, and technical consulting services
5418	Advertising and related services
55	Management of companies and enterprises
5611	Office administrative services
5613	Employment services
5614	Business support services
5615	Travel arrangement and reservation services
6211	Offices of physicians
6212	Offices of dentists
6213	Offices of other health practitioners
8131	Religious organizations
8134	Civic and social organizations
8139	Business, professional, labor, political, and similar organizations
GVF	Federal government

Source: Moody's Analytics.

Employment growth in industries that have a high share of office jobs has not been especially strong, even during a period of economic expansion. Because office construction activity has continued (and little existing space has been demolished or converted to other uses), double-digit vacancy rates are commonplace.

As many economists point out, several negative factors affected office-prone employment in recent years:

- The movement of customer service and call center jobs overseas,

- Corporate consolidations in key office-using industries (especially banking and insurance), and

- Greater workforce productivity (thanks to new technology, which allows businesses to meet their targets with fewer employees).

Space Standards: Square Feet per Worker

The changing design standards discussed earlier in this chapter are as important as changes in the size of the office workforce. Real estate professionals and office architects agree that, over time, the amount of space per employee has been declining. (See Figure 6-3.) As recently as 30 years ago, tenants were signing leases assuming an allocation of 200 to 250 square feet of space per employee or more, with top executives or partners assigned private offices with more than 300 square feet.

No universal agreement exists on today's office design standards, and variation by industry is still considerable. Some businesses are averaging as little as 125 to 150 square feet per worker, especially in the tech sector, with even less space for employees in call centers, customer service operations, open (shared) coworking spaces, and government offices. Open offices (with no enclosed/private spaces) may have as little as 60 square feet per desk seat. With increasing rents, allocating less space per employee is one important way that businesses can save money.

Figure 6-3
Shrinking Space per Office Employee

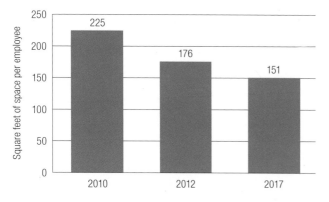

Source: Adrian Ponsen, "Trends in Square Feet per Office Employee: An Update," NAIOP Commercial Real Estate Development Association, Fall 2017.

Declining space allocations per employee, along with more people working at home or at nontraditional office locations, have contributed to less total demand for new space. Some companies have reduced their need for office space by permitting at least a portion of their workforce to share jobs, telecommute, or work during evening or night shifts. Consulting and accounting firms, as well as sales operations use office "hoteling"—where an area of the office is set aside and equipped for staff members who spend most of their time on the road and do not need a permanent space. Firms often find that it is easier to move (and take fewer square feet) rather than reconfigure space as their needs change. However, tenants often lease more space than they actually need during a booming market, hoping to lock in space for future expansion at current rents. Space standards evolve with technology, design innovations, workplace culture, and corporate employment policies.

Many businesses have rearranged existing space to provide more room for team projects; they also have reduced the number of cubicles and private office enclosures for top executives. This strategy also yields mixed results; although more collaboration and social interaction take place, managers and their staffs complain about distractions.

When preparing local projections of office space needs, the market analyst must obtain detailed employment estimates and forecasts. Chapter 3 discusses how to find employment data by industry and how to interpret the statistics. Occupational data are also helpful in distinguishing personnel who work in the field from those who work in the office. It is possible for office market analysts to estimate current levels of office-prone employment in a given submarket, but it will usually be necessary to purchase these data from a demographic data vendor, whose estimates are based on geocoded data from the BLS or state employment departments.

The Commerce Department's Bureau of Economic Analysis, state employment offices, and some regional planning agencies prepare employment projections for metropolitan areas and counties, but the frequency of updates varies widely among government agencies. Employment projections can be costly to obtain for areas smaller than a county or metropolitan area. However, firms such as CoStar and Reis sell this information for defined submarkets. In locations where these sources are unavailable, the analyst may need to allocate a share of projected growth in the county or metropolitan area to the submarket.

Replacement Demand

One reason that office construction continues to exceed growth in office employment is the need to replace obsolete facilities. Downtown submarkets in big cities contain numerous examples of vintage office buildings that have been converted to residential or hotel use. Other office buildings that lack character—and modern operating systems—have been demolished to make way for new projects if the site can be used profitably for new construction. No single source

One North in Portland, Oregon, comprises three architecturally distinctive buildings, developed collaboratively by two developers on three parcels, providing office space, retail space, and a common courtyard. *(Holst Architecture)*

of statistics exists on office or industrial demolitions or conversions, or the percentage of the total office inventory that these properties represent. However, companies that monitor the supply side of the office market delete these properties from the inventory when they are no longer being marketed for office use.

Use of Historical Net Absorption to Predict Future Demand

Office employment trends offer one approach to calculating the demand for office space. A second approach reflects net absorption trends. Net absorption—the change in the amount of occupied office space over a period of time—is a direct expression of recent demand. (Pre-leased space in buildings still under construction is not counted in net absorption statistics.) Historical net absorption data can be obtained from national and local commercial brokerage firms or purchased from data vendors or local consultants.

Both office employment trends and net absorption are imperfect proxies for office space demand, and neither approach should be relied on alone in market analyses. When used together, the two approaches can provide a reasonable picture of trends; however, the future may not replicate the past. It is important to look at what happened during periods of strong economic growth versus recession and consider what will likely happen in the regional economy when a proposed building is under construction and leasing activity is underway. Straight line projections are usually unreliable.

Changes in Space Use and Design: Law Firms

Law firms are a major source of demand for office space, and they typically have the most generous space allocations per professional among business services firms. Following trends seen elsewhere, law firms are also shifting toward more open space and collaborative work environments. They still want to be in new class A towers, but they want to use their space more efficiently. To save on cost, they are putting support functions on lower floors or in separate buildings in less expensive submarkets. Fewer private office spaces are provided, and less floor area is allocated for libraries and file storage. When they move, law firms are taking anywhere from 10 to 30 percent less space. And because fewer clients come to the office to meet with their attorneys, furnishings are less expensive.

By 2025, over half of the lawyers in the United States will be millennials. Law firms often sign leases of 15 years or more, so the spaces they take today need to appeal not just to current partners but to future ones as well.

Source: Julie Littman, "Goodbye Dark and Dreary, Hello Open and Well-Lit Law Office," Bisnow Bay Area, January 1, 2018, which is based on an interview with Sherry Cushman, executive managing director, Cushman & Wakefield.

Submarket Demand

Once the market analyst has thoroughly examined metropolitan or county demand, he or she must look at the relative advantages and disadvantages of the submarket in which a building is located or proposed. Several factors influence the attractiveness of one office location relative to others in the same metropolitan market:

- *Proximity to a business's client base or facilities it uses regularly.* This factor is why attorneys, title companies, and civil engineers tend to locate near the county office building or courthouse.

- *Availability of labor.* Skills needed will vary according to the types of tenants already found in the submarket, as well as the demands of prospective newcomers. A call center wants to know that it can find employees willing to take relatively low-paying, part-time jobs. In contrast, a tech company needs highly educated engineers and programmers. Such employers look for locations near university campuses and may seek out university-sponsored research parks.

- *Accessibility for workers,* both by car and by transit.

- *Proximity to employee amenities,* such as shopping, restaurants, and health clubs, which can be important in attracting executive talent.

- *Housing costs* in the surrounding community. Where workforce housing is scarce, employees spend more time commuting, and turnover rates may be higher. Companies that tend to hire young workers want to locate in areas with available apartments at affordable rents.

- *Image of the submarket* as a good place in which to do business.

- *Comparative rents.*

- *Real estate taxes,* which can vary not only by submarket but also by municipal jurisdiction.

- *Impact fees* (if any) levied in specific jurisdictions.

The sources of demand for a proposed multitenant office project can generally be segmented into two major categories: principal users and second-tier users. Principal users (a building's anchor or marquee tenants) are generally large and growing firms. Potential premium tenants will consider a new location if they are unable to expand into contiguous space at their current locations or if their current floor plans are inefficient. Much as their current landlords want to retain them, adjacent space for firms that want to expand may be occupied by other tenants who may be unable to relocate. If contiguous building floors are essential to a premium tenant's operations, moving becomes the only option. Developers must ascertain the presence of large, high-growth firms in the market area and their space needs. Relocation of corporate headquarters—within metropolitan areas or even across the country—can be another source of demand for large blocks of space.

The 1450 Brickell project is a 35-story, 586,000-square-foot office building located in downtown Miami. *(Robin Hill)*

A building's second-tier tenants are generally smaller firms, such as public relations companies, business consultants, and others that are drawn to a location near their major clients or one that provides access to potential clients. Small businesses have increased their share of total U.S. employment and now account for a larger share of total office occupancy. Leasing agents and property managers must be attentive to attracting and retaining dozens of small users, often those that will occupy less than 5,000 square feet apiece.

Demand analysis must go beyond general projections of future demand to identify and assess the sources of demand for the proposed office building. That should include the identification of potential tenants and their needs. Interviews with office brokers and economic development specialists will provide insight into the need for new space.

Use of Surveys

Surveying a sample of office tenants in a market area is always desirable before developers invest in a new or existing commercial building. For a prospective purchaser, conversations with tenants provide a sense of their overall satisfaction with the accommodations and with building management, as well as their plans at lease renewal time. Office developers benefit from learning about the needs of target companies, and those companies' perceptions about the metropolitan area and the proposed location.

For office buildings targeted to a particular tenant type, survey research can help determine the depth of demand. For a building targeted to medical services, for example, a short questionnaire can be sent by either email or U.S. Postal Service to health care professionals in the local market area, asking about their satisfaction with their current space and interest in expansion. They should also be asked about the years remaining on their leases. If a hospital is involved in the proposed project, it can encourage physicians to participate. Allied professions—such as physical therapists, laboratories, alternative medicine practitioners, nutritionists, and radiology centers—should also be contacted.

Tracking Supply

Four key metrics help analysts monitor office space supply changes: (a) inventory (the amount of existing space at a given point in time), (b) the percentage of inventory that is vacant or available as sublet space, (c) the amount of new space under construction that will be added to the inventory, and (d) trends in rent per square foot.

Market studies should include a brief summary of metro area and submarket office inventory by type of space and class, as well as background on the volume of recent construction. Next, the analyst would furnish descriptions of the most important competitive properties in detail, providing information on proximity to the subject site, ownership or management, building size and height, lease rates and terms, anchor tenancy (key tenants occupying the most space in a building), and vacancy rate.

A field survey may be needed to verify secondary data and to make certain that newly completed properties have not been omitted. When visiting an office building, the analyst may be able to check the tenant directory, note the types of tenants in the building, and observe the condition and attractiveness of the lobby. It must be noted, however, that the heightened security measures now typical in class A office buildings make fieldwork more difficult.

Building Inventory and Square Footage

It is important for the market analyst to understand property coverage and geographic delineations when citing third-party inventory statistics. Submarket boundaries can vary, depending on which firm is providing the data. If maps are not included in a report obtained from a brokerage or data vendor, analysts should contact the source to ascertain how local submarkets are defined. A clear sense of the minimum size of structures included in space data is important. (Data providers—be they brokerages or research companies—can have different definitions. National brokerages may rely on size cutoffs set by their local affiliates, which can vary from one metro area to another.) Analysts should use data that best address the submarket area that covers the subject building or future development site and should include the most important comparables.

Figure 6-4 shows how three national real estate brokerage and leasing firms rank the 20 largest U.S. markets by size of total space inventory. Note the differences. For example, Charlotte appears on the Cushman & Wakefield list, but not on the other two. The CBRE ranking separates San Jose from San Francisco, as does Cushman & Wakefield, but their relative positions are very different.

Leasing Activity

Leasing activity is the gross amount of space for which leases are signed in a specified time period. Leasing activity does not account for space that has been vacated during the period, so it is not a good measure of overall market strength. However, reports on major leases signed in the current period—whether from brokerage reports or the local real estate press—can offer insights into location shifts within submarkets, and in some cases, current rents. As discussed earlier, *net absorption* subtracts vacated space from new leases. For example, if a tenant moves out of 50,000 square feet of space in one building and moves into the same amount of space in a nearby building, 50,000 square feet of space has been leased but net absorption is zero.

Figure 6-5 shows the 10 business types responsible for the most new leases signed in the first three quarters of 2018, according to global brokerage firm JLL. Its analyst calls attention to the importance of coworking enterprises, ranking third on the list. This is a dramatic change from 10 years ago, when such firms did not exist in their current form.

Figure 6-4

Comparison of Top 20 Office Markets by Total Inventory

JLL ranking		CBRE ranking		Cushman & Wakefield ranking	
1	New York	1	Manhattan	1	Manhattan[a]
2	Washington, D.C.	2	Washington, D.C.	2	Washington, D.C.[b]
3	Chicago	3	Chicago	3	Chicago
4	Los Angeles	4	Boston	4	Dallas/Fort Worth
5	Dallas	5	Dallas/Fort Worth	5	San Jose
6	Houston	6	Houston	6	New Jersey[c]
7	Boston	7	Los Angeles	7	Houston
8	New Jersey	8	New Jersey	8	Los Angeles
9	Philadelphia	9	Atlanta	9	Boston
10	Atlanta	10	San Francisco	10	Cleveland
11	Denver	11	Denver	11	Atlanta
12	Orange County	12	Seattle	12	Denver
13	Seattle/Bellevue	13	Philadelphia	13	Detroit
14	Phoenix	14	Orange County	14	Charlotte
15	San Diego	15	Phoenix	15	Phoenix
16	Minneapolis	16	Detroit	16	Pittsburgh
17	San Francisco	17	San Jose	17	Orange County
18	Silicon Valley	18	San Diego	18	San Francisco
19	Baltimore	19	Pittsburgh	19	Sacramento
20	Detroit	20	Minneapolis/ St. Paul	20	San Diego

Sources: JLL Research Report, Office Outlook United States, *Q2 2018; CBRE Research,* U.S. Office Figures, *Q3 2018; Cushman & Wakefield,* Market Beat: U.S. Office, *Q3 2018.*

a. *Includes Midtown, Midtown South, and downtown.*

b. *Includes Maryland and Virginia suburbs.*

c. *Includes northern and central New Jersey.*

Vacancy Rates

The amount of vacant space and the vacancy rate (calculated as a percentage of inventory) are important indicators of market health. However, the overall vacancy rate in an office submarket does not, by itself, tell the analyst anything about the characteristics of existing space on the market. It is not unusual to see construction begin on new office buildings in areas where the vacancy rate exceeds 10 percent; if the area attracts large firms and if no sizable contiguous spaces (full floors) are available, developers will start new projects in order to capture key tenants that are seeking to expand. Similarly, if vacancies are concentrated in class B or C space, new construction of class A space might be justified.

If vacancy rates are stable or dropping despite additions to the supply inventory, then market conditions or trends can be viewed positively. If inventory is largely unchanged but vacancy rates are climbing, demand for office space is weakening.

Conditions in the local submarket should be compared with national, metro area, and county indicators to see whether declining demand is a purely local phenomenon or is indicative of a weakening economy. The market analyst must then consider how long this situation will likely last.

Two aspects of vacancy rate calculations bear mentioning:

- During economic downturns, tenants with long-term leases that are cutting jobs or dropping business activities will often have space available for sublet. The amount of sublet space on the market can have a significant impact on the strength of the market. Some firms report *available space* (which includes sublets) as well as *vacant space* (square footage that is already empty or will be when a lease expires).

Figure 6-5
Top 10 Sources of Leasing Transactions by Tenant Type
First Three Quarters of 2018

Tenant business	Leasing activity (million sq ft)
Technology	16.1
Finance and insurance	14.3
Coworking	12.8
Health care	6.0
Law	5.1
Life sciences	3.3
Media/entertainment	2.8
Professional services	2.6
Energy	2.4
Accounting and consulting	2.3

Source: JLL, "U.S. Office Market Statistics, Trends, and Outlook," www.us.jll.com.

Ascertaining the amount of space available for subleasing in a market area (sometimes called "shadow space") is an important element of the supply analysis. When markets are overbuilt, tenants may vacate before the end of the lease period to secure less expensive or more desirable space. If business is contracting during a recession, a company might lay off a portion of its workforce and consolidate operations in fewer locations.

- Sublet space, even if it is not occupied, is not technically vacant. It is still covered by a lease and the tenant is still paying rent. It is, nevertheless, part of the available inventory. Tenants that vacate before the end of their lease term generally attempt to sublease the vacated space. Often, space available for sublease is offered at a discount and thus is less expensive than other vacant space. The availability of large blocks of sublet space can impinge significantly on the viability of current and proposed office projects in the market area. It is important, therefore, to include an estimate of sublet space in the analysis of the competition that a prospective project will face. In response to this need, many sources now publish availability rates rather than vacancy rates.

- Vacancy varies by property class. When new class A buildings are being completed, and competition for tenants is strong, businesses located in lower-quality class B and C properties may see an opportunity to move to better buildings with little increase in rent.

Figure 6-6 shows the highest and lowest vacancy rates in the 25 largest U.S. downtown and suburban office markets, as identified by CBRE. Dallas registers the highest vacancy rates in both downtown and suburban areas. In the third quarter of 2018, 28 percent of downtown space and 20 percent of suburban space in metro Dallas were vacant, which are very high shares during a period of economic growth. In contrast, the figure shows that a number of downtowns had vacancy rates below 10 percent. Technology companies are key tenants in those markets. That factor also accounts for low suburban vacancies in San Francisco and San Jose.

Vacancy rates can exceed 10 percent in depressed areas, but also in vibrant economies with few constraints on development of new supply. Because of the several years it takes to build a high-rise office building, developers are unable to respond nimbly to sudden changes in demand. In a tight market where ample capital is available, a lender might require pre-leasing only 30 percent of an office building's space. However, if demand is softening, and new supply will soon be available, stricter pre-leasing requirements will apply. As figure 6-6 shows, office vacancy rates can be quite high, even in metropolitan areas with growing economies. Dallas is a good example. If occupancy is flat or declining, buildings that must be renovated in order to stay competitive will struggle to raise rents to cover increases in associated construction costs for both labor and materials. CBRE Research reported that construction costs increased over 2 percent per year between January 2013 and January 2018.[11]

If the market analyst is helping the developer prepare a feasibility study, the analyst will be required to give an opinion on stabilized occupancy on the basis of historical performance of similar properties in the submarket and new supply that will come on line at the same time. Lenders will be skeptical about overly optimistic occupancy scenarios, especially in locations where it is easy to build new space.

Construction Activity

CBRE Econometric Advisors tracks annual office space completions. The firm notes that the peak year for office completions was 1989, when a total of 121.1 million square feet of new space was brought to market. In subsequent economic cycles, peak-year new space was less than that of the previous peak: 110.3 million in 2001, 76.5 million in 2008, and 64.8 million expected in 2018 (the peak of the most recent cycle).[12]

Rent Trends, Lease Terms, and Concessions

Most office leases are expressed in square feet of net rentable area. Unlike apartment buildings, for which rent is quoted on a monthly basis, office rents are usually expressed on an annual basis. Market analysts should review trends in asking rents for the metropolitan area as a whole and for the submarket. These data are usually available in reports issued by brokerage firms or can be purchased from national data vendors. When evaluating office rent trends, the analyst should focus on properties in a comparable quality class, but it is also important to know the difference in average rent per square foot for class A, B, and C properties. The ability to retain a tenant at the time of lease renewal will be influenced by the gap in rent between property classes. If the gap is fairly narrow, a class B tenant might be willing to move up. If the gap is significant, the landlord of a class A building will be competing with more affordable space in class B buildings that have been upgraded.

During periods of market softness, building owners will offer concessions to attract tenants. Concessions can include free rent (for example, a year of free rent on a 10-year lease), an above-standard allowance to cover interior buildout costs, or an offer to pay for a new tenant's moving expenses. *Effective rents* are contract rents net of concessions.

Triple-net rents are typical in new buildings. Tenants are billed for a pro rata share of real estate taxes, insurance, and utilities on the basis of the amount of space leased. Office leases often include *escalator* clauses: the rent increases each year (or at some other specified interval) according to a commonly accepted index, such as the BLS's Consumer Price Index. In some buildings, the landlord may include certain utilities and taxes in the base rent and charge tenants only for actual increases above and beyond the initial base year of the lease. These rents are quoted as "modified gross."

When leasing a new building, the landlord will want to avoid having the same duration for all leases. Staggering the years that leases expire is a way to minimize the risk that the

Figure 6-6
Downtown and Suburban Office Vacancy Rates, 25 Largest U.S. Office Markets
3rd Quarter 2018

Highest downtown vacancy rates		Lowest downtown vacancy rates	
Market	**Rate (%)**	**Market**	**Rate (%)**
Dallas	28.0	San Francisco	5.2
Minneapolis/St. Paul	20.7	Boston	6.9
Phoenix	20.6	Austin	7.2
Los Angeles	17.5	Manhattan	7.6
Denver/Baltimore	17.2	Seattle	8.2
U.S. average[a]	**10.5**		

Highest suburban vacancy rates		Lowest suburban vacancy rates	
Market	**Rate (%)**	**Market**	**Rate (%)**
Dallas	19.8	San Francisco	7.1
Houston	19.5	San Jose	7.7
Chicago	18.8	San Diego	10.1
Atlanta	18.7	Orange County	10.9
Miami/Boston	18.3	Austin	11.0
U.S. average[a]	**14.1**		

Source: CBRE Research, Q3 2018 U.S. Office Figures.
a. All markets covered by CBRE.

building will need to find several new tenants in a single year, should leases not be renewed. For an existing property, the current rent roll should be reviewed.

Evaluating Competitive Buildings

High-rise office buildings are more prestigious, often because they offer attractive views and natural sunlight on the upper floors, as well as attractive styles (both classic and contemporary). Also, buildings in the best locations tend to be taller, if only because land will be expensive and developers will need to justify the additional expense by building higher. Corner properties are preferable to midblock properties that may lack good views and lose the light benefits of height. Several other important factors attract office tenants—and support higher rents:

- Building visibility.

- Compatibility of surrounding uses.

- Ease of access. In the suburbs, it is especially important for visitors to be able to enter and exit the property—and find parking—easily. In a downtown location, the cost of parking may also be a factor, both for employees and for visitors. Some tenants want valet parking. Covered parking can be helpful in extreme climates.

- Attractive, enduring exterior design. Although each tenant will have an opinion on architectural style, an experienced analyst can tell whether a building has long-term curb appeal, is attractively landscaped, and is well maintained. A good impression is important in attracting tenants. The durability of exterior finishes will be important when examining older properties. The appearance of the building should fit the rent level.

- Floor sizes and space configuration.

- Energy efficiency. Increasingly, tenants seek space in "green" buildings, not only to be socially conscious but also to save money on utilities.

If the analyst can visit a competitive building, he or she should also note the number of elevators and calculate whether it is sufficient to meet today's standards. In the past, one elevator was adequate for every 40,000 to 45,000 square feet of net rentable area above the ground floor. With more employees using a given amount of space, elevators will be more crowded; a sense of the density of workers helps determine the appropriate number of elevators. Also, prospective tenants will ask about cell-service reliability in the elevators, lest important business communications be lost.

Amenities such as a concierge, fitness center, restaurant or deli, shared conference room, dry cleaner, convenience store, and bank should be noted. If those amenities are not found in the building, they should be located nearby. The image of the lobby must be appropriate for the types of

tenants in the building. Some firms are sensitive to cost issues and therefore do not want to pay for an overdesigned, expensive lobby.

For the buildings that are deemed most competitive with a proposed development or acquisition, the market analyst should include tables that summarize building characteristics and comment on the advantages and drawbacks of the subject property. A comparison of rents (asking and effective) should be presented, along with information on vacancy rates, the size of vacant spaces, and recent absorption. Important tenants should be noted. (When considering an acquisition of a multitenant building, an investor will want to be sure that no one tenant occupies more than 30 percent of the space in a building, lest occupancy be vulnerable to a large move-out or corporate downsizing.)

Private data vendors, local commercial brokers, and online listings are the best sources of information on individual competitive buildings. Nothing substitutes for conversations with experienced leasing agents and property managers, who can verify information and provide insights. To predict absorption for a new property—or a property that is being substantially rehabilitated and re-tenanted—one must ask other managers about the absorption experience of their properties (the percentage of space that was pre-leased when construction started, during construction, and after the building opened). Absorption history for recently completed projects is one of the best indicators of what to expect when a new property enters the market, but it is important to remember that the balance of supply and demand can quickly change as businesses move in, contract or expand, or leave altogether.

Putting It All Together

A comparison of the current rate of net absorption of office space with the current (and planned) supply of space gives a fairly clear picture of the overall balance between demand and supply in the market. For example, if annual net absorption in the area has been averaging 50,000 square feet and 50,000 to 75,000 square feet of space are available, demand and supply are in balance. If, however, 100,000 square feet of space are available, the market has a two year supply of office space. And if the market contains 500,000 square feet of available space, it has a 10 year supply. This simple comparison of current demand and supply represents an expedient way of gauging the market's short-term supply–demand balance, but this snapshot should not be the basis for predicting future trends. The market analyst must look for factors that could affect absorption of office space in the future and interpret current market conditions accordingly.

In an office market study, the market analyst's conclusions will include estimates of absorption, rents, and stabilized vacancy rate. All three elements are vital to preparing a cash flow analysis. For determining absorption, analysts should use ranges rather than a precise number. The stabilized vacancy rate should reflect what is realistic in the local market. In an area where vacancies in good properties are typically higher than 10 to 15 percent, a stabilized vacancy rate of only 5 percent is inappropriate, even for a new class A building. The absorption pace will depend on the extent of pre-construction leasing. Concessions as a share of contract rent should also be estimated, although they may disappear as market conditions improve.

The analyst will also indicate the proportion of supportable demand that will be captured by the subject property and whether that proportion is reasonable and achievable. An initial proxy for a building's "fair share" capture rate is the share of competitive supply that it will represent once it is completed. This share of current supply method is a good first cut at estimating a building's capture rate. A building may absorb more or less than its share, depending on its location, design, and features, and how its proposed rents compare with competition of similar quality. Perhaps location and amenities that make the subject building superior to the competition or lower rents that make it more competitive will enable the proposed project to capture extra market share. It is important to be realistic, especially when economic conditions support below-average demand projections.

As indicated in previous chapters, the market study should include tables summarizing the features of comparable properties, along with photographs of the buildings and any unusual features of their surroundings. As was discussed in chapter 4, some analysts offer a "spec sheet" for each of the most important competitors, including photographs of the buildings and important nearby features; others list the properties and their characteristics in a table to facilitate comparisons. Maps should include (a) the boundaries of the local submarket and its location within the metropolitan area; (b) the location of the subject site within the submarket, surrounding land uses, and nearby transportation infrastructure; and (c) the location of comparable properties, existing and planned.

Data Sources

Data for metro areas, counties, and even submarkets are available online from national and local commercial brokerage firms that operate in the area. However, information on individual competitive office buildings will be more difficult to find without purchasing data from private vendors or obtaining listing sheets from firms representing buildings with available space. Descriptive information on buildings with available space for rent can also be found online, through such sources as Loopnet.com or Showcase.com, which aggregate listing information from multiple brokerages. However, sources that advertise available space will not provide information on buildings that are fully occupied.

In small markets, printed information may be available from local business organizations and economic development groups; market analysts will need to check to be sure that the best comparable properties are covered. Also, printed sources are not frequently updated. In contrast, vendors selling office market data usually conduct surveys quarterly, at a minimum. Local real estate agents, leasing agents, and property managers rely on such data for creating marketing

Figure 6-7
Example: Vacancy Rates and Asking Rents in Office Submarkets
Phoenix Metro Area, 1st Quarter 2018

Submarket	Vacancy rate (%)	Year-over-year basis point change	Asking rent (per sq ft)	Year-over-year % change
East Valley	11.0	−430	$24.42	2.5
West Phoenix	14.3	10	$24.78	9.7
East Phoenix	17.4	−120	$26.99	4.8
Scottsdale	17.4	−30	$25.37	4.5
Central Corridor	17.9	−270	$24.78	2.5
Airport area	19.8	−340	$23.82	3.8
Northwest Phoenix	20.8	110	$21.20	3.9
North Phoenix	22.3	390	$22.76	4.3
Overall metro area	17.0	−150	$24.53	5.0

Source: Marcus & Millichap, Office Research Market Report, *Second Quarter 2018.*

Note: basis point = 1/100th of 1 percent. Data are as of the first quarter of 2018.

materials; investors use these reports to make decisions on acquiring or selling individual buildings or property portfolios.

Metrowide and submarket data must be used carefully. Brokerage firms use varying criteria when tabulating inventory.

- Some inventories do not count buildings with less than 50,000 square feet of space or eliminate buildings with only a single tenant.

- One firm might use a 50,000-square-foot minimum in a small metro area but count only buildings with 100,000 square feet or more in larger markets.

- Firms define metropolitan areas differently, depending on which suburban areas are included. Local submarket boundaries may also be different, depending on the source.

Figures 6-7 and 6-8 show examples of information in Phoenix office market reports available on the internet from two different commercial brokerages. Using data from Marcus & Millichap, figure 6-7 shows vacancy rates and average asking rents for the first quarter of 2018 in eight submarkets and for the metro area as a whole. It also indicates changes in the previous year. The firm notes that demand has been rising rapidly in the Phoenix area; rents increased in all eight submarkets, with West Phoenix registering the biggest gain. It is noteworthy that the range of rents in Phoenix submarkets is fairly narrow; in many metropolitan areas, the rent differential between downtown and suburban submarkets is considerable. Not shown in figure 6-7 but noted in Marcus & Millichap's report, office market conditions improved in the Phoenix area despite a high volume of new space delivered in the previous three years. Similar observations should be part of a thorough market study.

Taken from a Colliers International report, figure 6-8 shows that nearly two-thirds of the office buildings in the Greater Phoenix market and 58 percent of the space are class B. Not surprisingly, construction activity is concentrated in the class A sector; space in class A buildings under construction but not yet completed is equal to just under 5 percent of the existing class A inventory and a much lower share of total office space. Barring a dramatic economic downturn, these numbers do not suggest overbuilding. New space deliveries in 2019 are expected to be below 2018 levels.

Although both reports provide useful snapshots of recent market conditions, they provide little historical context other than to indicate that vacancy rates declined, on average, in the previous year.

Figure 6-8
Example: Office Market Summary Statistics
Phoenix Metro Area

	Phoenix metro market	Class A	Class B	Class C
Number of buildings, 2Q 2018	2,908	317	2,027	564
Square feet (000s), 2Q 2018	147,591	49,651	85,161	12,779
Vacancy rate[a] (%)				
2Q 2018	14.7	14.4	15.7	9.4
2Q 2017	16.1	15.2	17.3	12.3
Asking rent, per sq ft, 2Q 2018	$24.69	$28.89	$22.69	$18.00
Net absorption, 2Q 2018 (sq ft, 000s)	1,112	352	527	232
New construction completed, 2Q 2018 (sq ft, 000s)	220	150	70	0
Under construction, 2Q 2018 (sq ft, 000s)	2,963	2,427	536	0

Source: Colliers International.

a. Includes sublease space.

Figure 6-9
Example: Milwaukee Area Office Inventory by Class
3rd Quarter 2018

	Buildings (Number)	Space inventory (sq ft, 000s)	Vacant space (sq ft, 000s)	Vacancy rate (%)
CBD	**142**	**19,849**	**1,411**	**7.1**
Class A	29	8,134	706	8.7
Class B	100	10,904	674	6.2
Class C	13	811	31	3.8
Class A share	20.4%	41.0%	50.0%	—
Other submarkets	**473**	**29,215**	**2,453**	**8.4**
Class A	97	11,310	826	7.3
Class B	334	15,972	1,558	9.8
Class C	42	1,933	69	3.6
Class A share	20.5%	38.7%	33.7%	—
Milwaukee market total	**615**	**49,064**	**3,864**	**7.9**
Class A	126	19,444	1,532	7.9
Class B	434	26,876	2,232	8.3
Class C	55	2,744	100	3.6
Class A share	20.5%	39.6%	39.6%	—

Source: Colliers International, https://www2.colliers.com/en/Research/Milwaukee/2018-Q3-Milwaukee-Office-Report.

Also using information from Colliers, figure 6-9 combines the market indicators shown in the previous two figures. It separates Milwaukee's downtown from its suburban submarkets and compares class A structures with class B and C space. Note that this table lacks information on rents and, like the information for Phoenix, offers no historical context. What it does tell a market analyst is that the Milwaukee market has low vacancies generally.

Private data vendors have more detailed information, especially the historical trend data that brokerage firms tend not to maintain online after a year or two. Analysts who purchase reports from CoStar, Reis, or other vendors can also define custom geographies and obtain data for areas that will be most comparable to a subject building or site. Such data can also be useful for a general overview of the commercial real estate supply–demand balance.

Figure 6-10 is an example of data purchased from Reis for use in a study prepared for a suburban municipality. The data show that buildings in the five-mile study area are small, rents are low, and vacancies are high, even by suburban standards. The office market in this area had yet to recover from the effects of the recession. Using this information, as well as interviews and field observations in the area, the market analyst could clearly demonstrate to the municipality that no demand existed for new office space.

Figure 6-10
Example: Office Market Data Available from Reis
Suburb X and Five-Mile Radius from Subject Site in Suburban Chicago

Inventory and rents		
	Suburb X	Five-mile radius
Number of buildings	14	25
Total square footage	441,517	1,091,048
Median building size (sq ft)	22,000	30,000
Median year built	1990	1983
Average asking rent (per sq ft)	$16.59	$15.00
Average vacancy rate (%)	19.7	28.0

Historical rent and vacancy rates: five-mile radius		
Year	Average asking rent (per sq ft)	Vacancy rate (%)
2013	$16.57	29.1
2014	$17.10	24.6
2015	$17.11	32.4
2016	$16.89	30.2
2017	$16.58	28.0

Source: Valerie S. Kretchmer Associates Inc., using data from Reis.

Notes

1. Colliers International, *U.S. Research Report: Office Market Outlook,* Q2 2018.

2. Colliers International, *U.S. Research Report: Office Market Outlook,* Q2 2018.

3. See Leslie Braunstein, "Inside the Office Space Revolution," *Urban Land* online, October 26, 2017.

4. See Ryan Ori, "Luxuries in Chicago Office Buildings: There's an App for That," *Chicago Tribune,* March 12, 2018; and C. J. Hughes, "In a Bid to Fill Office Buildings, Landlords Offer Kegs and Nap Rooms," *New York Times,* October 23, 2018. Tishman Speyer's Zo app allows employees in its New York City buildings to book personal services and classes, have meals delivered, reserve travel, and order prescription refills for delivery. The app is planned for rollout in Boston, Chicago, Los Angeles, Philadelphia, and Washington, D.C.

5. Washington, D.C., has taken the lead in discouraging garages in new office buildings.

6. This type of shared office space is still common, not only in the United States but also worldwide. Established in Brussels in 1989, Regus (now International Workplace Group or IWG) has 3,000 locations in 120 countries. In addition to private offices, Regus now offers "hot desks" subject to space availability and reserved spaces with a phone line and headset. It rents multiple desks for businesses needing satellite locations or for groups needing temporary space for special projects. Desks can be rented by the hour, day, or month. See the Regus website, www.regus.com, for more information.

7. Regus weathered two recessions, including a bankruptcy after 2001. Between 2008 and 2010, its occupancy rate dropped 5.5 percent. Cushman & Wakefield concluded that "the declines in occupancy were significant from a profitability standpoint but not sufficient to materially impact the long-term prospects of the organization."

8. Office Depot is creating coworking spaces, called Workonomy Hub, in some of its stores, starting with a location in Los Gatos, California. Staples has installed coworking spaces with 2,500 to 3,500 square feet of space in three store locations in the Boston area that had surplus space.

9. Brandi Pearce and Pamela Hinds, "How to Make Sure People Won't Hate Your New Open Office Plan," *Harvard Business Review* (online), January 11, 2018. See also Rebecca Knight, "Staying Focused in a Noisy Open Office," *Harvard Business Review* (online), October 11, 2018.

10. See Elaine Misonzhnik, "Commercial Assets in Walkable Locations Command Premium Prices, Rents," *National Real Estate Investor* (online), April 16, 2015.

11. CBRE Research, "U.S. Construction Costs & Office Development Trends," October 2018.

12. CBRE notes that construction cost indices cannot account for all factors that drive office development costs, such as land prices and regulatory compliance.

CHAPTER 7

INDUSTRIAL AND WAREHOUSE SPACE

Because shipping is usually a key activity at industrial properties, industrial sites are more transportation-driven than office sites. The market area for an industrial building might be the business parks surrounding an airport or near an intermodal rail facility. Industrial users cluster near airports, ports, rail freight yards, beltways around a metropolitan area, or points where interstate highways come together. A research and development (R&D) complex might depend on proximity to a university or other research center.

Traditionally, access to suppliers and delivery destinations has been more important for industrial users than access to workers. Warehousing and distribution functions are characterized by relatively low ratios of employment to building square footage, an important factor to note when selecting market analysis methods. However, when unemployment rates are very low, as they were in 2017 through 2018, the ability to hire warehouse workers and trained truck drivers become more important criteria when evaluating industrial or warehouse sites.

A production line for metal cans in a manufacturing plant.

Characteristics of Industrial and Warehouse Buildings

The line between office and single-story industrial space has blurred, because so many businesses today require flexible space to accommodate a wider range of activities. Industrial building types include a continuum from R&D facilities, which can closely resemble single-story office space, through big-box warehouse or distribution space with ceiling heights of 36 feet or more. Hybrid space mixes are characteristic of small industrial and showroom properties and do not fall neatly into one category of use. Newer industrial buildings have been built in business parks, most of which are dominated by warehouse/distribution activities rather than manufacturing, much of which takes place outside the United States.

Building Types

Industrial space is classified in four broad categories: manufacturing (both light and heavy); warehouse/distribution; flex space (including buildings combining offices with showrooms, storage, or both); and R&D facilities (engineering, design, and laboratories). Many subtypes exist, each with its own needs, including the following:

- *Manufacturing buildings* house specialized equipment to produce materials or finished products. Depending on the goods they create, factories will have unique needs for electrical power, water, drainage, ducting, ventilation, and exhaust systems; they may use chemicals in their production processes that need to be safely stored. Some observers would also classify freight forwarding and truck terminals as industrial space, although they may have little in the way of actual building space.

- *Warehouse/distribution buildings* are large facilities with high ceilings, multilevel racking, and increasingly sophisticated computerized inventory control and order assembly systems. They are typically single-story buildings, but new multilevel structures are being built in space-constrained, densely populated locations to be closer to delivery destinations. For big retail chains, *warehouses* are used for bulk storage; goods often remain in the warehouse for a long time (for example, long before the Christmas holiday's peak demand) to be sure they are available when needed. Inventory would then be shipped to *distribution centers* that service individual stores. Another example is a warehouse that stores parts for multiple automobile dealerships in a region; the parts are delivered to individual dealers as needed for repair work. A single warehouse often stores goods for multiple businesses.

A data center server room.

Data Centers

Data centers are a special type of industrial building designed as repositories for computing facilities (mainframes, servers, telecommunications equipment, backup systems). They house and maintain information technology systems and data storage. The need for data storage is coming not only from tech service providers (cloud providers) but also from companies in the finance and health care fields. A data center can serve a single user or rent space to multiple tenants. Many data centers locate in suburban business parks, but older office multistory space can be retrofitted for this use.

A property being considered as a data center must have fiber optic connectivity, cloud services, reliable electrical systems (and backup sources), sufficient water for cooling and fire suppression systems, and up-to-date security systems. Such properties often have raised floors for easy cabling and water damage protection. Although not labor-intensive, these facilities need highly skilled maintenance and operations staff—skills that are in short supply.

Unlike other industrial properties, data center inventory and vacancy rates are expressed in megawatts of capacity rather than square feet of space. Rents are based on kilowatts of usage per month. According to CBRE Research, the largest data center market by far is Northern Virginia, followed by Dallas/Fort Worth, Chicago, and Silicon Valley. Absorption was strong in 2017 and 2018.[1] A number of public data center REITs invest solely in data center properties.

Large e-commerce businesses rely on corporate-owned *fulfillment centers* where employees download online orders, pick items, and pack them for shipping to consumers. Amazon's many fulfillment centers are examples of this type of operation. Small e-commerce firms use fulfillment centers operated by third-party logistics companies (known as 3PLs). To be successful, a fulfillment center needs advanced computer and conveyor systems so that goods are delivered quickly to consumers. Fulfillment centers also handle returns. The need for speed often results in multiple shifts or even 24-hour operations.

A single warehouse/distribution building could house a mix of storage, distribution, and fulfillment operations for multiple companies that pay rent to the 3PL company, which in turn pays rent to the building owner.

Refrigerated warehouses provide freezer or cold storage space (or both) for perishable goods in transit to supermarkets, restaurant supply houses, and retailers.

- *"Wet" biotech labs* are used in R&D facilities. They are expensive to equip and need reliable water supply.

- *Showrooms* are generally single-story buildings that combine display space with offices or storage space, or both. They are similar in design to flex buildings.

- *Telecom and data centers* are large buildings with their own power supplies and reinforced floors capable of supporting generators, computer servers, and telephone switching equipment. Data centers are often located in business parks, but they can also use solidly built, older multistory office or industrial buildings; minimal windows are preferred.

The interior of Park 8Ninety in Missouri City, Texas, a 439,704-square-foot warehouse building that opened in 2018 as part of a 127-acre business park. *(City of Missouri City)*

A worker at a research laboratory.

Each type of industrial space has distinct characteristics. A market study for R&D space would not devote attention to warehouse/distribution buildings. However, market studies for flex space often contain information on nearby single-story and low-rise office buildings.

Figure 7-1 shows that industrial space is increasingly dominated by very large warehouse/distribution buildings. Special-purpose spaces (largely used for laboratories and research facilities) and manufacturing facilities are only a small fraction of recent additions to the industrial space inventory.

Ownership and Management

Most new factory buildings are designed and built to user specifications and are owned by corporations or investors through sale-leasebacks. Laboratories and warehouse facilities may be single user or multitenant, speculative or built to suit. Although large store chains and e-commerce retailers tend to operate their own warehouses, multitenant bulk warehouses run by 3PL management are very common.

Self-Storage

Self-storage properties—which used to be called mini-warehouses—are not warehouses in the traditional sense. Households that need additional space for seasonal items or a place to safely store sports equipment and household goods are the primary customers for self-storage properties. Small businesses also use self-storage for supplies. The best locations for self-storage are in areas with a high (or growing) concentration of nearby rental apartment buildings or condominiums and good visibility from major arterials so potential customers are familiar with the location.

Older office buildings and empty big-box retail space have been repurposed as self-storage. Individual spaces are as small as 25 square feet (typically eight feet tall) and as large as 250 square feet or more. Some locations have spaces large enough to store recreational vehicles or boats. These properties can be single story or multistory, depending on land availability and zoning. Single-story properties typically have multiple buildings with adjacent parking; access is through a gated security fence. In multistory structures, building entryways are secure and tenants access their units through a lighted corridor. Many properties are climate-controlled and have on-site managers.

Data vendors and trade organizations provide information on self-storage properties, including number of units, rents by size of unit, and new-supply pipeline.[2] Increasingly, national brokerage firms are providing market and investment insights for self-storage properties. Six REITs specialize in this property type.

Figure 7-1

Composition of U.S. Industrial Space Inventory by Purpose
Inventory (000s of Square Feet) as of Q3 2018

	Total stock	New deliveries	Under construction
Warehouse/distribution	9,651,902 / 73.5%	187,557 / 94.6%	242,376 / 94.4%
Manufacturing	3,440,970 / 26.2%	10,603 / 5.4%	13,951 / 5.4%
Special purpose	37,018 / 0.3%		

■ Warehouse/distribution ■ Manufacturing ■ Special purpose

Source: JLL Research, Industrial Outlook, Q3 2018.

Note: New deliveries are total for 2018 through the third quarter. Warehouse/distribution and manufacturing account for more than 95 percent of recent industrial construction.

Characteristics of Big-Box Distribution Buildings

- Precast or tilt-up concrete construction
- Primarily used for distribution
- Size of 200,000 square feet or larger
- Ceiling heights of 28 feet clear or greater

Design Features

Warehouse/distribution facilities are further distinguished by the proportion of space used for office functions (as opposed to package assembly, shipping, or storage). Small businesses often occupy flex space in which a high proportion of the space has office finishes (25 percent or more). Rents per square foot for high-finish industrial space will be much higher than for bulk warehouses, where less than 10 percent of the square footage is used for offices.

Industrial properties are distinguished by eight key features:[3]

- Building size,
- Site coverage,
- Loading capability,
- Parking for cars and trailers,
- Ceiling heights,
- Space buildout and extent of office-quality finishes,
- Power, and
- Floor load and floor levelness.

Because most manufacturing and flex industrial space is low-rise (less than 20 to 24 feet tall) and much of it is unfinished (or fitted out by the users), these buildings take less time to build than do office structures. The same is true of taller big-box warehouse/distribution buildings. As a result, industrial markets in small metro areas can quickly become imbalanced, with additions to supply exceeding demand.

Significant growth in big-box space occurred with the rise of e-commerce in the past decade (see figure 7-2). Yet despite the relative ease of constructing bulk industrial space, the warehouse property market has traditionally been less volatile than has the office market. Rents and occupancy will experience slow but steady increases during periods of economic expansion and slight declines when recessions are underway.

Because of greater automation and trends in construction techniques, today's warehouse buildings are different from those built 20 or 30 years ago:

- Buildings with 200,000 square feet or more are now the norm; a 500,000-square-foot or 1 million-square-foot warehouse is not unusual at all. (The metropolitan Atlanta

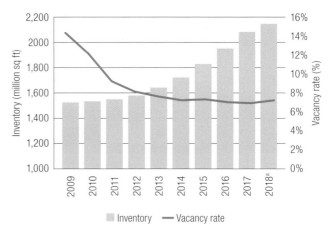

Figure 7-2

U.S. Big Box Industrial Trends, 2009–2018

Source: *Colliers International, U.S. Industrial Services,* North America Big Box Market Report: 2018 Mid-Year Review and Outlook, *October 2018.*

a. 2018 data are for the first half of the year.

market has 66 big-box warehouses with 750,000 square feet or more.)[4] Warehouses at logistics hubs can average more than 1 million square feet, especially where containers move from ship to train and truck or from train to truck.

- Businesses that do not handle perishable items are moving to fewer but larger warehouse buildings.
- New "high-cube" structures have ceilings at least 24 feet tall, with 32 to 36 feet being the current norm. Some are as tall as 60 feet. High ceilings require more costly racking systems, sprinklers, and sophisticated lighting systems.
- Tech capabilities are increasingly important. Order input, assembly, and distribution are now highly automated operations governed by the principles of just-in-time inventory control.
- Highly durable concrete floors are needed to accommodate tall, heavy stacking systems and pallets. In high-bay buildings, such floors are more expensive to build because the surface needs to be precisely level so materials that are stacked high will remain stable.
- Today's warehouses have more truck docks, essentially lining the two long sides of buildings (a 1 million-square-foot-distribution center will be 500 feet wide and 2,000 feet long), allowing simultaneous loading and unloading ("cross-docking"). The number of required docks is determined by the number of trucks being unloaded or loaded per shift, by the average time required to unload or load, and by when the trucks are likely to arrive (peak periods or slow periods). Site plans must provide for wider turning radii and longer parking bays to accommodate bigger trucks. The land planner and engineer must consider the size, dimensions, and shape

of a proposed building site; those factors affect the ability of trucks to maneuver on a site and within a business park.

- Tenants may require drive-in bays for smaller trucks that make local pickups or deliveries. In the past, such bays were more common for flex (office/warehouse or office/showroom) buildings. With a greater focus on "last-mile" delivery to nearby consumers, greater attention is given to drive-in spaces for small-load pickups (see discussion later in this chapter about how the logistics industry is dealing with last-mile delivery issues).

Changing design standards might suggest that much of the existing warehouse inventory is obsolete. However, the space requirements listed earlier reflect the needs of large national and multinational firms. Local businesses, which often combine light assembly with distribution and storage functions in one facility, do not require (and do not want to pay for) state-of-the-art facilities. A flexible facility that can be expanded or reconfigured easily to accommodate tenant needs will be preferable for both investors and users.

Manufacturing and laboratory space are usually designed to meet user specifications. The customized nature of each facility poses problems when tenants move out or when owners shut down operations. Because of the high cost of

Online Grocery Shopping Increases Demand for Refrigerated Warehouse Space

Supermarkets and the food service industry rely on smaller refrigerated warehouses. Food and floral distribution businesses must be close to their customers to ensure product freshness.

"The growing popularity of online grocery shopping could result in demand for up to 35 million square feet of U.S. cold storage space shifting from retail stores to warehouse/distribution centers within the next seven years, according to a report from CBRE. . . . CBRE estimates that the U.S. market for cold-storage space spans roughly 180 million square feet of industrial space—namely refrigerated warehouses—and about 300 million square feet of space in grocery stores and other retail venues. That ratio . . . will shift in the coming years as online grocery sales will grow from 3 percent of all grocery sales in 2017 to 13 percent by 2024. . . . Larger concentrations of food-grade cold storage facilities occur in states with substantial agricultural production, large populations, or both."

Source: Brett Widness, "In Brief: Growth in Online Grocery Sales Expected to Increase Demand for U.S. Cold Storage Warehouse Space," Urban Land online, April 2, 2018.

A big-box warehouse under construction in Burlington County, New Jersey. (Real Estate Strategies Inc./RES Advisors)

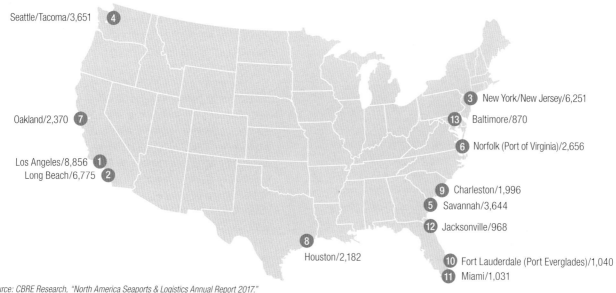

Figure 7-3
Busiest U.S. Ports
By TEU (000s), 2017

Seattle/Tacoma/3,651 **4**

New York/New Jersey/6,251 **3**

Baltimore/870 **13**

Norfolk (Port of Virginia)/2,656 **6**

Oakland/2,370 **7**

Los Angeles/8,856 **1**
Long Beach/6,775 **2**

Charleston/1,996 **9**
Savannah/3,644 **5**
Jacksonville/968 **12**

Houston/2,182 **8**

Fort Lauderdale (Port Everglades)/1,040 **10**
Miami/1,031 **11**

Source: CBRE Research, "North America Seaports & Logistics Annual Report 2017."

Note: TEU = 20-foot equivalent unit of cargo handled in 2016. Circled numbers indicate each port's rank by TEUs handled.

"Last-Mile" Distribution Facilities

"The key variables for multistory warehouse development are high population density, strong e-commerce penetration and tight market conditions for suitable last-mile fulfillment buildings and development sites. While efficiently accommodating the 53-foot trucks commonly used in U.S. logistics is a challenge (much smaller trucks are used in Asia and Europe), at least five multistory warehouses are underway or in the pipeline in New York [City], Seattle and San Francisco. If successful, these new projects could set an example for developers in other cities that face similar conditions."[a]

"Access to the 'last mile' of delivery in urban locations has become one of the most critical factors in site selection. Facilities must not only be the right size, they must also have access to a highway and/or waterway, appropriate zoning, an accessible employee base and be as close as possible to their customers . . . [B]uildings of several forms can be utilized, including former big-box stores; industrial sites in various stages of remediation; under-used office space; and, in one instance in Chicago, an underutilized parking garage. . . . A final frontier for e-retailers may be multi-story warehouses. . . . These urban centers are changing from replenishment warehouses that need five racks and 30-foot ceilings. Multi-story urban centers use mobile robotic storage, where individual products are picked off shelves."[b]

Source a: CBRE Research, "Going Up: Vertical Solutions in Industrial and Logistics," United States, October 11, 2018.

Source b: Joseph A. Panepinto Sr. "E-Commerce Industry's Last Mile Needs Create New Demand for Old Warehouse Space," National Real Estate Investor online, October 4, 2018.

retrofitting factory or high-tech buildings for new users, it takes longer to absorb vacant manufacturing or R&D space than warehouse/distribution space.

Increasingly, e-commerce operations are looking for ways to quickly reach their customers, even if their products are nonperishable. Expanding use of free same-day or next-day delivery as a marketing tool creates demand for distribution transfer facilities near dense urban population concentrations (where the customers are). Referred to in the logistics industry as *last-mile* distribution space, their primary function is to aggregate and deliver packages within a relatively small area. Such buildings still need room for trucks to maneuver; sufficiently large sites are rare (and expensive) in city neighborhoods. Some e-commerce businesses are looking at vertical (multistory) spaces, often involving reuse of old warehouses or office buildings. Goods reach the higher floors using ramps and cargo lifts.

Specialized Markets

Metropolitan areas often specialize in different types of industrial space. For example, Austin, Boston, Minneapolis, San Diego, Seattle, and Silicon Valley are well known as centers for high-tech research and laboratory space. Atlanta, Cincinnati, Columbus, Indianapolis, Kansas City, central New Jersey, and Sacramento attract warehousing because of their locations at the junction of two or more interstate highway routes.

Container shipments at the ports of Charleston, Jacksonville, Los Angeles/Long Beach, Miami, New York/Newark, Oakland, Savannah, and Seattle/Tacoma create strong demand for space to handle both imports and exports. (For a ranking of port activity by tonnage handled, see figure 7-3.) The transfer of containers from rail to truck generates demand in midcontinent locations such as Chicago, Dallas, and Kansas City.

Air logistics companies (UPS, FedEx, and DHL, with hubs in Louisville, Memphis, and Cincinnati, respectively) created demand for space in those markets. Manufacturing space is concentrated in both large and small metropolitan areas, primarily in the Southeast (where unionized factory labor is uncommon) and the Midwest.

Demand for Industrial Space

Unlike office demand, the need for most types of industrial space is difficult to determine using employment projections. Most industrial uses generate comparatively few jobs per square foot of leasable area, and space needs have little to do with changes in the number of jobs in NAICS codes for production or distribution businesses. In addition, manufacturing employment has been shrinking in most U.S. markets. R&D properties are the only industrial class in which demand can be tied to job growth. R&D buildings are more labor-centric than warehouses, and demand can grow in areas with a highly skilled, tech-oriented workforce and near universities that have strong reputations for research and product development.

Demand Determinants

Warehouse/distribution demand is usually generated by changes in corporate logistics, technical innovations, and freight volumes—not job growth. The need for modern space

that can accommodate computerized inventory control and order fulfillment generates replacement demand that is not evident in employment statistics. Expansion in global trade activity also propels warehouse demand. The desire for space near ports or air cargo terminals can create opportunities if suitable sites are available. Demand is also being driven by the continuing growth in e-commerce; warehouses are the "stores" that serve the online shopper.

As indicated earlier, distance to ports, air cargo facilities, and interstate highway interchanges are key factors in the demand for warehouse/distribution buildings. Examining trends in shipping tonnage going into and out of nearby airports and water ports can be a very useful way to look at demand growth.

Air freight handling facilities cluster near major international airports and the highways that service them. Figure 7-4 lists the 20 largest air cargo handling facilities. Memphis and Louisville are the worldwide hubs for FedEx

Figure 7-4
Ranking of Top 20 Airports, Air Cargo Handling
By Landed Weight

Airport	2017	2012
Memphis International	1	1
Anchorage Stevens	2	2
Louisville International	3	3
Chicago O'Hare	4	6
Miami Internatonal	5	4
Los Angeles LAX	6	7
Greater Cincinnati	7	9
Indianapolis	8	5
Dallas/Fort Worth	9	10
Ontario	10	13
Oakland Metropolitan	11	12
Newark Liberty	12	11
New York JFK	13	8
Atlanta Hartsfield	14	14
Honolulu	15	15
Seattle-Tacoma International	16	19
Philadelphia International	17	16
Phoenix Sky Harbor	18	18
Houston Bush Intercontinental	19	17
Portland	20	22
Denver International	21	20

Source: U.S. Department of Transportation, Federal Aviation Administration.

Demand for Port-Related Industrial Real Estate Is Growing on the East Coast

"The Panama Canal expansion project, which was completed in 2016, doubled the capacity of the canal by adding a new, wider lane of traffic, allowing larger ships to pass. This has increased the demand for larger container vessels, which are causing bottlenecks and customs delays at U.S. seaports. For years, California ports were the only ones in the U.S. that could accommodate the largest vessels from Asia. However, now that these largest ships can transit the expanded Panama Canal, some are making their way to East Coast markets. The increase in East Coast port activity is driving improvement projects at these locations, which in turn are raising the value of industrial real estate adjacent to the ports. . . . Owners and developers of modern distribution product near major ports have an opportunity to achieve strong returns as the renovations of those ports continue and global trade expands further."

Source: Eric Messer, "Expanding Port Activity Is Driving the Value of Adjacent Industrial Real Estate," Real Insight, Newmark Knight Frank, December 2018.

An Amazon fulfillment center in Kent, Washington, a suburb of Seattle. (*VDB Photos/Shutterstock.com*)

Demand for Warehouse/Distribution Space

"Demand for logistics space can be grouped into three main drivers: consumers' basic daily needs, cyclical spending, and structural trends. In the first half of 2018, . . . [t]ransportation companies were active lessees of space as they built out networks to accommodate greater parcel-delivery volumes resulting from e-commerce. Today, e-commerce fulfillment represents approximately 20 percent of new leasing, with online sales generating three times the demand for warehouse/distribution space compared with in-store sales. . . . In 2017, the U.S. market effectively hit capacity constraints, with users forced to wait for new product to come online before they could expand. . . . This lack of available space caused net absorption to decline in 2017 and early 2018, even as latent demand accelerated."

Source: PwC and the Urban Land Institute, Emerging Trends in Real Estate® 2019 *(Washington, DC: PwC and the Urban Land Institute, 2018), 71–72.*

and UPS package delivery operations, respectively. Anchorage is important because of its relative proximity to Asian exporters via the polar route. The other locations are served by international air carriers and are at the crossroads of multiple interstate highways.

Replacement Demand

As with office space, the replacement of obsolete facilities is a factor in estimating industrial demand. Today's manufacturing and warehouse buildings are largely single story; many older multistory buildings have been demolished, have been converted to loft apartments or condominiums, or simply are no longer actively marketed as industrial properties. However, the increasing need for last-mile distribution facilities may well resurrect demand for older warehouses and manufacturing facilities, especially if they have ample dock-high loading areas and can handle shipping containers.[5]

Although most attention is given to very large high-cube warehouses, local businesses still need storage space and will be content to rent inexpensive space with 12- to 18-foot ceilings. Less obvious is whether industrial properties built 30 to 40 years ago are still competitive for manufacturing or R&D use; most are not.

Using Historical Net Absorption

Using historical average annual net absorption as the basis for future demand projections is a common approach, but it must be used with caution. Demand for industrial space is sensitive not only to technology changes and the need to replace obsolete buildings, but also to national and regional economic conditions. Moreover, a weak economy can curtail industrial demand very quickly. As is the case for office space, the analyst needs to look at how net absorption changed during periods of economic slowdown or recession. Conversely, the comment from *Emerging Trends* suggests that high demand with little space availability will artificially reduce net absorption even in a strong market.

In assigning a share of metropolitan area absorption to a particular submarket, the analyst should also consider whether past trends will be indicative of future development patterns; new highway links, rail line improvements, government incentive programs, escalating land prices, or other factors could shift shares among submarkets. In all cases, the market study should describe the methods and assumptions behind future projections.

Government Incentives

To some extent, demand is influenced by the availability of government incentives to spur industrial development. The nature and extent of such incentives—be they tax abatements, revenue bonds, tax increment financing, infrastructure improvements, the new Opportunity Zone program, low-cost or free land, or workforce training—can make a business park or an individual building much more marketable. When passed through to tenants in the form of lower rent or to investors as a tax deduction, the value of these incentives can be considerable.

Although office tenants generate more jobs per square foot than most industrial space users, the focus of economic development incentives on production activity is a throwback to an era when factories employed workers earning good incomes. Today, attracting R&D facilities is a frequent goal for government officials because they provide high-paying jobs and generate few negative effects (such as truck traffic or noise). Whereas government incentives favored industrial properties in the past, municipalities and states are increasingly offering incentives to attract national and regional headquarters offices that will draw well-educated and highly compensated workers, as was seen in the competition for Amazon's second headquarters.

Defining the Market Area

Depending on the type of industrial property being analyzed, criteria for defining a competitive market area can be very different.

- Marketing a site for industrial development is often based on distance by highway from major population centers, expressed as drive time for trucks. Other locations a similar distance from the same key population centers would be the competition.

■ Because of the large amounts of land they require, most new manufacturing operations and big-box warehouses tend to be located away from downtowns and older neighborhoods, which accounted for the popularity of suburban and exurban business parks that were developed in the 1970s and 1980s. In more rural locations, economic development organizations encouraged creation of these parks and provided incentives (free land, workforce training, infrastructure improvements, and marketing support) as a way to keep good jobs in their jurisdictions. In such situations, the competitive market area for a new industrial development could consist of similarly sized sites or buildings in business parks in nearby locations.

■ For operations dependent on receiving, storing, packaging, and/or shipping imports or exports, competitive properties will be close to ports, airports, or rail freight terminals and near highway interchanges that can handle inbound and outbound truck traffic.

Because industrial properties can be highly specialized, the market area may need to be expanded so that truly competitive product is included in the research effort.

Supply Analysis

For industrial properties, the supply analysis starts with a review of past trends and current conditions in the metropolitan area and in the submarket where the subject site is located. Information (historical and current) on the size of the inventory, vacancy rates, net absorption, and rents is assembled by type of space and class of property. Space available for sublet is important as well as new or vacated space. The analyst should also contact local or county government agencies to find out how much space is approved but not yet under construction.

As with other land uses, field observations are important when the market analyst evaluates competitive properties. Security concerns have always made it difficult for market analysts to visit operating manufacturing or laboratory buildings. These properties are more likely to be single-user buildings rather than multitenant. In a business park, the analyst may be able to learn about the characteristics of firms occupying space through interviews with the park's leasing or management staff and learn about the age and sizes of spaces available at the time from broker listings.

Fastest-Growing Industrial Market

For 2016–2018, the East/Central Pennsylvania industrial market was the fastest growing in the United States. This area's attractiveness for warehouse development results from its proximity to major population centers in the Northeast and Midwest that are less than a day's drive from the Allentown/Bethlehem area and its ample supply of relatively inexpensive land.

Big-box warehouse buildings in a business park in northeast Pennsylvania. *(Real Estate Strategies Inc./RES Advisors)*

Figure 7-5
Largest Industrial Real Estate Markets
Based on Total Industrial Space Inventory, 3rd Quarter 2018

Rank	Market	Inventory (sq ft, millions)
1	Chicago	1,183.1
2	Los Angeles	801.7
3	New Jersey[a]	727.0
4	East/Central Pennsylvania	718.4
5	Dallas/Fort Worth	603.7
6	Atlanta	576.9
7	Inland Empire (CA)	538.1
8	Detroit	470.0
9	Houston	436.0
10	Cleveland	353.7
11	Kansas City	292.2
12	Charlotte	276.6
13	Phoenix	271.3
14	Seattle	267.1
15	Cincinnati	242.5

Source: JLL Research, "U.S. Industrial Market Statistics, Trends, and Outlook," third quarter 2018, www.us.jll.com.

a. Includes both northern and central New Jersey

Figure 7-6
Lowest and Highest Industrial Availability Rates
3rd Quarter 2018

Lowest rates (<5%)		Highest rates (>10%)	
Detroit	3.3	San Antonio	14.5
Cincinnati	3.4	Austin	12.4
San Francisco peninsula	3.7	Baltimore	11.4
Oakland	4.2	Greenville	11.2
Orange County, CA	4.4	Hartford	10.9
Milwaukee	4.5	Central Valley, CA	10.8
Los Angeles	4.6	Charleston	10.8
Portland	4.6	Boston	10.3
Savannah	4.6	Memphis	10.2
Salt Lake City	4.8	Walnut Creek/I-680, CA	10.2
U.S. average (%)	7.1		

Source: CBRE, U.S. Industrial & Logistics: Q3 2018 Figures.

Inventory

Figure 7-5 shows the top 15 industrial real estate markets according to total square footage. Inventory statistics from JLL include all types of industrial facilities, not just warehouses. The analyst needs to distinguish the performance characteristics of the property types most comparable to the subject development (existing or proposed buildings) from the industrial inventory in total.

Leasing Activity and Net Absorption

As indicated in previous chapters, net absorption is the change in occupied space over a specified time period. Analysts must distinguish between net absorption and leasing activity for industrial properties in the same way as was indicated for office buildings in chapter 6. By comparing trends in net absorption and leasing activity, analysts can reasonably describe the underlying strength and stability of an industrial market. For example, a market in which the rate of net absorption and the rate of leasing activity move in tandem over time is more stable than a market in which net absorption and leasing activity (sometimes referred to as gross absorption) exhibit widely varying rates. At the

same time, because so much industrial space is single user or corporate owned, the market analyst must be certain to understand the nature of space being built and absorbed.

As discussed previously, a straight-line projection that uses recent trends as the basis for estimating future events ignores the all-but-certain appearance of the next stage in the economic cycle. Nor can an analysis that relies on recent trends take sufficient account of cyclical changes in net absorption. Market studies should look beyond recent absorption to consider how shifting national and local business cycles will affect supply. Overly optimistic forecasts can lead to overbuilding; similarly, being too conservative can mean missing opportunities.

Vacancy and Availability Rates

Commercial brokerage firms typically provide information on industrial *availability,* not only vacancy. Because so much industrial space is corporate owned, vacant space is not always on the market. Available space is a better measure of full or partially occupied buildings that could be acquired or leased. Tenants often have excess space they do not currently need, or they might be planning on vacating in the near term and would be willing to sublet.

A strong industrial market is generally characterized by an availability rate no higher than 5 to 7 percent. The attractiveness of a submarket in a metropolitan area—and individual buildings within that submarket—is judged on the basis of how close it comes to this ideal range. Because industrial buildings are constructed more quickly than offices, projects can be put on hold when leasing activity slows and net absorption turns negative.

Figure 7-6 shows that 2018 industrial availability rates in major markets fell in a fairly narrow range. Only two metro areas shown in the figure (Austin and San Antonio) show more than 12 percent of their inventory available for sale or lease, and only three markets (Detroit, Cincinnati, and San Francisco) had extremely low rates under 4 percent. If one compares this with office vacancy rates reported by the same brokerage firm, a much higher share of office space is available. In general, demand for office space has been stagnant or declining, whereas demand for industrial space has been strong in recent years.

Although empty manufacturing buildings are a common sight in older cities, many of them are not suitable to modern production operations or cannot be economically reconfigured for a different industry. Modern, adaptable manufacturing space tends to have the lowest availability among the three main types of industrial buildings and shows little movement from year to year. In contrast, R&D space occupancy is the most volatile of industrial types.

Only a few market data sources provide industrial space information by subtypes. Warehouse data are the most widely available because the buildings are easiest to categorize. Most market data from secondary sources are lumped into a single category labeled "industrial."[6] Although data portrayed in this way explain little about actual market trends and the performance of individual subtypes of industrial property, the preponderance of multitenant industrial space is in warehouse or fulfillment buildings—a share that has grown significantly over the last decade. Analysts may have to make the best of imperfect data, but identifying a data source that accurately characterizes the industrial market is worth the time and trouble.

Rents

As with office space, rents per square foot for industrial property are quoted on an annual basis in most markets. An industrial market study should include analysis of rent trends, focusing on the types of space most similar to the subject property. Rents per square foot for R&D space, especially laboratories, will be much higher than for bulk warehouse properties, so the analyst must explain exactly what is included in industrial rent statistics presented in his or her report. Figure 7-7 shows lowest and highest rent per square foot for industrial facilities in large metro markets during the third quarter of 2018. Of the 10 markets with the highest rents, seven are located in California, where development constraints make adding supply in response to positive market conditions difficult. The lowest triple-net rents are seen in the South and Midwest.

Transactions

Another way to look at the health of industrial markets is to look at recent sales transactions, comparing the number of properties traded, amount of space, and average sale price per square foot to investment activity in preceding years. These data are important for investors who are considering the acquisition of an existing building. For new construction, having information on the cap rates associated with recent property trades helps developers and lenders estimate building values.[7] Transaction information is often reported in the real estate or general business press, but the amount of detail provided can be limited. Sales comparables can be purchased from sources such as CoStar and Real Capital Analytics. The market analyst should visit the buildings to see how they are similar to or different from the subject property.

Figure 7-7
Lowest and Highest Industrial Asking Rents
3rd Quarter 2018

Lowest	(per sq ft)	Highest	(per sq ft)
Greenville, SC	$3.33	San Francisco peninsula	$33.89
Louisville	$3.75	San Jose	$20.36
Columbus	$3.87	San Diego	$12.72
El Paso	$4.01	Walnut Creek/ I-680, CA	$11.76
Milwaukee	$4.05	Northern Virginia	$11.11
Dallas/Fort Worth	$4.29	Oakland	$11.04
Cincinnati	$4.32	Orange County	$11.04
Savannah	$4.32	Austin	$10.07
Indianapolis	$4.34	Los Angeles	$9.96
St. Louis	$4.51	Suburban Maryland	$9.26

Source: CBRE, U.S. Industrial & Logistics: Q3 2018 Figures.

Note: Rents are triple net per year.

A vacant manufacturing facility in Williamsport, Pennsylvania.
(Deborah L. Brett & Associates)

It is important to remember that transaction values reflect the availability of capital as well as the characteristics of the properties being traded. When the market is flush with funds for equity investment or mortgage loans, property prices are driven up even when property supply fundamentals— rent growth, net absorption, occupancy—are showing signs of weakness.

Future Additions to Supply

The inventory of competitive supply must include planned projects that may come on line and compete with the project under consideration. Such data are more difficult to obtain and less reliable than surveys of existing buildings. Not all approved projects are actually built, and others are modified before the project is completed (this is especially true of large, multibuilding industrial parks that are built out over many years). Some local economic development agencies and planning offices compile lists of submitted projects and track their progress through the approval, site preparation,

and construction process. Officials in these agencies are likely to know about proposed projects and should be able to provide some details. Market analysts can confirm and expand upon information from public agencies by questioning brokers and developers about building plans.

As with other property types, in market areas that contain a plethora of small government jurisdictions, assembling information on the status of projects approved, under construction, or planned for the future can be very time-consuming. Purchasing construction pipeline information from private data vendors may be more efficient. Companies such as CoStar and Reis may bundle this information with historical and current supply performance data. When the market analyst needs to provide preliminary answers quickly or has only a few weeks to complete a full report, purchasing data from third-party sources can be a time saver. The analyst should check the information against announcements in the real estate press or general business news outlets if time and budget permit.

Evaluating Competitive Industrial Space

The type of industrial property being studied will determine the nature of comparable buildings or business parks included in the market study. For R&D and office/showroom properties, emphasis should be placed on similar buildings, both new and old. Rent information for conventional office space or small warehouse buildings can also be useful for comparisons. Data on the market for high-cube distribution centers need not be included.

For all industrial building types, each competitive property's advantages and drawbacks should be discussed with respect to age, physical attributes, accessibility, building condition, proximity to highways, and parking. In a warehouse/distribution study, such elements as ceiling height, office buildout percentage, column spacing, building depth, the number of docks and ground-level doors, truck parking and turning space, and other functional components help define the property's marketability. Depending on the type of operation, water supply and sewer service are important (especially for food-processing and bottling operations). Reliable electric power is a must. At fulfillment centers, extra parking is needed to accommodate multiple shifts; these facilities are more labor-intensive than bulk storage warehouses.

Vacancy rates, tenant mix, recent lease signings, move-outs, and upcoming renewals should be noted to the extent that information is made available by property managers or through secondary sources. For business parks, the mix of building types and sizes should be described, as well as amenities (restaurants, health club, hotel) and site features (landscaping, trails). The report text should also indicate whether the business park includes corporate-owned/leased single-user buildings as well as multitenant leased space.

In analyzing an existing multitenant project proposed for acquisition, the analyst should review a rent roll or, at minimum, a leasing summary. These sources identify tenants,

Industrial Supply Information Available from CoStar

CoStar sells market data for all existing industrial properties and for a subset that excludes owner-occupied buildings. Quarterly indicators include the following:

- Number of properties;

- Rentable building area (square feet);

- New inventory delivered (square feet);

- Vacant space (total, available for direct lease, and sublet space)—square feet and percentage;

- Available space (total, available for direct lease, and sublet space)—square feet and percentage;

- Average asking rent, triple net, for direct versus sublet space, and total available space; and

- Gross and net absorption, quarterly and year to date, for direct and sublet space.

CoStar can provide data for predefined submarkets or custom-defined areas. The company also compiles detailed data sheets on individual properties, both existing and under construction, which are very useful for identifying the best comparable properties and their characteristics. Properties are rated on a scale of one to five stars, but are also identified as class A, B, or C. The data sheets contain information on building size, year built, ceiling height, number of high docks and drive-ins, number and sizes of available spaces, and ownership. Vacancy rates and asking rents per square foot are compared with submarket conditions overall and for properties of similar quality and age. Contact information for leasing agents is also included.

Processing cherries for packaging in the Yakima Valley, south-central Washington state. *(Trong Nguyen/Shutterstock.com)*

rental rates, lease terms and expiration dates, and other relevant factors. The client or the analyst obtains this information from the current owner or the listing broker. In the case of a project that is not yet built, the analyst's job will be to recommend the characteristics that are most desirable for the market by examining comparable properties.

Putting It All Together

As indicated in previous chapters, the market study should include tables summarizing the characteristics of comparable properties, along with photographs of the buildings and any unusual features of their surroundings. At a minimum, maps should include (a) the boundaries of the local submarket and its location within the metropolitan area; (b) the location of the subject site within the submarket, surrounding land uses, and nearby transportation infrastructure; and (c) the location of comparable properties, existing and planned.

Data Sources

Sources of information on the current economic base and historical employment statistics by NAICS code for counties and metropolitan areas are covered in chapter 3. The U.S. Bureau of Labor Statistics and state labor departments are the most important providers, along with the U.S. Census Bureau's County Business Patterns.

Although demand for industrial space is not directly related to growth in total employment, trends in employment in NAICS code 4841 (general freight trucking) and 493 (warehousing and storage) are good indicators of past growth in demand for warehouse/distribution space. For manufacturing (NAICS codes for sector 31–33), the analyst should look at the types of manufacturing businesses permitted under local zoning codes and then consider the number of such businesses included in the zip code where the subject property is located. These data can serve as proxies for identifying the types and sizes of manufacturing businesses in a county. Availability of workforce skills needed for manufacturing operations can be identified through state labor department offices. Information on top employers is often compiled by chambers of commerce and by the local business press; both are also sources of information on planned business expansions and closings. Although some state labor departments and larger metropolitan planning organizations prepare employment projections, they rarely have the resources to update the numbers every year in response to changing economic conditions.

Most market areas have at least one real estate brokerage firm that maintains a database of light industrial, flex, and warehouse buildings. Some economic development agencies and utility companies still publish industrial property guides online. The analyst must recognize that these sources may be incomplete, focusing only on buildings or business parks with available spaces, and they may not be current. Even so, obtaining published lists should be the first step in identifying competitive buildings.

Data on net absorption, rents, and occupancy can be purchased for a metropolitan area, for individual submarkets, and on a building-by-building basis, either from brokerage firms, local consultants, or data vendors such as CoStar or Reis.

Other firms sell construction pipeline information for both office and industrial properties—CMD (Construction

Figure 7-8
Example: Modern Bulk Warehouse Space Market
Columbus, Ohio, Market, 3rd Quarter 2018

Submarket	Rentable area (sq ft, 000s)	Construction completions, Q3 2018 (sq ft, 000s)	Under construction (sq ft, 000s)	Vacancy rate (%)	Availability rate (%)	Net absorption, last 4 qtrs (sq ft, 000s)	Direct avg. asking rent (per sq ft/yr)
East	794.6	0.0	0.0	11.5	11.5	168.8	$4.63
Northeast	3,050.2	0.0	0.0	0.0	0.0	0.0	—
Southeast	38,303.2	1,053.1	3,063.9	7.6	7.9	2,290.8	$3.77
Southwest	5,855.1	0.0	0.0	9.7	10.8	368.9	$4.33
West	490.0	115.0	0.0	—	—	490.0	—
Outlying	14,941.6	0.0	1,164.1	1.7	1.7	47.9	$4.45
Total	**63,434.8**	**1,168.1**	**4,227.9**	**6.0**	**8.1**	**3,366.4**	**$3.93**

Source: CBRE Research, MarketView: Columbus Industrial, Q3 2018.

Note: Figures are for space constructed in 1998 or later with at least 28 feet of clear height and a minimum of 100,000 square feet of space.

Market Data, formerly Reed Construction Data) and Dodge Data & Analytics.

The analyst must supplement published information with field visits to competitive properties and interviews with business park management staff as appropriate. It is important to remember that each private source defines submarkets and property classes somewhat differently.

Brokerages also publish reports covering areawide and submarket trends in net absorption, asking rents, and vacancies by property class or building size. Figure 7-8 provides selected data on modern bulk warehouses from a CBRE Research report on the Columbus, Ohio, market overall and for six submarkets.

Coverage can be inconsistent among firms and across metropolitan areas. Differences usually reflect the following:

- How metropolitan area boundaries and submarkets are defined geographically.

- The types of industrial properties included in brokerage inventories. Some sources include only warehouse/distribution facilities and not R&D or manufacturing space. The Columbus example in figure 7-8 includes only warehouse properties built in 1998 or later with a minimum height of 28 feet.

- Minimum building sizes included in the statistics. The minimum size might be 25,000, 50,000, or 100,000 square feet. In figure 7-8 for Columbus, the minimum size is 100,000 square feet.

- Whether the inventory covers owner-occupied as well as rented buildings.

- How the inventory treats available space not currently under lease or physically vacant. As discussed earlier,

the difference between vacancy rate and availability rate can be significant, especially during a recession when a significant supply of sublet space that tenants no longer need or want may exist.

National brokerage firms (JLL, CBRE, Cushman & Wakefield, Newmark Knight Frank, Marcus & Millichap, Colliers International, NAI) all have networks of local offices or affiliates. However, these firms are not represented in every metropolitan area. In addition, market data published in national research reports may be somewhat different from that provided by local offices. In smaller metropolitan areas or counties, local commercial and industrial brokers will be the best sources of market knowledge.

Public-sector economic development agencies and utility companies tend to be more active in providing industrial market data than office information. They often maintain data on available sites and can be useful sources for information on labor force availability and skills, training programs, and financial incentives to spur development or reuse of vacant buildings.

As indicated earlier in this chapter, interviews with local bank economists, chambers of commerce, and public-sector economic development agencies help the analyst identify manufacturers, 3PL providers, and other tenants who have indicated that they plan to expand or leave the area. Conversations with industrial brokers can provide insight into the types of firms that are locating in particular submarkets and what they are looking for—size of spaces, age of buildings, amenities, and features—and the rents they expect to pay. Lease announcements in the real estate press can also be valuable in pinpointing the types of locations that are attractive to different types of businesses.

Notes

1. See CBRE Research, "Surging Demand from Large Cloud Users Driving Record Absorption," *U.S. Data Center Trends Report,* H1 2018, https://www.cbre.us/research-and-reports/US-Data-Center-Trends-Report-H1-2018.

2. The Self Storage Association periodically publishes a *Self-Storage Demand Study,* which can help market analysts determine how to calculate demand and determine the best locations for self-storage. The most recent edition was issued in 2017 (see https://www.selfstorage.org/Products-Services/Research-Data). Data vendors covering the self-storage sector include Reis and STR.

3. Johannson L. Yap and Rene M. Circ, *Guide to Classifying Industrial Properties,* 2nd ed. (Washington, DC: ULI, 2003).

4. The mega-warehouses accounted for 16.7 percent of big-box buildings as of mid-2018. However, Colliers reported that 14 of the 66 buildings (more than one in five) were totally vacant, contributing to the overall 14 percent vacancy rate in big-box spaces.

5. See Patricia Kirk, "Demand for Smaller Industrial Buildings Surges in Coastal Markets," *National Real Estate Investor online,* August 13, 2018. The author cites strong interest from light industrial operations, entrepreneurs, and import/export firms as well as last-mile distributors seeking facilities in the 25,000- to 40,000-square-foot size range. The article suggests, however, that demolition and redevelopment of small industrial sites is often more attractive than renovating an older facility.

6. CBRE industrial reports for some individual markets (for example Columbus, as cited in figure 7-8) distinguish between bulk warehouse/distribution facilities that are at least 100,000 square feet and *modern* bulk warehouses completed in 1998 or later with clear heights of 28 feet or taller. Similar detail is not provided for every market covered by CBRE.

7. The *capitalization rate* (or cap rate) is the ratio between net operating income and original cost or current market value.

CHAPTER 8

CHAPTER 8

HOTELS AND LODGING

In 2018, the U.S. hotel market included more than 54,500 properties, with over 5.2 million rooms. Between 2014 and 2018, the number of properties increased by 2 percent and the number of rooms by 4.8 percent.[1] The hotel market is constantly changing, with properties being renovated, changing affiliation, or being repositioned to attract a wider source of demand, while others are closed, demolished, or converted to other uses. New properties are developed to follow demand generators. Older office buildings have been acquired, sold, and retrofitted as hotels. A property's affiliation, or "flag" (operating brand name), can change and with it the segment of the lodging market that it attracts. All these events demonstrate the importance of accurate market analysis.

U.S. hotel demand is easy to overestimate. Americans like to travel; they took nearly 2.25 billion person-trips of 50 miles or more in 2017. As seen in figure 8-1a, the U.S.

Travel Association projects that this number will reach nearly 2.45 billion by 2022.[2] But it is important to remember that more than half of all trips do not generate an overnight stay. And of those that do, a large percentage do not stay overnight at a hotel or bed-and-breakfast (B&B) lodging. Many travelers stay with friends or relatives, and the rest are camping, going to their second homes, or otherwise accommodated. As an example, figure 8-2 shows the mix of visits to the five-county Philadelphia metropolitan area in 2017. Only 40 percent of total visitors actually stayed overnight. Even among business visitors, a majority came only for the day.

When economic and political conditions are favorable, the number of visitors coming to the United States from other countries (for both business and pleasure) dramatically increases, a trend that should continue as the global middle class expands (as shown in figure 8-1b). However, the U.S.

Figure 8-1a
Trends in U.S. Domestic Travel
2011–2017 and 2018–2022 forecasts

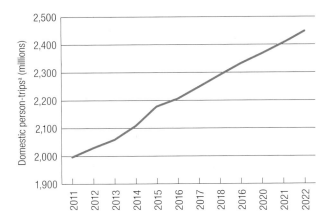

Sources: U.S. Travel Association, U.S. Travel and Tourism Overview, *2017;* Travel Forecast, *updated November 2018, www.ustravel.org.*

a. A person-trip is defined as one person on a trip away from home overnight in paid accommodations, or on a day or overnight one-way trip to a place 50 miles or more away from home.

Figure 8-1b
Trends in International Travel to the United States
2011–2017 and 2018–2022 forecasts

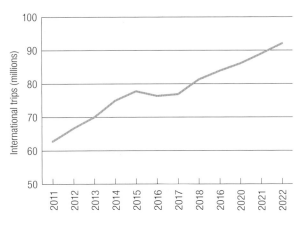

Sources: U.S. Travel Association, U.S. Travel and Tourism Overview, *2017;* Travel Forecast, *updated November 2018, www.ustravel.org.*

share of the international travel market has slipped of late. In 2015, the United States captured 6.5 percent of total international travel; by 2017, the share dropped to 5.8 percent. A decline in visitors from Mexico accounts for this trend.[3]

The hotel market is segmented by price, location, amenities, and available services.

- Brand loyalty is an increasingly important factor as travelers choose to stay where they can earn rewards or use their rewards from the various frequent-traveler loyalty programs.

- Even so, niche products abound. Some travelers want to be pampered, whereas others want an authentic local experience.

- Resorts can cater to a single demand driver—proximity to a beautiful beach, a spa, a championship golf course, ski slopes, a nearby national park, or natural wonders.

- In contrast, some hotel guests are on their way to a specific destination, don't stay long, and are price sensitive. They aren't interested in amenities and use few hotel services; all they want is a clean, comfortable, quiet room with a TV, internet, and wi-fi.

Travel in the United States in 2017

- U.S. residents logged 2.25 billion person-trips for leisure purposes and 462 million person-trips for business purposes (38 percent for meetings and events). These comprise both overnight and day trips, including those involving at least one night's stay in paid accommodations or a day trip of at least 50 miles one way.

- Domestic leisure travel increased 2.1 percent in 2017 and business travel increased 1.3 percent between 2016 and 2017. Leisure travel accounted for 80 percent of all domestic travel.

- Top leisure travel activities were (a) visiting relatives, (b) shopping, (c) visiting friends, (d) fine dining, and (e) rural sightseeing.

- International arrivals to the United States totaled 76.9 million persons. Top leisure activities for overseas visitors were shopping, sightseeing, fine dining, visiting national parks and monuments, and going to amusement or theme parks.

- Although the number of international arrivals increased by 0.7 percent between 2016 and 2017, the U.S. share of global international travel is declining. Canada (26.3 percent) and Mexico (23.1 percent) generate by far the largest shares of international visitors to the United States.

Source: U.S. Travel Association, "U.S. Travel Answer Sheet," updated October 2018, www.ustravel.org.

Hotels as Real Estate

Hotels are different from other investment property types in several ways:

- They are the only type of property that is rented by the night rather than leased by the year (or multiple years in the case of retail, office, and industrial buildings).

- For many hotels and resorts, business is seasonal; occupancy and achievable room rates fluctuate from month to month. Even when seasonality is not an issue, occupancy and rates can vary by the day of the week, with business travelers dominating patronage from Monday through Thursday, and leisure visitors prevailing on the weekends and holidays.

- A sudden downturn in the economy will have a negative effect on hotel occupancy long before its impact is seen in the apartment or office market.

- Special events in a given year (or season) result in room rate increases and can dramatically affect occupancy.

- Hotels have various revenue generators—not only room sales but also meeting space and banquet rentals, restaurants, parking garages, and leased shops. In contrast, apartments, office and industrial buildings, and shopping centers derive most of their revenue from leasing space. (Reimbursements from commercial tenants for utilities or real estate taxes do not generate profits.)

- Hotel corporations provide property branding, reputation, marketing resources, and operations expertise to individual properties in exchange for fees. Franchisees backed by single or multiple investors can brand a hotel, but the management of the hotel must be approved by the hotel brand.

Figure 8-2

Day Trips vs. Overnight Visitors in Greater Philadelphia
2017

	Visitors (millions)	Share of total visitors (%)
Day leisure	23.1	53
Day business	2.8	6
Total day	**25.9**	**60**
Overnight leisure	15.1	35
Overnight business	2.3	5
Total overnight	**17.4**	**40**
Total visitors	**43.3**	

Source: 2017 Greater Philadelphia Visitation and Economic Impact Study. Prepared by Econsult Solutions Inc., and Visit Philadelphia, June 2018, www.visitphilly.com.

Note: Data are for domestic visitors only. Includes only five counties in Pennsylvania; excludes counties in New Jersey and Delaware that are part of the Philadelphia metropolitan area.

Figure 8-3
U.S. Hotels by Size
2018

Size (rooms)	Properties	Share (%)	Total rooms	Share (%)	Average number of rooms
Under 75	28,318	51.9	1,233,898	23.6	44
75–149	19,716	36.2	2,059,003	39.5	104
150–299	4,745	8.7	946,976	18.1	200
300–500	1,193	2.2	443,014	8.5	371
Over 500	549	1.0	536,122	10.3	977
All properties	**54,521**		**5,219,013**		**96**

Source: STR.

- Hotels are labor-intensive and successful hotel management companies regularly review fixed and variable costs, as well as programs to maintain or increase occupancy, average daily room rates (ADRs), and other income-producing categories.

Because of the industry's complexity, hotel market studies are often conducted by analysts who specialize in the hospitality and travel industries. In addition to inspecting a proposed development site and visiting key competitors, the market analyst is often called upon to prepare demand projections, forecast room occupancy and rates, calculate food and beverage or meeting room revenue (depending on the type of property), and estimate operating expenses.

Product Types

Hotel development has followed paths taken by other types of commercial real estate in the United States. In the first half of the 20th century, most hotel development occurred in downtown areas where businesses were concentrated and where convention centers generated demand for thousands of room nights. Downtown locations and convention-oriented hotel market segments continue to offer development opportunities as older properties are demolished or converted to other uses and as tourism increases, business visitor demand grows, and convention centers expand or relocate.

As interstate highway systems served more communities and suburbanization spread, demand for hotel rooms followed the outward movement of employment and population—and continues to do so.

- Visitors can find a wide range of products—from budget to full-service hotels—at key interchanges along the interstates.

- New entertainment venues and outlet malls also draw limited-service hotel projects to the suburbs; suburban convention and exhibition facilities are yet another source of demand.

- Hotel development around airports caters to short-on-time business visitors and other travelers in transit.

- Including a hotel in or near a large suburban office park is now commonplace.

- Medical centers and universities often work with hotel developers to provide convenient rooms for their visitors and short-term teaching staff.

Figure 8-3 shows the distribution of hotel properties in the United States by number of rooms as of 2018. The average hotel had only 96 rooms, and a majority (51.9 percent) had fewer than 75 rooms. The large convention, conference, and business hotels—those with more than 300 rooms—accounted for only 3.2 percent of all properties but nearly 19 percent of total room inventory.

It is important for market analysts to understand that most hotels appeal to multiple consumer segments; a business traveler may select a more upscale lodging property on the basis of the location of his or her meetings or a frequent-traveler loyalty program, and then select a different type of hotel when traveling with family.

Classifying Hotels by Location

One way to classify hotel properties is by location. *Urban or downtown properties* are located in the central business district or a densely populated city neighborhood in large metropolitan areas. *Suburban hotels* are typically found at or near interchanges along heavily traveled highway routes or beltways in metropolitan suburbs. Examples are the White Plains submarket outside New York City; the Oak Brook and Schaumburg areas in suburban Chicago; or La Jolla, which is north of San Diego. Patronage at these facilities can be corporate or leisure oriented. As figure 8-4 shows, the suburban segment is by far the largest of all hotel locations, accounting for more than one-third of all properties and 36 percent of all hotel rooms in the United States in 2018. This distribution has not changed significantly since 2007, despite the proliferation of new suburban properties built as the economy improved post-recession.

Highway-oriented facilities in rural areas tend to be economy, budget, or mid-priced operations. They cater to price-sensitive business and leisure travelers. A hotel along the highway may be an intermediate stop on a long road trip or close to the driver's ultimate destination.

Airport-oriented hotels serve business visitors who want to get in and out of town quickly. Some are located on the grounds of the airport itself. These hotels are used primarily for business meetings, but secondary demand comes from travelers in transit, especially at airports that handle international flights. Airport hotels also host weddings, banquets, and other events on weekends when business visitor volume is slow; guests attending these events will get discounted room rates.

Vacation and resort properties are located in tourist destinations. Demand is primarily generated by leisure visitors, but many resorts are popular settings for conventions and conferences, corporate sales meetings, and executive retreats. They compete with urban or suburban convention hotels and conference centers for this segment of the meeting business. A resort hotel might feature golf courses, water sports, skiing, or spa facilities. Resort hotels have also been built in conjunction with theme parks, water parks, casinos, and other attractions. They usually include a range of restaurants, meeting rooms, and banquet space.

Depending on the climate of the resort area, lodging demand may be prone to seasonality, with distinct peak and off-peak periods. Peak periods generally yield maximum room rates and high occupancy levels. Off-peak periods are characterized by lower room rates and reduced occupancy levels. In certain market areas, intermediate periods marked by moderate demand are referred to as "shoulder" seasons.

Small metro areas and towns, in the aggregate, contain nearly as many lodging properties as the suburbs in large metro areas (29.4 percent of all U.S. hotels in 2018), but on average, these properties are much smaller (only 61 rooms per property on average compared with 100 in large metropolitan suburbs). Small town properties serve local businesses and leisure travelers but do not generate much overnight group meeting demand.

Classifying Hotels by Services Offered

Hotels can be classified as *full-service, select-service,* or *limited-service. Full-service hotels* offer a wide range of services, including valet parking, luggage assistance, concierge services, gift shops, fitness centers, three-meal restaurants, and room service. Many full-service hotels offer extensive meeting and banquet space, although that is not a requirement for this category.

Limited-service hotels encompass a wide range of property types and price points. They do not usually offer valet parking, luggage assistance, or concierge services but may provide luggage carts, small fitness centers and a pool, a "business center" area with one or more desktop computers and printers, and high-speed internet access. Limited-service hotel brands have little or no meeting space and no full-service restaurant; however, they usually offer a complimentary breakfast buffet. Casual restaurants are typically located nearby. Examples of limited-service chains include

Figure 8-4
U.S. Hotel Rooms by Location
2018

Location	Properties	Share of properties (%)	Rooms	Share of rooms (%)	Average property size
Urban	5,556	10.2	875,107	16.8	158
Suburban	18,883	34.6	1,889,339	36.2	100
Interstate/highway	2,453	4.5	332,886	6.4	136
Airport	7,793	14.3	538,082	10.3	69
Resort	3,834	7.0	608,960	11.7	159
Small metro area or town	16,002	29.4	974,639	18.7	61
Total	54,521	100.0	5,219,013	100.0	96

Sources: STR, American Hotel and Lodging Association.

The West Hotel in Jim Thorpe, Pennsylvania, a town in the Pocono Mountains. *(Khairil Azhar Junos/Shutterstock.com)*

Candlewood Suites, Comfort Inn, Element, Hampton Inn, LaQuinta, and Wingate by Wyndham. Demand comes from price-sensitive commercial and leisure travelers. Some limited-service hotels cater to extended-stay travelers.

Select-service properties combine some of the attributes of limited-service facilities with room amenities seen in full-service properties. They do not offer much in the way of banquet or meeting room space. Their restaurants do not offer three meals a day. Room rates are in between the full-service and the limited-service facilities. Examples are Aloft, Clarion, Courtyard by Marriott, Indigo, Hilton Garden Inn, and Hyatt Place.

Classifying Hotels by Physical and Functional Characteristics

Convention hotels have a minimum of 300 rooms and a minimum of 20,000 square feet of (divisible) meeting and banquet space. Such properties are often physically connected or adjacent to convention centers. They usually include several eating establishments of varying styles and price ranges. Most include a business center and substantial amounts of retail space. Large lobbies are needed to handle the check-in and check-out functions that occur in a concentrated period at the beginning and end of every convention. However, hotel chains now have smart phone apps that can be used for online advance check-in and room selection as well as digital "keys" that allow patrons to avoid long lines in the lobby. Commonly, up to 10 percent of the guest rooms may be suites. Guests can use the living rooms of the suites as hospitality rooms, or the hotel can arrange them as meeting spaces for small groups.

Many convention hotels have set aside concierge floors for valued patrons or for those paying higher rates for concierge services. With controlled access, concierge floors offer separate check-in areas, lounges, extra in-room amenities, and complimentary snacks, beverages, and services. (Concierge floors are also found in upscale properties that are not located

Hyatt House in Cupertino, California. *(Michael Vi/Shutterstock.com)*

near convention centers.) Frequent guests who are members of the hotel chain's loyalty program earn the privilege of being assigned to the concierge floor.

Conference centers meet the guidelines of the International Association of Conference Centers. Many are branded, others are independently owned and managed, and some are associated with universities or professional organizations. They tend to be located in the suburbs or exurbs, offering on-site or nearby recreational amenities such as golf courses, tennis courts, and spas. They are used for high-end corporate training and sales meetings, as well as trade and professional association functions. Although many hotels market themselves as conference centers, true conference properties are designed to provide a setting free of distractions. Conference centers usually contain 200 or more guest rooms and a large number of dedicated meeting rooms; they offer a full complement of audiovisual equipment, support services, and catering so as to make leaving the property unnecessary.

Guest units in *all-suite* or *extended-stay properties* consist of expanded studios with a divider separating the living area from the sleeping area or have one or two separate bedrooms with a living area. Units are larger than typical hotel rooms. Suites usually have a small refrigerator, sink, and microwave oven; an extended-stay hotel will also have a two-burner cooktop. Kitchens are equipped with cookware,

AC by Marriott in Asheville, North Carolina. *(Kristi Blokhin/Shutterstock.com)*

Bed-and-Breakfasts: An Alternative to Traditional Hotels

"Like other alternative lodging segments, the B&B industry is extremely fragmented with a long tail of small, independent operators. The average B&B has eight guestrooms—some have as few as two rooms or as many as 40. As with many industries, B&B operators of various sizes can have stark contrasts in business performance. Bigger operators tend to show higher occupancy, higher ADRs (average daily room rates) and higher technology adoption than smaller B&Bs.

"Regardless of size, B&Bs still serve a smaller segment of travelers than traditional hotels or private accommodation. . . . Average B&B occupancy for 2017 is 50 percent, peaking in the summer and dropping in the winter months. . . . Although B&Bs may be small properties, they provide a boutique value that travelers are willing to pay for. The average daily rate in 2017 was $173 (compared to $127 for hotels) but varies by region and property size."

Source: Brandie Wright, B&Bs Unbound: The State of B&Bs in the U.S., PhocusWright.com, February 2018.

utensils, dishes, a coffeemaker, and—in some cases—a toaster. The living area and the bedrooms will each have a television. All-suite properties typically offer complimentary hot breakfasts. Some brands offer a cocktail hour with a limited buffet or snacks. As with other hotels, all-suite hotels have an exercise room, business center, and often a pool. A self-service laundry room is another amenity; more upscale suite properties offer laundry and dry cleaning services for an extra fee. Properties of this type include Hilton's DoubleTree Suites, Embassy Suites, Homewood Suites, and Home2Suites as well as Marriott's Springhill Suites, Residence Inn, and TownPlace Suites.

The extended-stay hotel was developed to meet the needs of business travelers working in an area for more than a week; it also appeals to recently relocated corporate personnel. Many leisure travelers, especially families with children, also find these facilities desirable. (Suite hotels typically include a pullout sofa bed in the living area that can be used by children.) All-suite hotels and extended-stay properties can be found in both urban and suburban settings and range from two-story buildings to high-rises. Several hotel chains offer prototypes that mix conventional hotel rooms with suites.

Boutique or *lifestyle hotels* are small, intimate, urban, upscale, and trendy; great emphasis is placed on unusual interior design and room decor. Most have stylish bars and restaurants, which can be leased to a food and beverage operator. Although most boutique hotels are independent, a number of boutique chains have developed, including AC by Marriott, Canopy by Hilton, EVEN by IHG (Intercontinental), Hotel Indigo, Kimpton Hotels, and W Hotels.

Bed-and-breakfast inns operated by individual entrepreneurs also appeal to a niche market, but they offer a small number of rooms and do not provide a full array of services. They attract leisure travelers because of their historic character, neighborhood ambience, and proximity to visitor attractions.

Resort hotels are similar to full-service hotels but are typically situated in a scenic area (waterfront, mountains) and either provide or are near activities that attract leisure travelers. Resorts generally offer an extensive menu of spa services and recreational activities. These properties typically have significant meeting space and compete for group business. Like conventional hotels, resorts may have ballroom and meeting space that can easily be converted to accommodate a number of different uses.

Classifying Hotels by Price

Luxury hotels, located in large metropolitan areas or high-end resorts, are frequented by visitors who are willing to pay a premium price for accommodations. They typically have fewer than 300 rooms and cater to corporate travelers, convention delegates, and wealthy individuals, including overseas visitors. Such hotels are distinguished by high-quality furnishings, amenities, and personal service. Many luxury properties house fine restaurants and shops. Although luxury hotels may accommodate some meeting and banquet business, they do not target large groups. Examples of U.S. luxury chains include Fairmount, Four Seasons, Park Hyatt, and Ritz-Carlton.

Upscale commercial hotels are full-service properties that target individual business travelers during the week and leisure travelers on weekends. Although meetings may represent an important part of their business, the groups served by these hotels are smaller than those that use convention hotels. Compared with convention hotels, most upscale commercial hotels provide less public space and a more limited array of food and beverage outlets. Chains such as Hilton, Hyatt, Intercontinental, and Marriott all operate hotels of this type in both urban and suburban settings, as well as larger properties that cater to conventions.

Mid-price properties include most of the limited-service chains. As discussed earlier in this chapter, they do not provide the same array of personal services as luxury or upscale properties, and they have very limited shopping, dining, exercise, and meeting and banquet facilities. Most offer snacks and toiletries for sale and have small exercise rooms and a pool; many provide free breakfasts. Business and leisure travelers who want comfortable accommodations in convenient locations but do not want to pay for services

Changes in Hotel Design and Features: Catering to Millennials

With millennials accounting for an ever-increasing share of room demand, hotel design is changing to cater to their preferences. Young travelers are more interested in social spaces and interaction with peers than in spacious guest rooms with luxury furnishings. As a result, lobbies are providing conversation areas with comfortable chairs, couches, and communal tables along with spaces equipped for working on laptops. Bars, coffee bars and kiosks, and grab-and-go food pickup are common sights. Free wi-fi throughout the building is a must. Rooftop lounges are also popular. Although these hotels are very contemporary, millennial travelers are interested in authentic local experiences. Decor often reflects local history and culture.

The tradeoff for more common spaces is smaller guest rooms. Some hotels catering to young adults are more like upscale youth hostels, with shared suites and even bunk beds for price-sensitive travelers. Room furnishings may feature open cubbies instead of dressers with drawers; rooms need power connections for multiple devices. These chains have added automatic check-in using cell phone apps and digital room keys.

Examples of hotel chains that cater to the millennial demographic are Aloft and Moxy (both Marriott brands), Canopy (Hilton), Centric (Hyatt), Indigo (IHG), Radisson Red, and Selena. Aloft and Indigo have the longest track records of these brands. Others had only a few U.S. locations in operation as of year-end 2018, but more experience in Europe and Asia.

A rooftop bar at the InterContinental Hotel in Los Angeles. *(Kit Leong/Shutterstock.com)*

and amenities they do not use are the target market for mid-price chains. Examples are Comfort Inn, Fairfield Inn, Hampton Inn, and Holiday Inn Express.

Budget or *economy* hotels offer little besides rooms. Such properties usually do not have business centers or meeting space, and their fitness facilities are very limited. They do not operate restaurants but may serve a complimentary continental breakfast in a small common area. Budget hotels often locate close to shopping centers or freestanding eating and drinking places. This property type competes almost exclusively on the basis of price. Budget hotels cater to cost-conscious business travelers, price-sensitive vacationing families, and long-distance drivers. The first such hotels were built along highways outside metropolitan areas, but they are now frequently seen in suburban areas, near airports, and even in some downtowns. Rooms in budget hotels are often accessed by exterior corridors or directly from the parking lot, although many newer properties have secure internal corridors. Typical economy chains include Days Inn, Microtel, Motel 6, Red Roof, and Super 8.

It is important to recognize that the major hotel companies are always looking for new ways to serve their customers; as a result, new concepts are frequently announced and test-marketed. In the last decade, chains and independent operators have given much attention to developing new concepts targeted to the growing millennial travel market (see sidebar, page 179.) These hotels are characterized by smaller-than-average room sizes but have expanded space

Figure 8-5
Selected U.S. Hotel Chains by Price Points

Luxury	Upper upscale	Upscale	Upper midscale	Midscale	Economy
Andaz	Autograph Collection	AC by Marriott	Best Western Plus	AmericInn	America's Best Inns
Conrad	Canopy by Hilton	Aloft	BW Signature	Baymont Inn & Suites	America's Best
Fairmont	Club Quarters	Best Western Premier	Clarion	Best Western	Value Inn
Four Seasons	Curio Collection	Cambria Hotel	Comfort Inn & Suites	Candlewood Suites	Budget Host
Grand Hyatt	by Hilton	& Suites	Country Inn & Suites	Hawthorn Suites	Budgetel
InterContinental	Delta	Courtyard	Disney Value Resorts	by Wyndham	Country Hearth Inn
JW Marriott	Disney Deluxe Resorts	Crowne Plaza	Doubletree Club	Ibis Styles	Days Inn
Loews	Embassy Suites	Delta	Drury Inn & Suites	InnSuites Hotels	Econo Lodge
Mandarin Oriental	by Hilton	Disney Moderate	Drury Plaza	MainStay Suites	Extended Stay
Park Hyatt	Hard Rock	Resorts	Fairfield Inn	Quality Inn	America
Peninsula	Hilton	Doubletree by Hilton	Hampton by Hilton	Ramada	GreenTree Inns
Ritz-Carlton	Hilton Grand Vacations	Four Points	Holiday Inn	Red Lion Inn & Suites	Howard Johnson
RockResorts	Hotel Indigo	Great Wolf Lodge	Holiday Inn Express	Settle Inn	Knights Inn
Sofitel Luxury	Hotel Nikko	Hilton Garden Inn	Home2Suites by Hilton	Sleep Inn	Microtel Inn by
St. Regis	Hyatt	Homewood Suites	Moxy Hotels (Marriott)	Tru by Hilton	Wyndham
Trump Collection	Hyatt Centric	by Hilton	La Quinta	Uptown Suites	Motel 6
W	Hyatt Regency	Hyatt House	OHANA Hotels	Wingate by Wyndham	Red Carpet Inn
Waldorf-Astoria	Joie de Vivre	Hyatt Place	Oxford Suites		Red Roof Inn
	Kimpton	Iberostar Hotels	Park Inn		Rodeway Inn
	Le Meridien	& Resorts	Red Lion Hotels		Studio 6
	Marriott	Innside by Melia	Sonesta ES Suites		Super 8
	Marriott Conference	Melia	Spring Hill Suites		SureStay
	Center	Miyako Hotels	TownePlace Suites		Travelodge
	Millennium Hotels	Novotel	Tryp by Wyndham		
	Omni	Park Plaza	Wyndham Garden		
	Radisson Blu	Radisson	Yotel		
	Radisson Red	Residence Inn			
	Renaissance	Riu Hotel			
	Sheraton	Sonesta			
	Swissotel	Springhill Suites			
	Virgin Hotels	Staybridge Suites			
	Warwick Hotels	Tapestry by Hilton			
	Westin	Westmark Hotels			
	Wyndham Grand	Wyndham Hotels			
	Hotels	Wyndham Vacation			
		Resorts			

Source: STR Chain Scales 2019.

Note: Not all chains with U.S. locations are listed.

for socializing and networking on their lower floors. The real estate recession delayed the full rollout of these new brands (for example, Aloft and Indigo). Some chains grow their brands by acquiring and reflagging existing hotels in established locations rather than building from the ground up.

Figure 8-5 lists major U.S. hotel chains by service level and price points. Note that not all hotel brands with U.S. locations are shown.

Other Types of Lodging Properties

A number of other lodging types exist that resemble hotels in some ways but are more like residential properties in others.

Airbnb and Vrbo

Airbnb is a global online company that assists property owners in renting out all or part of their homes to visitors. Started in late 2007, it grew to a company with 550,000 listings by 2015 in the United States alone. Airbnb was originally envisioned as a way for homeowners or renters to earn extra cash to help pay bills. However, AirDNA (the leading short-term rental research and data firm) reported that 63 percent of Airbnb listings were for entire homes, with 34 percent for private rooms and 3 percent for shared rooms.[4]

Airbnb's rapid growth raised issues with local government officials. Initially, these properties were not subject to state and local hotel taxes, an important source of revenue for government. As participation shifted from renting spare rooms in individual homes to renting entire apartments or homes, investors saw the income potential and began acquiring multiple units to list on Airbnb. When affordable housing advocates insisted that these short-term rentals were reducing the inventory of available units in tight apartment markets (as in New York City), efforts at greater regulation ensued, and Airbnb operations became a political issue for both hosts and the hotel industry.

To date, the impact of Airbnb is largely confined to the leisure segment of demand, but the company is actively seeking to make inroads among commercial travelers. During peak periods with few available rooms in busy downtown areas, Airbnb listings can capture unaccommodated hotel demand that might otherwise go to more distant city neighborhoods or suburbs.

Vacation rental by owner (Vrbo) is a concept similar to Airbnb, but it handles only rentals of whole properties (not just condominiums and homes, but also villas, boats, and yachts). Vrbo matches renters with properties, provides reviews from prior users, gives property owners a 24-hour period to "vet" potential renters, and guarantees user satisfaction. It operates its own payment system.

Timeshares

For middle-income families who cannot afford to buy a second home, owning a timeshare (and banking or trading within multiproperty systems) is a way to experience different worldwide destinations at a relatively low cost. The traditional timeshare system, in which a buyer bought a specific week in a specific unit at a specific property, has been mostly supplanted by a more flexible system, in which owners amass points that can be used for different weeks at various locations. Long-established hotel management companies—such as Disney, Hilton, Hyatt, Marriott, and Wyndham—developed and marketed timeshare resorts. Some timeshares are in urban locations. From management's perspective, a timeshare operates like a resort hotel, except that visitors come for intervals of at least a week. However, buying a timeshare is not buying real estate; the purchaser does not receive a deed. Owners pay an annual maintenance fee.

According to annual research conducted for the American Resort Development Association (ARDA) International Foundation by Ernst & Young, 1,570 traditional timeshare resorts operated in the United States in 2017, offering approximately 205,100 units. Nearly three of every four units have two or more bedrooms, and the average unit size has more than 1,000 square feet. Beach resorts were the most popular location for timeshare properties in 2017, accounting for 34 percent. However, timeshare properties are also located at ski resorts, golf courses, casinos, and urban settings.

Short-Term Rentals in Memphis

AirDNA tracks short-term rentals available in communities throughout the United States. For January 2019, it reported the following information on rentals available in the Memphis area:

- AirDNA tracked 991 active rentals, with 485 hosts, of whom 143 had multiple listed properties.

- The average daily rate was $116.

- Seventy-three percent were entire homes, as opposed to a room in a home.

- Rentals averaged 1.9 bedrooms and could house 5.2 guests.

The company also provides details on the physical characteristics of short-term rental properties and how they perform (number of available and booked dates, number of unique reservations, ADR).

Source: www.airdna.co.

Marriott Vacation Club in Park City, Utah. *(M Outdoors/Shutterstock.com)*

Florida has the largest number of timeshare resorts in the United States (273); properties in Nevada are the biggest, averaging 249 units. A 2016 ARDA report estimated that 9.2 million American households then owned a timeshare. As with other visitor accommodations, timeshare sales are strongly tied to the health of the national economy; offshore buyers also generate demand. Sales declined during the recession but were growing again by 2016.[5] A key drawback of timeshares is their lack of liquidity; the absence of an organized, reliable resale market has negatively affected share values.

Fractional Ownership

A newer model is the fractional-ownership resort. The buyer owns a third or a quarter share of the unit and has use of the property for designated weeks or months. All buyers in the unit share the maintenance fee. A fractional-ownership unit has fewer owners than a timeshare situation, where many share owners could be entitled to no more than a week's use. For those who want the benefits of a deeded interest in vacation property, fractional ownership offers the opportunity to buy a share in a second home without the full ownership cost for a property that will be used only part time. Fractional-ownership properties tend to be developed

at more upscale locations than are traditional timeshares. State regulations covering the sale and management of timeshares and fractional ownerships vary, and laws applying to each type of property can be very different.

Condominium Hotels

Condominium hotels are a hybrid product combining hotel services and amenities within a condo ownership structure. The buyer purchases a room or suite in fee simple ownership. The building is managed by a national or regional hotel operator that places the unit in the pool of rooms or suites when the owner is not using it. The hotel handles advertising and reservations for visitors, who may not realize they are renting a condo and not a hotel room. Buildings have a staffed front desk, a concierge, and other personal services typically found in a top-quality hotel, along with restaurants and shops.

In a condo-hotel, unit rental income is split between the owner and the hotel management; the management firm charges a fee to market and maintain the unit and to provide housekeeping services. The management firm keeps any income from restaurant operations or retail shop rental. As in residential condo properties, the buyer has a deed and can obtain a mortgage. The owner of the unit also pays a monthly homeowners association fee.

Condo-hotels can be found in both urban and resort settings. They are attractive to hotel developers because deposits and signed contracts reduce equity requirements for construction loans. Additional cash comes in when the building is completed and ready for occupancy; a conventional hotel takes much longer to generate cash. However, the developer faces risks in an economic downturn when sales can grind to a halt if mortgage financing for second homes is difficult to obtain at reasonable interest rates. Complications can also occur if unit buyers fail to make their mortgage payments; foreclosed units are usually withdrawn from the rental program, reducing potential income for the hotel operator. In addition, owners in a condo-hotel may not want to contribute additional funds to renovate the units to the hotel operator's specifications or participate in property improvements or renovation efforts as the buildings age.

For the unit buyer, condo-hotels and fractional ownerships offer the advantage of deeded real estate ownership. Rents paid by visitors can be raised over time, as in any other hotel. However, some condo-hotel operating agreements limit the amount of time the unit owner can use the property during peak seasons. And finding a lender willing to write a mortgage for these property types may be difficult.

Preparing the Market Study

Hotel market studies require the analyst to examine six aspects of the property and the market:

- The outlook for travel generally, given national economic conditions;

- Access and proximity of the site (or existing hotel property) to demand generators such as tourist attractions, convention centers, airports, corporate headquarters, major medical centers, and universities;

- The types of businesses within the market area and whether they offer a growing source of room demand (to the extent that this potential can be determined);

- The sources and strengths of demand segments (business travelers, convention and meeting visitors, tourists);

- The attractiveness of competitive properties with respect to location, access, amenities, and management; and

- Unique local conditions and trends—future events (such as major sporting events or political conventions) that would increase demand for lodging in the metropolitan area or submarket.

In some ways, hotel analyses are similar to those conducted for other property types. As with those studies, the hotel market analysis includes an overview of metropolitan area economic conditions and an evaluation of site suitability. However, hotel analyses have important differences:

- The demographic characteristics of households in the surrounding area are not critically important to a hotel market analysis; however, the availability of labor, modes of transportation, access to the site, attractiveness of surrounding uses, and proximity to amenities (restaurants, shopping, outdoor recreation) are important factors in evaluating a hotel location.

- Noting specific local businesses, convention facilities, tourist attractions, hospitals, universities, and other "draws" that bring travelers to a hotel trade area is required.

- For a resort, the climate, natural features, and recreational amenities are the draws, but reliable, convenient air travel and ground transportation (to what are often remote locations) are also important.

- In the case of a resort or a conference center, the most significant competitors could be very far away.

(Clockwise from left: zimmytws/Shutterstock.com; Ceri Breeze/Shutterstock.com; Jer123/Shutterstock.com; Trong Nguyen/Shutterstock.com; Michael Vi/Shutterstock.com)

Few truly competitive properties (in terms of size, age, facilities, and target market segment) may operate in the local market area. Accurate information on the characteristics of nearby properties, their amenities, and performance should be provided.

Evaluating a Site

Increasingly, downtown hotels are becoming elements of mixed-use developments that may include rental apartments and condos, office space, retail and restaurant space, and entertainment venues (as described in chapter 9). Although downtown business hotels usually contain their own restaurants, they also need to be near other well-regarded eateries—places that would appeal to clients or customers.

For properties that cater to conventions, proximity to the convention center and easy, reliable transportation are obviously very important. Some convention hotels benefit from direct connections by covered walkways, but this amenity is not always possible. As a result, many conventions hire coach buses to transport attendees from hotels to the convention center. Properties designated as "official" convention hotels will enjoy this advantage when booking rooms. Freestanding downtown business-oriented hotels

want to be close to well-occupied office buildings and the best downtown shopping and entertainment venues.

Suburban hotels seek locations near traffic generators (corporate headquarters, office parks, tourist attractions). Sites need to be easy to reach, clearly visible from nearby highways, and big enough to provide sufficient parking for staff members as well as overnight guests. Proximity to restaurants and shops is also desirable. Like their downtown counterparts, suburban hotels are increasingly part of mixed-use developments.

Determining the Competitive Market Area

For most types of real estate development, market areas for supply and demand are either identical or overlapping. For hotel development, however, the two market areas are distinctly different, with considerable variation in geography. For example,

- The competitive *supply* for a convention hotel is the inventory of hotels with a similar price range and location in relation to the local convention center—perhaps a 10-minute walking distance or a short cab, Uber, or Lyft ride away. But the primary *demand* for rooms near a

The Mills House historic hotel in Charleston, South Carolina. *(meunierd/Shutterstock.com)*

convention center comes from meeting attendees and exhibition hall vendors from across the country. Many meetings also draw participants from overseas, which is one reason why large conventions are held in cities with frequent domestic and international service from multiple airlines.

- A typical U.S. beach-resort hotel with a regional draw would compete with comparably priced hotels with similar amenities and services that are located along the same strip of beachfront. Patrons might be drawn from a nearby metropolitan area or several nearby states.

- For other resort-type properties, demand generators would be nearby theme parks, ski slopes, lakes, scenic areas, golf courses, and other forms of outdoor recreation. Indoor water parks are growing in popularity with families. Pleasure visitors generate the largest number of room nights for resorts, but these properties also compete for business meetings.

- Competitors for an existing or proposed business-oriented hotel are properties catering to individuals visiting nearby corporate headquarters or regional offices, multitenant office buildings, manufacturing facilities, or government agencies. Identifying the best comparables may require a few phone calls to corporate travel offices or conversations with managers of existing lodging properties.

Analyzing Demand Segments

Room demand is affected by local, regional, and national economic trends in both the household sector and the business community. Market segments are defined in terms of the purpose of the trip, seasonality, length of stay, price sensitivity, nature of the facilities and amenities required, and number of rooms required.

- Individual business traveler demand comes from visitors who have clients, customers, or branch offices in a particular location (for example, downtown) or who need to be in a central or accessible location to visit multiple customers or clients.

- Group demand is generated by corporate meetings, convention activity, and weekend gatherings (social, military, educational, religious, and fraternal, often referred to as SMERF demand by market analysts).

- Leisure demand is driven by persons visiting family or friends who need (or want) to stay in hotels; attendees at special events (concerts, sporting events, and festivals); travelers drawn to historic sites, museums, or parks; shoppers from small towns and rural areas; and visitors to active recreation attractions.

Measuring demand is a complex process:

- Employment growth and income gains affect consumer confidence, which in turn influences leisure travel demand.

Looking at Airport Statistics

A number of factors must be considered when looking at airport arrival data: growth rate, seasonality, airlines adding new destinations, and (especially when evaluating the market potential for an airport-area hotel) the number of inbound flyers who are changing planes. Data on airline arrivals must be adjusted to reflect layovers or transfers that do not normally result in overnight stays.

- Some pleasure travelers are price sensitive; others are not. They may travel on their own or as part of a group tour. They may stay at multiple hotels on a single trip, especially if they are traveling by car.

- Vacationers include singles, couples, and families with children; these three household types can have unique space requirements.

- Women travelers are a growing share of the business travel market, and their hotel preferences are often different from those of men in the same age group.

Not surprisingly, factors affecting business travel decisions are quite different:

- Corporate and small business travel policies are periodically revised as business conditions improve or decline. The willingness of managers to authorize staff travel for meetings and conventions is especially sensitive to economic conditions; these trips can be considered as overhead items or benefits that are curtailed when the economy is weak.

- Moreover, businesses equipped with in-house video communication systems may see less need for in-person meetings that require out-of-town travel.

Historical occupancy patterns and room rate changes in a particular hotel market make a good proxy for how demand shifts in response to economic changes.

According to the American Hotel and Lodging Association, business travel accounted for 40 percent of hotel room–night demand in the United States in 2014, with 60 percent generated by leisure travelers.[6] Leisure travel is a growing share of the market as more business is transacted by email and videoconference and as retirees constitute a growing share of the traveling public.

The market study should begin with indicators of regional demand growth. Airport arrivals, convention attendance trends, new business formations and relocations, employment growth, office and industrial space absorption, population growth, and commercial building activity can all be factors to consider when looking at the growth of demand. Where a high degree of leisure visitation is anticipated, the analyst

Importance of Business Meetings

Meetings and events include gatherings sponsored by professional and trade associations or corporations, conferences designed for participation and problem solving, and exhibitions at which products and services are displayed or sold. They accounted for 12.7 percent of all travel spending in 2017 and four of every 10 dollars spent on business travel in the United States.

Source: Meetings Mean Business Coalition of the U.S. Travel Association, www.ustravel.org.

will want to examine trends in tourism activity as reflected in ticket sales or the number of admissions at major attractions, such as museums, sporting events, and theme parks in the market area. Conducting telephone interviews with staff members at such places will be helpful in determining whether these places draw patrons from out of town and, if so, whether those patrons stay overnight. The data collection effort will depend on proximity of the subject property to the attractions and events.

Because collecting demand information can be very labor-intensive, the analyst should focus on the economic data most relevant to the subject property. Data to be presented will depend on the type of hotel under consideration and its location. Not all trends need to be examined for every market study. For example, a report for a proposed limited-service hotel located 10 miles from the convention center does not need detailed information on convention booking trends or their seasonal patterns. A study for a hotel being built adjacent to a medical center needs information on overnight stays by patients' family members, new employees, and vendors; airport arrival and departure details are not necessary.

Although recent and historical data from local convention and visitors bureaus or state tourism agencies can be helpful, they are insufficient for gaining useful insights into the dynamics of a metropolitan or local lodging market. Analysts will need to purchase data from a business that specializes in hotel research, tour the submarket, and conduct interviews with staff members at the most comparable properties to get a qualitative sense of recent trends and future changes. To the extent possible, the analyst should learn the composition of patronage at competitive properties: what percentage comes from individual business travelers, leisure travelers, conventions, in-house groups (groups that use meeting rooms at a hotel and do not need space at a convention center), and any special sources of demand such as airlines, medical facilities, corporate contracts, and government. These tasks will vary depending on the type of hotel property being analyzed.

In large cities with multiple sources of demand and numerous submarkets, interviews may provide a general sense of trends but will not yield the detailed data needed to determine whether sufficient market support exists for adding more rooms.

Trends in the performance of the hotel inventory over time, both in the metropolitan area and in the local competitive market area, are helpful in gauging whether demand is growing. Looking at how room demand has changed over the preceding three to five years is important. Increases in occupancy and RevPAR are a good indication that demand is growing—especially in areas where new supply has been added. Analysts may need to purchase these data from hotel specialists.

Demand may shift because of developments in transportation, technology, or consumer habits. A thriving hotel cluster at a key highway interchange may lose dominance when a new interchange is built down the road and new competitive rooms are added. Hotels adjacent to an existing convention center will become less desirable when a new convention center is built, even if the new center is only a few blocks away. Conversely, older hotel submarkets can experience a renaissance. Miami Beach is an example of a thriving tourist destination that went through a long decline and then rebounded when the historic architecture of South Beach became a new draw for tourism. Old hotels were restored, and new ones were added.

For budget and economy properties, the demand analysis will be more limited. Traffic counts help in determining the potential to attract travelers who will make an overnight stop on their way elsewhere. For these product types, analysis based on traffic counts and performance of similar properties in the area usually suffices. Developers and investors will also want to know if surrounding uses are desirable amenities for the proposed hotel. Limited-service properties that lack their own restaurants will be more successful if they are located near freestanding food service establishments or shopping centers.

Commercial or Business Market

The commercial market segment, made up of individuals and groups, includes both domestic and international business travelers. Business travelers typically represent a major source of demand for downtown and suburban upscale hotels and a minor source for resorts. Business travelers can include executives and managers at all levels, tech staff and information specialists, sales representatives, and potential employees going to a job interview. Government agencies and nonprofits also have traveling personnel, but they are limited in how much they can spend for accommodations.

Most domestic business trips are only one or two nights in duration, from Monday through Thursday nights. However, business travelers may extend their stay over a weekend in a city or resort location with amenities.

A crucial criterion in the selection of business lodging is location. Primary location considerations include proximity to centers of business activity and ease of access to and from airports. Women are a growing share of business travel demand. They want to be sure their accommodations are secure, and attentive service is also important. Seasonality and price sensitivity are less significant factors in predicting business travel demand than in the leisure sector.

The business travel market has several subsegments of demand:

- *Corporate and commercial individual travelers:* This demand segment consists of those whose purpose in traveling relates solely or predominantly to their jobs or businesses. They book their own hotel arrangements either through corporate travel departments or travel agencies or on their own by phone or online. Their employer may or may not have negotiated preferred rates with major hotel chains. If convenient—and subject to their employers' policies—the individual business traveler may choose a hotel on the basis of membership in a frequent-traveler loyalty program.

- *Corporate groups:* This segment is distinguished from the corporate individual segment by virtue of booking rooms on a block basis. The specific purpose of travel is likely to be a company-sponsored meeting or training session in the hotel or at a nearby location. Because of the nature of the clientele and the source of business, room rates for this segment are negotiated and specify the number of rooms booked and the time of year that the rooms are available.

- *Convention and association groups:* Conventions and association meetings can have thousands of attendees, many of whom travel as corporate groups or book rooms on a block basis through the sponsoring organization. Although a limited number of resort hotels rely almost entirely on visits by independent travelers, most try to attract conferences and business meetings as an economic necessity.

- *Contract demand:* Airlines contract with hotels for crew lodging and emergency housing for stranded travelers. They typically reserve a block of rooms for this purpose and negotiate a very low rate. Businesses with employees who travel to perform low-budget tasks also frequently negotiate contract rates with hotels, which usually are heavily discounted. Construction crews, disaster relief workers, and truck drivers are typical types of contract guests.

- *Government and military personnel:* Government workers and members of the military travel with modest per diem allowances. They gravitate to establishments that offer special discounts to government and military personnel.

- *Extended stays:* As indicated earlier, hotels can serve as temporary residences for executives, corporate employees, or others who have relocated to an area and need lodging until they can make permanent living arrangements. Extended-stay facilities also house consultants, auditors, trainees, or other workers assigned to projects lasting several weeks or months. Families often accompany relocating employees. Rooms may be rented by the week or the month at a more attractive rate than for short-term stays.

Tourists and Leisure Travelers

This demand segment encompasses most pleasure travelers and family groups. It also includes people traveling for other nonbusiness reasons, such as medical care, weddings, or funerals. Lengths of stay vary widely from single-night stopovers a day's drive from home to vacations lasting a week or longer at a resort thousands of miles from home. Market subsegments include the independent traveler market, the group market, and the wholesale market:

- *Independent travelers:* These visitors have selected a vacation destination and arranged for their accommodations either online, directly with the hotel, or (less frequently) through a travel agent. Because individuals book their own accommodations, few or no discounts are available beyond those offered to loyalty members. However, many hotels offer discounts, subject to room availability, to members of groups such as AAA (American Automobile Association) or AARP (formerly American Association of Retired Persons). Peak seasons and weekends account for a significant share of independent traveler demand, which includes singles, couples, and families looking to travel at a range of price points.

- *Package travel sold online:* Online travel sites such as Expedia, Orbitz, and Travelocity, as well as "last minute" or "deep discount" specialists, identify available flights, rooms, and rental cars and bundle them to create packages that are less costly than separate bookings. Other websites, such as Hotels.com, specialize in lodging and offer rooms at both chain and independent properties. (Not all properties in each chain make their surplus rooms available to these sites.) Because hotel chains saw their share of direct bookings erode to the online discounters, many now guarantee that the rates available on their own websites will be comparable to or lower than those offered by the online aggregators.

- *Group market:* The group market for leisure travelers includes people attending weddings and other social and family events. Event organizers reserve blocks of rooms at discounted rates.

- *Wholesale market:* The wholesale market segment extends to tourists who purchase discount packages that include any combination of hotel, airfare, food and beverage, automobile rental, tours, and discounts at retail outlets.

Tour operators typically negotiate room rates with a range of properties on an annual basis. The negotiations specify the number of rooms booked and the time of year that the rooms are available. Accordingly, the rates paid can be much lower than for travelers in other demand segments. Discount packages are popular because of the assurance that travelers' full range of needs will be addressed without unexpected expenses. Some consumers purchase discount packages on the basis of the price/value relationship, while others like the convenience of paying just once for all their vacation needs. The wholesale market segment looks for the availability of a range of on-premise amenities coupled with a strategic location near recreational, cultural, and entertainment centers.

Growing Importance of Leisure Demand

"Leisure travel is increasingly important to hotels' strong financial performance. . . . Hotels had long earned the highest ADRs during midweek from business travelers on expense accounts, and weekend rooms were offered at a discount to attract leisure guests. . . . By 2016, weekend ADRs exceeded weekday ADRs, $120.87 to $118.54. . . . The oversized growth in leisure demand is partially explained by shifts in the hotel guest profile. . . . In 2015, well-heeled senior citizens contributed the largest share of total spending on lodging. Spending by seniors will likely continue to increase as the last cohort of baby boomers enters the seniors age group."

Source: CBRE Research, 2018 U.S. Real Estate Market Outlook: Hotel (2017), p. 4.

■ *Weekend-getaway guests.* Downtown and suburban hotels that cater to weekday corporate guests pioneered the getaway concept to bolster sagging weekend occupancies. The practice has been adopted by many nonresort hotels. Typically, guests are offered a package plan that includes the room, breakfast, garage parking with in-out privileges, and/or other perks. Rates often are discounted substantially. Hotels in resort areas will offer lower rates on weekdays than on weekends.

Figure 8-6 illustrates how sources of demand can shift over a relatively short period, using Center City Philadelphia as an example. Individual leisure visitors to Center City hotels increased from 922,000 in 2013 to 1,092,000 by 2017—a gain of 18.4 percent. As a source of occupied rooms, this demand segment accounted for 32.8 percent of demand in 2017, up from 30.8 percent four years earlier. Visit Philadelphia, which markets the city as a leisure destination, indicates that the number of Center City leisure visitors nearly quadrupled since the organization began its promotion efforts in 1997. Commercial business demand (primarily individual business visitors) also grew between 2013 and 2017, as did group business (primarily convention and conference attendees). Demand from airline staff members and government employees declined during the same period.[7]

A hotel often serves more than one market segment, potentially increasing its occupancy and making the property less susceptible to market downturns. However, broadening the target market might cause an increase in competition from other hotels. It might also weaken the product's appeal to the market segment originally targeted. Some examples of crossover niches include amusement park hotels, such as

Figure 8-6
Change in Room Demand, by Source
Center City Philadelphia, 2013–2017

Source of demand	Occupied rooms			
	2013 (000s)	2017 (000s)	Change (%)	Share of 2017 demand (%)
Individual leisure visitors[a]	922	1,092	18.4	32.8
Conventions/groups[b]	1,035	1,071	3.5	32.1
Commercial business[c]	914	1,021	11.7	30.6
Airline[d]	90	86	−4.4	2.6
Government employees[e]	64	62	−3.1	1.9
Total hotel demand	**3,025**	**3,332**	**10.1**	**100.0**

Source: Visit Philadelphia (www.visitphilly.com), using data from CBRE Hotels.

a. Persons traveling alone or in a group of fewer than 10 for leisure purposes.

b. Ten or more persons traveling together for leisure purposes.

c. Business travelers (individual and group).

d. Airline crew members staying overnight and rooms reserved to accomodate stranded travelers.

e. Government workers traveling on official business.

those at Disney World, which combine family entertainment with conference business, and Las Vegas casino hotels, which combine gaming and adult-oriented shows with family-oriented activities.

Commercial hotels often handle guest overflow that cannot be accommodated at convention hotels. By contrast, convention hotels can attract leisure visitors during the summer months or the Christmas holidays, when few conventions are held.

Analysts who specialize in the lodging industry stay informed about trends in recreational activity participation (such as golf or skiing); visitation at various types of museums, theme parks, and sports venues; and the extent to which these activities generate overnight hotel stays. As to destinations, interest has been growing in "green" travel, culinary vacations, exotic destinations, and adventure travel, but the impact on hotel occupancy is not always obvious.

Fluctuations in Demand

Annual room occupancy rates vary considerably from month to month by region, season, and product type. Of all demand characteristics, seasonal fluctuation in demand is the one most frequently overlooked.

Business travel remains relatively constant throughout the year, while the volume of pleasure travel changes with the seasons and peaks in the summer quarter when many families take vacations. In the United States overall, August is the month of peak hotel demand. June is usually second, followed by October, a popular month for meetings and conventions. The demand for hotel rooms reaches its lowest point in December, when business travel declines during the holiday season. In most U.S. markets, December, January, and February are "softer" months. However, local occupancy peaks and troughs might vary considerably from national ones.

Market seasonality can be determined using information from hotel data specialists and from interviews with local

Sofitel Hotel at Rittenhouse Square in Center City Philadelphia. *(Biddle Hotel Consulting)*

convention and visitors bureaus and property managers. Markets that primarily serve business customers experience less seasonality than those with high demand from tourists. Many markets dependent on commercial traffic see some seasonality in the summer months, depending on whether they can attract leisure visitors. Convention activity slows during the summer as well. When seasonality is examined in a tourism-driven market such as Bar Harbor, Maine, or Aspen, Colorado, dramatic differences in occupancies between in-season and out-of-season periods will be revealed.

Seasonal profiles for particular geographic areas tend to relate to weather. For example, the hurricane season brings the lowest occupancy rates in the Caribbean; it also affects New Orleans and the Florida coasts, but not as strongly. Seasonal fluctuations in demand in some U.S. visitor destinations are so extreme that some hotels or B&Bs stay open for only part of the year; for example, lodgings in very cold climates that do not feature ski slopes tend to open only during more pleasant weather. But the purely seasonal resort has become a rarity today. The most successful resorts have transitioned from seasonal to year-round operations by identifying market segments that could be attracted in their off-seasons. For example, ski resorts have added other recreational amenities such as spas, summer hiking, fall color tours, and even special events (local food and wine fairs, lectures, film festivals) to attract summer tourists. Others have pursued group meeting business when skiing is not in season.

In markets that depend on business visitors, demand can also fluctuate by the day of the week. Although business visitation is still very important in Center City Philadelphia, growth in tourist demand resulted in an average 90 percent occupancy rate on Saturday nights in 2017.[8]

Knowing the sources of demand and the weekly or seasonal patterns in a given market is a beginning. But the analyst must evaluate the potential for a new hotel on the basis of growth in economic activity, including new business activity generators, commercial and industrial development, new tourist attractions and recreational development, and new construction and expansion of convention centers and airports.

Because some demand cannot be accommodated during peak periods with limited room availability, occupancy alone will understate the true amount of demand available. The amount of apparent new demand during periods of hotel supply additions may reflect recapture of room sales potential that had been turned away in the past. In a supply-constrained area, real demand for hotel rooms may be lost for lack of available rooms in desired locations. In the hotel business, this concept is referred to as *unaccommodated demand*: demand that seeks rooms in the competitive market but must use properties outside the area because of capacity constraints.

The ultimate result of the market analysis process is the identification of an opportunity—that is, currently underserved market demand—or a new concept that the experienced analyst believes can be successful.

Competitive Inventory

Analyzing the inventory of the existing competitive lodging supply in the market area helps predict the likely success of a new lodging facility. For each existing and proposed facility that—because of its location, size, and price points—will compete with the subject hotel, the analyst should quantify the number of rooms, location, affiliation (chain or independent), orientation (convention delegates, business travelers, vacationers, etc.), amenities, average daily room rate, average annual occupancy, and competitive strengths and weaknesses.

Dual-Branded Hotels

The past five years have seen the emergence of dual-branded hotels. Initially, the concept of putting two separate hotel buildings (operating under the same flag) on a single site had appeal; some costs could be shared—perhaps a common garage, valet parking service, and laundry facilities, for example. Having the two chains together would capture a higher share of potential demand than if they operated independently at different locations in the same submarket. HVS, a global hotel consulting firm, points out that now two brands more commonly co-locate in the same building. "The most popular pairings are of select-service and extended-stay hotels under one roof, enabling the developer to offer two different products while maintaining relatively similar chain scales and guest profiles. . . . The operational benefit for dual-branded hotels is realized primarily when the management company can run both hotels and employ just one person for key positions."

Research conducted by CBRE Hotels Americas Research indicates that some expected labor efficiencies for dual-branded hotels did not materialize. One reason given is that each brand required its own check-in areas and its own uniformed personnel. However, cost savings were realized in administrative or back-of-the-house functions—general management, accounting, security, marketing, and maintenance. Other benefits included improved revenues from two reservation systems and from shared amenities (pool, gym, and meeting space).

Examples include Aloft/Element, Hilton's Homewood Suites/Hampton Inn, Hyatt House/Hyatt Place, and Marriott's Courtyard/Fairfield Inn.

Sources: J. Carter Allen, "Dual-Brand Hotel Market Overview," HVS, August 15, 2018, https://www.hvs.com/article/8330-dual-brand-hotel-market-overview; Robert Mandelbaum and Gary McDade, "Dual-Branded Hotels: Beware Expectations of Significant Operating Efficiencies," Lodging, December 13, 2018, https:// lodgingmagazine.com/dual-branded-hotels-beware-expectations-of-significant-operating-efficiencies.

Hotel market analysis uses four key indicators of market performance:

- *Occupancy:* Percentage of available rooms actually sold.

- *ADR:* A measure of the average rate paid for rooms sold, calculated by dividing room revenue by rooms sold.

- *RevPAR:* Total guest room revenue divided by the total number of available rooms. RevPAR differs from ADR because RevPAR is affected by the amount of unoccupied available rooms, whereas ADR shows only the average rate of rooms actually sold. Occupancy × ADR = RevPAR.

- *Revenue per occupied room (RevPOR):* Used in the conference center segment of the hotel market, RevPOR reflects the importance of revenue from food and beverage sales, equipment rental, and other elements of conference contracts in determining property performance.

Interviews with hotel managers can be particularly important in understanding how each hotel competes within its market. Interviews should include the following:

- Questions regarding the strengths and weaknesses of the subject property (if the market study is evaluating the future of an existing hotel before acquisition or renovation) and those run by competitors. Although property managers may be less than candid when discussing their own weaknesses, they typically are less reticent in discussing those of their competitors.

- Information about the most recent renovation and any planned changes to the property that might alter its future competitive position.

- Opinions regarding which hotels are considered to be the most important competitors.

The competitive set initially selected by the researcher should hold up after discussions with property representatives. A researcher may discover that a property thought to be competitive is not considered to be so by other hotel managers. Or interviews may reveal a competitive hotel that at first did not appear to compete with the subject property. Ascertaining a property's anticipated performance for the current year is also useful. The degree of competitor candidness will vary from property to property. In general, the more professional the management is, the more comfortable it is with sharing information.

In small metropolitan areas or rural counties where data are not available for purchase, some information may be obtained from state or local hotel associations. However, submarket averages may not be available; the market analyst will need to interview managers at those properties deemed most competitive by virtue of location, price points, and services offered. The researcher should ask if managers will share operating information, including occupancy and average room rate information for at least the past few years (up to five years if possible).

Figure 8-7 provides an example of how supply data can be summarized in a market study, again using data for the Philadelphia area. The table shows aggregate information for the central business district and the metropolitan area as a whole, including counties on the New Jersey side of the Delaware River. It shows that Center City properties command above-average ADRs and occupancy.

Figure 8-7
Example: Greater Philadelphia Hotel Performance Indicators
2012 and 2018

Indicator	2012	2018	Change, 2012–2018
Philadelphia CBD			
Occupancy rate (%)	73.6	79.6	6.0
Average daily room rate	$167.51	$191.30	14.2
RevPAR	$123.22	$152.36	23.6
Number of properties[a]	50	56	12.0
Number of rooms[a]	11,630	12,595	8.3
Philadelphia, PA-NJ, metro area			
Occupancy rate (%)	66.9	71.1	4.2
Average daily room rate	$119.14	$132.97	11.6
RevPAR	$79.68	$94.60	18.7
Number of properties[a]	379	414	9.2
Number of rooms[a]	45,153	49,250	9.1

Source: STR.

a. Numbers as of December.

Keeping Existing Properties Competitive

Hotel operators must keep abreast of changes in technology (for example, the need for sufficient outlets for personal communications devices, the reduced demand for business center services, and the need for wi-fi throughout the hotel). Hotel fitness centers need to provide up-to-date equipment and more space; guests will have different ways they prefer to exercise. New features are often introduced first in upscale properties, but they eventually make their way to more modest accommodations. For example, in the mid-2000s, many properties focused on pampering guests with new, more luxurious bedding, a trend that has since trickled down to midpriced, limited-service hotel chains.

Hotel Supply-and-Demand Metrics

STR is the largest research company specializing in hotel property performance. It sells detailed performance reports (with daily, monthly, and annual data) for metropolitan areas, submarkets, and user-defined competitive property sets, including (a) number of properties, (b) available room-night supply, (c) occupancy rate (accommodated room-night demand), (d) average daily room rate (ADR), (e) RevPAR, and (f) total revenue. Reports calculate the percentage change from the previous year. Information about projects under construction and in planning is also available.

STR's extensive database allows hotel analysts to track changes over time. In some cases, data can be sorted for different types of hotels—by size or price points. As with other property types, the analyst should field-check hotel information obtained from secondary sources to be sure that the inventory is complete.

Nationally, STR reports that average hotel occupancy in 2018 was 66.2 percent, at an average daily rate of $129.83. This finding represented an increase of 2.4 percent from 2017 results. RevPAR in 2018 was $85.96, up 2.9 percent from the previous year. For 2019, occupancy is projected to remain flat, with ADR at $132.81 (+2.3 percent) and RevPAR at $87.94.[9] CBRE Hotels sells similar data to hotel owners, investors, and managers after having acquired the hotel consulting practice of accounting firm PKF in 2014.[10]

Future Supply

Significant additions to supply can quickly change market performance, so the analyst will also need to find information about properties that are under construction or in the planning pipeline.

Interviews with competitive properties or information from data vendors may have revealed possible planned or rumored developments. Local governments should be asked about planning approvals and building permits issued for new hotels. The researcher should try to determine the likelihood of any rumored development actually being built; many announced projects do not proceed for a variety of reasons. Full-service and center-city properties in particular are much more difficult to bring to fruition than are suburban, limited-service properties.

The researcher needs to understand how far along such projects are in the development process. If only a small number of possible projects have been announced (and have submitted plans for government approvals), the analyst can investigate their status by talking to their developers or to municipal planning and building officials. Specific questions should be asked regarding the status of future projects where construction has yet to begin. Most property

Figure 8-8

Projected U.S. Hotel Openings, 2019

- 1,203 projects
- 150,169 rooms
- Top five markets by room openings: New York City, Orlando, Dallas, Las Vegas, Houston

Rooms by chain scale segment		
Segment	Number of rooms	Share of total (%)
Luxury	4,911	3.3
Upper upscale	17,563	11.7
Upscale	46,612	31.0
Upper midscale	50,351	33.5
Midscale	12,510	8.3
Economy	3,729	2.5
Independent	14,493	9.7

Source: Hotel News Now, *January 29, 2019. Data as of December 2018.*

sponsors claim their project is imminent when often it is far from certain.

An important factor in assessing the probability of a planned hotel is the sponsor of the project. If it is an experienced hotel developer with a proven track record, the project's completion is more likely than if the sponsor is an individual or organization with no experience developing hotels. However, the name of the developer listed on a planning document or building permit may not provide much insight into the organization behind the project. If the analyst determines that a future competitor is likely to be built within a period that will affect the proposed project, the researcher must evaluate that property's likely competitiveness with the proposed subject.

Figure 8-8 illustrates information available from STR on projected U.S. hotel openings in 2019 by chain scale segment. With more than 1,200 new hotels anticipated and over 150,000 rooms projected to open in 2019 alone, existing hotels in most markets will experience increased competition that could affect performance.

Hotels are attractive land uses from the perspective of municipal officials. Many states and localities levy room sales taxes, which can be a significant source of revenue (in addition to real estate taxes). Hotels also draw visitors who support local stores and restaurants. A desire for nonresident-generated tax revenues can result in new hotel plans being approved without consideration of whether demand is sufficient to support the hotel. Overbuilding of low-rise budget and limited-service properties can easily occur along highway corridors or in suburban business nodes where submarkets cross municipal boundaries.

Figure 8-9
Example: Calculating Penetration and Yield for a 300-Room Hotel

Year	Available Market	Available Subject	Occupied Market	Occupied Subject	% Market	% Subject	ADR Market	ADR Subject	RevPAR Market	RevPAR Subject
	Average daily rooms				Occupancy rate					
2016	1,500	300	975	165	65.0	55.0	$160	$120	$104.00	$66.00
2017	1,500	300	995	168	66.3	56.0	$163	$122	$108.12	$68.32
2018	1,500	300	1,010	175	67.3	58.3	$165	$122	$111.10	$71.17
2019[a]	1,700	300	1,050	180	61.8	60.0	$165	$124	$101.91	$74.40
2020[a]	1,700	300	1,070	185	62.9	61.7	$164	$125	$103.22	$77.08
2021[a]	1,700	300	1,070	185	62.9	61.7	$165	$126	$103.85	$77.70
2022[a]	1,700	300	1,110	185	65.3	61.7	$165	$127	$107.74	$78.32

Year	Fair share	Captured	Penetration	Yield
	Performance of subject			
2016	20.0	16.9	84.6	63.5
2017	20.0	16.9	84.4	63.2
2018	20.0	17.3	86.6	64.1
2019[a]	17.6	17.1	97.1	73.0
2020[a]	17.6	17.3	98.0	74.7
2021[a]	17.6	17.3	98.0	74.8
2022[a]	17.6	16.7	94.4	72.7

Sources: Deborah L. Brett & Associates; Biddle Hotel Consulting.

a. Projected

Projecting Performance

Once the competitors have been analyzed, the performance of the subject property should be projected. The most commonly used method is fair-share analysis, in which a percentage of market capture is estimated for the subject according to the number of rooms in the subject divided by the total number of rooms in the market. Projected market share must be tempered by qualitative factors, such as location, quality, and operator experience. The subject location and the proposed hotel (or one being evaluated for acquisition or repositioning) should be evaluated relative to its competitors with respect to many factors:

- Franchise affiliation ("flag"),
- Proximity to demand generators,
- Attractiveness of the building and its immediate surroundings,
- Visibility and ease of access,
- Traffic counts on adjacent streets or highways,
- Parking availability and cost,
- Guest room sizes and furnishings,
- Guest facilities and amenities (such as pools, gyms, dining, and meeting rooms),
- Average room rate, and
- Management and operations (to the extent that this information is available).

On the basis of this comparison and familiarity with market demand segments being targeted, the analyst should be able to estimate an achievable average daily room rate. Likely discounting for groups and contract demand must be considered. Using known local seasonality factors, projections of monthly occupancy can be made on the basis of the number of days per month and then summarized as annual occupancy.

Hotel market specialists are often asked to prepare financial pro formas for proposed properties or acquisitions. In addition to estimating room revenue, the analyst would include non-room revenue, such as banquet sales or restaurant operations.

In assessing the potential of an existing hotel being considered for sale or purchase, two key measurements are its *penetration* and *yield*. A hotel's penetration is its share of demand (occupied rooms) in relation to its share of supply (available rooms). Figure 8-9 provides an example of the penetration and yield analysis for a hypothetical existing 300-room hotel being considered for acquisition. It presents a picture of the recent and projected performance of the competitive market and the subject property. In 2016, for example, the subject hotel's share of demand (capture) was 16.9 percent (165 ÷ 975), and its share of supply (referred to as "fair share" in figure 8-9) was 20.0 percent (300 ÷ 1,500). Thus, its penetration was 84.6 percent (16.9 ÷ 20.0).

A hotel's yield in this analysis is its RevPAR divided by the competitive market's RevPAR. It reflects the property's relative performance in terms of occupancy and room rate compared with its competitors. As described earlier in this chapter, RevPAR is derived by multiplying the average daily room rate by the occupancy percentage. In 2016, the yield for the subject property was 63.5 percent ($66 ÷ $104), a figure based on its $66 RevPAR and the market's $104 RevPAR.

Future performance is projected on the basis of changes in general economic conditions, future additions to the competitive supply, and likely improvement in the subject property's competitive position after acquisition, while taking into account all planned improvements. The example in figure 8-9 projects increasing RevPAR for the subject property from 2016 through 2022. The market analyst has concluded that performance improvement will occur from a strong economy and gains in both business and leisure travel. Note, however, that the opening of a new 200-room property in 2019 will derail RevPAR growth in the market as a whole.

Figure 8-9 shows that the subject property will be able to improve its occupancy despite the growing supply of competitive rooms, probably because its room rates will remain below the average for the market. Both its market penetration and its yield rates will be significantly better in 2019 than in 2016, suggesting that the proposed acquisition and renovation has the potential to be successful as long as room rates are kept at the low end.

Data Sources

Trade associations serving the travel and lodging industries are the best source of national statistics on trends in domestic U.S. travel. The U.S. Travel Association tracks domestic person-trips and the number of international visitor arrivals. The American Hotel and Lodging Association provides summary information on business and leisure traveler characteristics; their state affiliates can also be helpful. The U.S. Department of Commerce's Office of Travel and Tourism Industries tracks foreign travel to the United States, and the United Nations' World Tourism Organization (www.unwto.org) publishes annual data on global travel and visitor spending.

Travel trends in local markets can be reviewed using data from local chambers of commerce, tourism and economic development agencies (both state and local), and various trade associations. However, the range of information provided is not consistent among markets. Private consulting firms specializing in travel market analysis and tourism studies are also useful as sources for industry-wide trends. Some firms sell local data for larger markets. One example is DK Shifflet (www.dksa.com).

Data on hotel supply and demand can also be monitored nationally and for individual metropolitan areas by purchasing reports from STR or CBRE Hotels Research. CBRE's annual *Trends in the Hotel Industry* covers hotel statistics for major markets. STR publishes *Lodging Outlook,* a monthly market summary and data on current trends in its online newsletter, *Hotel News Now.*

Information on new supply can be obtained from local convention and visitors bureaus or from planning and economic development agencies. It can also be purchased from data vendors, such as STR and CBRE Hotels.

Notes

1. STR (formerly known as Smith Travel Research) has the most extensive database on the U.S. hotel industry and provided 2018 data cited in this chapter (www.str.com). Statistics for 2014 were taken from the American Hotel and Lodging Association's *Lodging Industry Profile*, 2014 edition, www.ahla.com.

2. U.S. Travel Association, "U.S. Travel and Tourism Overview, 2017"; also "Travel Forecast," updated November 2018, www.ustravel.org.

3. The U.S. Travel Association mentions concerns from foreign travelers regarding negative political attitudes, mounting trade tensions, and higher oil prices. See Jaleen Christoff, "Domestic Travel Rises as US Struggles to Maintain International Market Share," U.S. Travel Association, August 8, 2018.

4. Scott Shatford, CEO of AirDNA, February 18, 2019, airdna.co. The firm collects information on more than 10 million Airbnb and HomeAway properties and their performance metrics (ADR, occupancy, RevPAR) in more than 85,000 locations worldwide, helping customers strategically price, optimize, and invest in short-term vacation rental properties.

5. Ernst & Young, *State of the Vacation Timeshare Industry: United States Study, 2018 Edition* (ARDA International Foundation, 2018), www.arda.org; press release, June 12, 2018.

6. More recent statistics were not available, but the leisure visitor share of total room demand has likely increased since 2014.

7. Visit Philadelphia, "2017 Hotel Performance: Center City Philadelphia," https://visitphilly.com, using data from CBRE Hotels.

8. Visit Philadelphia, *2018 Annual Report,* http://files.visitphilly.com/Visit-Philadelphia-Annual-Report-2018.pdf.

9. "STR: US Hotels Post Another Record Year in 2018," *Hotel News Now,* January 18, 2019; "STR, TE Downgrade US Hotel Forecast for 2019 and 2020," *Hotel News Now,* January 29, 2019. The hotel market is projected to continue to improve, but at a slower rate than in recent years.

10. PKF Hotel Experts still operates a separate international unit under the PKF International corporate umbrella.

CHAPTER 9

MIXED-USE DEVELOPMENT

Mixed-use development is challenging—and risky—for both the developer and the market analyst. In many ways, it consists of more than the sum of its parts: at best, it generates premium rents/prices because of cumulative attraction; at worst, it can fail because one or more uses were ill-conceived or failed to capture demand. Mixed-use developers must strategize the proper sizing, placement, connections, and timing of components. Site planners and architects must deal with myriad building code standards, density limits, parking requirements, and design issues that can differ for each proposed use. And market analysts must evaluate each property type individually and understand the synergies—both positive and negative—that can be created.

Financing is complex as the developer, investors, and lenders conduct their due diligence on the individual uses, as well as the composite project. Multiple uses lend excitement to a new development, but they also stretch out construction time. Supply and demand are cyclical, and the cycles for different property types do not necessarily move in tandem. A developer planning a mixed-use project in 2017–2018 would—depending on the location—feel comfortable including a variety of residential uses and a hotel, but would be more cautious about class A office space or big-box retail buildings. Ten years earlier, the housing market was shaky, but many potential retail tenants were in expansion mode.

Economic cycles and market conditions will likely change during the construction, stabilization, and holding periods for a mixed-use investment. This is a core reason why the projects are hard to finance and many lenders shy away from them. It also explains why many developers of larger mixed-use projects will create the master plan, obtain approvals, install any needed infrastructure, and then sell individual parcels to firms specializing in particular land uses. The development team needs the experience and financial resources to see the overall project to completion in order to maximize its success. And it needs a good working relationship with local government should plans need to be modified over time.

Background

Mixed-use buildings were common before World War II. Older structures with retail shops on the ground floor and apartments or offices on the upper levels can still be found in urban neighborhoods and on small-town Main Streets throughout the United States. Downtown office buildings usually included ground-floor space occupied by stores, restaurants, and banks, but only in the 1970s did truly multifunction high-rise buildings appear in the nation's densest central business districts. Redevelopment projects included buildings that incorporated a variety of uses in a single high-rise or a multiblock neighborhood.

The spread of transit-oriented development around commuter-rail stations in the 1990s brought the urban mixed-use concept to the suburbs, albeit at lower densities.

Mixed-Use Development Challenges

"Companies attempting to enter the mixed-development world will face a much different and more challenging experience and a more skeptical reaction from investors, at least initially. They note that those involved must have managerial mastery and staff experience for each different property type involved and be able to monitor and adjust to very different market cycles for each. . . . An eye for properties that make good candidates for such projects and the financial wherewithal to acquire the land in premium locations are also important. . . . You are dealing simultaneously with multiple different product types with different cycles, different demand generators and different fundamentals in the market for each form that are rarely in sync. . . . There is a ton of complexity."

Source: Don Briggs, executive vice president of development, Federal Realty Investment Trust, as quoted in David Tobenkin, "REITs and Mixed-Use Development," REIT Magazine, October 31, 2017. The author cites Federal Realty as "among the most experienced and skilled mixed-use practitioners."

Lifestyle centers combining housing, shops, eateries, and entertainment brought the mixed-use concept to suburban town centers that had no mass transit.

Today, mixed-use development is accepted and often encouraged by government agencies because of its vitality. In densely developed neighborhoods, combining apartments or condominiums with retail, hotels, and entertainment has created 24-hour locations that are safer for residents and more inviting for tourists and business visitors. In the suburbs, the smart-growth and new-urbanist movements promote mixed-use development because it reduces travel and parking demands and enhances the pedestrian experience.

In *Real Estate Development: Principles and Process* (5th ed., 2015), ULI defined a mixed-use project as "a development, in one building or several buildings, that combines at least three significant revenue-producing uses that are physically and functionally integrated and developed in conformance with a coherent plan. A mixed-use development might include, for example, retail space on the ground floor, offices on the middle floors, and condominiums on the top floors, with a garage on the lower levels."

A mixed-use project can cover a dozen acres or much more; it might have a few buildings with only one use (for example, freestanding restaurants, a hotel, or townhouses), and multiple taller buildings, each with two or more uses. The development will have pedestrian connections between buildings, open space (plazas, parks, walking/biking trails, water features), shared signage, and (to some extent) shared parking.

Mixed-use developments are not the same as the MPCs that were discussed in chapter 4. The latter, encompassing hundreds or even thousands of acres, usually will contain a variety of housing types and price points, as well as multiple commercial uses. MPCs may have pedestrian connectors and bike paths. But the primary focus—and profit generator—is housing. The community shopping centers, professional offices, health clubs, and other recreational facilities in an MPC are included primarily to enhance the marketability of homes and apartments.

Mixed-use developments are much smaller in scale than master-planned communities and are located in urban or mature suburban locations. Specialists may be brought in to handle the marketing of distinct components. Many mixed-use projects are built on redevelopment sites, requiring demolition of long-shuttered industrial buildings or rail yards, remediation of contaminants, and stabilization of waterfront locations so they can handle more intense use.

As discussed in chapters 6 and 7, large business parks often include warehouses, light assembly, flex office/showroom buildings, and limited-service hotels. Depending on their scale and the attractiveness of their locations, business parks can also attract convenience retail space, restaurants, health clubs, and daycare centers. However, in business parks, the office and industrial uses dominate and each building functions independently. The other commercial activities are supportive—they enhance the marketability of large parcels, while using portions of the property that might not be as attractive for primary space users. Business parks can be multiuse but not mixed use. A mixed-use project requires synergy among activities: residents patronize the restaurants and bars, as do shoppers, office tenants, and hotel guests. Service businesses rely on repeat customers (residents and office workers) but also generate revenue from hotel guests.

Three or More Significant Revenue-Producing Uses

Although many real estate projects have more than one use, mixed-use developments as defined in this chapter include at least three major revenue-producing uses. In most mixed-use projects, the primary revenue-producing uses are apartments, office space, stores, restaurants and other eateries, and hotels; condominiums can be included, as well as revenue-producing uses such as parking garages and commercial recreation facilities (health clubs, exercise studios, movie theaters). It is worth emphasizing that each use must be significant. A few shops at the base of an office building do not turn it into mixed-use development, nor does a fitness center in a residential complex.

Less common are mixed-use projects that include cultural facilities (performing arts centers, libraries, or museums) or civic centers. These uses may be supported (and managed) by nonprofit organizations or government entities. Note that convention centers are often developed in conjunction with one or more hotels, but these projects rarely have significant residential or retail components.

Each property type in a mixed-use development draws its own buyers, tenants, and patrons. In projects that involve residential uses, retailers generate sales from residents but also draw people who live outside the development. The same is true of arts and cultural facilities. A small number of people may both live and work in the same development, but this is more the exception than the rule.

Having at least three significant uses together in one development usually implies a project of considerable scale and impact. Typically, each major component will exceed 100,000 square feet, and total project size is usually more than 300,000 square feet. The largest developments can involve a million square feet or more.

Developers often seek a minimum critical mass for mixed-use developments, to create a strong public image and market penetration. The size and diversity of uses in these projects—if effectively programmed and designed—can result in a complex that becomes a significant new draw. Mixed-use projects are much more than simply developments; they are exercises in placemaking. A good mixed-use development can turn a lesser location into a prime one. A mixed-use project can also improve the chances of success for a socially desirable but economically risky activity because the more profitable uses can carry the less profitable. For example, higher prices charged for market-rate rental apartments provide funds to help subsidize less profitable units that are set aside for low-income households.

Local governments are becoming more comfortable with mixed-use projects; performance zoning is modifying or replacing the traditional list of permitted and prohibited uses.[1] However, even after numerous mixed-use successes have occurred around the country, many localities are still tied to old notions of separate-use zoning and are reluctant to modify their codes in ways that encourage multiple uses in a single structure or even on a single parcel or block.

Physical and Functional Integration

The second descriptive characteristic of mixed-use developments is a significant physical and functional integration of the project's components. All buildings and outdoor spaces should be interconnected by pedestrian links, although such integration can take many physical forms:

- Vertical mixing of project components into a single megastructure.

- Careful positioning of key project components around central public spaces (parks, fountains, plazas, amphitheaters) or open-air shopping areas.

- Combining single-purpose and multiuse buildings.

- Linking project components with sidewalks, interior walkways or trails, enclosed corridors, underground concourses, common lobbies, escalators and elevators, or even aerial bridges between buildings.

- Shared parking, which improves land use efficiency and reduces costs.

Mixed-use projects are usually envisioned from the outset in conformance with a coherent development strategy and an approved land plan. Master planning for a mixed-use development requires collaboration among specialists in site planning, architecture, engineering, market analysis, marketing, leasing, property management, and finance. The planning process is therefore far more complex and time-consuming than for simpler projects.

Parking, Circulation, and Transit

An integrated mix of on- and off-street parking is the most desirable goal for mixed-use centers. The convenience of short-term, on-street spaces in front of stores or outdoor play areas is a marketing plus, whereas off-street spaces (either in garages or surface lots—or both) are needed to accommodate residents, workers, and customers who will be staying for more than an hour or two. If land values and planned densities are high, parking decks, either above or below ground, can be justified—and are certainly more desirable than endless rows of open parking. In successful projects, parking garages can form the "base" for future building phases, to be developed using the air rights above. The ability to accommodate future changes to occupied buildings underscores the need for creative thinking and careful planning.

Mixed-use developments also offer opportunities for shared parking, especially in locations well served by mass transit. Although young adults are showing more interest in taking public transit or ride sharing, dedicated parking will still be needed for residents, office workers, and shoppers. The best opportunity to reduce total parking needs will be in the evening or on weekends, when shoppers, diners, and entertainment patrons can park in spaces used by daytime office workers. The overall number of spaces needed can be further reduced because on-site residents, office workers,

Creating a Place

Project for Public Spaces (www.pps.org) is a nonprofit organization, working with developers and municipalities on new mixed-use communities and town centers. PPS offers the following principles for creating successful mixed-use projects:

- Use public spaces as the framework around which housing, retail, and commercial buildings are planned and designed.

- Build a strong sense of community for residents and workers by creating social gathering places and space for community events.

- Reflect a consensus among members of the development team regarding public space goals and management policies.

- Provide a sense of place and a variety of destinations.

- Offer a wide range of uses and activities to create vibrancy and activity during all seasons, and to serve people of all ages and socioeconomic characteristics.

- Support transit options and smart-growth principles through design.

- Integrate the project into existing communities and surrounding neighborhoods.

- Manage and program the space carefully, taking advantage of public/private partnerships in operations.

According to PPS, places thrive when users have a range of reasons to be there. The reasons might include a place to sit, playgrounds to enjoy, art to touch, music to hear, food to eat, history to experience, and people to meet. Ideally, some of these activities will be unique to that particular place, reflecting the culture and history of the surrounding community. Busy plazas and pedestrian-friendly streets contribute directly to retail customer satisfaction. Those features can push building rents upward and reduce vacancy rates. PPS states that "it's not enough to have a single use dominate a particular place—you need an array of activities for people. It's not enough to have just one great place in a neighborhood—you need a number of them to create a truly lively community."

Mixed-Use Projects Enhance Long-Term Investment Stability

"The primary case for investing in mixed-use assets is that the combining of uses generates revenue and value premiums that exceed the incremental cost of delivery or acquisition. In other words, mixed-use assets get better rents.

"Market data largely supports this. Apartment buildings, for example, with a strong ground-level retail program can often generate a 5 percent or better rent premium to adjacent and similar buildings without this synergistic mix of uses occurring in the building.

"Mixed-use buildings also provide some product diversification within the same asset/investment. For example, if the office component of a mixed-use building suffers because that local market became soft, the residential and retail components of the same building may continue to produce revenue growth. . . . [T]he long-term performance of the assets is more certain . . . . Because the certainty of return over a longer period of time is perceived as greater, investors are willing to pay more for the same income stream."

Source: Adam Ducker, "How to Invest in Mixed-Use Real Estate Projects." Real Assets Adviser, January 1, 2018.

and nearby neighborhood residents will be able to walk to shops, restaurants, and exercise facilities. In addition, the explosive growth in ride sharing is already having an impact on parking demand. Developers also need to think about parking demand should driverless vehicles become a reality. Safe pickup and dropoff areas are also an important part of site planning for mixed-use development. For large projects, an experienced parking consultant should be part of the development team.

Pedestrian circulation is another critical element in the planning process; without it, the project will not achieve its desired synergies and sense of place—the hallmarks of successful mixed-use development. Yet security must be maintained for tenants of individual uses (for example, residences and hotels).

In the 1970s, transit-oriented development projects were a laboratory for mixing uses in urban settings. Private developers were eager to integrate new or renovated subway stations into their commercial buildings, and constructing offices adjacent to light-rail stations offered marketing advantages. Joint development projects involving transit agencies and private developers were promoted by Washington, D.C.'s Metro and San Francisco's BART; the transit agencies sold land adjacent to their stations or leased the air rights over them. Transit agencies were true partners in these projects.[2] The earliest examples of joint development projects were primarily office oriented, with one or two floors of aboveground retail space (and more in the subway concourses). Only later did apartments and condominiums

become part of the mix. What appears today to be a mixed-use project from the 1980s probably involved multiple developers over a long period. Today's transit-oriented developments are often built on underused privately owned parcels within a short walk of station entrances. Some projects involve a combination of new construction and adaptive reuse of older industrial or office buildings.

Plans must also carefully consider vehicular circulation into and within the project site, and the placement of parking entrances and exits (whether structured or in surface lots). Cars need to move in and out without affecting residential buildings adversely. If a transit station is part of a mixed-use project, residents and employees need a safe path to get to the station. Trucks need to be able to make deliveries to retail and restaurant spaces without blocking streets or generating noise. Lighting that enhances safety for commercial patrons visiting at night must be tempered by the need to protect residents from glare. Residential tenants and homebuyers come to mixed-use projects because they like the ambience, but they want to be shielded from adverse effects. These issues become even more problematic when marketing for-sale housing rather than rental units.

Analyzing the Market Potential of Mixed-Use Projects

Mixed-use developments present challenges for the market analyst. If conditions are optimal, the project's developer and investors can capitalize on the synergy among complementary uses and create an overall cumulative market attraction that exceeds what the individual project components would generate independently. However, each element's marketability must be able to stand on its own; the analyst must then determine whether any rent or price premiums might be achievable as a result of the project's varied elements. In some ways, the task is similar to determining the premiums a condominium buyer would pay for upper-floor units with attractive views or the enhanced privacy afforded by an end unit in a townhouse building. But it is easier to test whether tenants will pay premiums for an identical unit with a better view or on a higher floor in an apartment building than to quantify how much more a business will pay to be close to interesting restaurants and lively bars.

Considerable effort has been spent trying to identify whether mixed use justifies a rental premium—and to quantify its magnitude—with little success.[3] The theory is that potential apartment renters or office tenants will take advantage of co-located land uses to reduce the number of commuting, shopping, and entertainment trips, whether by private automobile, shared vehicle, or mass transit. Economies of scale are created from sharing the cost of infrastructure, off-site road improvements, on-site parking, and open space, as well as common services ranging from trash collection to marketing and advertising.

As suggested earlier, not all uses are equally compatible. Potential upper-floor residents may be concerned about odors, noise, and nighttime activity from street-level restaurants, bars, or clubs. Condominium owners will worry about security and need assurances that office workers or hotel guests will not have access to residential floors in a high-rise building. Hotel guests may also have security concerns in a mixed-use building.

Developers today have much more experience with mitigating negative effects through careful site planning, building design and materials, security systems, and management. Office and residential components of a high-rise mixed-use building will need their own lobbies with separate entryway security. Residents and office users want privacy, but retail tenants and restaurants want to be accessible to patrons who do not live or work in the building.

With sufficient scale, a mixed-use development can be a successful pioneer, generating consumer interest and investment in the surrounding neighborhood. But multiple uses are also riskier for developers:

- It is harder to time the market. Although large projects can be built in phases, the uses included in a single structure are started and completed (with the exception of interior finishes) at the same time. Mixed-use buildings are vulnerable to market shifts that occur during construction. For example, a single multiuse building might be ready for leasing at a time when the housing market is strong but the office market is overbuilt— or vice versa. One component may lease or sell more quickly than others. The developer cannot postpone the completion of a portion of the building because the prospect of finding tenants is poor.

- In a project with multiple buildings, proper phasing of project components is crucial, as is the need for flexibility in planning and design. Elements of the original plan may need to be revised in response to changing market conditions. For example, an initial plan that calls for two-thirds of the apartment component to be rental units and one-third condominiums might need to be altered if mortgage interest rates shift dramatically; 250,000 square feet of specialty retail space may no longer make sense now that e-commerce is capturing an ever-increasing share of sales. More entertainment uses or restaurants might have a better chance of success. Although a shift from rentals to condominiums in an apartment building would not, in and of itself, require a change in the development plan or zoning, condominiums are typically larger than rental units with the same number of bedrooms and baths. Floor plans would probably need to be reconfigured and the mix of unit types (number of bedrooms or bathrooms) could be changed.

- Buildings in the initial phase must function independently of future activity, because a considerable lag in construction completion could occur. The project should begin with the uses that have the strongest current market potential, thereby creating cash flow that can be funneled into later phases of the project.

- Making decisions about where to place different activities within a mixed-use site can be difficult. Every potential commercial tenant wants the storefront with the most visibility and the easiest access. A site plan for a large mixed-use project usually places offices on interior parcels and hotel, retail, and entertainment uses at the edges for the best visibility and access. Hotels need to be directly adjacent to or above their guest parking. This need is less critical for office or retail uses if the site has attractive pedestrian connections. Upscale restaurants will need space for valet parking.

- Different project elements may appeal to distinct socioeconomic groups. Prospective buyers of luxury condominiums might not like to see ground-floor retail space that caters to a less affluent demographic. Museums and cultural center patrons could be more affluent than office workers. Restaurants and coffee shops will need to cater to both groups. Casinos can attract affluent gamblers or elderly day-trippers who spend little at surrounding stores or restaurants. Marketing plans need to consider how to attract patrons who will maximize synergy among land uses.

- Even if interactions among uses make sense when the project is first planned, changing market conditions can cause tenant targeting to shift. For example, upscale shops might be the preferred retail tenants initially. But if they are unsuccessful, the tenant mix will change over time.

- In the current retail environment, the best projects are vulnerable to losing tenants if a store's parent company has to shutter underperforming locations or declare bankruptcy. Even in an attractive mixed-use development, it may take time to find new tenants and the rents they pay may be lower.

Notwithstanding the presumed advantages of mixed-use developments, the market analyst must start with the basics described in previous chapters: (a) the analysis of demand demographics, (b) an assessment of the subject site's attractiveness and accessibility, (c) evaluation of the strengths and weaknesses of competitive properties, (d) a review of market supply conditions, and (e) identification of "what's missing" in the area. These key steps are performed for each separate use as if each were to be independently located and built. The recommendations can then be refined to reflect the attraction among co-located uses and to estimate any cumulative attraction that might generate greater market penetration.

Analysts will then consider whether the mix of uses will result in higher capture rates from patrons who live outside the immediate area. An attractive mixed-use development with good road and transit access and an appealing location (for example, near a beach, an amusement park, a harbor, or an area with mountain views) will likely draw more out-of-town travelers and metropolitan area residents who live beyond the local trade area.

Understanding Synergy

Where strong market synergy exists among the various uses in a mixed-use development, opportunities arise for realizing market premiums from these combinations. Because every mixed-use development differs in design, scale, and sources of market support, there are no hard-and-fast rules. Nevertheless, certain land uses typically enhance the marketability of other uses. They are discussed briefly in the following sections.

Housing

Clearly, a powerful relationship can exist between residential development and retail space. Residents need a place to shop for basic necessities, creating demand for convenience stores and services such as dry cleaners or hair salons. Mixed-use projects that include housing are attractive to both young adults and empty nesters, creating support for restaurants, coffee shops, specialty food purveyors, and bars. A variety of housing types (rental apartments, condominiums, townhouses, and even single-family homes) can draw residents with a wide range of incomes. Mixed-use developments often include affordable housing components, which can generate local government support for the development plan.

It is unrealistic to expect that on-site housing alone will generate sufficient demand for shops and services to be successful. Most stores and restaurants will need to generate a majority of their market support from patrons living outside the mixed-use development at the time the project is started, and this may continue over time. Project residents will certainly not be the most important source of sales for retailers, although their support can be significant for convenience stores, coffee shops, takeouts, restaurants, and drinking places. Consider a project with 500 housing units and 150,000 square feet of store space. Assuming that the retail space would need sales of at least $400 per square foot per year, each residential unit would have to spend $120,000 annually at the development's retailers to make it successful—highly unlikely. Clearly, the shops and eateries in a mixed-use project would not survive if they failed to attract residents of other neighborhoods, nearby workers, and visitors.

Even so, residents are an important source of activity—and sales—for the retail space in a mixed-use project. In transit-oriented developments, residents patronize shops and restaurants during off-peak hours when commuters are at work or after they have gone home for the day. Because residents are on site, they will be the first to know about new store openings, and they will spread the word to peers who live within the larger metro area. However, mixing housing and retail uses is not always problem free. For example, mass-market stores can conflict with the image of quality sought by owners and renters; residents may not want to share outdoor plazas with shoppers and entertainment patrons.

Synergy between housing and office space is weaker, but fewer potential clashes exist between these uses. The option of walking to work will attract residents, especially entrepreneurs or self-employed persons who use coworking space (an increasingly important part of the office component of mixed-use developments). Employers may be intrigued by the idea of being able to find staff or freelancers who live in the development. However, the presence of on-site offices is unlikely to be a key factor in attracting renters or buyers—unless they already work for businesses that have space in the project. Focus groups with a sample of prospective residents and office employees will help refine the connection between place of residence and place of work. Census resources on commuting, including OnTheMap (described in chapter 3), can also be helpful but may not be current.

Office Space

Demand for office space was the driving force behind mixed-use projects in urban downtowns during the 1980s and 1990s; nearly all such developments included a significant office component. Before the Great Recession, demand for downtown living was not as widespread as it is in 2019, so office workers were viewed as the most important source of patrons for restaurants and retail space in mixed-use towers. That is not to say that mixed-use buildings appealed to all types of office tenants in past decades. Many preferred the image and corporate identity associated with a freestanding class A+ building in a class A location.

In low- and mid-rise suburban town centers, office space is often a secondary use, with retail and residential uses dominant. As indicated earlier, analysts should not assume that a high percentage of people who work in a mixed-use development will want to live there, or vice versa.

Office development has clear market synergy with hotels, bars, and restaurants, and to a lesser extent with many types of retail activity. Bars and restaurants obviously benefit from patronage by office employees, but the mix of establishments must be chosen to appeal to the ages, tastes, and income levels of nearby workers. If office tenants are already in place, focus groups can help identify the types of establishments that would perform best. Retail stores that are open in the evening can draw workers as they leave their offices, but major food shopping is more likely to occur closer to home.

Most offices have occasional (if not frequent) out-of-town visitors and find it practical to recommend nearby lodging. The extra boost of hotel patronage from office space in the same complex can be estimated from interviews with office tenants already committed to the mixed-use development or through conversations with marketing staff at hotels located near other office complexes in the area. As discussed in chapter 8, indicators of hotel patronage by individual business visitors can also be explored with staff at the area's convention and visitors bureau. The market analyst should explore the frequency with which businesses in both corporate and multitenant office space bring visitors for meetings and conferences, and the types of accommodations those visitors prefer.

City Creek Center in downtown Salt Lake City is a mixed-use project covering three blocks, with multilevel upscale retail space anchored by Macy's and Nordstrom, as well as 300 housing units (rental and condo), upper-floor office space, restaurants, a grocery, and a Marriott hotel. Distinctive features include a retractable roof and a skybridge. *(Ritu Manoj Jethani/Shutterstock.com)*

The Row, a condo-hotel building in the Assembly Row mixed-use development in Somerville, Massachusetts. *(Deborah L. Brett & Associates)*

Limited synergy can also be gained from the location of medical office space within a mixed-use complex that includes both residential and general office components. As is the case for retailers, health care professionals will need to draw patients from beyond the project's boundaries. Medical practices, dentists, physical therapists, imaging centers, testing laboratories, and kidney dialysis facilities can be attracted to multitenant office space, but they may prefer separate buildings. Outpatient clinics, urgent care centers, or day surgery centers could be part of a mixed-use project located near a hospital. Affiliation with the hospital can help in marketing space to health practitioners and draw prospective patients living in and near the development.

Hotels

Hotels can be vital components of mixed-use developments for several reasons. A quality hotel can enhance the project's image and provide immediate name recognition. In some cases, secondary uses such as health clubs can be shared by hotel guests, office tenants, and residents, saving the hotel the cost of providing its own facilities. In assessing the feasibility of the hotel component, it is important not to overestimate the room demand that will be generated by the project's office tenants or residents. Neither use will generate enough room demand to support a hotel. As was discussed in chapter 8, hotel and residential uses have been combined in "condo-hotels," which offer hotel services to residential owners or allow owners to put their residential units into the hotel room pool when they are traveling or living in another residence.

Hotel guests help support a mixed-use project's retail activity, especially unique specialty shops, bars and restaurants, sports arenas, and entertainment venues. However, the type of hotel can have a big influence on the amount of retail patronage generated. Failure to understand the market niche served by the proposed hotel can lead to serious misjudgments of hotel-generated demand for retail goods and services in a mixed-use project. Most business travelers have little time to shop, whereas conference attendees, tourists, and vacationers do. Limited-service hotels have a track record of success in suburban mixed-use developments because they can attract traveling families who will also enjoy the shops and entertainment.

Retail Space

Most mixed-use developments include a retail component, which can range from a small amount of convenience and service retail space ancillary to the project's housing mix to a lifestyle center with a mix of curated shops and services. Depending on the size of the residential component and nearby competition beyond the project's boundaries, a supermarket could be included (a full-size, natural foods, or smaller specialty operator).

In the past, some mixed-use projects included super-regional shopping malls, but, as discussed in chapter 5, few such spaces are now being built in the United States. Many of them were located in downtowns with the idea of attracting office workers, day-trippers, and tourists. Unfortunately, anticipated patronage did not generally meet projections, and retail performance in downtown mixed-use projects has been hard hit by anchor-store closings and the subsequent departures of smaller tenants.

Apartments, stores, and restaurants at the Domain in Austin, Texas. *(CBRE Austin office)*

Specialty retail uses (upscale apparel and shoe stores, children's items, unique craft and gift shops, local memorabilia and foods) are also included in downtown mixed-use projects. These stores can attract metro-area residents if they offer choices that are unavailable elsewhere in the area, and if they offer "experiences" in addition to shopping. Experiential retailing can also draw tourists who visit museums and entertainment venues (which may or may not be part of the mixed-use development). In downtown locations, retail space needs to be paired with entertainment and dining so that the development attracts patrons who live outside the central business district.

In suburban mixed-use projects, retailers tend to be an amalgam of well-known stores and new entrepreneurs, often including outlet stores and off-price merchants that sell discounted apparel, housewares, linens, and decorative items. Unique restaurants at a variety of price points are also important. For such projects, it is essential to engage market analysts who specialize in determining the best mix of restaurants and bars.

Depending on the scale and type of proposed retail space, the market analyst must determine the trade area that will be served, look at the demographics of demand, and evaluate competitive supply in the same way that would be done for a single-use shopping center. The following are key questions to ask:

▪ What are the key sources of patronage?

▪ What are the likely demographic and income characteristics of households that will live in the mixed-use development?

▪ From how far away can other metro-area residents be drawn and what would bring them to the stores? (The mix needs to differ from what is seen in typical suburban community centers.)

▪ Will the development as currently envisioned generate demand from tourists and other nonlocal visitors?

The size of the site, available building area, and parking needs will also influence how much retail space is actually built.

Entertainment, Culture, and Identity Creation

In addition to office, retail, residential, or lodging uses, several special property types can be part of mixed-use developments. Often the key factors affecting the success of a mixed-use development are related to the sense of place that the project can create and its ability to attract patrons on both weekdays and weekends, at lunchtime and in the evening, and through all four seasons. Entertainment, cultural facilities, and casinos serve this objective well and have become key ingredients in many mixed-use developments. Plazas, sculpture, green spaces, water features, unique lighting, and colorful signage are also important in creating a sense of place and an identity for the "brand." To attract visitors, mixed-use properties use outdoor concerts (targeting adults, teens, or children) and special events (fundraisers for local schools or charities, sidewalk sales, antique car or other hobby shows, five-kilometer races). Some offer skating rinks during the winter months.

Entertainment at the Assembly Row mixed-use development in Somerville, Massachusetts, includes Legoland and an AMC movie theater. *(Deborah L. Brett & Associates.)*

The most common commercial entertainment spaces in mixed-use projects are multiscreen movie theaters. However, the demand for movie theaters is easy to overestimate today, when so much entertainment is available at home on demand, or with subscriptions to Netflix, Amazon Prime, premium channels, and other providers. Also, theaters can strain parking and security for the entire project. Esports (video gaming) lounges are growing in popularity with teens and young adults. Bowling alleys and golf simulators are also seen in some locations and can be helpful in attracting visitors during cold or rainy weather. As with other specialty uses, experts in analyzing demand for theaters and other types of indoor entertainment and recreation should be consulted, although an experienced market analyst can use secondary sources and field research to identify competitive facilities.

From the developer's perspective, metrowide draws such as museums, arenas, or stadiums must be carefully studied to determine whether the facility would attract patrons, as well as how it would affect other uses. Museums or performing arts centers can add well-educated and affluent visitors to the mix of patrons, drawing people who might not be interested in midpriced or even upscale shops. Cultural facilities give the development a strong identity, marketing focus, and image of quality. However, including these facilities generally requires forging a public/private partnership involving the developer, one or more public agencies, and nonprofit arts organizations. One advantage of working with established arts and cultural facilities that are considering a move to a new location is that they will have data on their patrons, donors, and subscribers and will know whether they will support a new or expanded

space. They also know the location of their supporters, which is very helpful in identifying a market area.

Sports Facilities, Health Clubs, Spas, Marinas

As indicated earlier, health clubs and specialty exercise studios are often included in mixed-use developments because potential revenues from residents living in the project (and those residing nearby) can be augmented by marketing the facilities to office workers. A hotel located in the development may be willing to pay a fee to make a gym available to its guests rather than build its own exercise space or pool, thereby reducing its own capital expenditures. Upscale health clubs in mixed-use projects also sell fitness apparel and may include spas offering a wide range of personal care services.

Smaller fitness spaces devoted to cycling, yoga, kickboxing, karate, climbing walls, and high-intensity training are capturing a growing share of demand, as are exercise and swim facilities that cater to families. Because fitness centers are now commonplace (and increasingly overbuilt), the market analyst will need to interview managers of existing facilities to learn about growth in membership and fee trends.

In waterfront locations, mixed-use projects might include commercial marinas. Purchasers of condominiums often have first rights to buy boat slips, but docks should also be made available for seasonal or day use. Operators generate additional income from boat storage, fuel sales, and maintenance services. Analysts should study comparable marinas and learn about their sources of demand for an indication of how extensive the market potential might be. Slip usage statistics, seasonal and daily rental rate trends, and waiting lists for spaces at existing marinas are good indicators. State agencies will have information on boat registration trends, usually by county or zip code. As with other market sectors, it is crucial not to overstate potential and to understand that a new development cannot create demand— it can only capitalize on an untapped existing market that may currently be using facilities located farther away.

Examples of noteworthy mixed-use developments from the past decade are shown in figure 9-1. They represent a variety of urban and suburban locations throughout the United States. Some have not yet been fully completed.

Using Consumer Research and Social Media

Insights into consumer preferences and cross-sales potential can best be derived from direct user research involving each of the key constituencies to be represented in the mixed-use development. Focus groups are a good way to get consumer reaction to site plans, building designs, and materials. Interviews with representatives of potential retail and office tenant types—as well as operators of health/fitness and restaurant concepts—would also be advantageous.

Figure 9-1
Examples: Recent Mixed-Use Developments

Project name and location	Site size/previous use(s)	Residential development	Retail space	Other commercial development	Amenities
The Mayfair Collection, Wauwatosa, WI (suburban Milwaukee)	69 acres; vacant warehouses (some retained and renovated). Across Burleigh Street from Meijers supercenter.	269 mid-rise rental apartments.	270,000 sq ft; Whole Foods, DSW, Nordstrom Rack, Saks Off 5th, T.J. Maxx, Home Goods, Dick's Sporting Goods, and Ulta Beauty.	Homewood Suites hotel, Serendipity Labs coworking office space (30,000 sq ft, opening in 2019), eight local restaurants.	Summer concerts, outdoor movies, and children's events.
Avalon, Alpharetta, GA (suburban Atlanta)	86 acres.	250 rental apartments in two mid-rise buildings with concierge services; 101 attached and detached for-sale single-family homes.	570,000 sq ft; Whole Foods, Apple Store, West Elm, Urban Outfitters, Container Store, Pottery Barn, Crate & Barrel, apparel, banks, and personal care.	Office buildings and medical offices (570,000 sq ft), 300-room Autograph Collection hotel, 47,000 sq ft conference center, 12-screen movie theater.	Children's play area, skating, and dog park.
Downtown East, Minneapolis, MN	Five-block redevelopment area; public/private partnership.	195 mid-rise rental units in three buildings.	26,000 sq ft.	Two 17-story office towers with 1.4 million sq ft occupied by Wells Fargo, renovated four-story office building, 164-room Radisson RED hotel. Near transit stations.	4.2-acre public green space with summer splash pad, four skybridges with connections to the existing skyway system and football stadium.
Bellevue Place, Nashville, TN (10 minutes from downtown)	Redevelopment of former Bellevue Center Mall.	337 rental apartments.	400,000 sq ft; Sprouts Market, Ross, Michaels, Ulta Beauty, Home Goods, Off Broadway Shoes, Carter, Maurice, and Kirkland.	Home2Suites hotel (opening August 2019), Carmike Cinemas, restaurants.	90,000 sq ft ice rink (Nashville Predators practice facility) opening in summer 2019.

Source: Compiled by Deborah L. Brett & Associates from field visits, promotional materials, and press reports.

Developers can use social media to post a description of the concept, highlight the various land uses and public spaces in the site plan, and show building renderings and streetscapes. This is a good way to create "buzz," but it can also generate useful input about materials, colors, and signage. Respondents can sign up for news about the project and be contacted as work progresses, thus creating a pool of marketing leads. However, it is important to remember that people who respond to these posts may not be representative of all potential residents, shoppers, or office workers who may consider locating in a mixed-use development.

Consumer research meets two objectives: getting user reaction to project plans and determining whether tenants or users of one project component will likely take advantage of other uses. This information helps the analyst determine whether the array of uses will justify a rent premium.

Putting It All Together

The final step in the market analysis for a mixed-use development is to estimate its overall marketability on the basis of consumer demographics, the supply of key competitive

Project name and location	Site size/previous use(s)	Residential development	Retail space	Other commercial development	Amenities
Assembly Row, Somerville, MA (suburban Boston)	45 acres; river frontage; formerly industrial buildings and failing community shopping center.	Rentals: Avalon at Assembly Row (195 units), AVA Somerville (253 units), Montaje (447 units). Condos: Alloy (128 units; eight stories above Row Hotel) with 15 income-restricted ownership units.	45 stores, including factory outlets. The Assembly Square power center with T.J. Maxx/HomeGoods, Trader Joe's, Burlington, Bed Bath & Beyond, Kmart, and Staples was the first phase.	Row Hotel (195 rooms); 21 restaurants, cafés, bars, and small eateries; Legoland; bowling alley with bar and dining; paint bar; offices, labs, and medical offices, with 1.5 million sq ft after completion (sites still available); five fitness studios; 12-screen AMC movie theater.	Outdoor amphitheater/concert space, children's playground, and two parks (six acres along the Mystic River). Orange Line T station.
One Paseo, San Diego, CA (Carmel Valley neighborhood in north San Diego)	23.6 acres; opening March 2019.	608 rental apartments in three mid-rise buildings.	96,000 sq ft of specialty shops.	280,000 sq ft of class A office space in two buildings (four and six stories); 18 restaurants, cafés, and bars; fitness studios. Shared parking.	Internal shuttle to shops and restaurants, farmers market, outdoor actiivities (movies, music, and yoga), koi pond, and art displays.
The Domain, Austin, TX	300 acres; former IBM property; planned/ built in phases starting in 2003. First phase (57 acres) opened in 2007; second phase (45 acres) opened in 2008.	2,687 apartments as of 2019; six four- to six-story mid-rise properties; planned for an eventual 5,000 units. More than 400 units of senior housing.	1.8 million sq ft of retail and restaurants. Over 100 upscale/ designer and mainstream stores. Anchors include Dillard's, Macy's, Neiman-Marcus, Dick's Sporting Goods, Microsoft Store, Apple Store, and Whole Foods.	2.3 million sq ft of office completed. Nearly 1 million sq ft opening in 2019–2020. 5 million sq ft planned at full buildout. Four hotels: Westin (330 rooms), the Archer (171 rooms), Lone Star Court (123 rooms), and Aloft (140 rooms). iPic movie theaters, Punch Bowl Social, Top Golf, Rock Rose Entertainment District, and restaurants.	Great Lawn, nine-acre park, 1.5 miles of trails, farmers market, live bands, and yoga. Connected to downtown and growing north suburbs by commuter rail.

Source: Compiled by Deborah L. Brett & Associates from field visits, promotional materials, and press reports.

Avalon, located in Alpharetta (an Atlanta suburb), is an 86-acre mixed-use development that includes two mid-rise rental apartment buildings, 150 detached homes, 570,000 square feet of retail space, office buildings, a hotel and conference center, and a 12-screen movie theater. *(9Kowit/Shutterstock.com)*

properties, and the mix of tenant types at competitive locations. As in all market studies, this last step requires the application of informed judgment regarding the likely response of consumers to the development as envisioned. Large-scale mixed-use projects usually have few, if any, directly comparable projects in the same market area with a similar combination of uses. If such analogues exist, the performance of their key components should be analyzed in detail. Comparable properties in other markets can also help direct the developer toward choosing the right land uses and tenant types and avoid pitfalls. But as indicated previously, the market analyst needs to identify, document, and evaluate the inventory of competitive space for each use component.

Even if each component is marketable on its own, the analyst must determine whether higher rents/prices for any or all components can be attributed to the cumulative attraction of the mix. A business looking to rent office space may be impressed by the proximity of restaurants and shops, but that does not mean that the office tenant will be willing to pay rent that is significantly above-market for the general area. If the presence of mass transit, gyms, exercise studios, and interesting restaurants helps with recruiting high-caliber staff in a tight labor market, paying more for office space might be worthwhile—but not so much during a recession when it is easier to find qualified personnel.

In other words, the best mix of uses will not be enough to support a project component for which insufficient demand

or surplus supply exists in the market at large. After examining the market potential, the team of analysts will recommend refinements to the plan. These refinements could include changes in the size or location of project components, phasing, design, or marketing. Some elements might be dropped if synergy is insufficient.

Mixed-use concepts are exciting, and it is easy to be unrealistically positive about a project's potential. Many projects have underperformed compared with predevelopment forecasts; some components have failed outright. There are many reasons why:

- Individual buildings with multiple uses cost more to construct. Each use may need a separate lobby and a separate bank of elevators. Noise reduction, fire protection, and ventilation systems will be more expensive.

- In vertical mixed-use buildings, locating loading docks, freight elevators, and trash collection areas can be problematic. To make parking garages visually appealing, they are often "disguised" with attractive facades, so they appear to be office or residential buildings. Mixed-use design issues can be resolved, but recouping the additional costs of those solutions may be difficult.

- Apartments "above the store" have different floor plate and design requirements than shops on the ground floor. Apartments with odd layouts will not be marketable. View premiums will be important in generating revenue for residential buildings.

- Assumptions about shared parking may not work out as expected. Local governments unfamiliar with mixed-use development may resist the concept, requiring the number of parking spaces to reflect the amount of space in each separate use. If there are issues with parking availability, residents and office tenants will demand reserved parking areas. Developers will be reluctant to deal with retailers who insist on reserved spaces in front of their stores or typical suburban parking ratios. Fortunately, retailers are becoming familiar with shared parking in mixed-use projects and are willing to locate in walkable or transit-oriented neighborhoods.

- Demand for the component uses may not be equally strong. In the time it takes to plan and construct a multiuse project, the luxury residential market may weaken or competing office buildings may be started.

- Financial projections often include overly generous rent or price premiums for space in mixed-use projects.

- Property managers who have office or retail expertise may be unfamiliar with how to deal with complaints from condominium owners, apartment renters, or hotel operators. Even in relatively low-density projects, residents will not be happy with early-morning commercial deliveries, restaurant odors, or unsightly trash collection areas.

- The first mixed-use project in a revitalizing area may be very successful for a while because it offers housing, office space, shopping, or services unavailable nearby and because its rents are reasonable for the quality received. A successful pioneering project may be able to raise rents for a few years. However, as the area improves, more competition will come into the neighborhood; the new developments might be mixed use or have only one or two land uses. But as more choices are available to consumers, occupancy in the oldest property can slip.

Mixed-use developments are risk intensive and complicated to implement. But they can be highly desirable and worthwhile for developers, residents, and the community as a whole. Although the premiums are difficult to quantify, and will not be the same for all property types, experience indicates that developers may see rent or sales price premiums as high as 15 to 20 percent in a well-conceived mixed-use development compared with those for a single-use project—provided that local markets for each of the major uses are in balance. Much of this premium will be spent in advance on such features as high-quality public spaces, building finishes and signage, and structured parking—which accounts for the higher risk. The challenge is to carefully determine early in the development process the proper balance between higher costs and higher payback.

Notes

1. Under performance zoning, buildings must conform to site coverage and height restrictions. A wide range of uses is allowed as long as those practices do not harm surrounding properties by creating noise, generating fumes, blocking sunlight, increasing flood hazards, and so forth.

2. The process was complicated; joint development projects were subject not only to local land use controls but also to U.S. Department of Transportation rules, because the transit systems received federal funds. It took many years to move from the initial concept to the start of construction.

3. See Shohei Nakamura, Richard Peiser, and Raymond Torto, "Are There Investment Premiums for Mixed-Use Properties," *Journal of Real Estate Research* 40, no. 1 (2018): 1–39, and Dominic F. Minadeo, *Price Premiums and Mixed-Use Development*, report prepared for and funded by the NAIOP Research Foundation, April 2009. Also see David Tobenkin, "REITs and Mixed-Use Development," *REIT Magazine*, November/December 2017. Nakamura, Peiser, and Torto look at institutional-quality buildings within a mixed-use project and a half mile away, and model how their financial indicators compare with similar quality properties beyond the half-mile radius. They focus on investment returns, not on the ability of ownership to realize above-average rents on mixed-use properties at initial lease-up or over time. They conclude that office and retail properties within mixed-use areas have higher market values (37 percent and 48 percent, respectively) and higher total returns (67 percent for office and 63 percent for retail) than for similar properties outside the half-mile area. Minadeo focuses only on office space in eight markets. He concluded that office space in three of the eight markets showed statistically significant higher rents. In four markets, the rents in mixed-use projects were higher, but the difference was not significant. In one market, office rents were lower in mixed-use projects. He concluded that mixed-use developments were "an emerging market niche with strong potential" and "with depleting amounts of developable land in viable locations, mixing uses to increase investor returns and user satisfaction will become more predominant" (p. 5).

APPENDIXES

APPENDIX A

GLOSSARY

Absorption rate. The amount of real estate that will be leased or sold in a given time period—typically months for a residential property, years for commercial/industrial space. The rate is expressed in square feet for commercial/industrial properties and units for residential properties.

ADR. The average daily room rate for a hotel property.

Amenity. Property feature available for use by a resident or commercial tenant, typically recreational/exercise facilities, lounges, concierge services, social spaces/activities, storage lockers, or a combination of these.

Anchor tenant. The major space users in a shopping center, positioned to produce traffic for the smaller stores in the facility. Usually, the anchor has a minimum of 20,000 to 25,000 square feet of space.

Appraisal. An opinion or estimate of value substantiated by various analyses.

Asking rent. Advertised rent or stated rent prior to negotiations or concessions. Average asking rents are typically weighted to reflect the amount of space at each rent level.

Asset manager. A person who handles financial management for a property or portfolio. Asset managers either oversee property management or are responsible for it themselves. They advise owners regarding the appropriate time to renovate, retenant, or sell assets.

Attached housing. Two or more dwelling units constructed with party walls (for example, townhouses or stacked flats).

Availability rate. Total available space as a share of total rentable space or units. Available space can include an area that may or may not be currently vacant but will be at a future date. It can also include sublet space.

Base rent. In commercial properties, rent per square foot before pass-through charges for utilities, janitorial services, and other expenses. See also Percentage rent.

Benchmarking. Identifying and updating the standards by which data can be measured.

Broker. A person who, for a commission, acts as the agent of another in the process of buying, selling, leasing, or managing property rights.

Brokerage. The business of a broker that includes all the functions necessary to market a seller's property and represent the seller's best interests.

Buildout. Construction of specific interior finishes and built-in equipment to a tenant's specifications.

Build to suit. Construction of land improvements according to a tenant's or purchaser's specifications.

Capital. Money or property invested in an asset for the creation of wealth.

Capitalization. The process of estimating value by discounting stabilized net operating income at an appropriate rate.

Capitalization rate (cap rate). The rate, expressed as a percentage, at which a future year's net income is converted into a present value figure. It is calculated as a year's net income as a percentage of a property's sale price or value.

Capture rate. Percentage of total demand within a targeted market segment that a project can attract. See also Penetration rate.

Cash flow analysis. The analysis of income and expenditures, usually on a year-by-year basis, from the project's inception to completion and through the holding period until disposition.

Central business district (CBD). The center of commercial activity within a town or city; usually the largest and oldest concentration of such activity. The area is also referred to as "downtown" or "center city."

Client. The individual or group for which a market study is conducted. Developers, lenders, institutional or individual investors, government agencies, civic organizations, businesses, corporations, or individual property owners can be the client for a market study.

Cold storage facility. Warehouse used for perishable items (foods needing refrigeration or freezer space, flowers).

Commercial real estate. Improved real estate held for the production of income through leases for commercial or business use (for example, office buildings, freestanding retail space, shopping centers, and warehouse buildings).

Community development corporations (CDCs). Entrepreneurial institutions that combine public and private resources to aid in the development of socioeconomically disadvantaged areas.

Comparable or comparable property. Another property with which a subject property can be compared to reach an estimate of achievable rent or market value.

Competitive clusters. The aggregation of office and industrial land near highly traveled areas such as along major highway interchange; near ports or freight lines; or near surrounding centers of activity such as airports, universities, and hospitals.

Comprehensive planning. Long-range planning by a local or regional government encompassing the entire area of a community and integrating all elements related to its physical development such as housing, recreation, open space, and economic development.

Concessions. Discount given to prospective tenants to induce them to sign a lease, typically in the form of free rent or allowances for tenant improvements.

Condominium. A form of joint ownership and control of property in which specified volumes of air space (for example, apartments) are owned individually while the common elements of the building or property (for example, outside walls) are owned jointly.

Construction loan. A loan to be used for the construction of improvements on real estate, usually made by a commercial bank to a builder and usually running six months to two years or more (depending on the duration of construction activity).

Convenience goods. Items typically purchased at the closest or most convenient locations. They are usually not very expensive or long-lasting, and their purchase involves little deliberation. Convenience goods are distinguished from shoppers' goods when performing retail market studies.

Coworking. Flexible office space arrangements managed by third-party operators. Layouts provide open worktables, small-group areas, and common amenities. Users include individual entrepreneurs and freelancers, as well as companies needing temporary space.

Credit tenant. Strong national commercial tenants with solid credit ratings, which are needed to secure financing for a shopping center, office building, or multitenant industrial space.

Demographics. Information on population characteristics by location, including age, household characteristics, employment, income, and expenditures.

Density. Concentration of buildings or commercial space within a given area. It is often expressed as a ratio (for example, dwelling units per acre or floor area ratio). Term can also be used to describe the concentration of people, usually expressed as persons per square mile.

Detached housing. A freestanding dwelling unit, normally single family, situated on its own lot.

Developer. One who prepares raw land for improvement by installing roads, utilities, and other infrastructure. Term can also refer to a builder (one who actually constructs improvements on real estate).

Development fee. Compensation paid to a developer in return for managing a development project on behalf of a client such as a corporation or public sector agency.

Development process. The process of preparing raw land so that it becomes suitable for building construction. It generally involves clearing and grading land and installing roads and utility services.

Development team. The range of participants engaged by a developer or project sponsor to assist in the planning, design, construction, marketing, and management of a development project.

Digital native. A retailer that initially sells only online but adds physical stores after the brand is well established. See also Omni-channel retailer.

Direct space available. In multitenant office and industrial building statistics, refers to space being listed directly by the property owner/manager or leasing agent. It does not include space available for sublet. See also Availability rate.

Discounted cash flow. Present value of money to be received in the future. It is determined by multiplying projected cash flows by a discount factor.

Disposable personal income. Amount that persons have left to spend or save after taxes. This indicator is used to determine income available to spend on housing or retail purchases.

Draw. Any incentive or attractive feature—whether it be good schools; proximity to shopping or entertainment; or underlying social, economic, and environmental characteristics—that stimulates growth and development in a geographic area.

Due diligence. Analytical evaluation of all reasonable considerations, including economic and market indicators—as well environmental, financial, legal, and other aspects—that relate to developing or acquiring a property.

E-commerce. Purchases made online rather than in stores.

Economic drivers. Industries that stimulate growth and create both direct and spin-off jobs in a region. Sometimes they are called export industries because their products or services are exported beyond the local region.

Economies of scale. Financial advantages that result from business expansion. Concept refers to the market trend that occurs when the producer's or provider's average cost per unit decreases as the size or scale of the operation increases.

Effective rent. Rental income after deductions for financial concessions—such as no-rent periods or moving allowances—during a lease term.

Eminent domain. The power of a public authority to condemn and take property for public use on payment of just compensation.

Equity. That portion of an ownership interest in real property or other securities that is owned outright (that is, above the amounts financed).

Escalation clause. A provision in a lease that permits a landlord to pass through increases in real estate taxes and operating expenses to tenants, with each tenant paying a proportional share of said increases. It can also be a mortgage clause that allows the lender to increase the interest rate as specified in terms of the note.

Expense stop clause. A cap on annual increases in expenses that will be paid by the landlord or tenant, as stated in a lease.

Fair share. In analyzing hotel performance, a way of comparing an existing or proposed hotel with its competitors on the basis of size, room revenue, occupancy, and ADR.

FAR (floor/area ratio). The ratio of a building's total floor area to land area—expressed as a percentage or decimal—that is determined by dividing the total floor area of the building by the area of the lot. Typically, FAR is used as a formula for regulating building volume.

Feasibility study. A report designed to demonstrate a development or renovation project's probable cash flow and investment rate of return based on the findings of market and financial analyses. The report documents sources used and assumptions made in reaching conclusions. The feasibility analysis will be revised as plans are finalized.

Fieldwork. Visual inspection of a proposed development site and its competition, noting neighboring uses, building conditions, and transportation access. Can include on-site visits with property managers, brokers, and government officials.

Flex space. Low-rise commercial buildings that can be used for a combination of office, light assembly, showroom, and/or storage.

Focus group. Market analysis tool in which a moderator presents a set of prepared questions and visual exhibits to a small group in order to collect detailed, specific information about consumer attitudes and preferences.

Fractional ownership. In a resort or second-home community, a form of deeded ownership in which the buyer purchases a partial interest that includes specified weeks or months.

Freestanding retail. Individual stores not part of a strip shopping center, enclosed mall, or pedestrian-oriented business street. Buildings may be investor-owned and net-leased to occupants.

Fulfillment center. A type of automated warehouse/ distribution building that assembles, packs, and ships orders to customers. A fulfillment center can be owned and operated by a single store chain or online merchant, or it can have multiple users.

Full-service rent. Rate that includes all operating expenses (utility costs, janitorial service, taxes, and insurance).

GAFO. In retailing, an acronym for general merchandise, apparel and accessories, furniture and home furnishings, and other specialty stores. It also can be referred to as shoppers' goods stores (in contrast to convenience stores).

Garden apartments. Low density, two- or three-story walkup multifamily housing with on-site parking.

Gross income multiplier. Rule-of-thumb calculation to estimate the value of residential property. It is derived by dividing the sale price of comparable properties by their gross annual or monthly rent and is used most often by appraisers.

Gross leasable area. The total floor area of a commercial building, which may include restrooms, stairwells, elevators, basements, and other common spaces.

Gross leasing activity. The sum of all space leased during a given time period, including both renewals and leases signed in new buildings. It does not deduct space vacated by tenants who do not renew their leases. See also Net absorption.

Ground lease. A long-term lease on a parcel of land, separate from and exclusive of the improvements on that land.

Highest and best use. The property use that, at a given time, is deemed likely to produce the greatest net return in the forseeable future, whether or not it is the current use of the property.

High-rise. Tall building or skyscraper, usually more than 12 stories for office buildings or eight stories for apartments.

Housing start. A unit under construction but not yet completed or ready for occupancy.

Improved property. Land that has been developed.

Industrial park/business park. A large tract of improved land used for a variety of light industrial and warehouse uses. Users either purchase or lease individual sites. A business park combines commercial uses (office space, hotels, restaurants) with light industrial uses.

Inflow. Retail spending by persons living outside the trade area. See also Leakage.

Infrastructure. Services and facilities provided by a municipality, including roads, highways, water, sewerage, emergency services, parks and recreation, and the like. They can also be privately provided.

Intelligent building. A building that incorporates technologically advanced features to facilitate communications, information processing, energy conservation, security, and tenant services. Also known as a "smart" building.

Inventory. The number of buildings, square feet of space, or residential units in a market area that can be rented by a third party. An inventory may have minimum size criteria.

Joint venture. An association of two or more firms or individuals to carry on a single business enterprise for profit.

Land development. The process of preparing raw land for the construction of improvements, through clearing, grading, installing utilities, etc.

Last-mile distribution center. A fulfillment center, located close to customers, that aggregates and delivers orders within a relatively compact area.

Leakage. The portion of aggregate retail spending potential that is unsatisfied by a trade area's existing retail offerings and is instead captured by retailers beyond the local trade area.

Lease. A contract that gives the lessee (the tenant) the right of possession for a period of time in return for paying rent to the lessor (the landlord).

Lease-up. Period during which a rental property is marketed, leasing agreements are signed, and tenants begin to move in.

Lien. The right to hold property as security until the debt that it secures is paid. A mortgage is one type of lien.

Lifestyle center. A specialty center with a "main street" design. Tenants include specialty retailers, restaurants, and entertainment (for example, movie theaters or performance venues).

Lifestyle cluster. Population grouping based on consumer location (urban, suburban, rural, small town), employment (white or blue collar, retired), education (high school versus college degree), affluence and wealth, age, social status, or psychographics.

Limited partnership. A partnership that restricts the personal liability of the partners to the amount of their investment.

Loan-to-value (LTV) ratio. The relationship between the amount of a mortgage loan and the value of the real estate securing it. The loan amount is divided by market value.

Location quotient. Market analysis tool used to compare local employment estimates by industry with national averages. It is derived by taking the percentages of workers employed in each major industry locally and dividing them by the percentages of the workforce employed in those industry groups nationally. Location quotients can also be calculated for occupations.

Logistics. The process of obtaining, moving, and storing goods in the suppy chain.

Low-rise. A building with one to three stories.

Market analysis. The synthesis of supply and demand analysis in a particular market.

Market area. The geographical region from which most demand and the most competitors are located.

Market niche. A subgroup within a market segment that is distinguishable from the rest of the segment according to physical attributes or consumer characteristics (for example, co-living apartments as a niche in the general apartment market).

Market research. A study of the needs of groups of consumers used to develop a product that is appropriate for an identifiable market segment.

Marquee tenants. Major tenants in an office building, as indicated by exterior signage or lobby directories.

Metropolitan statistical area (MSA). An urban area containing multiple political jurisdictions grouped together for the purpose of tabulating U.S. Census Bureau statistics.

Mid-rise. An elevator-equipped building with four to 11 stories.

Mixed-use development. A development—in one building or several buildings—that combines at least three significant revenue-producing uses that are physically and functionally integrated and developed in conformance with a coherent plan.

Modified gross rent. Rent in a commercial or industrial building that includes some but not all utilities, taxes, or operating expenses (such as janitorial services).

Mortgage. An instrument that makes real estate the security for a debt and that spells out the terms of repayment. Mortgages are typically two-party instruments involving a mortgagor (a borrower) and a mortgagee (a lender).

Move-up housing. Typically, larger, more expensive homes that homeowners buy as their incomes increase. First homes, or "starter homes," are generally more modest in size and price.

Multifamily housing. Structures that contain more than one housing unit, regardless of tenure. Some data sources consider multifamily dwellings to have five or more units.

Net absorption. The net change in occupied inventory over a specified period of time, including the addition or deletion of building stock during that period of time. It is expressed in square feet of space for commercial and industrial properties and in units for residential uses.

Net leasable area. The floor area of a commercial building that is leased to a tenant and is usable. It typically does not include corridors, restrooms, elevator space, and utility rooms. See also Gross leasable area and Rentable building area.

Net operating income (NOI). Cash flow from rental income on a property after operating expenses are deducted from gross income.

Omni-channel retailer. A retail business that sells merchandise both online and in physical stores. These retailers may fulfill online orders from a warehouse or directly from in-store inventory.

Operating budget. A building's expense budget that lists projected outlays for building maintenance and repairs, utilities, marketing, security, and other ongoing costs.

Option. The right given by the owner of property (the optionor) to another (the optionee) to purchase or lease the property at a specific price within a set time.

Pass-through. Lease provision whereby certain costs flow through directly to the tenant rather than to the owner (for example, property tax increases on a long-term lease).

Penetration rate. Percentage of potential income-qualified demand within a targeted housing market area that is being captured by competitive projects while factoring in competition under construction or planned.

Percentage rent. In certain shopping centers, a lease provision whereby stores pay extra charges calculated as a percentage of sales.

Permanent loan. A long-term loan on real estate that is used to finance a completed development (as opposed to a construction loan).

Planned/proposed developments. The pipeline of future construction projects, including those that have already submitted approval requests and others that have announced but are still in the preliminary planning stage.

Planned unit development (PUD). A zoning classification created to accommodate planned developments that include a mix of uses, varied housing types and densities, or both.

Pre-leasing. Efforts to sign tenants before building construction is completed.

Present value. The current value of an income-producing asset, which is estimated by discounting all expected future cash flows over the holding period.

Pro forma. A financial statement that projects gross income, operating expenses, and net operating income for a future period on the basis of a set of specific assumptions.

Property manager. An individual or firm responsible for the operation of improved real estate. Management functions include leasing and maintenance supervision.

Proptech companies. Firms offering innovative real estate technology and data analytics, which can include construction and financing tools as well as pricing/marketing strategies. The companies help improve the reliability of information used in decisions regarding real estate purchases or sales, store openings or closings, setting rents, and forecasting future performance.

Psychographics. Segmenting consumers in a given market area on the basis of values, attitudes, interests, household characteristics, and lifestyles.

Purchasing power. The financial means that people possess to purchase durable and nondurable goods. See also Disposable personal income.

Pure-play retailers. Businesses that sell goods only online; they have no physical stores.

Quick-casual restaurant. Eatery with no table service; patrons order customizable meals at the counter.

Quoted lease rates. (Also known as asking rents.) Advertised rents still subject to negotiation.

Rack rate. In hotels, the published or highest room rate charged.

Raw land. Undeveloped land, without any infrastructure or other improvements.

Real estate investment trust (REIT). An ownership entity that provides limited liability, liquidity, and tax benefits. Ownership is evidenced by shares of beneficial interest similar to shares of common stock.

Redevelopment. The rehabilitation or repurposing of existing properties in need of improvement.

Rentable building area. In a commercial lease, calculated when the tenant pays rent for a pro rata share of common areas such as hallways, lobbies, restrooms, and utility rooms, in addition to its occupied space.

Rent control. Limitations imposed by state or local authorities on the amount of rent a landlord can charge in certain jurisdictions.

RevPAR. A hotel's revenue per available room. It is calculated by multiplying the number of available room nights by the average room rate.

RevPOR. Revenue per occupied room, which is a measure used in the conference center segment of the lodging market. It reflects the fact that a high share of conference center revenue comes from sources other than rooms (food and beverage sales, equipment rentals, etc.).

Risk. The possibility that returns on an investment or loan will not be as high as expected.

Same-store sales. A measure of retail performance over time based on sales for a store chain's locations that have been open more than a year.

Segmentation. The classification of a population group into segments for the purpose of identifying marketing subgroups.

Shoppers' goods. Items purchased after some degree of deliberation or comparison shopping. Generally differentiated through brand identification, retailer's image, or ambience of the shopping area. Such purchases are made less often, and the product is typically more durable and expensive than convenience goods.

Shopping center. Integrated shopping area with multiple stores, eateries, and service providers under central management. On-site (off-street) parking, either at ground level or in a multistory garage, distinguishes a shopping center from street-fronting neighborhood or downtown shopping districts.

Single-family housing. A dwelling unit, either attached or detached, designed for use by one household and with direct access to a street. It does not share heating systems or other essential building facilities with any other dwelling. A single-family residential development may have common area facilities shared by all property owners (for example, a clubhouse or playground).

Stabilized occupancy. For a new multitenant building, the point in time at which initial leasing is complete. That time is typically at 92 to 95 percent occupancy.

STEM jobs. Occupations in science, technology, engineering or mathematics fields.

Strip center. An attached row of stores, service businesses, or both under single management. The strip lacks common interior walkways or corridors.

Subdivision. Division of a parcel of land into building lots. It can include streets, parks, schools, utilities, and other public facilities.

Sublease. A lease made by the original tenant in a rented space to another lessee for all or a portion of the space. For example, the building owner A leases 5,000 square feet in an office building to tenant B for 10 years, who in turn subleases 1,500 square feet of that space to tenant C.

Submarket. A geographic area surrounding a site that will provide a substantial share of the customers for a real estate project.

Subprime mortgage. A loan issued to a borrower with a poor credit history, lack of adequate employment track record, or other circumstances that cause lenders to judge that person as a high risk. Subprime loans carry higher interest rates than do mortgages issued to more qualified borrowers. The loans may have very low "teaser" rates for one or more years but then rise steeply. There is a higher chance of default on these loans, especially if the economy weakens.

Tax increment financing (TIF). A way of providing public financial assistance to a development or redevelopment project. Increases in future property tax revenue from a TIF district are earmarked to back bonds that pay for upfront project costs. The taxing jurisdiction forgoes the revenue increment in the short run in order to encourage redevelopment that improves property values in the long run.

Tenant. One who rents from a property owner.

Tenant improvement allowance. A payment made by the developer to a tenant that enables the tenant, rather than the developer, to complete the interior work on the leased premises.

Tenant mix. The various types of tenants in a leased building.

Title. Evidence of ownership of real property to indicate a person's right to possess, use, and dispose of property.

Townhouse. Single-family attached residence separated from another by party walls, usually on a narrow lot with small front yards and backyards. It can also be called a rowhouse.

Trade area. Geographic area from which a retail facility consistently draws most of its customers. It is also called a market area or competitive area for residential, office, and industrial buildings.

Triple-net lease (NNN). A lease in which the rent does not include any utilities, property taxes, janitorial service, or other operating expenses. In a multitenant building, each tenant will pay for separately metered utilities (if any) and a pro rata share of other expenses on the basis of the amount of space occupied.

Warehouse. A building that is used for the storage, distribution, or both, of goods. Modern warehouses also assemble multiple items for shipment to a single user or consumer. The building can be owner occupied and operated or leased by an investor-owner to one or more tenants.

Zoning. Classification and regulation of land by local governments according to use categories (zones). It can often include density designations expressed as units per acre (for residential uses) or floor/area ratios. See FAR.

WEBLIOGRAPHY

Listed below are data and analytical resources for information cited in this book. The list includes URLs for finding such sources on the internet as of spring 2019. Note that internet addresses change frequently as new data items are added and as companies are sold, merge, provide new products, and eliminate old ones. Analysts will need to use search engines to find the most up-to-date URLs.

(The $ symbol indicates data are available for a fee or by subscription, although the site may offer basic information free of charge.)

Demographics
(Population, households, income, lifestyles)

Census Bureau
www.data.census.gov

Data portal to decennial census, American Community Survey, Current Population Survey, annual population estimates, and Census Bureau population projections. Data on population, age distribution, household and family characteristics, mobility, income. Some information (such as projections) available for the entire United States only; other data available for areas as small as a census tract or block group. Summary tables and customized data searches. Tract maps.

Claritas
www.claritas.com ($)

Decennial census data; current-year population, household, age, and income estimates; five-year projections. Age-by-income cross-tabulations. Available for states, counties, MSAs, municipalities, zip codes, and customized geographies.

Claritas
www.mybestsegments.com ($)

Current-year PRIZM psychographics by place of residence. Workplace PRIZM for employees by place of work.

Demographics Now
www.demographicsnow.com ($)

Decennial census data; current-year population, household, age, and income estimates; five-year projections. Available for states, counties, MSAs, municipalities, zip codes, and customized geographies, as well as lifestyle clusters.

Esri
www.Esri.com ($)

Decennial census data; current-year population, household, age, and income estimates; five-year projections. Age-by-income cross-tabulations. Available for states, counties, MSAs, municipalities, zip codes, and customized geographies. Current-year Tapestry psychographics (lifestyle clusters).

Internal Revenue Service
www.irs.gov/statistics/soi-tax-stats-migration-data

State and county mobility data, covering in-migrants and out-migrants, using addresses reported in tax returns.

Moody's Analytics
www.economy.com ($)

Historical data, current estimates, and long-term forecasts for states, counties, and metropolitan areas. Covers population by age, number of households, net migration, average and median household income, and per capita income.

PolicyMap
www.policymap.com (free and $)

4,000 variables, including decennial census and Census Bureau's American Community Survey. Covers demographics, housing, schools, residential real estate, and neighborhood conditions. Government data free; customized geographies and mapping by subscription.

Ribbon Demographics
www.ribbondata.com ($)

Preformatted data and graphs about population, households, families, housing units, and tenure from the decennial census. Current year employment status of residents and employed persons by industry and occupation. Estimates and five-year projections from Claritas. Standard census geographies.

Woods & Poole
www.woodsandpoole.com ($)

State, county, and metropolitan/micropolitan area forecasts for 900 demographic and economic variables projected to 2050. Updated annually. Historical data going back to 1970. Data available in print or on CD-ROM. No customized geographies.

Labor Force, Employment, and Business Statistics

Census Bureau
www.census.gov/programs-surveys/cbp.html

County Business Patterns—establishments and employment for counties, larger municipalities, and zip codes.

www.census.gov/programs-surveys/economic-census.html

Economic Census—data on businesses by NAICS code, including employment, payroll, and revenues; based on a sample. Conducted every five years. Data available for the nation, states, MSAs, counties, places, and zip codes.

https://onthemap.ces.census.gov

OnTheMap—maps, charts, and reports on job locations; demographic characteristics and commuting patterns for workers. Customizable geographies in all 50 states and D.C.

Department of Labor, Bureau of Labor Statistics
www.bls.gov
www.bls.gov/sae (current employment statistics)
www.bls.gov/bls/blswage.htm (wages by occupation)
www.bls.gov/cew/cewlq.htm (location quotients)

Portal to labor force data by place of residence, unemployment rates, and at-place employment by industry, wages, and location quotients. Annual data on employment by occupation. Data available by state, county, and MSA and for larger municipalities.

Emsi
www.economicmodeling.com

Labor market data analytics for use in site selection and workforce recruitment. Incorporates social media information; goes beyond government occupation codes.

infoUSA
www.infousa.com ($)

Employment and other information for individual businesses. Available for census tracts, zip codes, municipalities, and custom geographies. Sortable by NAICS code.

Moody's Analytics
www.economy.com ($)

Historical data, current estimates, and long-range forecasts for states, counties, and metropolitan areas. Includes employment by two- and three-digit NAICS codes, labor force, unemployment rate, and gross metropolitan product.

Housing

Housing Stock Characteristics, Tenure, and Construction Data Sources

Census Bureau
www.census.gov/housing/hvs/index.html

Housing vacancy and homeownership survey for states and 75 largest metropolitan areas.

www.census.gov/construction/chars

Characteristics of new housing (single family and multifamily) by purpose (own/rent). National and four multistate census regions.

www.census.gov/programs-surveys/ahs

American Housing Survey; data on housing stock, tenure, financial characteristics, and neighborhood indicators. National data collected every two years; data for 47 metropolitan areas collected every six years.

www.census.gov/const/permitsindex.html

Building permit data for states, counties, metropolitan areas, and permit-issuing places.

www.data.census.gov

Portal to housing-related data from the decennial census and the American Community Survey. Information on housing occupancy, tenure, building size, year built, units by number of bedrooms, rents, home values, mortgages, and cost burdens.

Housing Market Analysis

Department of Housing and Urban Development
https://www.huduser.gov/portal/ushmc/home.html

Metropolitan area housing market reports; 10 to 20 issued annually. Quarterly report covering national and regional market conditions. Each issue features a review of selected metropolitan markets.

www.huduser.org/datasets/usps.html

Quarterly vacancy survey conducted by postal letter carriers.

Harvard Joint Center for Housing Studies
www.jchs.harvard.edu

The State of the Nation's Housing, produced annually. Special reports on demographics, housing finance, and affordability.

Housing Trade Associations and Professional Organizations

Manufactured Housing Institute
www.manufacturedhousing.org

Annual statistics on production and shipments of factory-built housing by state and product type; comparisons with site-built single-family homes.

National Apartment Association
www.naahq.org

Publishes an apartment income and expense survey ($); compiles and analyzes government data on construction activity and vacancy.

National Association of Home Builders
www.nahb.org ($)

Magazines, newsletters, and special reports about housing design, finance, homebuyer characteristics, consumer preferences, and construction activity. Conducts monthly surveys of homebuilder sentiment and quarterly surveys of adults regarding their interest in buying a home, their perceptions of available product, and affordability. Also prepares forecasts of single-family and multifamily starts.

National Association of Realtors
www.realtor.com

Searchable base of for-sale housing listings.

www.realtor.org/research/research/metroprice

Median home and condominium sales prices for metropolitan areas, updated quarterly. Trend data older than three years require payment.

www.realtor.org/research/research/housinginx

Housing Affordability Index, monthly and quarterly, for metropolitan areas.

National Investment Center for Seniors Housing & Care
www.nic.org ($)

Reports about supply and performance of housing for seniors, by metropolitan area.

National Low Income Housing Coalition
www.nlihc.org

Information about housing affordability gaps for states and metropolitan areas.

National Multifamily Housing Council
www.nmhc.org

Research about national apartment market conditions and tenant characteristics. Many reports restricted to members only.

Other Data Sources for Rental Properties

Apartment websites and magazines
www.rent.com, www.apartments.com, www.forrent.com, www.apartmentguide.com, www.move.com

Consumer-oriented online apartment listings. Some publications still available in print.

CoStar
www.costar.com ($)

Historical and current data and forecasts for apartment market performance; information on individual properties.

Novogradac
www.novoco.com

Searchable database about low-income tax credit properties, New Markets Tax Credits, and new (2018) Opportunity Zone program. Information on fair market rents and income limits for affordable housing programs. Publishes *Journal of Tax Credits* ($).

RealPage (formerly M/PF Research)
https://www.realpage.com/analytics/topics/multifamily-research-trends ($)

Quarterly apartment market reports for 100 metropolitan areas and many more submarkets. Data cover supply down to the zip code level. Affiliated company (Axiometrics) provides detailed information about individual multifamily properties and student housing.

Reis (now part of Moody's Analytics)
www.reis.com ($)

Coverage of metropolitan markets and defined submarkets. Reports typically include demographic and employment background data. Searchable information on individual properties. Covers apartments, affordable housing, seniors housing, and student housing.

RENTCafé
www.rentcafe.com

Searchable rental listings (by zip code, number of bedrooms, rent, pet-friendly) for cities throughout the United States. Includes houses for rent. Also research, articles, and blog posts on topics of interest to renters. Affiliated with Yardi, which provides management software for multifamily properties.

VisionLTC

www.visionltc.com ($)

Current-year demand estimates and projections for senior housing industry segments: independent living, assisted living, memory care, and skilled nursing. Supply inventory uses NIC data; national, metro, and local geographies available. Subscription only.

Other Data Sources Covering For-Sale Housing

Attom Data Solutions

www.attomdata.com ($)

Information on home sales by zip code, city, and individual subdivisions. Updated monthly, quarterly, and annually. Parcel data, tax records, foreclosures, neighborhood, and school information.

CoreLogic Case-Shiller Index

www.corelogic.com/products/corelogic-case-shiller.aspx

Home price indices for the United States and 20 large metro areas; based on repeat sales; revised monthly.

Federal Financial Institutions Examination Council

www.ffiec.gov

Data regarding mortgage activity, submitted under the Home Mortgage Disclosure Act.

Federal Housing Finance Agency

www.fhfa.gov

Housing price index and home price calculator for nine Census Divisions, metropolitan areas, and nonmetropolitan areas by state. Does not show actual prices, only changes over time (one quarter, one year, five years, and since 1991). Draws from repeat sales of individual properties.

Hanley Wood Market Intelligence/Metrostudy

www.metrostudy.com ($)
www.hanleywood.com

Project-specific information on for-sale housing developments in 40 markets, as well as demographic and economic data, permits, and homebuilding news reports for the markets covered.

Trulia

www.trulia.com

Searchable online database and maps of current listings.

Zillow

www.zillow.com

Searchable online database and maps of recent home sales and current listings.

Retail Space and Retail Sales

Tenant Directories and Shopping Center Data

Chain Store Guide

www.chainstoreguide.com ($)

Searchable database of retail stores and their location and space size preferences.

Directory of Major Malls

www.shoppingcenters.com ($)

Online directory for centers larger than 225,000 square feet. Covers more than 8,400 centers.

Retail Tenant Directory Online

www.retailtenants.com ($)

Annual directory available online.

Retail Sales and Consumer Spending

Bureau of Labor Statistics

www.bls.gov/cex

Consumer Expenditure Survey program. Based on spending information recorded by a sample of consumers. Results cross tabulated by consumer unit demographic, location, and income characteristics.

Census Bureau

www.census.gov/retail

Annual Retail Trade Survey with data on sales and gross margins by store type; no longer includes food services. Bureau also publishes monthly sales and e-commerce reports.

https://www.census.gov/programs-surveys/economic-census.html

Economic Census covering retail and food services businesses conducted every five years.

Coresight Research

www.coresight.com

Weekly tabulation of store openings and closings. Reports on total sales and same-store sales changes.

CoStar

www.costar.com ($)

Information about individual shopping centers (size, tenants, age, ownership, management), construction activity, and market conditions. Searchable by state, metropolitan area, and place.

Esri

www.esri.com ($)

Reports on retail and restaurant expenditure potential by type of store; also sales, inflow, and leakage for user-specified trade areas.

Reis (now part of Moody's Analytics)
www.reis.com ($)

Information about individual shopping centers (size, tenants, age, ownership, management), construction activity, and market conditions. Searchable by state, metropolitan area, and place.

Space Jam Data
www.spacejamdata.com ($)

Proptech company using social media to identify shopper attitudes toward retail centers and stores. Used by property owners, chain stores, and municipalities.

Retail and Restaurant Trade Associations

Food Marketing Institute
www.fmi.org ($)

Information about construction trends, store design, and sales for the supermarket industry.

International Council of Shopping Centers
www.icsc.org ($)

Publishes reports about mall sales by type of store; provides research and publications (*Shopping Centers Today*) on retail trends and the shopping center industry.

National Restaurant Association
www.restaurant.org

Publishes annual *State of the Industry* report ($). Restaurant TrendMapper subscription series ($) tracks restaurant performance indicators, including sales, employment, and number of establishments (full service and limited service) by state. Does not provide data by city or county.

National Retail Federation
www.stores.org ($)

Represents store operators. Publishes *Stores* magazine; NRF Foundation sponsors research ($), tracks effects of online sales.

Retail Publications

Chain Store Age
www.chainstoreage.com

News and features on retail stores, shopping habits, store design, and retail real estate trends. In print and online.

eMarketer Retail
Retail_newsletter@emarketer.com

Online newsletter covering retail trends.

National Real Estate Investor
www.nreionline.com

News, features, and trend analysis for apartments, commercial, and industrial real estate. In print and online.

Plain Vanilla Shell
www.plainvanillashell.com

Online source for news about store expansion plans. Searchable retail tenant database. ($)

Shopping Center Business
www.shoppingcenterbusiness.com

Monthly magazine available in print and online. News on property sales and leasing, center openings, and development activity; features on industry trends and regional market conditions; capital market recaps.

Office and Industrial Properties

Government Sources, Trade Associations, and Professional Organizations

Association of University Research Parks
www.aurp.net

Represents university-affiliated research facilities.

Building Owners and Managers Association International
(BOMA International)
www.boma.org

Sets standards for measuring rentable area. Annual reports about income and expenses for office and industrial buildings (*Experience Exchange Report*). Data based on information shared by property managers. ($)

Bureau of Labor Statistics
www.bls.gov

Employment projections by industry and occupation. National employment and occupation matrix (for calculating office-prone employment).

NAIOP, the Commercial Real Estate Development Association
(formerly National Association of Industrial and Office Parks)
www.naiop.org

Newsletters on trends in office and industrial real estate. Research on special topics related to office and industrial space. Website includes a glossary of terms.

Leasing, Sales, and Investment Information

Green Street Advisors
www.greenstreetadvisors.com ($)

Independent provider of third-party research, data analysis, and mapping for apartments, industrial, lodging, malls and strip centers, office, self-storage, senior housing, and student housing in 50 largest U.S. markets. Investment/financial focus.

Loopnet
www.loopnet.com

Commercial and industrial property listings, for rent and for sale. Links to listing brokers. Subsidiary of CoStar Group.

Real Capital Analytics
www.rcanalytics.com ($)

Investment activity and property sales information for office, industrial, retail, hotel, multifamily and senior housing, and self-storage.

Reonomy
www.reonomy.com ($)

Proptech platform consolidating records on more than 47 million properties. Data include recent sales, debt, ownership, and contact information. Covers multifamily, office, industrial, retail, and land. Opportunity Zone maps. Used by a number of national commercial real estate brokers.

Self Storage Association
www.selfstorage.org

Represents the self-storage industry and publishes research.

Showcase
www.showcase.com

Commercial and industrial property listings, for rent and for sale. Owned by CoStar.

SquareFoot
www.squarefoot.com

Online listing service for small office landlords and tenants. Has space needs calculator. Rent guidance for submarkets. Assistance with lease negotiations. Currently focused on New York City.

Travel, Tourism, and Lodging

Government Sources and Trade Associations

American Hotel and Lodging Association
www.ahla.com ($)
https://lodgingmagazine.com

Research on topics of interest to the hotel industry, including impact of nonhotel facilities. Publishes *Lodging* magazine, with news and features on the industry.

American Resort Development Association
www.arda.org

Trade association representing the timeshare industry.

Department of Commerce, International Trade Administration, National Travel and Tourism Office
https://travel.trade.gov

Statistics covering international travel to the United States by origin and destination.

Hospitality Net
www.hospitalitynet.org

Online newsletter and feature stories covering the lodging and tourism business

International Association of Conference Centers
www.iacconline.org

Trade association representing conference center properties.

U.S. Travel Association
www.ustravel.org ($)

Statistics and news about travel purpose, traveler volumes, and characteristics.

Local hotel associations

Websites for local tourism promotion organizations provide valuable information, often free of charge.

Hotel Consulting Firms and Data Providers

AirDNA
www.airdna.co ($)

Searchable location-specific information on short-term lodging such as Airbnb and HomeAway (ADR, occupancy, RevPAR). Reports covering the impact of Airbnb on hotel markets.

CBRE Hotels
www.cbrehotels.com ($)

Quarterly *Hotel Horizons* reports on hotel performance, nationally and for 55 large markets, by type of hotel and submarket. Publishes *Trends in the Hotel Industry* annual report, forecasts, and *Benchmarker* income/expense reports.

DK Shifflet
www.dkshifflet.com ($)

Consumer travel research, traveler profiles, guest satisfaction surveys, and trend analysis.

STR (Smith Travel Research)
www.strglobal.com ($)

Customizable reports about local hotel market performance. Pipeline Report on future supply. "Comparable set" performance data for specific properties. Glossary of hotel industry terminology used in STR reports. Publishes weekly *Hotel News Now* newsletter, with updates on U.S. hotel performance.

Tourism Economics
www.tourismeconomics.com ($)

Travel data for all 50 states and cities. Publishes *North America Inbound Tourism Outlook*. An Oxford Economics company.

TravelClick
www.travelclick.com ($)

The Demand 360 program monitors demand segments.

National and Global Commercial Real Estate Brokerages

Global, national, and metropolitan area–level data and analysis of commercial markets and apartments. Inventory, leasing activity, net absorption, vacancy rates, rents, and sublet space. Reports often compare market conditions across U.S. metropolitan areas. Geographic coverage varies by firm, as does minimum size of properties included in inventories.

CBRE (formerly CB Richard Ellis)
www.cbre.com

Colliers International
www.colliers.com

Cushman & Wakefield
www.cushwake.com

JLL (formerly Jones Lang LaSalle)
www.us.jll.com

Marcus & Millichap
www.marcusmillichap.com/services/research

NAI Global Commercial Real Estate Services
www.naiglobal.com

Newmark Knight Frank
www.ngkf.com

INDEX

INDEX

Figures and illustrations are indicated by italic page numbers.

A

Absorption rates, 21, 23, 25*n*6, 65, 96–97
    See also Net absorption
ACS. *See* American Community Survey
Active adult communities, 63, 90, *92–93*
ADRs. *See* Average daily room rates
Affordable housing
    capture rates, 94
    data sources for, 53, 100, 101
    demand for, 37
    feasibility analysis of, 63
    financing for, 7, 62
    in mixed-use developments, 202
    penetration rates for, 95
    for seniors, 22, 63, 64
Age-restricted housing. *See* Senior housing
AHS. *See* American Housing Survey
Airbnb, 181
Air cargo handling facilities, 163, *163*
AirDNA, 181, 195*n*4
Airport-oriented hotels, 176, 185
Airport retail, *115*, 117
All-suite hotels, 177–78
Amazon, 108, 111–12, 118, 158, 164
American Community Survey (ACS)
    access to, 25*n*3
    on affordability, 82
    on age of housing stock, 67
    data provided in, 42–43
    information on foreign-born U.S. residents, 78
    income data, 56*n*12
    scope of, 15
American Hotel and Lodging Association, 185, 194
American Housing Survey (AHS), 67, 87, 102*n*2
American Planning Association (APA), 9
American Resort Development Association (ARDA), 181, 182
American Seniors Housing Association (ASHA), 99

Anchor tenants
    characteristics of, 134*n*16
    in community centers, 117
    as percentage of gross leasable area, 23, 118
    in regional and super-regional malls, 113, 117
Apartments
    absorption rates for, 23, 25*n*6, 65, 96–97
    age of, 67, *67*
    amenities offered by, 4, 65–66, 75
    building permits for, 55
    capture rates for, 95–96, *95–96*
    classification of, 51, 65
    co-living, 80
    data sources for, 99–101, *101*
    demand for, 19
    existing competitive projects, 88–90, *89 91*
    field observation of, 54
    in mixed-use developments, 208
    parking at, 51, 65, 74
    penetration rates for, 96
    size of, 72, *72*, 74, 77
    as student housing, 66
    vacancy rates for, 5, 54–55, 91, 101
ARDA. *See* American Resort Development Association
ASHA. *See* American Seniors Housing Association
Asset estimates, 41, *41*, 87
Assisted-living facilities, 64, 78
At-place employment statistics, 29, 30
Autonomous vehicles. *See* Driverless vehicles
Average daily room rates (ADRs) for hotels, 175, 178, 188, 191, 192
Axiometrics, 99–100

B

Baby boomers, 69, 78, 188
Barriers to entry, 54
Bed-and-breakfasts (B&Bs), 178, 179
Boutique hotels, 179
Brokerage reports, 9–10, 52, 134, 151, 170
Budget hotels, 180, *180*, 186, 192
Building permits, 16, 42, 55, 93–94, 100–101
Built barriers (in defining market areas), 16–18, 84, 124
Built to suit, 139

Bureau of Economic Analysis (BEA), 126, 145, 146
Bureau of Labor Statistics (BLS)
    Consumer Expenditure Survey, 20, 40–41, 56n11, 125–26, 132, 135n28
    Consumer Price Index, 151
        Current Population Survey, 43–44, 64
        employment statistics from, 15, *29*, 29–30, 35
        location quotients from, 34, 56n5
Buyers, as users of market analysis, 9

C

Campus housing, *See* College student housing
Capitalization rate, 167, 171n7
Capture rates, 22–23, 94–96, *95–96,* 131, 153
Cash flow analysis, 8, 9, 152
CBP. *See* County Business Patterns
CBRE
    brokerage reports from, 52
    on construction cost indices, 155n12
    coworking space created by, 142
    on data center market, 158
    on dual-branded hotels, 190
    economic indicator data from, 10
    hotel market data from, 192, 194
    industrial market data from, 170, *170,* 171n6
    office market data from, *149,* 149–51
    on refrigerated warehouses, 161
    retail data from, 133
CCRCs. *See* Continuing care retirement communities
Census Bureau, U.S.
    absorption reports from, 25n6
    American Housing Survey, 67, 87, 102n2
    building permit data from, 16, 100–101
    County Business Patterns, 31, 31, 56n4, 169
    Current Population Survey, 43–44, 64
    Economic Census, 128, 133
    household data from, 41, 60, 80–81, *81*
    housing construction data (permits, starts, completions) from, 100–101
    OnTheMap program from, 16, 31, 32, 202
    population projections from, 77–78, *79*
    Public Use Microdata Sample, 44
    restaurant types by, 106
    retail sales data from, 106–8, *107*
    U.S. regions as defined by, 69
    Zip Codes Business Patterns, 31
    See also American Community Survey (ACS)
CES. *See* Current Employment Statistics
CEX. *See* Consumer Expenditure Survey
Child-oriented households, 80–81, 88
Claritas, 15, 41–42, 44–45, 57n13, 67
Co-living apartments, 80
College student housing, 66
Colliers International
    examples of metro office market reports, 154–155, 155nn1–2
    industrial inventory and vacancy, big boxes, 160, 171n4
    market data from, 10, 52, 57n18, 155, 170
    office space in downtowns vs. suburbs, 138, 139
    size of U.S. office markets, 137
    space needed for amenities, 140
Commerce Department, 36, 126, 146, 194
Community centers, 23, 112–13, *114,* 117–19, 122, 124

Commuting, changing attitudes toward, 82–83
Competitive clusters, 18
Competitiveness. *See* Marketability
Condominium hotels, 182–83, 203
Conference centers, 177
Congregate housing, 63–64
Construction data, 16, 23, 55, 131, 151, 192
Consumer Expenditure Survey (CEX), 20, 40–41, 56n11, 125–26, 132, 135n28
Consumer Price Index, 151
Consumer research. *See* Focus groups; Survey research
Continuing care retirement communities (CCRCs), 63, 64
Convenience centers, 113, *114,* 117, 124
Convenience stores, 106, 113
Convention hotels, 175, 177, 179, 184–90
CoreLogic Case-Shiller Index, 99, 102n27
CoStar, 53, 99–100, 133–34, 146, 155, 167–69
Cotenancy provisions (in leases), 122
Counselors of Real Estate (CRE), 9
County Business Patterns (CBP), 31, 31, 56n4, 169
Coworking spaces, 27, 112, 137, 141–43, 146, 155n8
Current Employment Statistics (CES), *29,* 29–30, 145
Current Population Survey (CPS), 43–44, 64
Cushman & Wakefield
    brokerage reports from, 52
    on coworking trends, 141
    economic indicator data from, 10
    on food as anchor in retail centers, 121
    office market data from, 149, *149*
    retail data from, 117, 133

D

Data centers, 158
Data mining, 130, 131
Data vendors
    absorption information from, 23
    competitive office building information from, 152
    construction pipeline data from, 55, 168–70, 192
    demand and supply data from, 20
    demographic data from, 15, 36, 40, 44–45, 146
    employment statistics from, 33
    housing data from, 51, 99–100
    income and asset estimates from, 60, 87
    industrial market data from, 159, 168–70
    lifestyle profiles from, 41, 88
    mapping programs from, 85
    market areas created by, 16
    methodologies of, 53
    office market data from, 147, 151–53
    population projections from, 85
    rent and price trends from, 51
    sales estimates by store type from, 132
    as source of market information and analysis, 10
Demand
    for affordable housing, 37
    analysis of, 19–20, 27, 59
    for apartments, 19
    for college housing, 66
    determination of supply/demand balance, 23, 131
    hotel market analysis of, 20, 185–90, *188*
    housing market analysis of, 85–88

industrial market analysis of, 20, 163–64
office market analysis of, 20, 144–48
reconciliation with supply, 21–23
replacement demand, 28, 37, 87, 146–47, 164
retail market analysis of, 20, 125–29
for second-home properties, 61, 62
for senior housing, 19, 64–65
unaccommodated, 190
Demographic data, 36–45, 77–78
    age composition, 39
    future projections, 36
    for hotel market analysis, 36
    for housing market analysis, 36–40, 85–88
    importance of, 27
    for industrial market analysis, 36
    mobility rates and migration patterns, 81–82, 102n10
    for office market analysis, 36
    population growth, 37–39, *38*, 77–78, *79*
    psychographic profiles, 41–42, 88
    racial and ethnic, 39
    for retail market analysis, 36, 39, 125–27, *126–27*
    sources of, 15, 42–45, *44*
    tenure estimates, 42
    See also Employment statistics; Households; Income data
Department of ____ . *See specific name of department*
Developers, as users of market analysis, 7–8
Dining. *See* Restaurants
Directories, 20, 32, 53–54, 83, 133–34
Discount stores, 115, 124
Disposable income, 126, *126*
Distribution centers, 158, 160, 162–64
Diversity. *See* Immigrants; Race and ethnicity
Dodge Data & Analytics, 55, 134, 170
Driverless vehicles, 83, 141, 200
Drugstores. *See* Pharmacies
Dual-branded hotels, 190
Due diligence, 6, 45, 59, 105, 197

E

E-commerce, 106, *108,* 108–10, 158, 162–64
Economy hotels. *See* Budget hotels
Effective rents, 151
Emerging Trends in Real Estate® (ULI & PwC), 57n19, 164
Employment statistics, 27–35
    at-place, 29, 30
    demand analysis based on, 27
    for full-time vs. part-time workers, 56n1
    for housing market analysis, 85
    industrial classifications (NAICS) used in, 30, *30*
    interpretation of, 32, *33,* 35
    key employers and new industries, 34
    labor force participation rates, 56n6
    labor force profile, 34–35
    location quotients, 34, 56n5
    nonfarm employment, 28, *28, 33*
    office-using industries, 144–46, *145*
    seasonally adjusted, 30, 35
    sources of, 15–16, *29, 29–33*
    unemployment rates, 15, 34, 35, *35,* 56n7
    worker-based, 29
    See also Income data

Energy-saving features, 140–41, 152
Escalator clauses, 151
Esri, 15, 41, 44–45, 57n13, 67
Ethnicity. *See* Race and ethnicity
Executive summaries, 25
Extended-stay hotel properties, 177–78, 187

F

Factories. *See* Manufacturing buildings
Factory-built housing, 70
Factory outlets, *115,* 115–16, 125
Fair housing laws, 57nn23–24, 79
Fair Market Rents (FMRs), 82, 102nn15–16
Fair-share analysis, 153, 193
Fast-food restaurants, 113, 120
Feasibility analysis
    absorption rates in, 23
    of affordable housing projects, 63
    generation of inputs for, 5
    of mixed-use developments, 203
    of office space projects, 144, 151
    supply factors in, 28
Federal Housing Administration (FHA), 59
Federal Housing Finance Agency (FHFA), 99
Field observations
    cost of, 12
    in hotel market analysis, 184
    in housing market analysis, 19, 92, 100
    importance of, 18–19
    in industrial market analysis, 165
    limitations of, 57n23
    of market conditions, 54–55
    in office market analysis, 19, 144, 149
    of proximity to amenities, 19
    in retail market analysis, 130
    of site advantages and disadvantages, 19
Flex space, 3, 50, 137, 157–61
FMRs. *See* Fair Market Rents
Focus groups
    advantages of, 45
    examples of, 48–49
    in housing market analysis, 84, 88
    for mixed-use developments, 202, 206
    moderators for, 12, 48
    in retail market analysis, 130
Food courts, 113, 115, 118, 120
Food deserts, 129
Food halls, 121, 135n21
Food Marketing Institute, 109, 134n12
Foreclosures, 69, 73, 75–76, 183
For-sale housing
    assessment of market for, 59
    customization of, 3, 76
    data sources for, 98–99
    existing competitive projects, 90, *92–93*
    in multifamily buildings, 71–72
    for seniors, 63
    signs of downturn in market for, 69
    single-family homes, 98, *98*

Fractional-ownership resorts or vacation homes, 182
Freestanding retail stores, 112–13, 118, 120, 121, 124, 134n18
Fulfillment centers, 158, 167, 168
Full-service hotels, 176

G

GAFO stores, 106, 134n4
Geographic information system (GIS) programs, 125
Government officials, as users of market analysis, 8–9
Grocery stores. *See* Supermarkets
Gross leasable area (GLA), 23, 51, 105, 113, 117–18, 134nn1–2

H

Highway-oriented hotels, 176
Homeownership rates
    by age, 74, 75, 102n30
    data sources for, 42
    downward trend in, 73, 75, 102n4
    for immigrants, 39, 78
    by race and ethnicity, 76–79, 77, 102n30
Hotel market analysis, 183–94
    business segments in, 185–87
    data sources for, 194
    of demand, 20, 185–90, 188
    demographic data for, 36
    field observations in, 184
    market area identification for, 17–18, 184–85
    objectives of, 183
    penetration rate calculation in, 193, 193–94
    performance projections in, 193, 193–94
    of supply, 50, 190–92
    visitor and tourism data for, 15, 185–89
    yield calculation in, 193, 193–94
Hotels and lodging, 173–83
    Airbnb properties, 181
    classification of, 51
    condominiums, 182–83, 203
    dual-branded, 190
    fractional-ownership resorts, 182
    location of, 175–76, 176
    in mixed-use developments, 184, 203
    new construction prospects, 192, 192
    performance measures for, 191, 191–92
    physical and functional characteristics, 177–79
    as real estate, 174–75
    room rates for, 51, 179–81, 180
    seasonality of occupancy, 189–90
    services offered by, 4, 176–77
    timeshares, 181–82
    and travel trends, 173–74, 173–74
    Vrbo (vacation rental by owner), 181
    See also Hotel market analysis
Households
    child-oriented, 80–81, 88
    expenditure potential of, 127, 127
    growth in total number of, 37, 38, 78
    lifestyle data for, 41–42, 88
    net worth of, 41, 41, 102n21

nontraditional, 81, 88
    sizes of, 79–80, 80
    tax return data for, 82
    types of, 80, 81
    See also Income data
Housing, 59–83
    affordability gap in, 82
    age of, 67, 67
    college housing, 66
    cyclical nature of new construction, 68, 68–69
    demographic trends affecting markets, 77–83
    factory-built, 70
    fair housing laws, 57nn23–24, 79
    homeownership rates, 39, 42, 73–79, 74, 77, 102n4
    infill development, 61, 71, 83
    market areas for, 16, 17
    market conditions for, 27
    master-planned communities, 60–61, 84, 91, 198
    in mixed-use developments, 202, 208
    multifamily buildings, 71–73, 72–73, 75
    occupied housing stock in U.S., 67, 67
    overview of product types, 60
    proximity to amenities, 19
    replacement demand for, 28, 37, 87
    retirement, 17, 36, 39, 63–65
    single-family homes, 68, 69–71, 70, 76, 98, 98
    in subdivisions, 59–60, 71, 84
    See also Affordable housing; Apartments; For-sale housing;
        Homeownership rates; Housing market analysis; Mortgages;
        Second-home properties; Senior housing
Housing and Urban Development, Department of (HUD)
    affordable housing data from, 53
    "Comprehensive Housing Market Analysis" reports, 8
    Fair Market Rents, 82, 102nn15–16
    market overview reports from, 101
    safety and energy efficiency standards from, 70
Housing market analysis, 83–101
    absorption rate estimation in, 96–97
    building permit data for, 16, 42, 55, 93–94, 100–101
    capture rate calculation in, 94–96, 95–96
    data sources for, 98–101
    demand, 85–88
    demographic data for, 36–40, 85–88
    employment statistics for, 85
    field observations in, 19, 92, 100
    illustrations, maps, and photos, use of, in reports, 25
    income and assets in, 86–87, 86–87
    market area identification for, 83–85
    monitoring market conditions, 97–98
    objectives of, 59, 83
    penetration rate calculation in, 95–96
    population and household data for, 85–86
    recommendations in, 97
    supply, 88–94, 89–93
Housing wage calculations, 82
HUD. *See* Housing and Urban Development, Department of
Hybrid outlet centers, 115–16

I

ICSC. *See* International Council of Shopping Centers
Immigrants and foreign-born
  homeownership among, 39, 78
  projections regarding, 102*n*10
  as rental housing consumers, 39, 76
  settlement patterns for, 81
Income data
  by age, 40, *40*
  calculation of, 56*nn*9–10
  disposable income, 126, *126*
  household and family, differences in, 39
  importance of, 39, 85, 87
  limitations of, 60
  median and average income, 86, *86–87*, 129
  by property type, use of, 39–40
  regional differences in, 86, 87
  sources of, 40–41
Industrial and warehouse space, 157–63
  classification of, 51
  design features, 160–62
  government incentives for, 164
  inventory of, 159–60, *159–60*, 170, *170*
  ownership and management of, 159
  parking at, 168
  port- and airport-related, *162*, 162–63
  proximity to amenities, 19, 168
  specialized markets for, 162–63
  types of, 3, 50, 157–59
  vacancy and availability rates, *166*, 166–67, 171*n*4
  See also Industrial market analysis
Industrial market analysis, 163–70
  data sources for, 53, 169–70
  of demand, 20, 163–64
  demographic data for, 36
  field observations in, 165
  leasing activity, 166
  market area identification for, 16, 18, 164–65
  net absorption in, 164, 166
  rent trends, 167, *167*
  supply, 50, 165–69, *166*
  transactions as a measure of market strength/weakness, 167–68
Infill development, 61, 71, 83
Inflow, 17, 127, 132
InfoUSA, 32–33, 54
In-line tenants, 113, 117, 118, 121, 131
Intercept interviews, 48, 49
Intercept surveys, 48, 130
Internal Revenue Service (IRS), 41, 82, 102*n*13, 135*n*20
International Council of Shopping Centers (ICSC), 9, 52, 105, 108, 112, 116, 132
Interviews, importance of 48–49, 54, 130, 170, 191, 206

J

JLL, 10, 52, 112, 133, 149, *149*, 152, 166
Job statistics. *See* Employment statistics
Joint Center for Housing Studies (Harvard University), 76, 78, 81
Jumbo mortgages, 102*n*29

L

Labor force statistics. *See* Employment statistics
Labor market areas (LMAs), 16, 44
Lambda Alpha International, 9
Last-mile distribution facilities, 162, 164
LAUS. *See* Local Area Unemployment Statistics
Leadership in Energy and Environmental Design (LEED) ratings, 140–41
Leakage, 127, 128
Leasing activity, 149, *150*, 151, 166
Leisure travelers, 185–89
Lenders, as users of market analysis, 9
Lifestyle centers, *115*, 116, 118, 121–22, 124, 198
Lifestyle data, 41–42, 88. *See also* Psychographics
Lifestyle hotels, 179
LIHTCs. *See* Low-income housing tax credits
Like-kind exchanges, 135*n*20
Limited-service hotels, 176–77, 179, 186, 192, 203
LMAs. *See* Labor market areas
Local Area Unemployment Statistics (LAUS), *29*, 30
Location quotients (LQs), 34, 56*n*5
LODES database, 31–32
Lodging. *See* Hotels and lodging
LoopNet.com, 52, 153
Low-income housing tax credits (LIHTCs), 54, 62–64
Luxury hotels, 179, *180*

M

Mail surveys, 47, 129
Main Street America program, 133
Malls, 109, 113–18, *114–16*, 121–25
Manufactured homes, 70
Manufactured Housing Institute (MHI), 70, 99
Manufacturing buildings, 157, 159, 161–63, 167
Marcus & Millichap, 10, 52, 133, 153–54
Marinas, 205–6
Marketability
  barriers to, 19
  and competitive clusters, 18
  features for enhancement of, 6, 198
  and household income, 41
  of industrial space, 168
  of mixed-use developments, 202, 207–8
  presentation of findings regarding, 55
  recommendations for, 97
  of senior housing, 41, 87
Market analysis. *See* Real estate market analysis
Market areas
  competitive clusters in, 18
  defined, 5
  demographic data for, 36, 37, 39–40
  determination of, 16–18, 61
  factors affecting size and shape of, 16–17
  for hotel market analysis, 17–18, 184–85
  for housing market analysis, 83–85
  for industrial market analysis, 16, 18, 164–65
  for mixed-use developments, 5, 17
  for office market analysis, 143–44
  primary, 17–18, 24, 84, 123–24
  psychographic profiles for, 41–42, 88

for retail store analysis, 16, 17, 123–25
    secondary, 17–18, 24, 84, 123–24
    for shopping centers, 17, 113, 115–16
Markets, defined, 3
Market screening, 7
Master-planned communities (MPCs), 60–61, 84, 91, 198
MHI. *See* Manufactured Housing Institute
Mid-price hotels, 179–80, *180*
Migration patterns, 81–82, 102*n*10
Millennials
    hotels catering to, 179, 180
    housing for, 69, 70, 73–81
    in workforce, 139–40, 147, 152
Minorities. *See* Race and ethnicity
Mixed-use developments, 197–209
    challenges related to, 197, 208–9
    consumer research on, 202, 206–7
    defined, 198
    entertainment and cultural activities at, 106, 122, 204–5
    examples of, 206, *206–7*
    health clubs and spas in, 205
    history of, 197–98
    hotels and lodging in, 184, 203
    housing in, 202, 208
    long-term investment stability of, 200
    marinas in, 205–6
    market areas for, 5, 17
    market potential of, 200–201, 208, 209*n*3
    office space in, 137, 138, 198, 202–3
    parking, circulation, and transit in, 199–200, 209
    physical and functional integration of, 199
    retail stores in, 116, 198, 203–4
    revenue-producing uses of, 198–99
    and social media use, 207
    sports facilities in, 205
    synergy among, 202–6
Mobility rates, 81–82
Model Content Standards for Rental Housing Market Studies (NCHMA), 83
Modular homes, 70
Moody's Analytics, 30, 44, 56*n*3, 57*n*20, 145
Mortgages
    access to, 68, 76
    and affordability, 82
    in assessment of for-sale market, 59
    interest rates for, 75, 99
    jumbo, 102*n*29
    lending standards for, 73, 86
MPCs. *See* Master-planned communities
Multifamily buildings, 71–73, *72–73*, 75

N

NAICS codes. *See* North American Industrial Classification codes
NAI Global, 10, 52
National Apartment Association (NAA), 13*n*1, 99
National Association of College Stores, 132
National Association of Home Builders (NAHB), 10–11, 13*n*1, 52, 99, 102*n*30
National Association of Industrial and Office Properties (NAIOP), 13*n*1, 52
National Association of Realtors (NAR), 10, 13*n*1, 61, 98, 99
National Bureau of Economic Research, 129
National Council of Housing Market Analysts (NCHMA), 9, 83

National Investment Center (NIC), 100
National Low Income Housing Coalition (NLIHC), 82, 98
National Multifamily Housing Council (NMHC), 13*n*1, 52, 99
National Retail Federation (NRF), 133
Natural features, importance in defining market areas, 16, 18, 84, 124
Neighborhood centers, 113, *114*, 117, 122, 124
Net absorption, 23, 96, 143, 146–49, 164, 166
Net-lease properties, 120
Newmark Knight Frank, 10, 52
New-urbanist movement, 61, 198
NIC. *See* National Investment Center
NLIHC. *See* National Low Income Housing Coalition
NMHC. *See* National Multifamily Housing Council
Nonconforming loans, 102*n*29
Nontraditional households, 81, 88
North American Industrial Classification (NAICS) codes
    in employment statistics, *30,* 30–33, 169
    for GAFO stores, 134*n*4
    for office-using industries, 145, *145*
    for restaurants, 106, 134*n*5
    sales data reported by, 106, *107,* 134*n*3
Novogradac & Co., 100
NRF. *See* National Retail Federation

O

Office market analysis, 142–55
    capture rate calculation in, 153
    of construction activity, 151
    consumer research in, 148
    data sources for, 153–55
    of demand, 20, 144–48
    demographic data for, 36
    field observations in, 19, 144, 149
    identification of office-using industries in, 144–46, *145*
    illustrations and maps used for, 25
    leasing activity information used in, 149, *150,* 151
    market area identification for, 143–44
    net absorption in, 143, 146, 147, 149
    objectives of, 142–43
    reporting rent trends and concessions in, 151, 153, *153*
    space standards in, 146
    submarkets in, 143–44, 146, 148
    supply side, 50, 149–52
Office space, 137–43
    classification of, 51, 137–38
    coworking spaces, 27, 112, 137, 141–43, 146, 155*n*8
    directories for, 20, 53
    energy-saving and environmentally friendly features in, 140–41, 152
    features and amenities, 4, 21, 138–41, 152
    inventory of buildings and square footage, 149, *149,* 153, *154*
    location profile, 138–39, *139*
    in mixed-use developments, 137, 138, 198, 202–3
    parking and transit concerns, 19, 141, 151–52
    proximity to amenities, 19, 144, 148
    replacement demand for, 146–47
    security considerations for, 138, 140
    size and layout, 139, 146, *146,* 147
    technological capabilities in, 140
    use and ownership of, 139
    vacancy rates for, 22, 146, 150–55, *151, 153*
    See also Office market analysis

Off-peak periods (for hotel demand), 176
Omni-channel retailers, 20, 106, *108,* 108–10, 119
One-on-one interviews, 48, 49
Online shopping. *See* E-commerce
Online surveys, 46–48, 129
OnTheMap (Census Bureau program), 16, 31, 32, 202
Outlet malls, *115,* 115–16, 125

P

Parking
    at apartment communities, 51, 65, 74
    at industrial and warehouse space, 168
    in mixed-use developments, 199–200, 209
    in new urbanist communities, 61
    for office space, 19, 141, 151–52
    at shopping centers, 54, 113, 120, 122
    at supermarkets, 106, 116, 122
    valet, 122, 152, 176, 190, 201
Peak periods (for hotel demand), 176, 190
Penetration rates, 22, 95–96, *193,* 193–94
Pew Research Center, 47, 57n16
Pharmacies, 106, 113, 117, 118, 129
PKF Hotel Experts, 192, 195n10
Population density of market areas, 17
Population growth, 37–39, *38,* 77–78, 79
Port-related industrial space, *162,* 162–63
Power centers, 106, 112–13, 115, *115,* 122, 124
Primary market areas, 17–18, 24, 84, 123–24
PRIZM psychographic system, 41–42
Project for Public Spaces (PPS), 199
Psychographic profiles, 41–42, 88
Public Use Microdata Sample (PUMS), 44
Purchasing power
    leakage of, 127
    retail, 20, 45, 105
    sources of, 41
    and sales, 131
    translation of demographic and income into, 132
    in underserved neighborhoods, 28, 129

Q

Qualitative research, 4, 46, 48–49, 131
Quantitative research, 45–48
Quarterly Census of Employment and Wages (QCEW), 29, 29–30, 34, 145
Quick-casual restaurants, 120, 135n26

R

Race and ethnicity
    demographic data on, 39
    homeownership rates by, 76–79, 77, 102n30
    population growth by, 78, 79
    spending patterns and, 129
    in survey research, 47
RCLCO Real Estate Advisors, 61, 76
Real Capital Analytics, 53, 167
Real estate investment trusts (REITs), 66, 76, 131, 158, 159

Real estate market analysis
    construction activity data for, 16, 23, 55, 131, 151, 192
    cost of, 11–12
    defined, 5
    demographic data for, 15, 27, 36–45
    in development process, 7
    employment statistics for, 15–16, 27–35
    field observations in, 12, 18–19, 54–55
    illustrations, maps, and photos, use of, 24–25
    market areas defined, 5, 16–18
    objectives of, 3, 5–7
    presentation of findings, 25, 55–56
    providers of, 9–11
    qualitative data for, 4, 46, 48–49, 131
    quantitative data for, 45–48
    recommendations in, 23–24, 97, 131
    regional or metropolitan setting for, 15–16
    of supply, 20–21, 59
    users of, 7–9, *10*
    visitor and tourism data for, 15, 36
    See also Hotel market analysis; Housing market analysis; Industrial
        market analysis; Mixed-use developments; Office market
        analysis; Retail market analysis
RealPage, 99–100
Refrigerated warehouses, 158, 161
Regional malls, 113, 114, 116, 117, 121–22
Regus, 142, 155nn6–7
Reis
    apartment data from, 99–100, *101*
    construction pipeline data from, 55, 168
    employment projections from, 146
    history of, 53, 57n20
    industrial market data from, 169
    office market data from, 155, *155*
    property types covered by, 52, 53
    retail data from, 133, 134
    self-storage sector data, 171n2
REITs. *See* Real estate investment trusts
Rental housing
    absorption rates for, 23, 25n6, 65
    consumer characteristics, 76
    demographic data for, 39–40
    Model Content Standards for market study of, 83
    monitoring activities for, 97–98
    occupied housing stock in U.S., 67, *67*
    retirement housing, 65
    single-family homes, 76
    See also Apartments; Tenants
Replacement demand, 28, 37, 87, 146–47, 164
Resort properties
    business segment in, 186, 187
    characteristics of, 176, *176,* 179
    demand for, 185
    fractional-ownership, 182
    market areas for, 17
    proximity to amenities, 19, 183
    timeshares, 181–82
    as year-round operations, 190

Restaurants
    classification of, 106, 134n5
    fast-food, 113, 120
    in hotels and lodging, 4
    in office locations, 19, 25
    quick-casual, 120, 135n26
    in shopping centers, 120–21
Retail market analysis, 123–34
    absorption rates in, 23
    capture rate calculation in, 131
    consumer research in, 44, 45, 129–30
    data sources for, 131–34
    of demand, 20, 125–29
    demographic data for, 36, 39, 125–27
    field observations in, 130
    household income and expenditures in, 126–27, *126–27*, 129
    illustrations used for, 25
    market area identification for, 16, 17, 123–25
    objectives of, 105, 122
    potential and estimated sales, 127–28, *128*
    recommendations in, 131
    shopper data analytics in, 129–30
    supply, 130–31, *133*
    visitor spending estimates in, 36
Retail stores, 105–22
    artificial intelligence in, 130
    classification of, 106
    downsizing of, 112, 119
    and e-commerce, 106, *108*, 108–10
    location criteria for, 122, *123*
    market conditions for, 27
    in mixed-use developments, 116, 198, 203–4
    net-lease properties, 120
    new construction prospects, 121–22, 131
    omni-channel, 20, 106, *108*, 108–10, 119
    opening and closing of, 110–11
    performance measures for, 109–10
    sales data for, 106–10, *107, 109*
    security considerations for, 122
    as showcases for online shopping, 111–12
    strategies for staying competitive, 119–21
    See also Retail market analysis; Shopping centers; Supermarkets
Retirement housing, 17, 36, 39, 63–65
RevPAR (revenue per available room), 51, 186, 191, 192, 194
RevPOR (revenue per occupied room), 191
Ride sharing, 141, 152, 199, 200
Rosen Consulting Group, 44

S

Sale-leasebacks, 139, 159
Sales-per-square-foot metric, 109, *109*, 131
Same-store sales, 109–10
Seasonally adjusted employment data, 30, 35
Secondary market areas, 17–18, 24, 84, 123–24
Second-home properties
    capture rates for, 94–95
    condominium hotels, 182–83
    demand for, 61
    fractional-ownership resorts, 182

    market areas for, 17, 83
    market conditions for, 27
    motivations for purchase of, 62
    proximity to amenities, 19
    timeshares, 181–82
Security considerations, 122, 138, 140
Select-service hotels, 177
Self-storage properties, 159, 171n2
Senior housing
    affordable, 22, 63, 64
    amenities offered at, 4, 63
    assisted-living facilities, 64, 78
    capture rates for, 22–23, 94
    congregate properties, 63–64
    continuing care communities, 63, 64
    data sources for, 100
    demand for, 19, 64–65
    for-sale, 63
    marketability of, 41, 87
    market conditions for, 27
    See also Retirement housing
Shadow rental market, 75–76
Shadow space, 150
Shopper data analytics, 129–30
Shopping centers, 112–22
    absorption rates for, 23
    classification of, 112–16, *114–15*
    data sources for, 132–34
    defined, 105
    entertainment activities at, 106, 118, 121
    gross leasable area of, 23, 51, 105, 113, 117–18, 134nn1–2
    in-line tenants at, 113, 117, 118, 121, 131
    market areas for, 17, 113, 115–16
    new construction prospects, 121–22
    parking at, 54, 113, 120, 122
    performance measures for, 118–19
    rent costs at, *118*, 118–19
    restaurants in, 120–21
    reuse of vacated spaces in, 111, 112
    sales-per-square-foot in, 109, *109*
    space trends, 117, *117*
    store mix in, 117–18
    strategies for staying competitive, 119–21
    vacancy rates for, 118, 134
    See also Anchor tenants
Short-term rental properties, 181
Shoulder seasons (for hotels and other lodging), 176
Showcase.com, 52, 153
Showrooms, 158, 168
Single-family homes, *68*, 69–71, *70*, 76, 98, *98*
Single-family subdivisions, 59–60, 71, 84
Single-tenant net-lease properties, 120
Site assessment. *See* Field observations
Small-format stores, 119
Social media, 47, 130, 207
Speculative construction, 59, 139
STEM occupations, 34
STR, 171n2, 192, 194, 195n1
Strip centers, 113, *114*, 117
Student housing, *See* College student housing
Subdivisions, 59–60, 71, 84

Sublet space, 150, 165
Subsidized housing. *See* Affordable housing
Summary tables, 21, 55–56, 154, *154*
Supermarkets
    classification of, 106
    in community centers, 113, 117
    as key employers, 29, 34
    market share estimations for, 131
    in mixed-use developments, 203
    parking at, 106, 116, 122
    refrigerated warehouses for, 161
    in regional malls, 116
    sales-per-square-foot for, 109
    size of, 134n12
Super-regional malls, 109, 113, *114,* 116–18, 121–22, 124
Supply
    analysis of, 20–21, 59
    by property class, 51
    data sources for, 51–54, 98–99, *101*
    determination of supply/demand balance, 23, 131
    documentation of historical and current trends, 49–54
    for geographic submarkets, 50
    hotel market analysis of, 50, 190–92
    housing market analysis of, 88–94, *89–93*
    industrial market analysis of, 50, 165–69, *166*
    office market analysis of, 50, 149–52
    by property type, 50
    reconciliation with demand, 21–23
    rents and prices in relation to, 51
    retail market analysis of, 130–31, *133*
    Survey research, 12, 45–49, 88, 129–30, 148

T

Tapestry psychographic system (Esri), 41
Telecom centers, 158
Telephone surveys, 46, 47, 129
Tenants
    affordable housing income limits for, 63
    cotenancy provisions, 122
    in-line, 113, 117, 118, 121, 131
    in mixed-use developments, 201
    multitenant offices, 138, 139, 148, 152
    net-lease, 120
    as users of market analysis, 9
    See also Anchor tenants
Third-party logistics companies (3PLs), 158, 159
Timeshares, 181–82
Tishman Speyer, 152, 155n4
Tourism data, 15, 36, 185–89
Town centers, 116, 198, 202
Trade area. *See* Market area
Transit-oriented development (TOD), 65–66, 82–83, 138, 197, 200, 202
Triple-net rents, 51, 151, 167

U

Unaccommodated demand (in hotels), 190
Unemployment rates, 15, 34, 35, *35,* 56n7
Upscale hotels, 179, *180*

Urban Land Institute (ULI)
    Emerging Trends in Real Estate®, 57n19, 164
    mixed-use projects as defined by, 198
    research commissioned by, 52
    residential market area as defined by, 84
Urban street retail, 116
U.S. Travel Association, 173, 194, 195n3

V

Vacancy rates
    for apartments, 5, 54–55, 91, 101
    for industrial and warehouse space, *166,* 166–67, 171n4
    for office space, 22, 146, 150–55, *151, 153*
    in reconciliation of demand and supply, 21, 23
    for shopping centers, 118, 134
Vacation properties. *See* Resort properties; Second-home properties
Vacation rental by owner (Vrbo), 181
Valet parking, 122, 152, 176, 190, 201
Visitor data, 15, 36, 185–89

W

Wages. *See* Income data
Warehouses. *See* Industrial and warehouse space
"Wet" biotech labs, 158
WeWork, 142, 143
Woods & Poole Economics, 30, 45
World Tourism Organization (United Nations), 194

Y

Yield analysis (in hotel market studies), *193,* 193–94

Z

Zip Codes Business Patterns (ZBP), 31